AF837590

Verb-governed infinitival complementation in the recent history of English

Linguistic Insights

Studies in Language and Communication

Edited by Maurizio Gotti,
University of Bergamo

Volume 287

ADVISORY BOARD

Vijay Bhatia (Hong Kong)
David Crystal (Bangor)
Konrad Ehlich (Berlin / München)
Jan Engberg (Aarhus)
Norman Fairclough (Lancaster)
John Flowerdew (Hong Kong)
Ken Hyland (East Anglia)
Roger Lass (Cape Town)
Françoise Salager-Meyer (Mérida, Venezuela)
Srikant Sarangi (Cardiff)
Susan Šarčević (Rijeka)
Lawrence Solan (New York)

PETER LANG
Bern · Berlin · Bruxelles · New York · Oxford

Sofía Bemposta-Rivas

Verb-governed infinitival complementation in the recent history of English

PETER LANG
Bern · Berlin · Bruxelles · New York · Oxford

Bibliographic information published by die Deutsche Nationalbibliothek
Die Deutsche Nationalbibliothek lists this publication in the Deutsche Nationalbibliografie; detailed bibliographic data is available on the Internet at ‹http://dnb.d-nb.de›.

Library of Congress Cataloging-in-Publication Data
A CIP catalog record for this book has been applied for at the Library of Congress.

Spanish Ministry of Science and Regional Government of Galicia (project/grant nos. FPI BES-2014-069851, FFI2009-11274/FILO, FFI2013-44065-P, FFI2016-77018-P, CN2012/294, R2014/016, 431D017/19 and ED431C 2017/50)

ISSN 1424-8689
ISBN 978-3-0343-4227-8 (Print)
E-ISBN 978-3-0343-4443-2 (E-PDF)
E-ISBN 978-3-0343-4444-9 (EPUB)
DOI 10.3726/b19020

© Peter Lang Group AG, International Academic Publishers, Bern 2022
bern@peterlang.com, www.peterlang.com

All rights reserved.
All parts of this publication are protected by copyright.
Any utilisation outside the strict limits of the copyright law, without the permission of the publisher, is forbidden and liable to prosecution.
This applies in particular to reproductions, translations, microfilming, and storage and processing in electronic retrieval systems.

Table of contents

1. Introduction

1.1 Clausal complementation in the recent history of English: An introduction

This monograph deals with morphological, syntactic, semantic/pragmatic and discursive variation between *to*- and bare-infinite (BI) verbal complementation in English. It investigates the reasons that lead certain verbs (specifically, *dare*, *need* and *help*) to opt for one solution or the other in the recent history of English. Non-finite complementation is a highly productive area of research (see Fanego 1996, 1998, 2004; Mair 2003: 329; Taeymans 2004a, b, 2006; Schlüter 2005; Cuyckens and De Smet 2007; Loureiro-Porto 2009, 2010; Lohmann 2011; van der Auwera and Diewald 2012: 131; Levshina 2018). While there are numerous studies examining *to*-infinitive vs BI complementation from a syntactic, semantic or cognitive perspective (see Section 1.2), this volume is an attempt to provide a comprehensive analytic analysis of the possible grammatical, structural, semantic/pragmatic, processing, period and identity-avoidance factors affecting *to*-infinitive/BI complement alternation.

Some historical background regarding the origin and rise of non-finite complementation is in order to put the analysis in context. Los (2005: 301) distinguishes three different infinitives in OE, based on distribution, structural and positional evidence:

> (i) the bare infinitive; (ii) the *to*-infinitive as complement of the verb *wesan* 'be', as in the PE fossil *he is to blame*; and (iii) the *to*-infinitive as purpose adjunct, and as theme- or goal-argument of verbs other than *wesan*.

Los contends that the BI (type (i)) is a verbal head even though it occurs in positions reserved for case-marked nouns in the clause and therefore has nominal traits. With respect to the *wesan-to*-infinitive construction in type (ii), Los explains that the *to*-infinitive constituent behaves like an Adjective Phrase in terms of position, distribution and structure and "occurs as a predicate in a small clause". In ME this infinitive undergoes re-analysis as an overtly passivised *to be*-infinitive. Type (iii) is restricted to control constructions and functions "as the non-finite counterpart of the subjunctive clause" (p. 301); this *to*-infinitive has clausal characteristics. The assumption that the *to*-complementiser derives from the homonymy preposition *to* is supported by Fanego (2004: 26), who observes that "cognitive research on complementation has generally argued that *to*-infinitival complements evoke aspects of imagery inherent in the source-path-goal image schema associated with prepositional *to*".[1] According to Verspoor (1999: 511), "*to*-infinitive expresses that the subject, figuratively speaking, moves towards the state of being expressed, is not there yet, but is projected towards it". From a diachronic perspective, Fanego (2004: 27) points out that there are records that show that the source of the *to*-infinitive was a "directional adverb/preposition with the meaning 'toward'", but that "by Late Old English or Early Middle English (1100–1300) *to* had lost its prepositional character and had grammaticalised to an infinitive marker, so that it began to occur where previously only the bare infinitive was". Los (2005: 303) suggests that the rise of the *to*-infinitive may have been influenced by its reanalysis as a non-finite subjunctive, together with the gradual loss of Object-Verb word order, and more importantly, by the obsolescence of finite subjunctive forms. As will be explained in Chapter 2, modal verbs, which typically select BI clauses, are also favoured as periphrastic markers of the subjunctive mood.

The outline of this chapter is as follows: This section provides a general description of non-finite complementation in English, specifically in relation to its morphological, syntactic and semantic/cognitive

1 Fanego (2004: 44) observes that, from a cognitive perspective, *to* "reflects aspects of source-path-goal image schema" and therefore includes " 'notion[s] of futurity' (Langacker [1991]: 446), 'future orientation' (Verspoor 1996), 'conceptual distance' (Smith and Escobedo 2001: 561) or 'subsequence or posteriority' (Hamawand [2003]: 74)". Egan (2008: 96) points out that the meaning of *to*, which on its own means 'towards / in the direction of', when preceded by main verbs such as *manage* or *remember*, shows that the target mentioned has been reached.

features. Section 1.2 deals with *to*-infinitive and BI clausal complementation and the determining features of each complementation alternative. Finally, Section 1.3 outlines and justifies the research questions that underlie this study.

1.1.1 Complementation: Morphological features

This volume presents an exploration of verb-governed non-finite clausal complementation in the history of English. Non-finite clauses are characterised by the absence of verbal inflection and characteristically fulfil a subordinate function in the syntactic constituents to which they belong. In fact, Huddleston and Pullum et al. (2002: 89) view non-finiteness as a 'desententialization' strategy since it involves the loss of properties that are associated with a clause standing alone as a full sentence. Unification and bonding are the minimal process, "at least pragmatically", in clause combining and most often take place in subordination, showing "hierarchical downgrading and desententialisation" (Hopper and Traugott 2003: 178). As a consequence, one member of the complement structure is decategorialised and becomes syntactically non-canonical. In their cline of dependency, Hopper and Traugott place finite constructions on the leftmost end of the cline (lowest degree of dependency), and non-finiteness, expressed by clausal remnants such as infinitives and participles, on the right (lowest degree of grammatical integration).

1.1.2 Complementation: Syntactic features

Hopper and Traugott (2003: 175) point out that "ordinary discourse does not consist of isolated, context-free utterances but of linked discourse units". 'Clausal complementation' refers to the process of embedding a clause so that it becomes a complement within another syntactic unit (Hamawand 2002: 1). Complement clauses are embedded clauses in the complement position of another clause or phrase, and are "regularly introduced by a complementizer, a morpheme or a paired morpheme, whose function is to identify the structure as a complement" (Hamawand 2002: 1). Hamawand (2002: 87; 2003: 66) claims that "complementisers iconically encode different degrees of distance between the referents of the main and complement clauses", and analyses them as complex categories comprising "a central prototypical meaning from which other meanings are derived" (2003: 70). As Matthews (2007: 42) explains, the term 'complementiser' dates from the mid-1960s, and was known in the beginning as 'marker' specific to a 'predicate complement'. Under this definition, Matthews (2007: 42) includes *that*, as in example (4), morphemic markers such as *-ing* (5), 'POSS' (6) and *to* (7):

(4) I suppose *that it barked.*

(5) It liked *barking at night.*

(6) I was *angry about the animal's barking.*

(7) I ordered it *to be put down.*

As pointed out in Hopper and Traugott (2003: 175), the "development of markers of clause linkage" and complementisers, such as those in (4)–(7), has been attributed to the total or partial grammaticalisation of lexical items that led to the integration of initially separate clauses within larger main units,[2] where the embedded clause fulfils a syntactic function (Hamawand 2002: 1).

Hamawand (2002) analyses clausal complementation as a type of subordination: the process of linking individual clauses so that they adopt a different, dependent syntactic status. He uses the term 'superordinate' clause to refer to the main clause and 'subordinate' for a complement clause. Subordinate clauses are characterised by syntactic incompleteness because interpretation of a subordinate clause often relies on inference from the main clause or from a broader context

2 According to Matthews (1981: 170), "a clause is a main clause if it forms a sentence or is one of two or more coordinated elements that together do so. Otherwise it is a subordinate clause". In example (i) below, the clause *GENERAL Accident is bidding* is the main clause, while the clause *to stem claims losses and bring down premium costs with the launch of customised household and motor insurance policies* is the complement clause, introduced by the *to*-infinitive verb.
(i) GENERAL Accident is bidding to stem claims losses and bring down premium costs with the launch of customised household and motor insurance policies. (BNC Baby, CBD)

(Huddleston and Pullum et al. 2002: 89). Matthews (1981: 174), for example, explains that in (8a) the incomplete clause *to get him to the airport*, which lacks a subject, can be transformationally related to the complete non-finite clause *(for) it to get him to the airport*, in (9a), or the finite clause in (9b). Clauses such as that found in (8a) are classed as 'reduced units': they are "incomplete (...) in that at least one potential element of a main clause, or at least one of the potential categories of its predicator, is excluded" (Matthews 1981: 174).

(8) a. *a*[I hired a taxi *b*[*to get him to the airport*]*b*]*a*. (Matthews 1981: 173)
    b. The taxi got him to the airport / I will get him to the airport. (Matthews 1981: 173)

(9) a. *a*[I hired a taxi *b*[*for it* to get him to the airport]*b*]*a*. (Matthews 1981: 174)
    b. He got to the airport. (Matthews 1981: 174)

The matrix verb of the main clause functions as the 'licenser' of different types of complementation (Matthews 2007: 77). Terms such as 'valency' or 'valence' (Tesnière 1969: 238), 'complementation' (Quirk et al. 1985: 65–67) and 'argument structure' (Fromkin 2000: 685) are used variously to refer to verbs that require complements (e.g. *love*), verbs that may take complements but do not have to (e.g. *sing*), verbs that require a complement and may take an additional locative (e.g. *throw*), and verbs that only require a locative (e.g. *put*). In other words, verbs may be intransitive or transitive with one or two complements. Among transitive verbs, some permit or require clausal constructions comprising a subordinate finite or non-finite verb (Matthews 2007: 85).[3]

---

3 According to Matthews (1981: 169), depending on the type of matrix verbs, the dependents can be strongly obligatory as in (i), latent as in (ii), or excluded as in (iii):
(i) I mentioned they were coming.
(ii) They didn't tell us.
(iii) I read they were coming vs. *I persuaded they were coming.
Hilpert (2014: 44) uses 'null instantiation' to indicate that "not all the arguments that a verb has in its event structure are overtly expressed", as in (iv). Ruppenhofer (2005) contends that verbs can be classified into indefinite, such as *read* in (iv), and definite with null instantiation, such as *understand* in (v), depending on whether the speaker knows the exact identity of the omitted argument, i.e. depending on the definiteness of the argument that may be omitted:

Matthews (2007: 92) explains that complements are defined relationally as parts of a construction that are either required or 'licensed' by specific lexical units, in line with Huddleston and Pullum et al. (2002: 219), who state that "the most important property of complements in clause structure is that they require the presence of an appropriate verb that licenses them". According to Matthews (1981: 148), that the complement clause and the main clause enter into an exocentric construction relationship, where none of the constituents can substitute for a whole, or into a 'directive' relationship, in Hockett's (1958: 191) terminology, in which the verb is a 'director' and the complement is the 'axis'. Modifiers, by contrast, are dependent but not specifically 'licensed'. Matthews (1981: 147) adapts Bloomfield's (1933: 194) notion of 'endocentricity' in his definition of modification, applied to constructions where at least one of the elements may be substituted for the whole.

Hamawand (2002) identifies three word classes that license subordinate or complement clauses: nouns, as shown in (11) below, adjectives, as in (12), and verbs, as in (13).[4] Huddleston and Pullum et al. (2002: 1176) add prepositions to the list, as illustrated in (14) – I will not consider examples such as (14) as complement clauses but as an adjunct, because the main verb is intransitive and does not license a complement clause.

(11) At the meeting there was *a desire to change section 3 of the agreement.* (Rudanko 2000: 7)

(12) He was *determined to commit himself.* (Rudanko 2000: 90)

(13) John *forced* me *to perform menial tasks.* (Rudanko 2000: 3)

(iv) Kim was reading. I just don't remember what.

(v) Kim understood. *I just don't remember what'.

4 Biber et al. (1999: 658) do not consider the type of noun-complementation in their definition of complement clauses since they do not distinguish between complementation and modification in the case of nouns: "a complement clause is a type of dependent clause used to complete the meaning relationship of an associated verb or adjective in a higher clause". They claim that these types of complements are called nominal clauses "because they typically occupy an NP slot as subject, object or object predicative".

(14) She left at *six in order to catch the early train.* (Huddleston and Pullum et al. 2002: 1176)

As mentioned before, this study focuses on verbal complementation and the determinants of variation when a verb may select different types of verbal complements. Rudanko (2011: 3) identifies a role of dependency or correlation between the main verb and the type of predicate in the complement, observing that "saying that a head selects its complement or complements means that a head selects the head of each complement". For instance, in the transitive *into. . .-ing* pattern illustrated in (15), the matrix verb *fool* selects as its complements both the NP *him* and the *-ing* clause introduced by *into.*

(15) They *fooled him into believing he was fast enough.* (Rudanko 2011: 2)

Biber et al. (1999: 658) identify three types of non-finite clauses according to the inflectional form of the verbs and the grammatical roles they play in the clause. As regards the inflectional properties of main verbs, non-finite clauses may be headed by gerund-participials, infinitivals (subdivided into *to*-infinitives and bare infinitives) and past participials (Biber et al. 1999: 198); in this study, I focus on the two types of infinitivals. As far as their syntactic roles are concerned, infinitival complement clauses can be placed in pre-predicate, extraposed and post-predicate position, the last of these being the most frequent according to Biber et al. (1999: 693). Huddleston and Pullum et al. (2002: 1176) argue that the function of *to*-infinitives and BI-clauses is similar to the function of content clauses: they may be objects of the main verbs, as in (16), extraposed objects, as in (17), or catenative complements, as in (18). Huddleston and Pullum et al.'s 'catenative complements' are governed by so-called 'catenative' verbs such as *hope.*

(16) I found *talking to her* quite helpful.

(17) I found it distressing *to see her so ill.*

(18) She hopes *to hear from them soon.*

My analysis does not adopt this catenative interpretation and treats *to hear from them soon* in (18) as a complement clause functioning as the object of the main clause. For the purposes of comparison, however, in what follows I will summarise the relevant literature on catenative constructions and comment on any overlaps with my own research. In Huddleston and Pullum et al. (2002: 1177), 'catenative' refers to constructions that take non-finite internal complements where the main and subordinate verbs are chained or concatenated, as in (19). In (19), the notional subjects of the first three catenative verbs (*intend*, *try* and *persuade*) co-refer with *she*, whereas *him* is the subject of the last catenative verb *help*. Two types of catenative constructions are present, simple and complex, depending on the absence or presence of a Noun Phrase (NP) intervening between the main clause and the subordinate clause that functions as the complement of one of the clauses.

(19) She intends to try to persuade him to help her redecorate her flat. (Huddleston and Pullum et al. 2002: 1177)

Matthews (1981: 186) uses 'catenative' to refer to the fusion of a dependent verbal construction with a transitive or intransitive construction. He analyses example (20) as a fused construction (i.e. a construction in which a single element is the complement of both a controlling and a dependent predicator) where *him* is the object of *made* and the subject of *do*. Matthews claims that the relationship between the subject and the object reveals the fusion between the transitive and the secondary predication. According to this interpretation, it does not matter whether the first predicator in (20) controls the second predicator plus its object, *do it*, which is considered a reduced clause, or the second predicator (*do*) by itself (Matthews 1981: 186). Following Haegeman (2006) and Rudanko (2011), however, I consider that the main verb *make* in (20) selects the whole predicate *him do it* as its complement, which functions as the direct object. Pronoun substitution supports this analysis, as in (21), where *this* replaces *him do it*. Example (22) is a representation of the syntactic analysis adopted in my study: *him* (NP2) is the overt subject of the complement clause headed by *do* (Vb2) and *it* (NP3) is the direct object of the lower-clause verb *do* (Vb2). In intransitive constructions, the covert NP2 is a PRO form co-referent with the NP1 subject of the main clause, as in (23). In (24), the subject of the infinitival coordinated verbs (*ventilate* and *remove*) has *the tube* as its referent in the main clause headed by *has*.

(20) They made him do it. (Matthews 1981: 185)

(21) I made this

(22) [NP1 [Vb1 [NP2 Vb2 NP3]obj S2]S1

(23) [NP1$_i$ [Vb1 [PRO$_i$ Vb2 . . .]obj S2]S1

(24) The tube has about an inch of clearance around the mirror to *help ventilate* the tube and *remove* heat from the light path. (COHA, mag_1995_394838)

Matthews argues that predicates headed by *dare to* and *want to* illustrate catenative constructions, whereas Quirk et al. (1985: 138) classify *dare* (*to*) as a marginal modal. *Dare* can exhibit properties typical of either modal auxiliaries, such as co-occurrence with bare infinitives and lack of inflection, as in (25), and homomorphic verbs constructed as main verbs when followed by *to*-infinitive forms, in (26), and/or with inflected realisation: *-s*, in (27), *-ing* and past forms.

(25) I [*daren't visit*] *him*. (Matthews 1981: 183)

(26) I *didn't dare to* visit him. (Matthews 1981: 183)

(27) or else I am afraid you will not meet a great while, for he *dares* not com down any more: therfore I shall wish for som good ocasion that may bring you together, and make a harty frendshippe amongst us. (PCEEC, CORNWAL,233.146.2031)

According to Matthews (1981: 183), *dare* and *visit* form unitary verb phrases in examples (25) and (28), respectively, with *dare* showing modal-like features and behaving like a blended category between a modal and a lexical verb with *do*-support. By contrast, example (29), which illustrates a catenative construction, is not an instance of clausal complementation but a simple clause with four constituents in which there are direct links between the subject and *dare*, between *dare* and the infinitive, and between the infinitive and the object. As noted by Haegeman (2006), Matthews' analysis is disconfirmed by pronoun-substitution, in (30), and VP-deletion, in (31). Complement Clause (CC) pronoun-substitution shows that *dare* is the head of the clause, as in (30), with *that* replacing *visit him*, and VP-deletion corroborates that *dare* plus the *to*-infinitive complement form a unit, as in (31), where the complement of *dare to* is retrievable from the post-verbal complement of the previous clause (*raise*).

(28) I [*didn't dare visit*] him. (Matthews 1981: 183)

(29) [I] [*didn't dare*] [*to visit*] [him]. (Matthews 1981: 183)

(30) I didn't dare *that*

(31) Yet Mr Smith is not only proposing to *raise* tax in one go by more than anyone *has ever dared to* before but also concentrating the effect on a relatively small group. (BNC Baby, AHB)

Additionally, whereas Matthews (1981: 183–184) analyses the verb *want* as a catenative verb, Quirk et al. (1985: 550) describe it as a complex transitive verb, claiming that *want* in this construction is not a main verb but a sort of pragmatic particle (1985: 148). Quirk et al. (1985: 147) also include verbs such as *may* and *let* in this category of 'pragmatic particles' that mark a sentence with an expression of wishing or an optative mood, as in (32) and (33).

(32) You *want to be careful* with that saw. (Quirk et al. 1985: 148)

(33) I *want to tell you* how much we enjoyed last night. (Quirk et al. 1985: 148)

Quirk et al. (1985: 148) explain that, in example (32), "*you want to* expresses a warning or piece of advice", whereas in (33), "*I want to* introduces an expression of wish, which, in effect, tones down a performative verb". They (1985: 148) point out that the fact that changing the tense of example (32) into the simple past or into the progressive aspect implies a variation in the meaning of the sentence evinces that *want to* behaves like a pragmatic particle, as evidenced in (34) and (35). According to Quirk et al., these examples "no longer have a particular advice-giving function, and have to be interpreted simply as statements about the hearer's wishes". The stative meaning of *want* results in the unacceptability of examples such as (34). Examples (32) and (35) are both possible but convey different meanings: the former refers to an unrealised proposition and an event that has not taken place yet, whereas the latter conveys an unrealised fact (*be careful with that saw*). In other words, in example (35) the speaker knows that the main-clause subject *you* was not careful and that it has consequences at the time the utterance is made (see Chapter 2, Section 2.2.3).

(34) ?You *are wanting to* be careful with that saw. (Quirk et al. 1985: 148)

(35) You *wanted to be* careful with that saw. (Quirk et al. 1985: 148)

In his so-called 'gravitation' theory, Krug (2000: 214) hypothesises the rise of an 'emerging auxiliaries' (or 'emerging modals') subcategory within the class of modal verbs (see Chapter 3, Section 3.2). Since the classification of a verb in this way is determined by its modal function and interpretation rather than by its syntactic properties, Krug (2000: 238–239) classifies *want to* as a prototypical emerging modal. As regards *dare*, Krug argues that this verb, like *need to* and *ought to*, oscillates between a central modal and an emerging modal. Even though, diachronically, all three verbs have moved towards the emerging modal type, the features that *dare* shows synchronically place it the "nearest to the central modals" category (Krug 2000: 238).

Matthews (1981: 187) provides examples of marginal subordination, in which it cannot be determined whether or not they contain a lower clause. His findings show "no effective difference among speakers if the recursion [in sentence (36)] is learned as one involving successive layers of subordination, or as purely linear". In his view, examples such as (37) and (38) are cases of marginal codification: in (37) the predication of 'try' is applied to the speaker, whereas in (38) the happening refers to a predication of the process, not of the individual. *Try* takes two complements (the subject *I* and the object *to see her*), whereas *happen* takes a single complement, *to see her* (Matthews 1981: 188).

(36) They forced *him to make John do it.*

(37) *I* tried *to see her.*

(38) I happened *to see her.*

Constructional ambiguity is illustrated by Matthews (1981: 189) in (39), which may refer to a promise that the third-person subject is making (in contrast to example (40)), or to something that promises to be so with a meaning closer to that found in (41). Another ambiguous case is illustrated by the verb *begin* in (42), which may mean either that the discussion was begun by them (in contrast to example (43)) or simply something that began to happen (cf. (44)). Matthews points out that the difference between examples (37), with matrix *try*, and (38), with matrix *happen*, lies in the different meanings of these verbs. The constructional ambiguity illustrated in *promise* in (39) and *begin* in (42) also reflects different senses of these verbs (Matthews 1981: 189):

(39) He *promises to be a pianist.*

(40) He *is trying* to be a pianist.

(41) He *happens* to be a pianist.

(42) They *began to discuss it.*

(43) They *pretended* to discuss it.

(44) They *seemed* to be discussing it.

Quirk et al. (1985: 146) take an alternative approach to catenative verbs. Firstly, they define constructions headed by *appear to*, *come to*, *fail to*, *get to*, *happen to*, *manage to*, *seem to*, *tend to* and *turn out to* followed by infinitives as catenative, as in (45). These constructions "have meanings related to aspect or modality, but are nearer to main verb constructions than are semi-auxiliaries", since they come under the category of so-called *do*-support, as in (46) (Quirk et al. 1985: 146).

(45) Sam *appeared/ came/ seemed to* realize the importance of the problem. (Quirk et al. 1985: 146)

(46) Sam *didn't* appear to realize the importance of the problem. (Quirk et al. 1985: 146)

Secondly, they use the term 'catenative' because of "the ability of these verbs to be concatenated in sequences of non-finite constructions", but point out that this "chain-like structure is not, however, confined to catenative verbs but is also" applicable to semi-auxiliary verbs and "main verbs followed by non-finite clauses functioning as objects" (1985: 987). They define a complex sentence as a sentence in which one of the core constituents is realised by a subordinate clause, i.e. which contains what Huddleston and Pullum et al. (2002: 1177) call a catenative verb.

This study analyses constructions composing a verbal group followed by a non-optional, non-finite clausal constituent, and will adopt Dixon and Aikhenvald's (2006: 15) criteria for the recognition of clausal complementation. According to the first criterion, a clausal complement should have the internal structure of a clause, that is, it comprises subject, verb and possible objects and arguments; if these arguments are not omitted by specific grammatical rules, they "should be marked in the same way as in a main clause [. . .] and will have much the same grammatical properties". Secondly, the complement clause functions as a core argument of a higher clause, as an object argument or an extended argument, typically marked by the dative case. Thirdly, a complement clause should materialise a proposition.

1.1.3 Complementation: Semantic and cognitive features

Fanego (2004: 29) lists a number of semantic features of (English) complementation. For example, main verbs "with similar or related meanings" tend to select "the same kind or kinds of complements". Contexts of non-factuality and verbs denoting volition (*intend*, *want*, *wish*) thus favour or require *to*-infinitive constructions, whereas verbs denoting sensory perception tend to co-occur with BI clauses (see also Dirven 1989). However, Smith and Escobedo (2001) argue that there is often little difference in meaning between different types of complements, as in the case of *to*-infinitive and *-ing* complements with the aspectual verbal groups headed by *begin*, *start* or *cease*, and the emotive verbs *love*, *hate*, *prefer*, *like* and *can't stand*.

Egan (2008: 19) classifies *to*-infinitive/BI complement clauses according to the semantics of the main verb and the tense-aspect-modality (henceforth TAM) correspondence between the main verb and the situation conveyed by the complement clauses with respect to the subjects in the constructions: same subject (SS) and different subject (DS). The subjects in DS constructions are identified as Sl, in reference to the trajectory of the main verb, and S2, the trajector of the complement-clause predicator or, less commonly, the landmark of the matrix verb, as in (47) (Egan 2008: 20). The landmark of the main clause may also be the complement clause as a whole, and not specifically the S2, as shown in (48):

(47) My father *taught me to shoot*, I can't imagine why he *didn't teach me to drive*. (H8X 2660) (Egan 2008: 19)

(48) Certainly, but I *should hate you to forget* that he has scored more runs in Test cricket than any other Englishman. (K3X 873) (Egan 2008: 20)

Egan's categorisation of the main verbs in DS constructions is based on Langacker's (1991: 284) stage model. Two situations are possible depending on how S1 is profiled. Firstly, S1 may be "an observer of the onstage situation" it may "observe it (Perception constructions), think about it (Mental Process constructions) or form an attitude towards it (Attitude constructions), but does not influence its unfolding", as in (49). This situation can also take into account minority communication constructions in which "the addressee of the communication is a fellow member of the audience, rather than S2".

(49) John *wants/expects Mary to propose* the toast. (Dixon 1991: 192–3)

If S1 "mounts the stage", Egan (2008: 22) states that S1 can "issue advice or instruction to S2 (Communication constructions)", "facilitate the realisation of the complement construction situation (Enablement constructions)" or "enforce its realisation (Causation constructions)", as shown in (50).

(50) John *forced/permitted/helped Mary to propose the toast*. (Dixon 1991: 192–3)

When the subjects of the main clause and complement clause coincide, Egan (2008: 26) claims that the subject encodes the trajector of both predicates. He distinguishes six categories of "same-subject constructions": Effort, Mental Process, Attitude, Communication, Aspect and Applied Attitude. Egan uses Givón's (1995: 118) term "non-implicative modality verbs" to refer to the first four categories, given that the event of the complement clause in these does not necessarily have to be realised. As an exception, Egan mentions the Effort construction verbs *manage to* and *contrive to*. Aspect constructions contain an aspectual main clause, which usually refers to the actual (non-)occurrence of the situation. The sixth category, Applied Attitude, refers to constructions that share certain characteristics of both attitude and aspect constructions.

Egan (2008: 92) notes that "the semantic content of the infinitive will be taken to be identical to that of the verbal stem". Langacker (1990: 80) characterises this infinitive/stem as "a complex 'atemporal relation' which is scanned summarily rather than sequentially". According to Egan, the term 'summarily' implies that the process is viewed as "unfolding in time", whereas 'sequentially' involves "an atemporal relation frozen in time".

With respect to the semantic and cognitive development of non-finite complement solutions, *to-* and BI-clauses profile a situation as a "whole" (Egan 2008: 92) but differ in relation to the "*focused* or *targeted* alternative" (p. 96). Unlike *to*-clauses, BI complement clauses refer to "an almost certain, rather than to a merely possible, or perhaps probable, eventuality" (Egan 2008: 91). *To*-clauses are profiled as the more likely of two or more alternatives in an explicit domain, as in example (51) (Egan 2008: 103):

(51) We expected people to just come and go, *but most didn't* –they had a great get together.' (GX2 302)

According to Egan (2008: 93), the *to*-infinitive occurs in three types of constructions: Forward-looking, when the situation is "profiled as expected to occur after the time of the matrix verb", as in example (52); General, when the "situation is profiled as likely to occur on a more or less regular basis", as in (53); and Judgement, if the "situation is hypothesised to be true", as in (54) (Egan 2008: 39–40). BI clauses, on the other hand, can only occur in Same-time and Forward-looking constructions because they encode "a situation that is located in temporal proximity to the time of the matrix verb" (Egan 2008: 91). BI clauses are attested in Same-time constructions if they are realised at the time of the main verb or are located in the time after that of the matrix verb, as in (55). BI are found in Forward-looking constructions because these profile situations "incorporating force-dynamic relations which ensure the immediate realisation of the complement situation" (Egan 2008: 92).

(52) He then *requested Lucy and Jean to come* into the kitchen. (HHB 4158) (Egan 2008: 39)

(53) God's own country, as the Canadians *delight to call* it. (A0P 217) (Egan 2008: 39)

(54) Theodora *judged her to be* in her early forties... (HA 2 802) (Egan 2008: 40)

(55) Cecilia Darne, who lived round the corner, said she*heard a bell toll* once at about eight in the morning. (EDN 355) (Egan 2008: 91)

As Hamawand (2002: 11) observes, superordinate verbs must involve a "direct interaction between the referents of the main and complement subjects" in order to be compatible with a BI. In most cases, the event of the main and complement clause are coincident in time, as illustrated in (56), where *he* joined *she* in performing the event of the complement clause, thus denoting "an action that is direct and coincident" (Hamawand 2002: 11).

(56) He helped *her* achieve success. (AmE NEWS) (Biber et al. 1999: 736).

To support this coincident actualisation meaning between the BI and the main verb, Hamawand (2002: 93) applies the following two tests: according to the first test, adding *but he didn't* to example (57) would result in an ungrammatical sentence, whereas inserting *and he did* would not. The second test shows the impossibility of introducing time adverbial expressions which do not coincide in time, as in (58).

(57) She made him clean the floor, *and he did/ *but he didn't.* (Hamawand 2002: 93)

(58) **Last week* she made him clean the floor *yesterday.* (Hamawand 2002: 93)

The way in which BI-clauses profile the situation is related to the meaning involved in the semantic class of causation or modality verbs such as *make*, *let* and *have*, the perception verb group comprising *feel*, *hear*, *notice*, *observe*, *overhear*, *see* and *watch*, and a residual class of verbs which includes *help* and *know* (Quirk et al. 1985: 1205).

Nonetheless, the semantics/pragmatics of the non-finite complement constructions does not always lead to a clear-cut explanation of infinitival choice, as in the case of my examples with *dare*, *need* and *help*. To give an example, Egan (2008: 237–278) observes that *need* (see also Chapter 3) occurs in Forward-looking and Applied Attitude sentences, where it selects *to*-infinitive and BI complements. In the case of Applied Attitude, the *need to*-infinitive construction expresses "the necessity of the subject's realising the targeted alternative in question", as in (59). In Forward-looking constructions, Egan (2008: 278) notes that the *to*-infinitive is usually used to encode at least the possibility that the targeted alternative might not be realised. However, with *need* the distinction between *to*-infinitive/BI complementation is less clear (cf. example (60)). Egan suggests that the reason for this lack of distinction between *to*-infinitive/BI clauses is that *dare*, *need* and *help* have "clear implications with respect to the realisation of the complement situation".

(59) You *need to check* on the tax position. (B08 217) (Egan 2008: 240)

(60) Don't you think you *need actually stand* in the mud, though –if we get back to the hard it will be all right' (H0D 69) (Egan 2008: 240)

1.2 Determinants of infinitival complementation: A review of the literature

This section describes the most significant processes and factors identified by the literature regarding the *to*-infinitive/BI complementation alternation in English: iconicity and distance, the Complexity Principle, the inflectional form of the main verbal group, the principle of avoidance of identity and text-type features.

ICONICITY AND DISTANCE. Smith and Escobedo (2001) argue that in *to*-infinitives, *to* "marks the conceptual distance between the matrix and the subordinate clauses by iconically separating them in the grammar" (p. 556) and reflects aspects of imagery "inherent in the source-path-goal image schema" (p. 561).

COMPLEXITY PRINCIPLE. Rohdenburg's (2003: 205) Cognitive Complexity Principle states that "in the case of more or less explicit constructional alternatives [. . .], the more explicit option(s) will tend to be preferred in cognitively more complex environments". He notes that this principle also predicts that "more explicit novel constructions are first established in more complex environments and that more explicit recessive (or obsolescent) constructions survive longer in exactly the same type of context". Hence, the *to*-infinitive is expected in the following contexts: main- and lower-clause complex subjects; when there is distance between the main clause main-verb and the infinitival verb and/or the transitive construction (NP2 subject); in relative-clause formation with relative pronouns functioning as the subject of the main clause or the object of the subordinate clause; passivisation of the main or lower clause; presence of *not*-negation, complement clause complexity, non-indicative mood and non-present tense (Mustanoja 1960: 526, 529, 533; Rohdenburg 1996, 2009: 317–319, 2014, 2018; Schlüter 2005: 185–206; Vosberg 2006; Callies 2013: 4; see also Chapter 2, Section 2.2).

Inflectional form. Particularly in relation to the Cognitive Complexity Principle, certain paradigmatic forms are found to facilitate or delay the spread of new complementation types. As modal verbs, non-explicit (base and old) forms are attested with BI clauses, whereas explicit ones (*-s*, *-ing* or *-ed* inflections) are found more frequently with the *to* infinitival marker (cf. Callies 2013: 4).

Principle of avoidance of identity. Three realisation/performance/phonetic factors are claimed to have a bearing on infinitival alternation: the *horror aequi* effect, the Principle of Rhythmic Alternation and the optimal syllable. *Horror aequi* refers to the avoidance of repiting "identical lexical or morphological forms in immediate adjacency" (in Lohmann 2011: 2; cf. Vosberg 2006: 45–46; Rohdenburg 2009: 317, 2018: 137). In the case of infinitival complementation, this refers to the "tendency to avoid the coincidence of two (near-)adjacent marked infinitives" (e.g. *to help* + *to* infinitive; Rohdenburg 2018: 137). The Principle of Rhythmic Alternation denotes "an idealized state" in which "an ideal rhythm alternates between maximally constraining units, i.e. between stressed and unstressed syllables" (Schlüter 2005: 18–19). In infinitival complementation, the *to*-infinitive acts as a stress clash buffer in contexts in which both the preceding and the initial syllable of the infinitive are stressed. Finally, the optimal syllable structure refers to the avoidance of sequences of vowels or consonants

(Rohdenburg and Schlüter 2000: 472; Lohmann 2011: 6; see also Chapter 2, Section 3.4).[5]

1.3 Modelling infinitival complementation in the history of English

This research seeks to advance the study of non-finite clausal complementation, particularly in relation to *to*-infinitive/BI alternation in post-verbal position in English. Previous studies have focused on the origin and rise of the *to*-infinitive and the competition with other forms (BI, *–ing*, subjunctive *that*-clauses; see Los 2005; Fanego 2004; Cuyckens and De Smet 2007), on specific main-clause complement-taking verbs (Mair 2003; Taeymans 2004a, b, 2006; Loureiro-Porto 2009, 2010; Lohmman 2011; Callies 2013; Levshina 2018), and on the semantic/cognitive differences between the two complement alternatives (van der Auwera and Diewald 2012: 131) and other textual, dialectal and periodisation predictors. The aim of this research is to investigate the determinants of infinitival alternation in American and British English across time. The following chapters will present a comprehensive analysis of the influence of morphosyntactic, semantic/pragmatic, processing, identity-avoidance and period-related factors on the variation and its evolution and distribution over time.

The purpose of this study is to answer the following research questions:

1. Is the variation categorical (one-to-one correlation between main-clause verb and infinitival solution) or probabilistic? Are the variants interchangeable?
2. Does frequency play a role? Is frequency related to the success of specific probabilistic constraints?

5 In this monograph, I only deal with strictly linguistically variables. In the literature other factors have been studied, such as the emergence or obsolescence of complement types in relation to textual variation (Palmer 1990: 128; Rohdenburg 1996: 159; Denison 1998: 170; Biber 1999: 736–737) – BI clauses are considered more informal than those with the *to* infinitival marker.

3. Does diachrony affect the variation? Does it affect American English and British English in the same way?
4. Is dialectal or regional (American vs British) variation a determining factor in the model?
5. Is the variation influenced by language-internal and language-external constraints?
6. Is the variation influenced by the meaning of the main-clause verb?

More specifically, this study explores the variation between *to*-infinitive/BI complementation governed by the verbs *dare*, *need* and *help* in American and British English from ME to PDE. It adopts a corpus-based/related approach, which investigates a number of morphosyntactic, semantic/pragmatic, processing and identity-related features, as described in Chapter 2, Section 2.2. The theoretical interpretation of the results does not follow any specific framework, but instead draws on different theoretical approaches to describe and explain the variation, and bases its findings on real (native), written and spoken data extracted from the Penn-Helsinki Parsed Corpus of Middle English (1150–1550), the Penn Corpus of Early English Correspondence (1410–1681), the Penn-Helsinki Parsed Corpus of Early Modern English (1500–1710), the Penn Parsed Corpus of Modern British English (1700–1914) and the British National Corpus Baby (1994) for British English, and COHA (1810–2000) for American English. These corpora will provide evidence for research questions (RQ) 1–4, while descriptive and statistical analysis of the variables will answer RQs 5–6, with information about lower-clause verbs, metalinguistic and main-/complement-clause, constructional and semantic/pragmatic features. Logistic regression will serve to identify the type of variation (categorical, probabilistic or free) and reveal the factors responsible for the choice. Distance, complexity and avoidance of identity will be central to the analysis in relation to RQ 5. Direct interaction between *dare*, *need* and *help* and the *to*-infinitive/BI clause will offer insight into the conceptualisation of the construction as a unit (see Matthews 1981: 183; Egan 2008), as will distance issues between the main and lower clause, *horror aequi* and stress patterns (Rohdenburg 1996, 2003: 205, 2009: 317–319, 2014, 2018; Schlüter 2005; Vosberg 2006: 45–46). The aim of RQs 2 and 3, related to frequency and diachrony, respectively, is to assess the impact of the economy vs expressivity dichotomy on the variation (Langacker 1977: 106–107; Fischer and Nänny 1999: xix). The same RQs will examine the regularisation of the variants and the consolidation of the processes in progress (Denison 2004). A study of American and British English (RQ 4) constructions has been conducted to check whether Mair's (2002) conclusions for *help* may be extrapolated to the other verbs investigated in this dissertation. As regards semantic/pragmatic features (RQ 6), I analyse the relationship between the meaning of the main-clause (main) verbs and the *to*-infinitive/BI complement (Driven 1989; Egan 2008; Fanego 2004, among others).

In what follows, Chapter 2 explains the adoption of a corpus-based/related methodology, describes the corpora and tools used for the retrieval/extraction of examples (Section 2.1), and presents the factors that may have a determining effect on the infinitival alternation (Section 2.2) and the statistical techniques used for their analysis (Section 2.3) examines the effect of diachrony and regional variation on infinitival complementation alternation and identifies the most relevant factors affecting the variation in American and British from ME to PDE. Chapter 3 focuses on the constructions headed by the verbs *dare* and *need*. The chapter begins with a review of the literature on the status of *dare* and the ancestors of modal verbs (Section 3.2) and continues with a descriptive and quantitative analysis of *dare* and *need* in ME and EModE and of the role of *tharf* and its influence on *dare* and *need* in the ME period (Section 3.3). Section 3.4 presents the synchronic and diachronic study of the *to*-infinitive/BI clauses governed by *dare* and *need* from EModE to PDE in American and British English, and Section 3.5 explores the development of the *dare*- and *need*-construction plus infinitival complementation in terms of the predictors that have been claimed to have an effect on the alternation and analyses the few transitive construction types in which the verbs are attested, mainly from LModE onwards. Chapter 4 is devoted to constructions with *help*. The literature review provided in Section 4.2 summarises the main findings on *help* plus infinitival complementation and the analysis of the various complementation choices in *help* sentences from ME to PDE in American and British English is presented in Section 4.3.1. Section 4.3.2.1 explains the methodology used and the factors selected in the statistical analysis for *help* from ME onwards; the multivariate analysis per period and variety is justified in Section 4.3.2.2. Section 4.4 analyses the factors that have affected the variation diachronically and diatopically; these findings are summarised and commented on in Section 4.5. Chapter 5 rounds off the investigation by summarising the main findings and identifying future lines of research.

2. Data and methodology

This chapter provides information about the methodology and data used in this study: the corpora used for the empirical analysis, the process of data retrieval, the factors and variables examined, and the statistical analysis. Section 2.1 describes the six corpora selected for the diachronic and synchronic analyses of British and American English. Section 2.2 examines the variables claimed in the literature to influence the distribution of *to*-infinitive/BI complement clauses governed by *dare*, *need* and *help*, and the characteristics of main and complement clauses and other construction-based/related predictors. Section 2.3 explains the statistical analyses carried out in Chapters 3 and 4, and Section 2.4 offers an analysis of the overall effect of verb, diachrony and regional variation on infinitival complement choice in American and British ME to PDE.

2.1 Data selection

The following sections present a description of the corpora selected for British and American English, the tools used to retrieve the data, and the coding process applied.

2.1.1 British English

The Penn Corpora of Historical English and the BNC Baby are the main sources of data used for British English to trace the evolution of infinitival complementation from ME to PDE.

Middle English. The PPCME2 (https://www.ling.upenn.edu/histcorpora/PPCME2-RELEASE-4/index.html) comprises approximately 1.2 million words and covers the time period M1 to M4, with each subperiod spanning approximately one hundred years (M1: 1150–1250, M2: 1250–1350, M3: 1350–1420, M4: 1420–1550). When the dating of some of the texts in the PPCME2 is ambiguous between the date of composition and that of the earliest manuscript, I follow Taeymans (2006) in suing the manuscript date. Texts which are labelled MX/1 are therefore classed as M1; MX/2 and M1/2 texts, as M2; MX/3, M1/3 and M2/3, as M3; and MX/4, M1/4, M2/4 and M3/4, as M4.

Early Modern English. For the Early Modern English period, I have used the PPCEME (https://www.ling.upenn.edu/histcorpora/PPCEME-RELEASE-3/index.html). It contains 1.7 million words and divides the EModE period into E1 (1500–1569), E2 (1570–1639) and E3 (1640–1710).

I have expanded the data for the ME and EModE periods with examples retrieved from the PCEEC. The PCEEC is based on the Corpus of Early English Correspondence. This corpus consists of roughly 2.2 million words (over four-fifths of the original corpus word count) and covers the final years of M3 (1410–1419), M4 (1420–1550) and the three subperiods of Early Modern English. Since the letters included in these collections usually date from different years, the PCEEC identifies them according to the date range in which the collections were written. I have taken as my reference point for each source the first year of the date range provided. The PCEEC uses the same annotation conventions as the PPCME2 and the PPCEME. To avoid the minor overlap between the PCEEC and PPCEME corpora, 27 texts from the PPCEME were omitted from my database because the examples found in these texts were also attested in the PCEEC and the corresponding PPCEME texts are smaller than those of the PCEEC.

Late Modern English. The data for British LModE were retrieved from the PPCMBE (https://www.ling.upenn.edu/histcorpora/PPCMBE2-RELEASE-1/index.html). The PPCMBE contains just under one million words and spans just over 210 years (1700–1914) (see Kroch et al. 2010). The corpus is divided into three periods of 70 years, labelled as L1 (1700–1769), L2 (1770–1839) and L3 (1840–1914).

Present-Day English. The data for Present-Day English were retrieved from the BNC Baby (http://www.natcorp.ox.ac.uk/corpus/baby/manual.pdf), a database of 4 million words extracted from the 100 million-word British National Corpus.

2.1.2 *American English*

The database for the empirical analysis of American English is sampled from COHA. COHA is a 400-million-words database of texts from 1810 to 2000. Given the vast size of COHA, I have compiled a subcorpus consisting of two periods of ten years each, and a third period of six years (1810–1819, 1910–1919, 1995–2000). These periods correspond to the final years of the L2 and L3 LModE subperiods and the PDE period in my British English database. The texts from each period were selected randomly. In attempt to ensure representativeness and balance, each period contains roughly 1,001,000 words and the size of each genre and year are also similar, where possible.

2.1.3 *Data retrieval and coding*

I began by reading the whole PPCMBE in order to identify all of the verbs that select *to*-infinitive and BI clauses in British LModE and all relevant examples of this construction. The second stage was to retrieve all instances of the verbs selected following this initial examination of the British and American varieties using WordSmith Tools and Corpus Studio. The 'Concord' option in WordSmith Tools was applied to the raw texts of the BNC Baby and COHA (for *help*, for example, the verbal forms *help*, *helps*, *helped* and *helping* were retrieved from the PDE data). The data from the Penn Corpora of Historical English was processed using Corpus Studio (Komen 2014). In Corpus Studio, I selected the type of language to be analysed (English histCS), the historical periods and their groups, the definition file with all possible spelling variants of the target verb, the different types of IP, the verbal, adjectival and noun phrase categories, coreferencing, conjunction types and other default values. In order to retrieve all possible occurrences of even rare dialectal forms, spelling variants were identified using the information and textual sources in the OED, the MED and Visser's ([1963] 1973) grammar.

After manual pruning, the database was then enriched with information about complementation types (NP, *ing*, *ed*, *that*-clauses, zero complementation, BI clauses, *to*-infinitive clauses, etc.) and a number of grammatical, structural, semantic/pragmatic and periodisation variables. When an example contains more than one complementation pattern, each predicate is recorded in a database entry; this convention is applied even to instances of ellipsis.

2.2 Database variables

The variables considered in this dissertation are categorised as follows: verb, metadata, periodisation, main-clause, complement-clause, construction and semantic/pragmatic variables. The categorisation of the variables was done bearing in mind the reduction or simplification of the levels to avoid problematic scenarios owing to the (potential) scarcity of data. For statistical purposes, binary levels are the preferred option whenever this does not involve the loss of relevant information.

VERB categorises the subordinate verb in the complement clause, and the 'metadata' variables provide information about the texts: author, file, period, production/recording year(s), corpus and geographical variety (British or American English). PERIODISATION reflects time periods: ME, EModE, LModE and PDE. In what follows I focus on the variables that convey more complex information.

2.2.1 Main-clause variables

These variables analyse the syntactic structure of the construction, i.e. SYNTAX, the occurrence of relative clauses and inversion, i.e. RELATIVE and INVERSION, and the main constituents of the subject and verb group. The syntactic structures in which the construction occurs are classified into three types: (i) 'main', when the main verb and the infinitival complement occur in a main clause, as in (61); (ii) '(optional) adverbial' (62). (iii) 'Dependent' refers to: apposition, in (63); cleft sentences; right-dislocation, in (64); relative clauses, with an elided relative *which* or *that*, as in *I durst not owne* in (65); tag questions, as in (66); dependent-phrases, of an adjective phrase, as in (67) where *ready* is the head of the AP and *to help further develop* is its complement; of an adverb phrase, as in (68); of a noun phrase or of a preposition, as in (69); clausal complements, in examples where the construction is an obligatory element of the clause: subject, as in (70), in which *what needs to be emphasised* is the subject of the main verb *is*; object; obligatory element in an intransitive predicate, as in (71), where *helpe rescue þe toune of Bathe* is the obligatory adjunct or adverbial of *go*;[6] extraposed subject, as in (72), or object; subject or object predicative, as in (73), in which *help* plus the *to*-infinitive complement functions as the object predicative of *found*; and parentheticals, as with *need* in (74).

(61) Raleigh. He may be, my Lord. Ld. Cecil. But *dare you challenge* it? Raleigh. No. (PPCEME, RALEIGH-E2-H,I,215.C1.551)

(62) And *yf thou dare truste the wether*, lette it lye so all nyghte: and on the nexte daye, tourne it agayne before none, (PPCEME, FITZH-E1-P2,34.226)

(63) "You need to be fair to that friend and realise it's your responsibility to handle it," says Betty Youngs, Ph.D., a family counselor from San Diego, and author of Stress and Your Child: *Helping Kids Cope With the Strains and Pressures of Life*. (COHA, mag_1997_398785)

(64) There 's one thing only of you I beseech, *To help me pay the printer* -- write thy speech. (COHA, fic_1818_8886)

(65) I am not for disguises, it looks like Guilt, and I would not doe *a thing I durst not owne*. (PCEEC, OSBORNE,57.026.1293).

(66) Oh. I daren't leave them that, *dare I*? (BNC Baby, KD3)

(67) "[. . .] It is *ready to help further develop* American shipping either by operating U. S. Shippmg Board vessels or in any ether way." (COHA, news_1919_684696)

(68) Mrs. Purcell. I can remember it as well as any thing in the World. Oates. I desire, my Lord, that she may tell how she does remember it. Mrs. Purcell. That's enough, and *as much as need to be said*, I remember very well. Oates. But I desire to know how you come to remember it? Mrs. Purcell. I remember it, I tell you, very well; (PPCEME, OATES-E3-H,4,83.C1.435)

(69) When it comes *to helping clean up* soils contaminated with heavy and toxic metals, nature has ARS plant physiologist Leon V. Kochian to thank. (COHA, nf_2000_746930)

6 Unless otherwise indicated, translations are mine.

(70) *What needs to be emphasised*, though, *is* that direct experience - becoming part of a way of life that includes the alien in a wider definition of what it is to be human - seems to be almost the only way of achieving demystification. (BNC Baby, CRS)

(71) WHen Arthure herde þis tydynges, he lete honge anone þe hostages, [. . .] and him-self *went helpe rescue þe toune of Bathe.* (PPCME2, CMBRUT3,71.2144)
when Arthur heard these events, he let hang immediately the hostages, [. . .] and himself went help rescue the town of Bath.
'when Arthur heard these events, he let hang the hostages immediately, [. . .] and he himself went help rescue the town of Bath.'

(72) As for pill popping, *it* 's now clear *that we need to down a few supplements a day to fill nutritional gaps.* (COHA, mag_1999_407850)

(73) The most important fact on the German side of the southeast front is the tremendous personality of General von Linsingen, *which I found* animating the whole gingery, scrappy staff and permeating to the farthest mud outposts, chiefly accounting for the exuberant morale and terrific optimism of the Volhynian front and *helping to explain the Volhynian campeign.* (COHA, news_1916_682619)

(74) The present,*we hard*ly need to be told, is extremely tense. (BNC Baby, B17)

Examples are classed as RELATIVE when the subject or object of the construction is a relativiser, as in (75) and (65), respectively, or when the construction containing the complement is part of a relative clause, as in (76).

(75) How many vaine wordes are spoken and *who dare speake* for me? (PCEEC, STUART,173.012.429)

(76) Constantly ask yourself *what key questions reading this book is going to help to answer.* (BNC Baby, HXH)

Another main-clause variable is (main-clause) verb-subject inversion (INVERSION), as in (77), where *dare* inverts with the subject *I*. The possibility of inversion is characteristic of modal/auxiliary verbs.

(77) Arch. I humbly beg leave to be excused: My Master, Madam, pays me; *nor dare I take* Money from any other Hand without injuring his Honour, and disobeying his Commands. (PPCEME, FARQUHAR-E3-P2,34.604)

Two aspects of main-constituent subjects are analysed: syntactic structure and animacy. The syntactic structure of the subject, i.e. SUBJECT COMPLEXITY, has eleven levels: (i) 'pro_personal', when the subject is a personal pronoun, such as *I* in example (77) above and *us* in (78) below. In example (78), the oblique personal pronoun *us* functions as the subject of the Experiencer construction *nedith not to excuse Judith*. This type of construction has a separate category of its own: 'experiencer' (see Chapter 3, Section 3.3.1); (ii) 'pro_indefinite' is used to code indefinite subject pronouns, such as *something* in (79); (iii) 'pro_demonstrative' labels subject demonstrative pronouns; (iv) 'pro_relative' corresponds to the relativisers *that*, zero, *when*, *where*, *what*, *which*, *who*, *whom* and their historical variants (e.g. *þat* in (80)); (v) 'imperative_subject' refers to contexts in which the main clause has imperative force and contains either an explicit *you* subject or an implicit second-person subject referent; (vi) 'NP' is used to label noun phrase subjects without a post-modifier; (vii) 'clausal' refers to *-ing* clauses (*trading down* in (81)), *to*-infinitive clauses (*to have it swell in volume, and rise higher and higher* in (82)), and *that*- and *whether*-clauses functioning as subjects (in (83) and (84), respectively); (viii) 'expanded subject' is used when the subject contains a postmodifier, as in the case of *any one of you* in (85); (ix) 'coordinated' is used to label examples of noun-phrase coordination (examples containing both post-modification and coordination are classified according to the strategy that is displayed by the subject; for instance, in (86) *Theodore Price and other bears who had turned bulls earlier in the declines* is coded as coordinated since the postmodifier follows the coordinator); (x) 'expletive' is used in examples with dummy/expletive *it*, as in (87), and *there* subjects, as in (88) (in (87), for example, the *that*-clause *that coping with such multiple databases on which modelling is to be carried out is not a trivial exercise* is the logical/semantic subject of the main verb *need*, while *it* is a mere slot-filler); (xi) 'unexpressed' refers to non-explicit subjects, except in the case of imperative clauses, as in (71) above and (89) below, in which the implicit subjects of the non-finite main verb *help* are 'he' and 'the co-op', respectively – non-explicit subjects of clauses functioning as the object of the matrix verb have been classified as unexpressed as well, as in the subject of the complement clause governed by *want* in (90), which does not apply in the case of examples such as (91), since the matrix verbal group is not *'re going* but *'re going to need* because *'re going to* is a modal ('modal') auxiliary.

(78) *Vs nedith not to excuse* Judith fro lesingis and tresoun to Olofernes, but we moun fauorably excuse hire fro deedly synne in this doinge, for the greet loue that sche hadde to Goddis peple, and to slee Olofernes, a blasfemyere of God, and distroiere of his lawe and peple; (PPCME2, CMPURVEY,I,36.1692)

(79) Widmann said he told Hamrick that "*something* needed to be done" about him. (COHA, news_2000_622049)

(80) he fourþe is: 'Þou schalt worschyp þy fadyr and þy modyr þat han broght þe ynto þys world, and þy god-fadyr and þy god-modyr *þat holpen to make* þe a cristen man, and thy faydr vndyr God þat haþe þe charche of þy soule, and schall ġeue vnswar þerof befor God.' (PPCME2, CMMIRK,103.2786)
'the fourth is: "you shall worship your father and your mother who have brought you into this world, and your god-father and god-mother, who helped to make you a Cristian man, and your father under God who has the charge of your soul, and shall give answer therefore in front of God"'

(81) *Trading down helped* the firm grab business from smaller operators and more than made up for falling sales of its classier Gainsborough furniture in the six months to end September. (BNC Baby, CBD)

(82) and then *to have it swell in volume, and rise higher and higher, helps* hasten disaster. (COHA, mag_1911_430486)

(83) It is clear that the actual behaviour of a church bell differs widely from that of a bell infinitely thin; and*that this should be the case need* not surprise us when we consider the actual ratio of the thickness at the sound-bow to the interval between consecutive nodal meridians. (PPCMBE, STRUTT-1890,3,330.246)

(84) *Whether this has or has not been a wise desire need* not be discussed here. (PPCMBE, TROLLOPE-1882,170.239)

(85) (--) and if *any one of you dare* call me by any other name, I 'll bring my action against you for defamation. (COHA, fic_1814_8564)

(86) Theodore Price *and* other bears who had turned bulls earlier in the declines were heavy buyers and helped maintain prices. (COHA, news_1910_678775)

(87) *It* need hardly be pointed out *that coping with such multiple databases on which modelling is to be carried out is not a trivial exercise.* (BNC Baby, B1G)

(88) *There need* not in all cases be an actual breach of the contract.' (BNC Baby, FSS)

(89) *To help* parents and children get to know one another-thus broadening the number of sitters each child will feel comfortahle with-*the co-op* organizes group activities like trick-or-treating at Halloween. (COHA, mag_1998_401804)

(90) *I* wanted to *help* these women to "find a voice" and no longer to place their needs at the bottom of the list of priorities. (BNC Baby, A7Y)

(91) How many roadside interview sheets do you think we*'re going to need* to order? (BNC Baby, KD8)

In Chapter 4, the different subject types are grouped into four categories: 'pro', in reference to the four types of pronouns, (c-)overt imperative subjects and expletive subjects; 'complex', in reference to clausal, expanded and coordinated subjects; 'NP', and 'unexpressed'. This reduced classification of the original factors is further simplified to basic vs non-basic subjects, with basic subjects comprising the pro and NP levels, and non-basic subjects referring to complex and unexpressed subjects, which are more difficult to process (see Chapter 3).

My analysis of subject animacy follows Zaenen et al.'s (2004: 1) animacy hierarchy, which is "hypothesized to influence the grammatical prominence that is given to the realization of entities within a discourse". My analysis is condensed to three values: 'animate', 'non-animate' and 'unexpressed'. In cases of indeterminacy, I have opted for animate categorisation when the verb is in the plural form, as in (92); when the subject serves as the antecedent of a plural pronoun (*them*, *these*, *those*), when the subject co-refers with a plural noun; when the subject serves as the antecedent of an animate pronoun (*who*), and, from a semantic perspective, when the collective subject focuses on the members' animate dimension, as in (93). By contrast, I analyse the subject as non-animate when the verb is in the singular form (as in (94) and (95)), when the subject serves as the antecedent of a singular pronoun (such as *its* in (95), which refers to *the county council's tourism department*), when the subject co-refers with a singular noun, when the subject serves as the antecedent of an inanimate pronoun (*which*), and when the subject may be replaced by either 'the members of. . .'· or 'the organisation/administrative body. . .' in cases of collective subjects (for more details about animate subjects, see Section 2.2.2). Also, subjects which comprise both inanimate and animate referents are classified as either animate or non-animate, depending of the animacy of the first element of the coordination, as illustrated by the subjects *a pensions ombudsman and a tracing service* in (96) and *people and businesses* in (97). Finally, unexpressed is used when the construction lacks a subject because the construction itself functions as the subject of the main clause, as in (98), where the non-finite clause *HELPING VERY YOUNG CHILDREN learn pre-academic skills* is the subject of the main verbal group *can be*.

(92) *Petersfield Rugby Club are helping* Mrs. Bulmer organise a May Ball as a fund-raising event, and it will take place in a specially erected marquee at Penns Place adjacent to the club on May 1st. (BNC Baby, BM4)

(93) And the *council's housing department* is *asking* tenants thinking of moving on to *help* them make the most of the housing stock by giving early notice when they intend to leave. (BNC Baby, K4S)

(94) More recently, *CSE has* joined the battle against the Kyoto treaty, *helped* lead the fight against the Microsoft anti-trust prosecution, and launched a number of other anti-regulatory campaigns in the areas of liability law, technology, and heal (COHA, mag_1999_399060)

(95) The *county council's tourism department has released* a new edition of *its* guide, Essex – Places to Visit, *to help* local families or visitors to the region choose their destination. (BNC Baby, E9S)

(96) There will also be *a pensions ombudsman and a tracing service to help* people track down pensions held with previous employers, he told Mr Gerrard Neale (C. Cornwall N) in a written reply. (BNC Baby A7W)

(97) TEC managing director Dr. Max Wilson said: 'In the current recession, more *people and businesses need to* have instant and accurate information about vocational training opportunities. (BNC Baby, BM4)

(98) *HELPING VERY YOUNG CHILDREN learn pre-academic skills* can be ticklish business. (COHA, mag_1998_390828)

The variables PARADIGM, MORPHOLOGY, PRESENT, INDICATIVE, DO-SUPPORT and VOICE depict features of the main-clause verbal groups. PARADIGM identifies the grammatical form of the main verb (MV_FORM) according to eight levels- 'Present general' is used with verbal forms in the present tense with subjects other than the third-person singular, as illustrated by *dare* in (99), and with third-person-singular present-tense contexts in which the main verb and the subject do not show overt agreement, as in (100), where *need* does not show third-person -*s* inflection. 'Present third', when the verb agrees overtly with a third-person subject in a present-tense context, as in *is going to* in (76) above. If the verbal construction is in the past tense, the main verb or the first auxiliary form of the verbal group is labelled as 'past', as illustrated by *might* in (101). 'Base form' covers infinitives (with or without *to*) and imperative forms, as in (75) and (76) above. *Ing* forms may be '*ing*_progressive', if the verb is part of a continuous tense, such as *helping* in (102), and '*ing*_general' in other cases, such as *needing* in (103). The levels '*ed*_perfect' and '*ed*_passive' refer to the use of the past participle in a perfect and a passive construction, respectively. In the present perfect continuous construction illustrated in (102), therefore, the first auxiliary *'s* is labelled as 'present third', *been* as *ed*_perfect and the main verb *helping* as '*ing*_progressive'. A combination of up to four main verbal forms is attested in (101): the past form *might* is followed by the base form *have*, the *-ed* perfect form *been able to* and the base form *help*.

(99) *I dare* not resort to such an unworthy experiment. (PPCMBE, BROUGHAM-1861,12.414)

(100) [. . .] -yet *that need in no way occur*, if only I am properly informed, through you and Stockmar, of the true state of things. (PPCMBE, VICTORIA-186X,1,206.469)

(101) If they had investigated thoroughly at the time they *might not only have been able to* identify other elements of the fraud but also *help* secure some of the lost assets. (BNC Baby, K2C)

(102) He'*s been helping* Mark put together the Business Plan and the presentation. (BNC Baby, AC2)

(103) *Needing* to borrow £50,000 million this year, Mr Lamont had to promise his creditors that he would put his accounts in order as soon as possible. (BNC Baby, E9S)

Paradigm cannot be added to the multifactorial study because its levels cannot be reduced without the loss of relevant information, and are therefore discussed in quantitative terms only. The predictors MORPHOLOGY,

PRESENT and INDICATIVE also describe features related to paradigm. MORPHOLOGY contains the levels 'explicit' and 'non-explicit'. To give an example, *s/he/it dare*, *you dare* and 'other' forms are considered 'non-explicit', whereas *dares*, *darest*, (non-)finite *dared/durst* (simple past), *to dare*, bare *dare* and *daring* are 'explicit'. To simplify the analysis of the main-clause verbal group, only the binary 'present' vs 'non-present' tense is considered by the variable PRESENT.

As regards mood, finite verbal constructions may be factual, non-factual or counterfactual (see Quirk et al. 1985: 149, and Section 2.2.3). Three moods are traditionally identified in English: indicative, considered to be the unmarked alternative, subjunctive and imperative (see Quirk et al. 1985: 149 and Denison 1998: 160, among others). Indicative refers to facts whereas subjunctive refers to "the set of forms chosen typically to mark doubt, unreality, wishes, commands, and so on" (Denison 1998: 160). Imperative mood "expresses a request which the speaker expects to be fulfilled" (Mustanoja 1960: 473). Mustanoja observes that the formal differences between the indicative and the subjunctive started to be lost or abandoned as early as Old English, though the process was not completed until the fifteenth century. In EModE, therefore, the only "distinctive subjunctive forms are restricted to the verb *be* and to the second and third person singular of non-auxiliary verbs (thou lovest/love; he loves (loveth)/love; thou lovedst/loved)" (Rissanen 1999: 228; see also Mustanoja 1960: 452). This decline in inflectional forms favoured the use of modal auxiliaries (*sculan*, *willan*, *magan*, *motan*, *þurfan*, *uton*, *hatan* and *durran*) as periphrastic markers of the subjunctive mood, as a clearer, more emphatic alternative to the old inflectional forms (Mustanoja 1960: 453). In ME the inflectional present subjunctive is attested in the third- and second-person singular in non-dependent clauses, though in the latter case, the subjunctive and imperative forms are similar and sometimes indistinguishable (Mustanoja 1960: 455–456). The present subjunctive is volitional (i.e. it expresses wish, exhortation, command and concession), whereas the preterite subjunctive normally "expresses non-volitional verbal activity the reality or realisability of which is conditioned by a hypothetical dependent clause or is otherwise subject to doubt", such as *dide* in (104) (Mustanoja 1960: 456).

(104) ȝiff Crist itt nolde þolenn himm, Ne *dide* he nohht tatt dede (Orm. 11812) (in Mustanoja 1960: 456)
If Crist it not-wanted thole him, not did he not that deed
'If Crist did not allow it to him, he [the Devil] would not perform that action'

Mustanoja (1960: 458–70) describes nine dependent clause types in which the subjunctive may occur, regardless of the subject person: noun, relative, place, time, comparison, result, purpose, concession and condition. As regards conditional sentences, the indicative mood is used when the condition is conceived as a fact, while the subjunctive is attested when the main clause expresses volition. According to Mustanoja (1960: 469), the subjunctive became increasingly frequent in conditional clauses with a main clause in the indicative in the thirteenth and fourteenth centuries. Sometimes the indicative and the subjunctive are used in the same context without any marked difference as regards modality, as in (105). If the clause conveys a purely hypothetical, unreal statement, Mustanoja states that the verb is likely to be preterite subjunctive, as in (106). Rissanen (1999: 230) claims that the preterite or pluperfect subjunctive was frequent in the apodosis, as illustrated by *were* in (107), and remained common until the eighteenth century.

(105) and *if he bereth* a spere, hoold thee on the right syde, and *if he bere* a swerd, thanne shul ye kepe yow wisely from all swich peple (Ch. CT B Mel. 2502) (in Mustanoja 1960: 470)
'and if he carries a spear, keep youself on the right side, and if he carry a sword, then you should keep yourself wisely from all such people'

(106) *and I were* a pope… every myghty man Sholde have a wyf (Ch. CT B Mk. 3140) (in Mustanoja 1960: 470)

(107) *I were* a verie vnworthye man to hold that place… if I were to be touched in that sorte. ([HC] Essex 16)

In PDE, the remnants of the subjunctive are found in third-person present-tense forms, as in (108), with bare *be* forms, as in (109), and with the past subjunctive *were* form with first- and third-person singular verbal groups, as in (110) (Hundt and Gardner 2017: 105). Hundt and Gardner (2017: 105–108) point out that the subjunctive is limited to four contexts: in formulaic expressions such as *Long live the Queen if need be. . .*; after certain subordinators such as *on condition that* and *lest*; in mandative subjunctives following 'suasive' verbs (*advise*, *ask*, *beg*, *demand*, *desire*, *direct*, *insist*, *move*, *order*, *propose*, *recommend*, *request*, *require*, *stipulate*, *suggest*, *urge* and *wish*), nouns (*demand*, *desire*, *proposal*, *recommendation*, *request*, *requirement*, *suggestion* and *wish*) and adjectives (*anxious*, *essential*, *important*, *necessary* and *sufficient*), and in the protasis of conditional sentences. The verbal form is therefore indeterminate as regards subjunctive or indicative mood in affirmative clauses dominated by a matrix expression that requires the subjunctive, which the subject is not in the third-person singular, as in (111) (Hundt and Gardner 2017: 108).

(108) . . . he turned upon her with his mock fury and demanded that *she give* him another pickled peach before the jar was disposed of. (1913 COHA: FIC) (Hundt and Gardner 2017: 105)

(109) She felt that her position as a future poet demanded that *she be* finely dressed. (1911 COHA: FIC) (Hundt and Gardner 2017: 105)

(110) you were shifting the gears as if *this were* an ordinary car . . . (Hundt and Gardner 2017: 105)

(111) I *propose we/they/you* all *use* fewer subjunctives in the future

Therefore, mood comprises six levels: indicative, imperative, non-finite, subjunctive, modal subjunctive and underspecified. The main verbal group is indicative in the following contexts: if it features the inflectional *-s* ending in third-person present forms, as in *he bereth* in (105); if the verbal form is unambiguously indicative, as in the case of the inflected second-person singular form *hast* in (112); and if the linguistic context/construction is not eligible for subjunctive mood (113).

(112) *Thou hast* carried me in thy arms, and *hast* helped me to climb for many a bird's nest (COHA, fic_1815_9352)

(113) Hoover knew how the Mob helped Kennedy buy votes; (BNC Baby, K5C)

The imperative value applies in the case of imperative sentences, while non-finite refers to non-finite verbal groups, such as *needing* in (103) above. The classification of the verbal group as subjunctive varies depending on period and context. In ME, the label subjunctive is assigned to sentences in which: (i) the verbal group occurs in a non-dependent context expressing preterite subjunctive, as in (104) above, or in a non-dependent context with a third- or second-person singular subject expressing present subjunctive; (ii) the verbal group is found in one of the nine dependent clauses described by Mustanoja (1960: 458–70), as illustrated by the subordinate clause introduced by *that*, dependent of the subject noun clause *resoun and tyme* in (114); and (iii) the verbal group inverts with the subject, as in (115). In EModE the label subjunctive is restricted to dependent contexts expressing subjunctive meanings and third- or second-person singular subjects, as in (116). From LModE to PDE, the subjunctive is restricted to cases in which the verbal form is a third-person present tense in a mandative subjunctive construction following suasive verbs, nouns and adjectives (Hundt and Gardner 2017: 105–108).

(114) now it is resoun and tyme that I shewe yow… (Ch. CT B Mel. 2413) (in Mustanoja 1960: 458)
'Now there is reason and time to show you…'

(115) Wretyn at Sustede on þe Satyrday nexst after Seynt Valentynys day. Here *dare noman seyn* a gode wurd for ġou in þis cuntrè, Godde amend it. (PCEEC, PASTON,I,230.063.1870)
'Written at Sustede on the Saturday after Saint Valentine's day. Here dares no man say a good word for you in this country, God amend it.'

(116) Wherefore if there be any Apothecaries of Lo~don, that dare take in hande to make these noble compositions, they may know now where to haue the~: (PPCEME, TURNER-E1- P2,E6V.12)
Wherefor if there be any apothecaries of London, that dare take in hand to make these noble compositions, they may know now where to have them
'For that reason, if there be any apothecaries in London who dare take the responsibility of making these noble compositions, they may know now where to find them.'

Verbal groups introduced by modals are analysed as modal subjunctive, since modals convey subjunctive meaning, as in (117). Following Hundt and Gardner (2017: 108), the verbal form has been classed as unspecified: when it may be (morphologically) indicative or subjunctive and the context/construction admits subjunctive mood, as illustrated by the past tense *needed* in the protasis of the conditional sentence in (118); with third-person singular forms involving cliticisation of the negative particle *n't*, such as *needn't* in (119); and, in the EModE period, with subjects other than third- or second-person singular in dependent constructions that express subjunctive meaning, as in (120).

(117) That is what no man, of the common timid feelings of mankind, *would have dared* say or feel, and what's the world's opinion of Nelson? (PPCMBE, HAYDON-1808,1,36.926)

(118) *If she needed to hang out the wash*, all she had to do was tie Ann's harness line to the post. (COHA, fic_2000_27711)

(119) Lady Markby: That is quite true, dear. But one *needn't* know them. (PPCMBE, WILDE-1895,61.595)

(120) I speake my cleear thoughts; had I not taken my journy when I did, to carry me from the inquisition of owr examiners and from thedejectednes that the continewall renewing thereof did urge upon me, I was in a fayre or fowle way to a dangerous feaver, and so ill was I that I protest *I durst not have taken* a journy had not my judgment tould me that I had no other outward meanes left to preserve my selfe. (PCEEC, BARRING,217.156.2700)

Indeterminate mood is used when it is not possible to determine whether the verbal group has a periphrastic subjunctive mood, it is a relic of an old verbal form, or the verbal form is undergoing regularisation or modalisation/auxiliarisation. These contexts are restricted in ME and EModE to third- and second-person singular subjects that lack *–s* or *–st* inflection, respectively, in non-dependent clauses, as in (121), and in EModE to dependent clauses that trigger indicative mood, as in (122); in LModE and PDE, indeterminate applies to forms with third-person singular subjects. In EModE, subject-verb inversion may be considered unspecified or indeterminate, depending on the type of subject, as in (123). This is also the case of the old form *durst* and the regularised *–ed* forms of *need*, *dare* and *help* in contexts expressing subjunctive meaning from EModE onwards, as in (124) and (125). In any case, for statistical needs, mood has been coded as a binary feature in the INDICATIVE variable in my analysis. INDICATIVE takes 'indicative' as its reference level and combines imperative, subjunctive, modal subjunctive and unspecified/indeterminate mood into 'non-indicative'.

(121) *The Priest* is now in the Cellar, and *dare not refuse* to do the work. (PPCEME, FARQUHAR-E3-H,64.662)

(122) I merveyl meche þat ġe send me nomore tydyngys þan ġe haue sent. Rogere Foke of Sparham sent to me and *seythe* þat *he dare nott gon owt* of his hows for be kawse of þe sewte þat Heydon and Wymdam haue aġens hem, for he is thrett þat if he may be gette he xal be ladde to preson. (PCEEC, PASTON,I,232.064.1909)
'I marvel much that you send me no more pieces of news than you have sent. Rogere Foke of Sparham sent me and said that he dare not go out of his house because of the suit that Heydon and Wymdam have against him, for he is threatened that if he may be got he shall be sent to prison.'

(123) So that they being on all occasions very useful to us, we find it absolutely necessary to caress 'em as friends, and not to treat 'em as slaves, *nor dare we do* other, their numbers so far surpassing ours in that continent. (PPCEME, BEHN-E3-P1,151.63)

(124) I am not for disguises, it looks like Guilt, and I would not doe a thing *I durst not owne.* (PCEEC, OSBORNE,57.026.1293)

(125) I had a whore on on side and a pitifull rogue on the other; and two schollars in the opposit seat violated my ears with such horrid, dissolute, and profane discourse, as I scarce should have thought *the divell himselfe dared either use or teach others*, were it not that I was soe unfortunate as to have this miserable experience thereof. (PCEEC, PRIDEAU,5.001.5)

The parameter DO-SUPPORT codes the presence/absence of primary auxiliary *do* in negative or interrogative sentences and in emphatic uses; the old strategies of direct negation and inversion are classified as 'other' in this factor. Finally, the variable VOICE identifies 'active' and 'passive' verb groups.

2.2.2 Complement clause

As was the case with the main clauses, a number of variables were designed to account for the syntactic structure, subjects and verbal groups of the complement clauses in the database. Following Cuyckens et al. (2014: 189), I have classified the syntactic structure of the complement clause (CC) into three patterns within the factor VALENCY:

- 'Intransitive': subordinate verb without complement(s) and with/without modifier(s), such as *dy* in (126)

- 'Transitive': subordinate verb with complement(s), as in (127), with/without modifier(s), as in example (127), where the subordinate verb *maintain* selects *a constant interior temperature* as its object and is followed by the adverbial *in the appliance.* In (128) *so* replaces the subject predicative *well-dressed and attractive at all times* of the previous sentence, also headed by the subordinate verb *be.*
- 'Coordinated', as in (129), which shows the coordination of two subordinate BI clauses (*confront him* and *deny a charge More hateful*)

(126) and if you remember of olde *I dare dy* so I be not guilty of my owne death, and oppresse others with my ruine too if theare be no other way. (PCEEC, STUART,258.062.1087)

(127) This practice eliminates needless openings and closings of the refrigerator door, and *helps maintain a constant interior temperature in the appliance.* (COHA, mag_1997_428180)

(128) And yet at Millfield she had been more than ever concerned about her appearance, wanting to *be well-dressed and attractive at all times.* And I have *helped her to be so,* Ruth thought, jealousy surging through her. (BNC Baby, CB5)

(129) *Dare* you *confront him,* and *deny a charge More hateful,* if in guilt of such black hue Degrees exist, than perjury itself. (COHA, fic_1812_8551)

The label 'unclear' has been used here when the tag <unclear> is found in the example; in other words, when part of the subordinate verb complementation is missing (as in (130)). Examples of this type are only found in the spoken section of the BNC Baby, which uses this tag when one or more words are unclear to the corpus annotator.

(130) DOROTHY: there is golden syrup in this thing, I need to get <-|-> *<unclear>* <-|-> CHRISTOPHER: and I'm, I'm having the bowl and he's having the DOROTHY: OK (BNC Baby KBW)

As mentioned in Chapter 1, infinitival subjects may be overt or covert. The construction is referred to as overt when the NP is explicit and as covert when the NP is not present. These options are coded by the levels of the predictor SUBJECT OF INFINITIVE.

As was the case of main-clause subject, the types of complement-clause subject are: (i) 'pro', in reference to the four types of pronouns (personal pronoun objects or 'pro_personal'; 'pro_indefinite'; 'pro_relative'; 'pro_reflexive', as *themselves* in (131)); (ii) 'NP's; (iii) 'complex', in reference to clausal, expanded and coordinated subjects, such as *the Kynge and the realme* in (132); or (iv) 'unexpressed', in examples that lack an NP between the main verb and the infinitival complementation. Again, examples featuring both coordination and postmodification are classified according to the strategy displayed by the subject, as in (133), which is coded as coordinated. This reduced classification is further simplified to basic versus non-basic subjects in the variable OBJECT_COMPLEXITY, with 'basic' subjects comprising the pro and NP levels, and 'non-basic' subjects referring to complex and unexpressed subjects, which are more difficult to process.

(131) they drank to help *themselves* deal with a crisis; and they missed meals because they wanted to drink instead. (BNC Baby, ALP)

(132) But yet this fable for his parte, did in his daies helpe *the Kynge and the realme* to spende many a faire peny. (PPCEME, MROPER-E1-P1,518.62)

(133) The county council's tourism department has released a new edition of its guide, Essex – Places to Visit, to help *local families or visitors to the region* choose their destination. (BNC Baby E9S)

The animacy levels for the CC are 'animate' and 'non-animate'. Subjects are coded as 'animate' for linguistic and semantic reasons. Ambiguity is linguistically resolved in favour of the 'animate' level (i) when the verb is in the plural form, (ii) when the subject acts as the antecedent of a plural pronoun (*them*, *these*, *those*), such as *they* in (134), (iii) when the subject co-refers with a plural noun, such as *winners* in (135), and (iv) when the subject serves as the antecedent of an animate pronoun (*who*). Semantically, subjects are 'animate' when the CC verb more commonly selects animate subjects, as in the case of *recover* (*from*) in (136) and *raise* in (137), and when the subject refers exclusively to the members of a collective subject and to the members' animate properties.

(134) "We must get back to the high standards of self-discipline that we have set ourselves in the past," said Cooke. Inspirational Richards *helped Leicester* storm back from 18–3 down to 18–11" and *they* could have snatched victory in the dying stages. (BNC Baby, CH3)

(135) "When I came I said I wanted to *help Glamorgan* to become *winners* and that is still my aim." (BNC Baby, CH3)

(136) VIV ANDERSON called on all his European know-how *to help Sheffield Wednesday recover from* the shock of their lives last night. (BNC Baby, CH3)

(137) Chairman David Simpson, who appealed to supporters *to help the club raise* the money, said: 'We had some reaction. But we had to move quickly otherwise Colin would have gone back to Barnsley because his loan spell was over.' (BNC Baby, CH3)

'Non-animate' CC subjects are distinguished formally in the following cases: (i) the verb is in the singular form, such as *has* in (138), which agrees with *Vodafone* and its antecedent, *the company*; (ii) the subject may be replaced with a singular pronoun (*it*, *this*, *that*), as in (139) and (140), where *it* refers to *the party* and *British Rail* is the antecedent of *its*, respectively; and (iii) the subject serves as the antecedent of an inanimate pronoun, as in (141), where *which* replaces *the group*. Semantically, 'non-animate' CC subjects refer to either 'the members of. . .' or 'the organisation/administrative body. . .', such as *Sheffield* in (142).

(138) The new service helped *the company* boost pre-tax profits to £322.5m from £271.76m previously. *Vodafone* presently *has* 838,000 subscribers, swelled by the introduction of Low Call which is aimed [. . .] (BNC Baby, K39)

(139) His unconventionality, his unorthodoxy and his accent all helped *the party* to feel that *it* had made a step forward: "the dawn of the new regime". (BNC Baby, EW1)

(140) TINKER Dill, the sidekick on TV of wheeler-dealer Lovejoy, helped *British Rail* consign some of *its* antique trains to the history books. (BNC Baby, E9S)

(141) A stronger second half when turnover was up 12% helped *the group* recover from a disappointing performance in the first six months, said chairman James Millar. Shares responded with a 15p rise to 239p. *The group, which* has 65st (BNC Baby, CEL)

(142) The 32-year-old helped *Sheffield* stay in big time soccer but Dave Bassett wouldn't stand in his way if a move back South came up. (BNC Baby, CH3)

Indeterminate/mixed subjects, which comprise both inanimate and animate referents, are classified as either animate or non-animate, depending of the animacy of the first element of the coordination, such as the non-animate subject *businesses and individuals* in (143). Finally, 'unexpressed' is used for intransitive constructions, i.e. where the subject of the CC is absent and co-refers with that of the main clause.

(143) HAMPSHIRE Training and Enterprise Council have relaunched a counter-wide computer network to help *businesses and individuals* tap into thousands of training opportunities. (BNC Baby, BM4)

The verbal group of the CC is analysed in terms of voice in the variable PASSIVISATION and has the levels passive, as in *to be punished* in (144), or active.

(144) and þanne by riġtwysnesse of God nediþ þis synnere *to be punyschid.* (PPCME2, CMWYCSER,388.2931)
'and then by righteousness of God this sinner needs to be punished.'

2.2.3 Construction-based variables

I have grouped distance, realisation/performance/phonetic and semantic/pragmatic variables as construction-based predictors. Distance between the main verb and the infinitival complement clause, encoded as words_mv_inf, reflects to the number of words between the end of the main-clause verbal group and the beginning of the infinitive clause. Distance in example (145) is one word, with the intervening pronoun *us* between *helped* and *to go*. If the *to* infinitival marker is reinforced by *for*, *for to* is considered a single unit, as in (146), where only *nat* is counted. When the main-clause verbal group is coordinated, only the material after the end of the second part of the coordinated main verbal group and the beginning of the infinitive clause is considered. When the lower clause consists of two coordinated infinitival verbs and each has its own subject, the example is recorded twice in my data and analysed independently according to the lower-clause infinitival verb features of each example. Distance is thus calculated based on the intervening material between the main-clause main verb and the lower-clause infinitive verb in each example.

(145) "Playing regularly in south Wales has helped *us* to go places and 10 years on it's nice to crown it with a win like this." (BNC Baby, A1N)

(146) [. . .] and pulled at hit egirly, but the swerde wolde nat oute. 'Sir,' seyd the damesell, 'ye nede *nat for to* pulle halffe so sore, for he that shall pulle hit oute shall do hit with litill myght.' (PPCME2, CMMALORY,46.1511)

I consider two cases of avoidance of prosodic identity: the Principle of Rhythmic Alternation and the *horror aequi* principle, also analysed by Lohmann (2011) in her study of *help* in British PDE. In her discussion of the Principle of Rhythmic Alternation, Schlüter (2005, 2009) states that the ideal rhythm alternates between stressed and unstressed syllables (2005: 18). Stress clash and stress lapse are the two major deviations from rhythmic alternation. The former refers to the sequence of two stressed syllables whereas the latter is a sequence of two or even three unstressed syllables (Schlüter 2005: 19–20). Following Schlüter (2005), I distinguish between stressed and unstressed syllables preceding the *to*-infinitive/BI complement and between stressed, unstressed and overshadowed syllables following the infinitive. My hypothesis is that the *to*-infinitive acts as a stress clash buffer in contexts in which both the preceding and the initial syllable of the infinitive verb are stressed.[7] If the preceding syllable is stressed and the infinitive verb is

7 The incidence of the possible text types potentially affected by rhythm in the LModE period were measured in COHA. The data were classified into prose and non-prose. Prose consists of non-fiction, magazine, news and fiction texts, which only contain narrative texts such as novels, tales or short stories. Non-prose was used with the texts that COHA classifies as fiction, but that are indeed drama, comedy, tragedy, plays, (musical) farce and poetry and which may comprise verse, as in the blank verse in (i).
(i) General. French General I speak as man. -- High Priest High Priest And I, as heavn 's own organ, A priest inspir 'd by gods. -- General. French General And do thy gods Incite thee to such crimes? High Priest. High Preist And who are you, Who dare to judge the manners of my country; And seek to change the customs of old times!! -- Think'st thou thy proud, but feeble hand, can pluck The rooted groves of India from their place? (COHA, fic_1815_8716)
A multivariate analysis was carried out with each individual verb, i.e. *dare*, *need* and *help*. The infinitival complementation alternative was taken as the dependent variant and the following predictors as the independent ones: DISTANCE, INDICATIVE, POLARITY, RHYTHMIC ALTERNATION, SYNTAX, MORPHOLOGY, SUBJECT ANIMACY, NOTIONAL CHARACTERISATION and PROSE. The models revealed that the

overshadowed or non-initially stressed, the *to*-infinitive may be omitted. Finally, if the syllable preceding the infinitive verb is unstressed, the BI clause option is unproblematic. On this basis, four patterns are possible: uncritical, unproblematic, neutral and critical stress patterns. Uncritical patterns consist of two unstressed syllables: one preceding the infinitive verb and the other, the initial syllable of the infinitive verb, as in (147) with *me* and the second stressed syllable verb *achieve*. Example (147) is an instance of stress lapse because the *to*-infinitive provokes a sequence of three unstressed syllables.

(147) "If industry doesn't help *me* to *achieve* the objectives of the Government, we will have to take appropriate alternative steps", she had said with a steely smile. (BNC Baby, AC2)

The negative particle *not* and the intensifier *well* are classified as unstressed and act as stress clash buffers in stressed-stressed contexts, as in (148). However, the insertion of the conjunction *but* between the main and the lower verb leads to a neutral stress pattern because it results in a pause and thus avoids a stress clash, as in (149), where *but* is placed between *durst* and *speake*.

(148) Mail. Vicomte de Maillac Perhaps you will command me to read to you? I have here a volume of Rousseau 's "New Hlose."
Ad. Adelaide That I *dare not read*; papa does not permit it. But tell me, my lord vicomte, why is your book called the "New Hlose"? (COHA, fic_1815_9352)

(149) Lady. I barren, o` life that I durst *but* speake now, In mine owne Iustice, in mine owne Right, I barren, (PPCEME, MIDDLET-E2-P1,40.611)

Four stress patterns are classified as unproblematic: critical-uncritical, uncritical-critical, uncritical-overshadowed and critical-overshadowed. Critical-uncritical is illustrated in (150), with the stressed monosyllabic form *need* and the second-syllable stressed verb *eliminate*. The uncritical-critical stress pattern is shown in (151), with the unstressed

factor PROSE did not significantly influence the variation (*dare*, P= 0.5756; *need*, P=0.3015; *help*, P=0.8648). In fact, the step 'backward' reduction of variables with no loss of explanatory force suggested that PROSE could be discarded from the models.

pronoun *them* and the stressed monosyllabic verb form *cope*. Example (152) exemplifies the uncritical-overshadowed context, with the negative particle *not* and the overshadowed stressed syllable *come*. The last unproblematic context is critical-overshadowed and it consists of a stressed syllable preceding the infinitive verb and an overshadowed stressed syllable following it. The following contexts downgrade the stress of the infinitive verb: (i) when the infinitive verb is monosyllabic and selects a complement with an initially stressed syllable, as in (153), where *honest* functions as the subject predicative of *be*; (ii) when the infinitive is a phrasal verb, the particle receives higher stress than the verbal form, as in the case of *clear up* in (154); and (iii) when the infinitive clause has passive voice or perfect aspect, and the infinitive form of the auxiliaries *be* and *have* receive less stress, as in (155).

(150) Mr Lambert said: 'The two men and car were seen in the area on separate occasions near the suspected time of the attack, and we *need* to *eliminate* them from our inquiry.' (BNC Baby, CFC)

(151) COPING: Alison Hillhouse says poorer women think smoking helps *them cope*. (BNC Baby, K5C)

(152) The Dutch say, y=e= French Fleet has been ready a good while, but dares *not come out* without an English Convoy. (PCEEC, FLEMING,191.063.1079)

(153) I think you besides noble, just, temperat, a man that dares *be honest* in ill times; (PCEEC, DUPPA,20.013.289)

(154) Afterwards, when Billie had helped *clear up* and Adam had finished the list of instructions for Lily, they settled down in the living room with a large jug of coffee. (BNC Baby, G0L)

(155) and no one's feelings need *be hurt* by her fixing herself near some public school for her sons' education. (PPCMBE, YONGE-1865,169.279)

The label 'neutral' is used in six contexts: (i) when the verbs *dare*, *need* and *help* have disyllabic forms because the second syllable is unstressed and acts as a stress clash buffer for the stressed syllable, such as with *helping* in (156); (ii) when the negative particle is cliticised to the main verb, resulting in an initially stressed disyllabic word, such as *daren't* in (157); (iii) in examples with intervening material that consists of more than one syllable, such as *scarcely* in (158), or more than one word, as such *not yet* in (159); (iv) when an NP intervenes between the main-clause main verb and the infinitive clause, as in (160) (contexts (iii) and (iv) create pauses and, consequently, mitigate the stress clash between the stressed monosyllabic form of the main-clause main verb and the infinitive verb with an initially stressed syllable); (v) when the infinitive clause does not follow the main clause, as in (161), where *Overlode mi frends with mi burden* is moved to front position; and (vi) in contexts of main-clause main-verb coordination, where the verb does not immediately precede the infinitival verb because it is the first element of the coordination, as is the case of *need* in (162).

(156) Such awareness becomes important in *helping* clarify one's place in society and, thus, one's relationship to others in that society. (BNC Baby, J57)

(157) Manager Howard Wilkinson admitted: "You *daren't* think about what it means" if you do that you end up thinking about what you might lose. (BNC Baby, CH3)

(158) especially in the winter-season, when vigorous health dares *scarcely* look abroad. (PPCMBE, BARCLAY-1743,38.275)

(159) Sir, I dare *not yet* adventure to come up, my purging and stone payne hath made me feeble. (PCEEC, COSIN,I,87.025.899)

(160) Unfortunately, this attitude doesn't help *the average person* make such a judgment. (COHA, nf_1999_773819)

(161) What were best to be dun in so desperat a case I se not. Ride yit to London mi self I can not. Differ the time ani longer I ouht not. *Overlode* mi frends with mi burden I dare not. And what other wai I shuld take I know not. (PCEEC, HARVEY,21.002.329)

(162) The authorities plainly establish that he *need* not *and cannot* do so. (BNC Baby, A7Y)

Finally, the contexts consisting of stressed monosyllabic main-clause main verbal forms followed by initially stressed syllable infinitive verbs are coded as critical, as in the case of *help* and *make* in (163).

(163) Frequent droughts also *help* to *make* them unprofitable. (COHA, nf_1913_773672)

These five stress patterns are eventually coded into 'unproblematic' (uncritical, unproblematic, neutral and critical-overshadowed) and 'critical' in the factor rhythmic alternation in my study in an attempt to ensure consistency with the binary levels of the logistic regression, even though these five stress patterns constitute a cline of well-formed stressed sequences which can be used to test the influence of the Principle of Rhythmic Alternation on the distribution of BI/*to*-infinitive complementation with the verbs *dare*, *need* and *help* diachronically and synchronically.

The *horror aequi* effect refers to the "tendency to avoid the use of formally (near-)identical and (near-)adjacent (noncoordinate) grammatical elements and structures" (Rohdenburg 2003: 236). This principle can be observed in example (164), where the non-finite infinitive form *to help* selects the BI *carry* as its complement. A violation of this principle is found in (165), with the *to* infinitival marker immediately preceding and with the *to*-infinitive complement following it. The effect of this principle is analysed by the variable horror aequi. Examples (164) and (165) are *horror aequi* contexts, whereas the level 'other' in this predictor refers to contexts in which the main-clause main-verb forms are not *to*-infinitive, as in the case of *needing* in (166) and the infinitival alternation cannot, therefore, be explained by *horror aequi*.

(164) The driver is even willing *to help carry* the newborn through the closest door, he 's so eager. (COHA, fic_2000_38830)

(165) Wherfore I requyre your maistership to come hider in your persone with suych as ye seme not to that intent to take party in the mater but to that intent *to help to set* peas in the shire and to stire my lord for his honour. (PCEEC, PASTON,II,46.256.7481)

(166) Now, the elder brother was kind almost to patronizing, though evidently persuaded that Colin was a gay careless youth, with no harm in him, but *needing to* be looked after; (YONGE-1865,184.628)

The binary variable POLARITY classifies as 'negative' instances in which the construction is negated by *not* or its spelling variants and forms (*ne*, *nought*, *ne... nawt/nohht*, etc.), as in (167), by the clitic *n't*, as in (168), by *neither* or by *never*. In example (168), the clitic *n't* is attached to the verb *need*, whereas *not* cliticises with the primary auxiliary *do*. In contrast, positive polarity constructions are tagged as 'affirmative', as in the case of *to help* and *needing* in examples (164)–(166) above.

(167) But, I think, I *need not labour* much to recal these things into thy Memory; (PPCEME, BOETHPR-E3-P1,42.209)

(168) MARJORIE: Where are you going?
TIM: To the post office.
MARJORIE: Yes I want to pay for me er papers so
DOROTHY: Oh well there we are, that's
TIM: That's handy.
DOROTHY: It is handy. You're right.
MARJORIE: And then I *needn't* go round that way tomorrow. If I want to go into town I *don't need* to worry about. Are you
TIM: Got it.
MARJORIE: Are we going now then? (BNC Baby, KBW)

Semantic/pragmatic features are shown to affect the polarity of the construction (see Hoelvet 2020). In example (169), the main verb *need* is negated and the proposition is non-factual and irrealis since the situation described did not take place at the time at which the utterance was produced. The main verb *need* is also negated in (170), but the event conveyed by the infinitive clause *tell you that* is realised and the proposition is a fact. Like (170), example (171) shows main-verb negation and the proposition is factual, but the action *call it to mind* is unrealised. The event described in the subordinate clause of example (172) (*doubt that*) is unrealised and the proposition is a fact; this example differs from examples (169)-(171) because the negator *not* does not negate the main verb but the subordinate clause, so example (172) is a positive-polarity construction. Also, intervening material between the negator and the complement clause creates unambiguous polarity contexts, as in (169), where the insertion of *even* restricts the scope of the negative particle over the main-clause main verb (*need*). The lightly stressed adverb *never* does not behave like other members of this group of negative items, such as *hardly* or *seldom*. Whereas *hardly* and *seldom* convey presupposition or doubt meanings, *never* refers to facts. Hence, *never* accompanies negative main-clause verbal groups, unrealised infinitive clauses and factual propositions, as in (173). In my analysis, the construction may be (non-)factual and (un)realised independently of the polarity of the clause.

(169) Wie. Mr. Wieland: That is a business not taught in the military school.
Mail. Vicomte de Maillac: You may love, sigh, and languish as much as you please. *You need not even wait for the end of the honeymoon.* The l'ami de la maison shall always be welcome. (COHA fic_1815_9352)

(170) The services I have receaved from you hath beene *so eminent*, and is lykely to have so great an influence upon all my Affaires, *that I need not tell you* that I shall never forgett it, but alwais looke upon you as a principall instrument in keeping the Crowne upon my heade. (PCEEC ORIGIN3,293.030.303)

(171) Bo.: I remember well that that was demonstrated.
Ph.: Canst thou call to mind that it hath been shewed, that Happiness is the Sovereign Good, and that when Happiness is sought for, Good is desired of all?
Bo.: *I need not call it to mind, because it is always fixed in my Memory.*
Ph.: All Men then, the good as well as the bad, with one and the same Intention, endeavour to arrive at Good. (PPCEME BOETHPR-E3-P2,164.363)

(172) Jo.: Be not angry my dear, if thou hast not a Smock to thy back I would have thee, but in knowing what each other hath, we shall know the better how to improve it, do thou the same by me.
Ka.: Truly I have but ten pounds my father left me, and that is in my Uncle Hodge's hands.
Jo.: 'Tis sure I hope.
Ka.: *You need not doubt that*, for he cannot keep it from me, and five pound I have gathered since I came to service, besides my Mistress owes me above half a years wages. (PPCEME, PENNY-E3-H,116.14)

(173) Diuers of the Noble men did in like sort entertaine some of those children into their seruices, so that in the end not one was left to picke wool, but were all so prouided for, that their *Parents neuer needed to care for them*: and God so blessed them, that each of them came to be men of great account and authority in the land, whose posterities remaine to this day worshipfull and famous. (PPCEME, DELONEY-E2- P2,49.260)

Likewise, examples (174) and (175) convey affirmative factual realised interpretations realised by interrogative designs. In (174), the event of *say I'm not one* already happened and the speaker is only asking about the person that provoked the situation involving the relative pronoun *who*. Similarly, subject *he* in (175) did perform the action expressed in the infinitive clause and the construction *dare touch* is factual, hence rhetorical questions such as (175) are classified as factual realised, too. Unlike (174) and (175), example (176) expresses uncertainty and the constructions with *dare admit* and *dare risk* have affirmative polarity and a non-factual unrealised interpretation.

(174) Cha. Now, if you had only played your part half as well, you might have passed for a woman. Lady C. Passed for a woman! *who dares to say I'm not one*? Stamps her foot with rage. Cha. Why you betray yourself by your violence did any one ever see a woman stamp and rave, in such a manner? (COLLIER-1835,20.671)

(175) Rook. Rook The same, my lord --While grey haired men, And boys, and all between, stock still, agape, Their greasy caps in hand, his words devoured, While he, with gestures fierce, and eyes like beacons, Of Hotspur spoke.
West. Lady Westmoreland Of Hotspur!
Rook. Rook Ha! --he comes! --Ever, my lord, he named him –
West. Lady Westmoreland Peace! begone! When the stir's past of this day and the next, I'll more of this. Begone! Exit Rook. *How dare he touch That theme among my vassals*? -- Hotspur! ha! Enter Percy.
Per. Percy Joy to my lord and his illustrious dame, That conquering Henry draws so near to Warkworth West. Lady Westmoreland Thou'rt well encountered (COHA, fic_1819_8706)

(176) This conclusion summarizes the continuing choice: True education is not for every man the scrap of paper he leaves school with. *Dare we* as teachers *admit* this? *Dare we risk* our existence by forcibly expressing our views on this? (BNC Baby, CLW)

My taxonomy considers the polarity of the main verb (negative vs positive/affirmative), the factuality of the proposition (factual vs non-factual) and the realisation of the event described in the subordinate clause (realised vs unrealised). The analysis of the semantic/pragmatic features takes into account both the context preceding the construction and the context that follows it. This classification yields six possible combinations (see Table 1): 'negative non-factual unrealised' constructions, as in (169) above; 'negative factual realised', as in (170); 'negative factual unrealised', as in (171); 'affirmative factual unrealised', as in (172); 'affirmative factual realised', as in (174) and (175) above, and 'affirmative non-factual unrealised', as in (176) above and (177) below. Example (177) is affirmative because the negation has scope over *reveal* rather than over the main-clause main verb, and the proposition refers to an event which may or may not happen in the future (non-factual unrealised interpretation).

	Factual		Non-factual	
	Realised	**Unrealised**	**Realised**	**Unrealised**
Negative	✓	✓		✓
Affirmative	✓	✓		✓

Table 1: Notional characterisation of the construction

(177) Are you in love unless on ruin bent, Sit not like patience on a monument, Fancy's pernicious visions to indulge, A prey to feelings you dare not divulge, But to some prudent common friend impart The sentiments, which agitate your heart, By whom, with proper management, no doubt, An eclaircissement may be brought about, And *yet your confident need not reveal*, A sentiment, which honor would conceal. But, if by these, or other means you learn, That your partiality meets no return, Let none discover that you have been slighted, Or that affections' blossoms have been blighted; (COHA, fic_1818_7631)

The options 'negative non-factual realised' and 'affirmative non-factual realised' are darkened in Table 1 because, by definition, non-factual propositions cannot be carried out when the instance has been uttered. Even though these are statistically marginal cases, the polarity domain also contains ambiguous examples where it is not possible to determine whether the negative particle is affecting the main or the lower clause, as in (178), where two readings are possible: either negation has scope over the main verb *need* and the construction conveys negative non-factual unrealised meaning, as in (179), or the negative particle has scope over the subordinate clause, leading to an affirmative non-factual unrealised interpretation, as in (180). Owing to this ambiguity, (178) is labelled as ambiguous non-factual unrealised in my database.

(178) This topic is too recent for there to be many guidelines available but for a particular topic the designer can assume that *he need not be inhibited* in allowing his imagination to run to many kinds of novel solutions. (BNC Baby, CLP)

(179) 'the designer can assume that it is not necessary that he is being inhibited in allowing his imagination to run'

(180) 'the designer can assume that it is necessary that he avoids being inhibited in allowing his imagination to run'

2.3 Statistical analysis

Section 2.3.1 describes the multivariate analysis and the coding conventions applied to some of the variables described in Section 2.2 so that they can enter the statistical model. Section 2.3.2 explains the measure conventions adopted in the analysis of the corpora for comparability purposes.

2.3.1 Multivariate analysis of the data

The aim of the qualitative-quantitative continuum methodology adopted in this study is to reflect the gradual nature of most of the diachronic and diatopic linguistic variation. Rohdenburg and Schlüter (2009: 6) point out that the quantitative analysis of corpora helps "uncover a number of hitherto unnoticed differences in the functional load carried by identical structures". In view of the probabilistic nature of complement choice in a context where different factors are at play, the statistical method used is logistic regression by means of the generalised linear model function ('glm') in R (R Core Team 2020) and the generalised linear model with mixed effects ('glmer') in R. According to Gelman and Hill (2007: 79), "logistic regression is the standard way to model binary outcomes (that is, data y_i that take on the values 0 or 1)". A generalised linear model is a multilevel model in which the parameters (i.e. regression coefficients) are given a probability model and this second-level model "has parameters of its own – the *hyperparameters* of the model – which are also estimated from data" (Gelman and Hill 2007: 1).

In this study, the dependent variable is the infinitival complementation alternation with the levels *to*-infinitive and BI complements, and the independent variables are the factors that are suspected to influence the alternation. The categorisation of the variables PARADIGM and PASSIVISATION (see Section 2.2.1), proving problematic at times owing to the scarcity of data, requires the reduction or simplification of levels. As a result, the parameter PASSIVISATION codes the voice of main and lower clauses with the values active and passive.

As mentioned in Section 2.2.3, the variable DISTANCE as designed to measure the distance between the main and infinitival subordinate verb. To avoid skewing the data with a high concentration of values when distance is low and lower values when distance is high, the 'log' function with natural base has been applied to the predictor DISTANCE as follows: zero values are assigned a score of –1, which transforms the data into a more normal pattern; to determine the number of words corresponding to an increase of one unit of distance, that figure is raised to 2; average distance is expressed by the mean, and the quantile (with a 90 % probability percentile) groups the least frequent cases.

Before running 'glm', the most frequent value in the dependent variable is taken as the reference level so that negative results in the estimate refer to the most productive level. The P-value obtained in the model measures the significance of the factors and the Odds Ratio (OR) calculates the probability that something may happen over the probability that it may not.

2.3.2 Data comparability

For the purposes of data normalisation and comparability, I used the IP-MAT unit for the Penn Corpora of Historical English and the <-s> unit for the BNC Baby rather than a baseline relying on word counts. Word counts are not optimal normalising measures here since the linguistic phenomenon investigated in this dissertation is not lexical but syntactic and affects predicate or clausal units. For this reason, I have opted for normalising frequencies by selecting a baseline focused on frequency of words not clauses. IP-MAT annotates declarative matrix clauses with inflected main verbs. In contrast, the <-s> unit is the basic category in the BNC Baby and is defined as the "sequence of words and punctuation marks making up a complete segment" (Burnard 2008: 10). The comparability of these two metrics is also supported by the fact that neither of these two tags is applied to subordinate or embedded clauses in the corpora.

Since clauses or sentences are not annotated in COHA, these data have to be normalised by means of word count. To allow for the comparison between IP-MATs, <-s> units and word frequencies, I established equivalences between the metrics. IP-MATs were identified in COHA by applying the definition adopted in the syntactic annotation of the Penn Parsed Corpora for Historical English for the PPCME2, PPCEME, PCEEC and PPCMBE (https://www.ling.upenn.edu/hist-corpora/annotation/ index.html), and analysed a sample of 300 IP-MATs (100 IP-MATs per subperiod) in the American corpus. To ensure textual balance, I randomised the texts from each subperiod, selected the first five, and then analysed the first 20 IP-MATs in each text. Table 2 shows the texts analysed per period and the number of words in which IP-MATs were found. Since the file news_1918_683819 only contains 6 IP-MATs, I had to select a sixth text for the L3 subperiod and analyse 14 additional IP-MATs.

Period	File	Words analysed	Total number of words analysed	IP-MATs	Number of IP-MATs per subperiod
L2	fict_1819_8815	419	2419	20	41403,969
	fic_1815_8796	591		20	
	fic_1815_8708	364		20	
	fic_1812_8987	358		20	
	fic_1813_7433	687		20	
L3	news_1918_683780	343	2414	20	41473,902
	news_1918_683819	229		6	
	mag_1910_487039	478		20	
	news_1919_684739	498		20	
	news_1919_684601	525		20	
	fic_1917_13903	341		14	
PDE	news_1998_657587	433	2749	20	36447,472
	mag_1998_401608	744		20	
	news_1995_631290	621		20	
	fic_1995_39246	384		20	
	news_2000_633204	567		20	
Total		7582	7582	300	119325,34

Table 2: Sample of 300 IP-MATs from COHA

Finally, I estimated the total number of IP-MATs in the American corpus by multiplying the total number of words per subperiod by the 100 IP-MATs analysed in that subperiod, and dividing this by the number of words in which those IP-MATs were found. For example, the total number of words for the L2 subperiod (1,001,562) was multiplied by 100 and divided by 2,419, resulting in 41,403.969 IP-MATs (see Table 2). Table 3 summarises the corpora used for British and American English in this study, the periods and subperiods, number of words per subperiod and number of IP-MATs or <-s> units.

Period	Subperiod	Words	IP-MAT/<-s> units	Corpora
ME	M1	338952	12214	PPCME2
	M2	125986	6102	PPCME2
	M3	796732	33560	PPCME2 + PCEEC
	M4	648046	26247	PPCME2 + PCEEC
EMODE	E1	1119268	32198	PPCEME + PCEEC
	E2	1643014	60388	PPCEME + PCEEC
	E3	1079310	38244	PPCEME + PCEEC
LMODE	L1	382623	11089	PPCMBE
	L2	1001562	41403,969	COHA
		467199	17113	PPCMBE
	L3	1001180	41473,902	COHA
		348167	13549	PPCMBE
PDE	1994	3895894	333045	BNC BABY
	1995–2000	1001941	36447,472	COHA

Table 3: Corpora comparability

2.4 *To*-infinitive and BI complementation: An overall diachronic and synchronic assessment of the variation

The aim of this chapter is to determine the overall effect of verb, diachrony and regional variation on infinitival complement choice in American and British ME to PDE. For this purpose, a fixed regresion analysis (Multivariate Model 0) analyses the influence of the three verbs, i.e. *dare*, *need* and *help*, and all the relevant variables mentioned in Chapter 1 and in the previous sections of Chapter 2. In addition, a mixed regression analysis (Mixed Multivariate Model) with the predictor VERB, comprising the levels 'dare', 'need' and 'help', as a random factor is carried out in order to corroborate whether the individual verbs play an important role in the infinitival choice.

Multivariate Model 0 takes the two infinitival variants as the levels of the dependent variable, and as independent variables, the predictor VERB, as well as the commonly cited predictors of infinitival alternation governed by these verbs: PERIODISATION, REGIONAL VARIANT, DISTANCE, INFINITIVAL SUBJECT, INDICATIVE, RHYTHMIC ALTERNATION, HORROR AEQUI, POLARITY, SYNTAX, VALENCY, PASSIVISATION, RELATIVE, SUBJECT COMPLEXITY and NOTIONAL CHARACTERISATION. To avoid collinearity, DISTANCE and SUBJECT OF INFINITIVE are analysed separately. BI clauses are taken as the reference level of the dependent variable since they are more frequent than the *to*-infinitive complement in my data; negative estimates thus indicate a preference for BI complementation. ANOVA confirms that the differences with the collinear factors are not statistically significant.

Table 4 shows the weight of the significant predictors after the step 'backward' reduction technique with the variable DISTANCE. INDICATIVE, RELATIVE and SUBJECT COMPLEXITY are not explanatory of the infinitival complementation alternation in Model 0 (for the distribution of the variants with respect to the determinant factors of the alternation, see Tables 134, 135 and 136 in Appendix).

Predictor	Estimate	P-value	OR
Intercept	-0.75305	0.013980 *	1/0.4709302=2.1234
Verb (ref.: *Dare)*	1.41280	< 2e-16 ***	4.1074555
Help	2.71904	< 2e-16 ***	15.1658278
Need			
Period (ref.: *ME*)	-0.41336	0.009647 **	1/0.6614235=1.5118
EModE	-0.30017	0.101588	1/0.7406933=1.3500
LModE	-0.05311	0.735868	1/0.9482759=1.0545
PDE			
Regional variant	0.48035	2.47e-06 ***	1.6166394
(ref.: *American*)			
British			
Distance	-0.59749	< 2e-16 ***	1/0.5501923=1.8175
Rhythmic Alternation	-0.35389	0.000258 ***	1/0.7019503=1.4246
(ref.: *Critical*)			
Unproblematic			
Horror Aequi (ref.: *Other*)	-1.70107	< 2e-16 ***	1/0.1824877=5.4798
Yes			
Polarity (ref.: *Affirmative*)	-1.50642	< 2e-16 ***	1/0.2217026=4.5105
Negative			
Syntax (ref.: *Adverbial*)	-0.47636	0.000141 ***	1/0.6210408=0.2217
Dependent	-0.53690	8.66e-06 ***	1/0.5845597=1.7106
Main			
Valency (ref.: *Coordination*)	-0.75634	0.001585 **	1/0.4693795=2.1304
Intransitive	-0.93747	1.32e-05 ***	1/0.3916184=2.5535
Transitive			
Passivisation (ref.: *No*)	0.31201	0.087107 .	1.3661680
Yes			
Notional characterisation	0.83265	2.01e-06 ***	2.2993985
(ref.: *Factual realised*)	0.68693	5.57e-13 ***	1.9876037
Factual unrealised			
Non-factual unrealised			

Table 4: *To*-infinitive/BI complementation in LModE and PDE (step "backward")

Model 0 shows that VERB is a significant factor of complementation choice. The odds of the *to*-infinitive clause increase by 15.16 percentage points with *need* and by 4.1 with *help* in comparison with *dare*. When *help* is taken as the reference level, the results show that this verb significantly prefers BI clauses by 3.51 percentage in comparison with *need* (Pr(>|z|)=< $2e^{-16}$).

In addition to VERB, the variables shown to have the strongest effect on my data are PERIODISATION, REGIONAL VARIANT, DISTANCE and SUBJECT OF INFINITIVE, RHYTHMIC ALTERNATION, HORROR AEQUI, POLARITY, SYNTAX, VALENCY and NOTIONAL CHARACTERISATION. As for the variable PERIODISATION, the odds of the BI clause are 1.51 per cent higher in EModE than in ME. The propotions of the infinitival alternation are similar in EModE and in LModE (Pr(>|z|)= 0.43). In contrast, when LModE is taken as the reference level, the incidence of the *to*-infinitive is 1.28 percentage higher in PDE (Pr(>|z|)=0.046). In other words, BI clauses decrease significantly in PDE and show a similar distribution to that of *to*-infinitive complements. This result justifies the study of the alternation in different models, one per period of time, in order to identify the most significant factors affecting the alternation over time.

Table 4 also indicates that the factor REGIONAL VARIANT affects the alternation with British English showing a significant preference for *to*-infinitive clauses (Pr(>|z|)=2.47e^{-06} and 1.61 percentage points). The productivity of BI clauses increases in the SUBJECT OF INFINITIVE predictor when there is intervening material between the main and lower clauses, in examples encoded as unproblematic stress patterns, *horror aequi* contexts, negative clauses, dependent and main syntax and intransitive and transitive lower verbs (by 1.82, 1.42, 5.48, 4.51, 0.22, 1.71, 2.13 and 2.55 percentage, respectively; see Table 4). The *to*-infinitive is significantly favoured when the main or lower verbal groups are in the passive voice and has a factual unrealised or a non-factual unrealised meaning (1.36, 2.29 and 1.98 percentage, respectively).

In the Mixed Multivariate Model, VERB is taken as a random variable. This analysis sticks to the same procedure and takes the same independent variables as Multivariate Model 0. The results of the Mixed Multivariate Model corroborate that strong effect of the same predictors as in Multivariate Model 0 (PERIODISATION, REGIONAL VARIANT, DISTANCE and SUBJECT OF INFINITIVE, RHYTHMIC ALTERNATION, HORROR AEQUI, POLARITY, SYNTAX, VALENCY and NOTIONAL CHARACTERISATION) and also reveal that the verb itself, i.e. *dare*, *need* and *help*, is explicative of the model (Variance=1.213, C-index=0.84), which justifies the analyses per verb undertaken in the ensuing chapters.

3. *Dare* and *need* revisited

3.1 Introduction

This chapter focuses on the semantic and structural changes undergone by the verbs *dare* and *need* in the history of English, particularly in relation to their lexical, auxiliary and modal features (already explored in, for example, Warner 1993; Beths 1999; Loureiro-Porto 2009). My decision to analyse *dare* and *need* in the same chapter is based on their occurrence in essentially the same contexts and with the same features from Late Middle English onwards. This period sees the pre-modal verb *dare* start to exhibit lexical features, the lexical verb *need* attested with modal features, and both verbs occurring in so-called 'blend' constructions (Denison 1998), where they display modal and lexical features (see Section 3.3). However, the literature on these blends pays little attention to the factors responsible for the divergence of *dare* from other pre-modal verbs and the influence exerted on it by *need*. The analysis in this chapter focuses on three aspects of the question: (i) the emergence of lexical features in the pre-modal verb *dare* and the interruption of its grammaticalisation at the end of the Middle English (henceforth ME) period; (ii) the grammaticalisation of *need* from Late Middle English onwards and its influence on *dare* at that time; (iii) and the alternation of *dare* and *need* with BI and the *to*-infinitive complements and in what contexts. The main sources of my qualitative analysis of the Old English period include the Oxford English Dictionary, the Middle English Dictionary and Visser (1963-73). In addition to these, the study also uses data from the Penn Corpora of Historical English, BNC Baby and COHA for the description of *dare* and *need* in the periods between Middle and Present-Day English.

The chapter is divided into five sections. Section 3.2 provides a review of grammaticalisation theory from synchronic and diachronic perspectives, with a focus on the distinctive features of pre-modal verbs in general and *dare* in particular. Section 3.3 compares *dare* and *tharf*, mainly as Experiencer verbs, and looks at the influence that *tharf* and *need* exert on *dare* in Late ME and Early ModE. Section 3.4 analyses the various morphosyntactic, semantic/pragmatic and textual determinants of infinitival choice from EModE to PDE in American and British English from qualitative and quantitative perspectives using univariate and multivariate analyses. Finally, Section 3.5 summarises the main issues and compares the complementation choices of *dare* and *need*, and explores the behaviour of both constructions diachronically and synchronically.

3.2 Literature review: The status of *dare* and the ancestors of the modal verbs

The historical evolution of the verb *dare* has been used as evidence against the unidirectionality principle of grammaticalisation (Beths 1999; Taeymans 2004a; Schlüter 2010; Norde 2011). In OE, *dare* is classified as a pre-modal verb but from ModE onwards it starts to exhibit full-verb features. The group of modal auxiliaries begin to conform a separate grammatical category only in the ME period, but this process is not completed until the second half of the fifteenth century or the first half of the sixteenth century (Warner 1993: 92–235; Wischer 2019).

In what follows, I will provide an overview of the morphological, syntactic and semantic features shown by *dare* in OE which support its categorisation as a pre-modal. Morphologically, *dare*, as well as most PDE modal verbs (other than *will*), shows preterite-present morphology and a defective paradigm. The origin of a pre-modal verb is the preterite of a strong verb, which, after losing its past-time reference, develops a new preterite, following the productive weak conjugation in OE (Loureiro-Porto 2009: 56). For this reason, scholars differ on whether or not to include OE *dare* and other modals as 'irregular' verbs "within the general classification strong, weak and irregular" verbs or in a class of their own (Loureiro-Porto 2009: 55). In this vein, Denison (1993: 296) characterises them as a "set of verbs with a present tense just like the past (preterite) tense of a strong verb (apart from the –*st* of the 2SG) and a past tense formed on an irregular stem with the endings of the weak". Preterite-present verbs consist of 'non-modals' and so-called 'pre-modals' (Loureiro-Porto 2009: 57, quoting Traugott 1992: 193 and Denison 1993: 296).[8] The pre-modals group that concerns us here comprises *agan* 'own', *cunnan* 'can', **durran* 'dare', *magan* 'may', **motan* 'must', **sculan* 'shall' and *þurfan* 'need' (Mitchell 1985: § 990).[9] Most of these verbs have survived in PDE, and belong either to the class of central modal verbs or to what Krug (2000: 167) calls the group of 'emerging modals' or 'neomodals'.[10]

The non-finite forms of OE pre-modals are very infrequent. **Durran* 'dare', **motan* 'must' and **sculan* 'shall' do not have infinitive, present or past participle forms in OE. They also lack third-person singular *-þ* inflection, as in (181), and simple past forms. In (181), *dear* does not show overt agreement morphology with the third-person subject pronoun *he*.

(181) Gif *he* gesecean *dear*. (OE Beowulf 684) (OED s.v. *dare* v.1 c. α.)
If he seek dares
'If he dares seek'

As pointed out above, coordination is a syntactic strategy that, already in OE, distinguishes modal verbs from the other group of verbs selecting BI complementation (Warner 1993: 103). Also, VP-deletion, where the complement of the coordinated verbs is retrievable from the post-verbal complement of the previous clause, is a syntactic characteristic of modals and *dare*.

8 The modal/non-modal distinction in preterite-present verbs is important because the latter disappear in the late fifteenth century. Preterite-present non-modal verbs include *beneah/geneah* 'suffice', *deah* 'avail, be of use', *gemunan* 'remember', *(ge)unnan* 'love, grant' and *witan* 'know' (Denison 1993: 296).

9 The symbol '*' means this form has not survived to PDE.

10 Krug uses the term 'neomodal' for cases in which the new process of modalisation does not produce elements that share all the characteristics of the central modals, i.e. *can, could, may, might, shall, should, will/'ll, would/'d* and *must*.

Semantically, according to the Oxford English Dictionary (OED) and the Middle English Dictionary (MED), *dare* means ‘to have boldness or courage (to do something); to be so bold as’ when it selects an infinitive clause as its complement, as in (182), or when it occurs with covert complements for different reasons, i.e. ellipsis or in so-called event-integration/conflation constructions (Fanego 2017: 45–46), as in (183). Contexts triggering meanings of ‘fear’ or ‘doubt’, as in (183), which are typical of subjunctive use, suggest that the lexical meaning of *dare* has been bleached and that the verb has acquired a modal undertone. Duffley (1994: 234) observes that modal meanings and subjunctive mood are closely related in that both evoke an event as merely potential or virtual. In addition to these two meanings, the MED also registers the use of *dare* in emphatic questions and asseverations, as in (184). In these contexts, *dare* usually expresses courage.

(182) *Hwa durste slepen* hwil his deadliche foa heolde an itoġe sweord up on his heaued. (PPCME2, CMANCRIW-1,II.240.3494)
Who dare sleep while his implacably enemy holds a drawn sword up on his head
‘Who dares sleep while his implacably enemy holds a sword drawn against his head?’

(183) Ferrer ne *draste* þay noȝt for fere. (c1380 Sir Ferumbras (1879) l. 3725) (OED s.v. *dare* v1. 9)
Further not dare they not for fear
‘They don’t dare further for fear’

(184) *How dare* [other MSS: dar] ȝe *come* in godis hus! (a1400 (a1325) Cursor (Vsp A.3) 17304) (MED s.v. *durren* 1b. (a))
‘How dare you come in God’s house?’

As for modality and auxiliarisation, in OE the semantics of pre-modal verbs mainly consist of the expression of their basic root meanings and, in some cases, of temporal meanings (Loureiro-Porto 2009: 69). Loureiro-Porto remarks that, at times, pre-modals are semantically empty when accompanied by synonymous non-pre-modals, as in (185). In this example, the third-person singular form of the pre-modal form **durran* (to *dare*) is followed by the infinitive *gedurstlæcan*, which also conveys the meaning of ‘to dare’. This indicates that the meaning of the pre-modal is “totally bleached, since otherwise it would be redundant to have two verbs expressing the same meaning in the same verbal unit" (Loureiro-Porto 2009: 69).

(185) Hwa *dear* nu *gedurstlæcan*, þæt he derige þam folce? (Æ HomI vii, 306) (Loureiro-Porto, 2009: 69) (example and translation from Beths 1999: 1081)
Who dare-3SG now dare-INF, that the harm-SBJV this people-DAT
'who would now dare to harm these people?'

Loureiro-Porto goes on to argue that there is a cline from fully lexical verbal status in OE to partially grammaticalised verbal status. In their fully lexical state, verbs keep their original meaning and occur as heads in their syntactic constructions. In contrast, when they have a more grammaticalised status, they behave as auxiliaries to the infinitive which follows them, and express their root modality and temporal meanings.[11] She supports the view that in OE some of the pre-modals, such as *magan*, **sculan*, *motan*, *willan* and **durran*, undergo two of the processes reported by Heine (1993: 58 ff) as part of the grammaticalisation chain: decategorialisation and desemanticisation.[12] Since OE *dare* does not have full argument structure (i.e. it does not determine the way in which the participants in the verbal event are conveyed in the clause), I will argue that *gedurstlæcan* in example (185) above has a double function.[13] On the one hand, it conveys lexical meaning, i.e. courage

11 For a detailed description of modality meanings, see, for example, van der Auwera and Plungian (1998), who suggest that *dare* implies a deontic possibility within the participant-external possibility domain.

12 Hopper (1991: 22) defines 'decategorisation' as the tendency for forms to undergo grammaticalisation when they "lose or neutralize the morphological markers and syntactic privileges characteristic of the full categories Noun and Verb, and to assume attributes characteristic of secondary categories such as Adjective, Participle, Preposition, etc". As regards 'desemantisation', Loureiro-Porto (2009: 38–39) explains that the term refers to a change in the semantic features of a given element either in relation to the loss of specificity or to ever-increasing generalisations (see Heine 1993: 54).

13 Within the Principles-and-Parameters framework, Beths (1999: 1075, 1080) distinguishes two uses of modals in OE. She claims that modals show argument structure when they select a non-verbal complement, but do not seem to generate external arguments when they select infinitive clauses as their internal arguments.

and, on the other hand, it provides the arguments of the sentence, i.e. the subject *Hwa* and the complement *þæt he derige þam folce*. The defective paradigm of *dare* is therefore complemented by its semantic equivalent *gedyrstl*, which exhibits non-finite forms as a result of the OE translation of the Latin non-finite form *audens*.

3.3 The status of *dare* and *need* in Middle English and the role of *tharf*

The changes undergone by *dare* and *need* in ME mirror the transformations and the significant degree of variation that characterise this period. This section offers a qualitative and quantitative description of the status of *dare* and *need* in ME, focusing in particular on infinitival complementation. As mentioned in Section 1, *dare* acquires new lexical features from ME onwards, such as the adoption of non-finite forms, complementation by *to*-infinitive clauses and occurrence in blend constructions (Denison 1998: 170; see Section 3.3.3). I will argue here that this dual lexical and modal function is due not only to the phonological similarity between *dare* and the pre-modal verb *tharf* but also to the relationship between *tharf* and the verb *need*, and their influence on *dare*. For this reason, a closer analysis of *tharf* and *need* in ME is necessary in order to shed light on the evolution of *dare*.

3.3.1 Morphosyntactic and semantic features of *dare, tharf* and *need*

Like *dare, tharf* is classified as a pre-modal verb (Mitchell 1985: § 990; see also Section 2 above). Morphologically, *tharf* exhibits a defective paradigm; in fact, Campbell (1959: § 767) only mentions the infinitive form *þurfan* and the present participle *þearfende*, with no illustrations of either. Syntactically, *tharf* selects NPs and BI clauses as its complement in OE and ME, but ceases to select NPs after ME, when it becomes restricted to BI clauses with a modal meaning (186) (Taeymans 2006: Chapter 3). Semantically, it conveys meanings of necessity (186), obligation based on duty, superior authority, divine law, etc., and possibility with meanings close to the PDE modals *may*, *can* and *could*, as in (187) (MED s.v. *thurven* 2a, 3a, 4a, 5, 6a,7a, respectively).

(186) that were popys of Rome, reseyved þis writyng and sayd, "Hosoeuer bere þis writyng abowte hym, *he thar not drede* hym of non enmy ner sodeyn deth, ner fyer, ner watyr, ner poyson" (PPCME2, CMREYNES, 247.412)
'who were popes of Rome, received this letter and said, 'whosoever has this letter with him, he needs not fear him about no enemy nor sudden death nor fire nor water nor poison''

(187) Þou ert full meke; A meker man *thar noman seke.* (a1425 NPass.(Cmb Gg.5.31) 35/324) (MED s.v. *thurven* 7a(a))
'You are really humble; A more humble man who anyone can seek'

Tharf is also found in constructions in which one of its syntactic arguments is in the oblique form and the other is an infinitival verb (as *þe* and *dread*, respectively), as in (188); the form *þe* functions as the semantic subject of the clause.

(188) On þe þird maner: he tourmentes a mans body, als we rede þat he has done job. Bot wytt þou wele, if he begyle þe noght wiþin, *þe þar noght drede* what he may do þe wiþouten, for he may do na mare þan God gyfs hym leve for to do. (PPCME2, CMROLLEP,89.415)
On the third manner: he tourments a man's body, in the way that we read that he has done job. But know you wel, if he beguile you not within, you-obl.exp need not dread what he may do you-obl.exp without, because he may do no more than God gives him leave to do
'Thirdly: he torments a man's body, as we read that he has worked. But you know well, if he do not beguile you inside, you need not fear what he may do you outside, because he may do no more than what God allows him to do'

This and other verbs of necessity have been variously labelled as 'impersonal' (Wahlén 1925; Visser 1963–1973; Denison 1990), 'subjectless', 'true impersonals' and 'quasi-impersonals' (Lightfoot 1979: 229), 'nominative-less' (Bennis 1986) and 'verbs of natural phenomena and verbs of experience' (Méndez-Naya 1997: 191). Anderson (1986: 167–168) calls them 'impersonal' constructions and proposes the following definition:

> An Impersonal verb is one which can appear in predictions which are finite but which, unlike in other such predications in the language, shows no variation in person/number: the verb is always in the form associated with the third person singular [. . .] Associated with this is a further property of all these sentences: they all lack an argument inflected for the nominative.

Allen (1995: 20–23) objects to the term 'impersonal' on the grounds, firstly, that some authors use it as synonymous of 'subjectless', while others extend it to sentences with a formal subject; and, secondly, that it may be extended to constructions with nominative arguments normally seen as playing the role of subject, as in (189). According to Allen, these verbs are considered similar to subjectless verbs because they do not assign the Experiencer role of the subject and "enter in constructions generally agreed to be impersonal when the non-human argument is a clause, rather than an NP". On the basis of these arguments, I use Allen's (1995: 20) term 'experiencer' in my analysis (see also Loureiro-Porto 2009, 2010).

(189) Gif ðe licode his dysig (Bo 27.62.12) (COE)
If you liked his foolishness
'If you/thou liked his foolishness'

Allen (1995) classifies Experiencer verbs according to the nature of the Experiencer and the theme, which may be nominal or sentential. Given that *tharf* is not attested with nominal themes in my data, I have restricted the analysis to sentential ones.

Confusion and overlapping of function and form between *dare* and *tharf* in ME is observed in the entries, examples and/or etymological sections for these two verbs in the OED (s.v. *dare*, v.[1] 9) and the MED (s.v. *thurven* 8). In the etymology section of the verb *dare*, the OED points out that *dare* and *tharf* were used interchangeably to a certain extent in ME, "*dar* being sometimes written for *thar*, while, on the other hand, [the] *th*- forms [. . .] appear with the sense of *dar*: see Forms 9" (s.v. *dare* v.[1]), as in (190), where the form *þerst* is used in a context expressing 'courage' where the form *derst* would be expected.

(190) Was þer þan no man þat in wraþþe *þerst sen* ys fas. (c1380 Sir Ferumbras (1879) l. 2668) (OED s.v. *dare* v[1] 9)
Was there then no man who in worth dare see his face
'There was nobody then who dared see his face in wrath'

The MED also notes some confusion in the entry for *tharf* when it expresses modal auxiliary meaning:

> volition, determination, free choice, etc.: to have the will (to do sth.), be willing; venture (to do sth.), have the courage, *dare*; – usu. in negative contexts; ~ seien, venture to say (sth., that sth. is so), *dare say* [many quots. in 8. show confusion with, or influence from, *durren* v.] (MED s.v. *thurven* 8).

Furthermore, the MED indicates that *dare* is found expressing "to be under necessity or obligation; (one) must (do sth.), ought, needs, should; – with neg., (one) need not (fear, blame, seek, say, etc.)", as in (191). Example (191), dated around the year 1200, corresponds to the first instance of *dare* attested in the MED with a meaning related to necessity/obligation. The orthographical similarity between *dare* and *tharf* explains the confusion attested in (190) and (191) in a period in which orthographical variability was common. In ME the letter which represented the sound <v> is sometimes dropped and/or the initial dental fricative consonant is replaced with the plosive stop *d-* (Molencki 2002: 378, 2005; Loureiro-Porto 2009: 71–72).

(191) Ne *dert þu nauere adrede...* þæt æuere æine modi cniht at þine borde makie fiht. (c1275(?a1200) Lay. Brut (Clg A.9) 22923) (MED s.v. *durren*, 2a (a))
Not need you never fear... that ever any brave knight at your table fight
'You need never fear... that any brave knight ever fight at your table'

The classification of the same example under both the entry of *dare* and *tharf* in the citations of the OED, MED and in Visser (1963–73) confirms the confusion between *dare* and *tharf*. Seven of the nine examples in the MED (s.v. *durren*, 2 (b)) are also found either in the OED or in Visser (1963-73) under the entry for *thurven*. Examples (190) above and (192) below, two of the three instances found in both the OED and the MED, show the difficulty of determining which verb or combination of the characteristics of *dare* and *tharf* is at work.[14] In (192), the form *dar* occurs in an Experiencer construction, with the non-nominative *The*,

14 Example (56) is found under the entries OED (s.v. *dare* v^1 9) and MED (s.v. *thurven*, 8 (c)).

which functions as the subject of the clause, and the BI complement *drede.*

(192) Soden deth. . . *The dar not drede.* (?a1425 Const.Masonry(1) (Roy 17.A.1) 674) (MED, s.v. *durren*, 2 (b))
Sudden death. . . You-obl.exp. dare-3SG not fear
'Sudden death. . . You need not fear'

Need behaves as a full verb in ME. The examples show inflection for third-person singular, simple past (193) and non-finite forms ((*to*) *need* and the BI form, *needed* and *needing*). As for complementation, *need* selects a wider range of types than *dare* and *tharf*: it is attested with *to*-infinitive clauses, *that*-clauses, prepositional phrases and NPs (193). However, it starts to select BI clauses as its complement from 1350 onwards, as in (194), and also to exhibit features typical of (pre-)modal verbs, such as the rejection of non-finite forms and inflections. In addition to these features, in ME *need* is found in Experiencer constructions, as in (194). In example (194), *need* selects two complements: the oblique pronoun *me* (which is the understood subject) and the BI complement *telle of nowþe*, and the preposed relative *which*, the object of the subordinate verb *telle.*

(193) & hem dede arraye hors armure, & schippes, & al thing *þat hem neded* to þat viage. (PPCME2, CMBRUT3,46.1381)
and them did array horse armour, and ships, and all things that them-obl.-exp. neded to that voyage.
'and they arrayed the horse's armour, the ships and all the things that they would need for that *voyage.*'

(194) Also it comeþ for many oþer causes of þe whiche *me nedeþ not telle* of nowþe. (PPCME2, CMHORSES,117.312)
Also it comes for many other causes of the which I-obl.-exp. need not tell about now
'Also there are many other causes which I need not mention now'

Loureiro-Porto (2010: 685–686) contends that the only verb in the group of necessity verbs (*tharf, betharf, need, behove* and *mister*) which can actively select an oblique Experiencer in OE is *need* (OE *neodian*). She suggests that three different factors account for the evolution of *need* from impersonal to personal verb status (2010: 696). The first factor corresponds to Harris and Campbell's (1995: 81–82) three-way stages of the actualisation of reanalysis. The first of these stages, 'stage A', refers to an 'input' stage in which the structure is unambiguously impersonal, since "the input structure has all the superficial characteristics of the input analysis". In 'stage B', actualisation, "the structure is subject to different analyses, i.e. exhibits variation, and gradually acquires the characteristics of an innovative analysis". Example (195) from M4 (1420–1500) still exhibits the impersonal characteristics of stage A, as variation is found from M3 (1350–1420) to E1 (1500–1570). The subject in example (195) corresponds to the oblique form *me*, which is in the dative rather than the nominative case, as in PDE. The final stage, from E2 (1570–1640) to E3 (1640–1710), 'stage C', refers to the completion stage, in which there is only one possible analysis, which differs from stage A in terms of its structure (196). The other two factors which may have led to the personalisation of *need* are its low frequency with dummy subject *it* (OED *hit*) and the preference for volitional Experiencers.

(195) *Me nedes* fro hire presence *withdrawe* me prively. (1450 Mirour Saluacioun 939) (OED sv *need* II. 5.a)
I-obl.-exp. need for her presence withdraw me privately
'I need withdraw myself privately for her presence'

(196) Or rather, it is a pity the same fashion don't subsist now, when *one need not be* at the trouble of invention, nor of turning the whole Roman history into romance, for want of proper heroes. (PPCMBE, WALPOLE-174X, 5, 25.571)

However, it remains unclear whether the main verb *need* is a personal or an Experiencer verb in origin. In contrast to Loureiro-Porto (2010), Taeymans' (2006) analysis of Experiencer *neodian* (OE *need*) in the Helsinki Corpus (henceforth HC) reveals that the occurrence of the verb in the Experiencer construction is a late or a rare innovation in OE. Taeymans' corpus does not contain any instances of Experiencer *need* and only five occurrences of Experiencer *neodian* are attested in the entire Dictionary of Old English Corpus (DOEC), four of which are identical to the examples found in the OED, the Bosworth and Toller Dictionary and Supplement (BTD/BTS), and Visser (1963-73). For this study, suffice it to say that *need* is attested in two different constructions since OE: as a personal verb and in the Experiencer construction.

In terms of semantics, *need* is classified under two entries in the OED (*need* v.[1] and *need* v.[2]). Loureiro-Porto (2009: 204) maintains that the most common *need*-verb in OE and ME is *need* v.[1], which initially expresses physical forces and then conveys social forces. With this second meaning, *need* v.[1] coalesces with *need* v.[2] in M3 (1350–1420) (see Section 3). During M3, *need* v.[2] replaces *need* v.[1] with a meaning of force based on external, internal, general and logical factors (Loureiro-Porto 2009: 204). Once *need* acquires these new meanings, it starts to compete with *tharf* (see Taeymans 2006 and Loureiro-Porto 2009) since both verbs occur in personal and in Experiencer constructions, and when followed by infinitive clauses, they convey participant-external and participant-internal necessity senses (Taeymans 2006: Chapter 3).

3.3.2 Distribution of *dare, tharf* and *need*

The changes in the frequencies of the verbs *dare, tharf* and *need* in ME and EModE support the confusion attested between *dare* and *tharf* and the morphosyntactic and semantic changes undergone by these two verbs and *need* during that time. As Table 1 shows, the verb *dare* is the most frequent of the three from M1 to E2, a period during which the use of *dare* increases continuously.[15] This increase is very significant if we compare M1 with M3 ($\chi^2(1)=10.39$, P=0.0008) and M4 with E1 ($\chi^2(1)=18.89$, P=<.0001); the incidence of *dare* is relatively stable in the periods M3-M4 and E1-E2 ($\chi^2(1)=1.6$, P=0.167 and $\chi^2(1)=1.18$, P=0.2453, respectively). The verb *tharf* is the second most frequent verb in M1, but it shows a significant slump in use in later periods of ME, before becoming obsolete in EModE.[16] Given that the incidence of *need*

15 Table 1 includes all the occurrences of *dare, tharf* and *need*, i.e. cases in which these verbs have covert complements or other types of complementation other than BI clauses (*to*-infinitive clauses, *that*-clauses, NP and PPs).

16 The chi-square test indicates a very significant decrease in the use of *tharf* between M1 and M3 ($\chi^2=50.49$, P=<.0001). Between M3 and M4 its use remains stable ($\chi^2=0.11$, P=0.522), but no further instances of *tharf* are found in my data from 1500 onwards; example (186) above is the last recorded instance.

between M1 and M4 is not statistically significant ($\chi^2(1)=0$, P=0.8625), the growing tendency of the *d*-spelling forms and the decrease of the *th-/þ* forms in ME is due to the confusion between *dare* and *tharf.* In comparison to *dare* and *tharf,* the verb *need* shows a lower incidence in M1 but a rising trend, which from M4 to E1 becomes statistically significant ($\chi^2(1)=26.55$, P=<.0001). *Dare* and *need* show the same distribution in E1 (154 (n.f. 47.83) each), but the incidence of the former decreases significantly from E2 to E3 whereas the latter increases significantly ($\chi^2(1)=11.12$, P=0.0007), as shown in Figure 1.

	M1	M2	M3	M4	E1	E2	E3
D'are	30 (24.56)	13 (21.3)	124 (36.95)	113 (43.05)	154 (47.83)	295 (48.85)	133 (34.78)
Th'arf	25 (20.47)	0	5 (1.49)	6 (2.29)	0	0	0
Need	17 (13.92)	0	63 (18.77)	39 (14.86)	154 (47.83)	250 (41.4)	183 (47.85)
Total	72 (58.95)	13 (21.3)	192 (57.21)	158 (60.2)	308 (95.66)	545 (90.25)	316 (82.63)

Table 1: Distribution of *dare, tharf* and *need* from ME to EModE (n.f./10,000 IP-MATs)

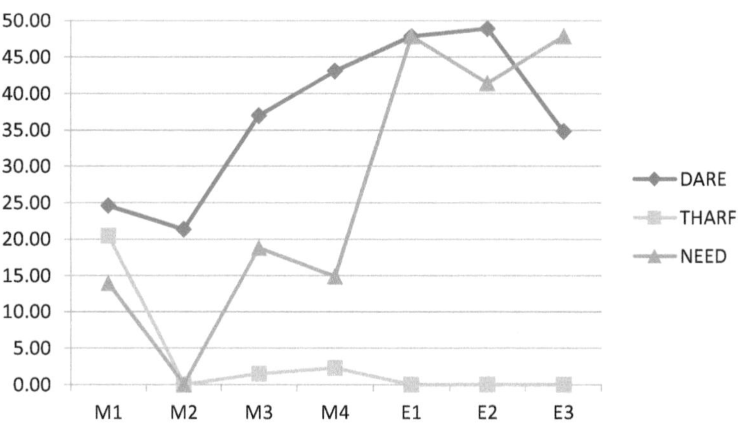

Figure 1: Distribution of *dare, tharf* and *need* from ME to EModE (n.f./10,000 IP-MATs)

The changes observed in the distribution of *dare, tharf* and *need* can be analysed according to six criteria: (i) spelling and pronunciation; (ii) type of subordinate verb selected; (iii) contexts of use; (iv) occurrence of these verbs in Experiencer constructions; (v) occurrence in (non-)assertive contexts; and (vi) semantics. The analysis of these six features is restricted to the occurrence of *dare*, *tharf* and *need* with either the *to*-infinitive or BI complementation (Table 2). Other types of complements have been disregarded because it is only with infinitival complementation that all three verbs show modality-related meanings. Examples of extraposition are not explored either because in these constructions the *to*-infinite is the clausal subject occupying a clause-final position and not an internal clausal complement of the verb, as in (197), with a syntactic dummy *it* in subject position and the semantic subject in the form of a *to*-infinitive clause in post-verbal position. Given that the elided elements in instances of covert complementation may be arguments other than infinitival clauses, these examples are also discarded. Finally, parenthetical uses or fixed expressions, as in (198), are not included in the analysis because they function as frozen units and their purpose may be different from that of the verb plus infinitival complement in other constructions. In contrast, examples of *how dare* plus BI clause are investigated here because *dare* has not been idiomaticised in such instances (199). Table 2 displays the total number of examples which have been considered in my analysis of these criteria in *dare*, *tharf* and *need* constructions.

(197) *It* nedeth not *to telle ġou the names of the cytees ne of the townes þat ben in þat weye* For the weye is comoun & it is knowen of many nacyouns. (PPCME2, CMMANDEV,35.869)
It needs not to tell you the names of the cities nor of the towns that been in that way because the way is common and it is known of many nations.
'It is not necessary to either tell you the names of the cities or of the towns that have been in that way because that one is common and it is known for many nations.'

(198) For to the worlde, wronge may seme right sometyme by false coniecturing, sometimes by false witnesses, as that good Lorde sayd vnto you, which is *I dare say* my very good lorde in his mynde, and said it of very good wyll. (PCEEC, MORE,541.039.700)

(199) þis is al þt we dođ i cristemen & eggiđ eauer to vuele. Me ġe eateliche wihtes. qđ þt eadi wummon. hu *durre ġe* eauer *neomen* ow to cristes. icorene; Me sei me seli meiden qđ he hu derst tu halde me & hondlin se heterliche bute þuh þt tu art trusti o þi lauerd. (PPCME2, CMJULIA,112.271)

This is that we do to Chistianmen and urge ever to evil. But you horrible creature, said the blessed woman, how dare you ever approach to Christ's selected. But tell me blessed maiden said he how dared you hold me and handle so violently but that you are trusty on your lord
'"This is all that we do to torment Chistianmen, and urge them always to evil." "But how do you loathsome creatures ever dare to fasten on Christ's chosen?" said that blessed woman. "But you tell *me,* blessed maiden," said he, "how you dare hold me and handle me so violently-unless it is because you have trust on your Lord."'

	M1	M2	M3	M4	E1	E2	E3	Total
'D'are	27 (22.11)	13 (21.3)	117 (34.86)	97 (36.96)	128 (39.01)	258 (42.49)	121 (31.61)	761 (228.34)
'Th'arf	22 (18.01)	0	4 (1.19)	6 (2.29)	0	0	0	32 (21.49)
Need	5 (4.09)	0	40 (11.92)	20 (7.62)	84 (25.6)	149 (24.54)	106 (27.69)	404 (101.46)

Table 2: *Dare*, *tharf* and *need* and *to*-infinitive/BI clause (raw and n.f./10,000 IP-MATs)

In relation to criterion (i), spelling and pronunciation, my data are in line with the dictionary entries for *dare* and *tharf*, and also with the observations made in Loureiro-Porto (2009: 71–72) and Molencki (2002: 378; 2005) (see Section 3.1): *d*-spelling expressing necessity meanings is found in one instance from M4, in (200), whereas *th*- spelling with a 'courage' meaning related to the verb *dare* is attested in instance different example from M3 (201).

(200) 'So God me helpe,' seyde the quene, 'ye *darfnat* shame, for he ys the goodlyest knyght, and of the beste men of the worlde commyn, and of the strene, of all partyes, of kynges.' (PPCME2, CMMALORY, 636.3826)
'So God me help', said the queen, 'you need not be ashamed, because he is the most good-looking knight, and of the best men of the world coming, and of the offspring, of all parties, of kings.'
''So God, help me!' said the queen, 'you don't need to be ashamed, because he is the most good-looking knight and the best men of the forthcoming world and their offspring, of all parties and of all kings''

(201) And ells thay say that they *thernot* take it vppon hem, for they dwelle so ney to the othere many that thay knowe well thay shold neuer be in ease yf

thay dyde soo whyle that thay dele amongys hem. (PCEEC, PASTON, I, 304.101.2991)
And else they say that they dare not take it upon them, because they dwell so near to the other many that they know well they should never be in ease if they did so while that they deal with them.
'In addition, they say that they dare not take it upon them because they dwell so near to many of them that they know well that they would never be in ease if they did so while they were dealing with them.'

Since *dare* can convey necessity when verbs such as *fear*, *blame*, *seek*, *say*, etc. occur in its complements (MED s.v. *durren* 2a.(a)), criterion (ii) focuses on the type of verbs selected by *dare*, *tharf* and *need*.[17] Taking the MED as my point of reference, I searched for occurrences of *dare*, *tharf* and *need* with the subordinate verbs *eisian* 'to frighten', *fear*, *shame*, *doubt*, *dread*, *grieve* and *seek* and expressions such as *be afraid*, *be ashamed* and *be frightened* (Table 3). The verb *tharf* shows the highest frequency with these verbs and expressions in M1 and M4 (13 out of 32 examples in ME; see Table 2), as in the Experiencer construction illustrated in (202) with the pronoun *us* in the oblique form and the subordinate verb *dreden*.

	M1	M3	M4	E1	E2	E3	Total
Dare	1 (0.82)	0	1 (0.38)	0	2 (0.33)	1 (0.26)	5 (1.79)
Tharf	8 (6.54)	1 (0.29)	4 (1.52)	0	0	0	13 (8.37)
Need	0	3 (0.89)	1 (0.38)	15 (4.57)	27 (4.44)	25 (6.53)	71 (16.82)
Total	9 (7.36)	4 (1.18)	6 (2.28)	15 (4.57)	29 (4.77)	26 (6.79)	89 (26.98)

Table 3: *Dare*, *tharf* and *need* plus 'fear' subordinate verbs (raw and n.f./10,000 IP-MATs)

(202) ġef we hire halded þenne ga we sikerliche ne *þerf* us nowđer for deađ ne for deouel *dreden*. (PPCME2, CMSAWLES,176.146)
if we it hold then go we safely nor need us-ACC neither for death nor for devil fear.
'if we hold it, we go safely and we don't need to fear either death or the devil.'

17 Examples of *dare* plus the verb *say* in the lower clause were not considered within this criterion because of the difficulty of determining whether *dare* really means necessity or courage in such cases.

The verb *dare*, on the other hand, is found in just 5 occurrences: 2 (out of a total of 254) in ME, illustrated in (203) with the lower verb *eisian* 'to frighten'; and 3 (out of 507) in the last two periods of EModE, as illustrated in (204) from E3 with the verb *waver* 'to hesitate'. In example (203), *dare* shows pre-modal features with the old negative form *ne* and the presence of the BI complement governed by *eisian*. In (70), *dare* exhibits morphosyntactic features related to lexical verbs, i.e. *do*-support for negation and *to*-infinitive complementation. However, in 4 of the 5 instances, including (203) and (204), *dare* expresses 'necessity', compared to only one instance in which *dare* means 'courage', as in (205), with the verb *seek* in the subordinate clause. As the n.f. in Table 3 reflect, whereas *dare* roughly shows the same low distribution in M4, E1 and E2, the frequency of *need* gradually increases from the last two periods of ME to EModE. In EModE *need* is the most frequent verb of the three with these subordinate verbs, and with *doubte*, as in (206).

(203) þet he his men *eisian* ne *der* ne to nane wisdome heom nule wissien. (PPCME2, CMLAMBX1, 111.1060)
That he his men frighten not dare not to none wisedom them not-will teach
'That he does not dare frighten his men or wish to teach them any wisdom.'

(204) I charge thee, therefore as thou wilt answer it to the great God, the Judge of all the Earth, that thou *do not dare to waver* one tittle from the Truth, upon any account or pretence whatsoever: (PPCEME, LISLE-E3-P1,4,108.142)

(205) The old man answeres, A poore Shropshire man; and demands if there were not a gentleman in the court dwelling, called by the name of M. Will Sommer? for the country hearing him in fauour in the court, said hee was so at least. The courtier answered, Here is such a one indeede. For fault of a worse, saies hee, I am his uncle; and wept with joy that hee should see him. Marry, sayes the man, I'll help you to him straight; for, I tell you, *not any in the court durst but haue sought him*, which this man did, and it was told him. (PPCEME, ARMIN-E2-H, 43.282)

(206) Wherfore there is nothynge that *thou nedest to doubte* in any maner, for all thynges that be: desyreth naturally stedfast dwellyngs, and to eschewe distruction. (PPCEME, BOETHCO-E1-H,81.515)
'Consequently, there is nothing that you need to doubt in any manner because all the things are as follows: it naturally desires firm dwellings, and to avoid destruction.'

For criterion (iii), I investigated the occurrence of the verbs in contexts expressing 'fear' and 'doubt', as denoted by collocates such as *terrible, fearful, be afraid, make doubt* or *dangerous.* Unlike *dare* and *need,* no instances of *tharf* were attested in my data. Table 4 illustrates the presence of *dare* in these contexts in ME and EModE, and that the most frequent meaning it conveys is 'courage' or 'boldness', in (207). *Need* is recorded in these contexts from M4 onwards, as in (208), but its frequency is lower than that of *dare* in ME and EModE.

	M1	M2	M3	M4	E1	E2	E3	TOTAL
Dare	6	1	13	11	11	18	8	68
Need	0	0	0	1	3	6	4	14
Total	6	1	13	12	14	24	12	82

Table 4: *Dare* and *need* in 'fear' contexts (raw data)

(207) Þe peas is weel kepte, but þe straungiers ar soore *a-dradde* and *dar nought come* on brode. Here is all þat I knowe as yet. (PCEEC, PASTON,II,143.319.8778)
'The peace is well-kept, but the strangers are sure afraid and dare not come on board. Here is all that I know right now.'

(208) Haveing here under consideration how great the influence of company is, and how prone we are all, espetially children, to imitation, I must take the liberty to set down one thing though *I doubt not* but *you need not be advised of it,* but if that were a reason for me $to passe it in silence I might very well be excused from writeing at all. (PPCEME, LOCKE-E3-P2,68.54)

In relation to criterion (iv), Table 5 shows that no examples of *dare* in the Experiencer construction were attested in my data (cf. MED s.v. *durren* 2 (b)). *Tharf,* on the other hand, is attested in 3 (out of 22) instances in M1, as in (202) above, increasing to 3 out of 4 instances in M3 and to 3 out of 6 in M4. *Need* occurs in the Experiencer construction in both periods, as illustrated in (193) and (194) above, with frequency highest in M3 and M4 (see M3 (209)). Loureiro-Porto (2010: 689) reports the occurrence of *need* throughout the whole period from OE to EModE, claiming as its last occurrence an instance of *need* with a non-nominative Experiencer in E1 (1500–1570). Taeymans (2006: Chapter 4) pushes this date forward to E2, observing *need* with an oblique Experiencer and a clausal complement, i.e. *to*-infinitive or BI.

	M1	M3	M4	E1	E2	E3	Total
Tharf	3	3	3	0	0	0	9
Need	1	9	9	1	1	0	21

Table 5: *Tharf* and *need* in the Experiencer construction with sentential theme (raw data)

(209) Bot in þis sorow *nedeþ þee to haue discrecion* on þis maner: (PPCME2, CMCLOUD, 83.441)
But in this sorrow needs you-obl.exp. to have discretion in this manner
'But in this pain you need to be discreet in this manner'

Criterion (v) is designed to test Molencki's (2002: 369–370; 2005) assertion that *þearf* and *dearr* are restricted to non-assertive contexts, except for a few instances in poetry. In the literature, 'non-assertive' clauses include negative, interrogative, conditional, as in (210), comparative, as in (211), concessive, *before*-clauses, clauses with lightly stressed adverbs such as *hardly*, *never* or *seldom*, as in (212), clauses with negative items, putative *should*-clauses, as in (213), and restrictive relative clauses with conditional meaning, as in (214) (Jacobsson 1974: 62; Quirk et al. 1985: 138–139; Duffley 1994: 219; Beths 1999; Taeymans 2006; Schlüter 2010).

(210) Anything sent to my House will find me for reply *if need be* before you go in the morning. (PPCMBE, GLADSTONE-1873, 2, 388.315)

(211) And as the Advantage will be great in forbearing to give them Battle, so, on the other side, the Danger will be more (said she) than we *need venture*, and the Loss, in case it fall upon us, greater *than the Advantage of the Victory*, if we should obtain it. (PPCMBE, HIND-1707, 319.244)

(212) The many excellent Uses of this Custom need *scarce* be hinted to a Reader who hath any Knowledge of the World: (PPCMBE, FIELDING-1749, 3, 7.348)

(213) It is embarrassing that such a truth *need be stated* at all. (Duffley 1992: 100)

(214) All study *whatsoever* needs a similar exercise of patient application; (PPCMBE BAIN-1878, 370.172)

According to Molencki, in affirmative sentences *þearf* is replaced with periphrastic constructions containing the nouns *þearf/tharf*, *nedþearf* or *neod/ned*, as in (215), whereas *gedyrstigan* is used as an equivalent to *dearr* (see also Taeymans 2006: Chapter 3). Loureiro-Porto's (2009: 79) study contradicts Molencki's by providing three examples of *tharf* in affirmative contexts, two of them expressing external obligation and one conveying internal necessity. However, she points out that these meanings are not very common, either because of the general decrease of this verb over time, or because of the verb's specialisation as a non-affirmative verb, given that other necessity verbs such as *behove* were used in affirmative contexts.

(215) þæt ic æe wel herige ond þe to geoce garholt bere, mægenes fultum, þær ðe bið manna þearf. (Beowulf 1836) (Molencki 2002: 378)

As discussed in Chapter 2, polarity and semantic/pragmatic context have been taken here as two separate factors that may influence the evolution and behaviour of *dare* and *need*, when followed by infinitive clauses. As far as polarity is concerned, even though *d'are* is slightly more frequent in negative clauses in M1 and in affirmative clauses in M4, this distribution is not statistically significant when the M1 and M4 subperiods are compared ($\chi^2(1)=0.52$, P=0.3482; see Figure 2). This situation changes in E1 when the incidence of *d'are* increases significantly in affirmative clauses in contrast to M4, i.e. $\chi^2(1)=5.98$, P=0.0098. This increasing tendency of *dare* in affirmative clauses comes to a halt in E2 when the proportion of *d'are* in negative clauses increases significantly in comparison to E1, i.e. $\chi^2(1)=13.92$, P=0.0001, and *d'are* occurs in negative and affirmative clauses.

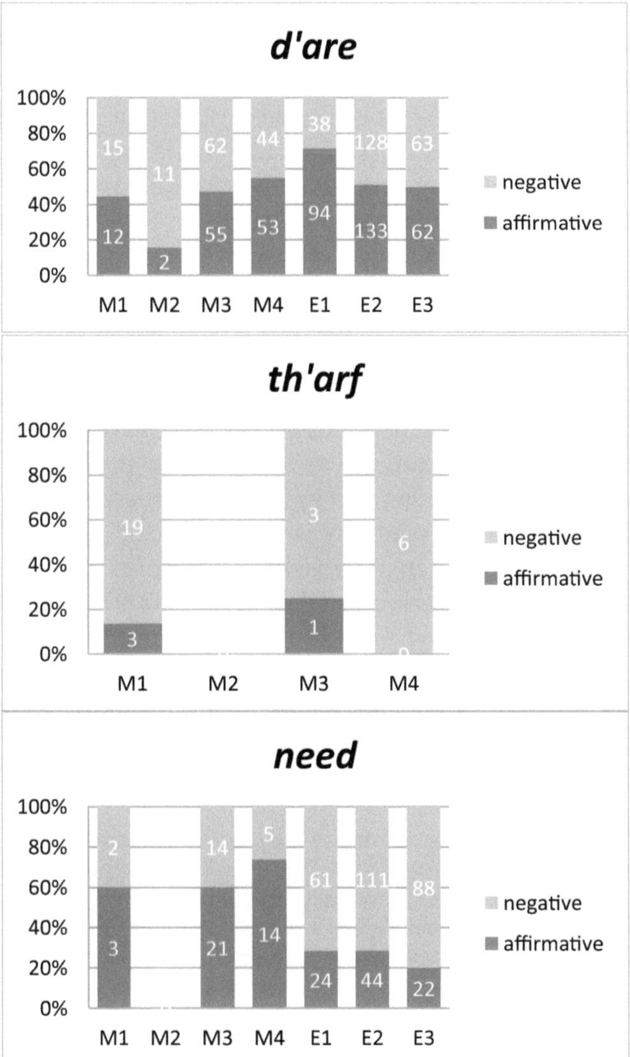

Figure 2: Polarity and *'d'are*, *'th'arf* and *need* plus infinitival complementation in ME and EModE (raw data)

Figure 2 shows that *th'arf* is restricted to negative clauses in my ME data set. In contrast, the distribution of *need* in affirmative clauses in the ME period is higher than that of negative ones, representing more than 60 per cent of the data. Variation in *need* and *d'are* with respect to polarity is not statistically significant in M4, i.e. when *d'are* shows its highest frequency in affirmative clauses in the ME data ($\chi^2(1)=1.65$, P=0.1245). However, the incidence of *need* in affirmative clauses decreases in E1 in favour of negative clauses and this distribution remains stable in the following two subperiods of EModE.[18]

I have also analysed these three verbs with respect to the factuality of the proposition and the realisation of the event described by the subordinate clause (Table 6 and Figure 3). *Dare* is attested in the three contexts, but in the first two subperiods of ME it more frequently conveys non-factual unrealised meanings, as in (216). The number of examples with factual unrealised meanings gradually increases in M3 and M4, as in (217); however, this tendency is not significant unless the factual unrealised and the non-factual unrealised examples from the subperiods M1 and M4 are compared ($\chi^2(1)=5.49$; P=0.0097).[19] This situation changes again in E1, when factual unrealised meanings significantly decrease in use in favour of factual realised and non-factual unrealised ones ($\chi^2(1)=18.52$, P=<.0001 and $\chi^2(1)=12.9$, P=0.0002, respectively). This distribution remains stable during EModE.[20]

---

18 The distribution of *need* in affirmative and negative clauses does not vary significantly from E1 to E2 ($\chi^2(1)=0.02$, P=1) or from E2 to E3 ($\chi^2(1)=1.99$, P=0.1198).

19 The increase of factual unrealised meanings vs non-factual unrealised ($\chi^2(1)=2.06$, P=0.0949) and factual realised meanings ($\chi^2(1)=0.05$, P=0.5716) from M1 to M3 is not statistically significant. The difference between non-factual unrealised and factual realised meaning in these periods is not statistically significant either ($\chi^2(1)=0.3$, P=0.4096). Similarly, the proportions of the factual realised contexts did not change from M1 to M4 when compared with either factual unrealised or non-factual unrealised meanings ($\chi^2(1)=0.38$, P=0.3375 and $\chi^2(1)=0.75$, P=0.2524, respectively).

20 The proportions of *dare* and the *to*-infinitive/BI clause remain stable from E1 to E2. The distribution is not statistically significant when non-factual unrealised and factual unrealised meanings are compared ($\chi^2(1)=1.68$, P=0.1512). This is also the case in the comparison between non-factual unrealised and factual realised meanings ($\chi^2(1)=0.02$, P=0.8065), and between factual realised and factual unrealised ($\chi^2(1)=2.2$, P=0.1042).

	M1			M2	M3			M4		
	d'are	*need*	*th'arf*	*d'are*	*d'are*	*need*	*th'arf*	*d'are*	*need*	*th'arf*
Factual Realised	5	0	0	0	24	7	1	19	0	0
Factual Unrealised	7	0	0	1	48	4	0	49	1	0
Non-factual Unrealised	15	5	22	12	45	29	3	29	19	6

	E1		E2		E3	
	d'are	*need*	*d'are*	*need*	*d'are*	*need*
Factual Realised	49	4	86	22	44	24
Factual Unrealised	26	5	73	20	40	12
Non-factual Unrealised	53	75	99	107	37	70

Table 6: (non-)factual (un-)realised and *'d'are*, *'th'arf* and *need* plus infinitival complementation in ME and EModE (raw data)

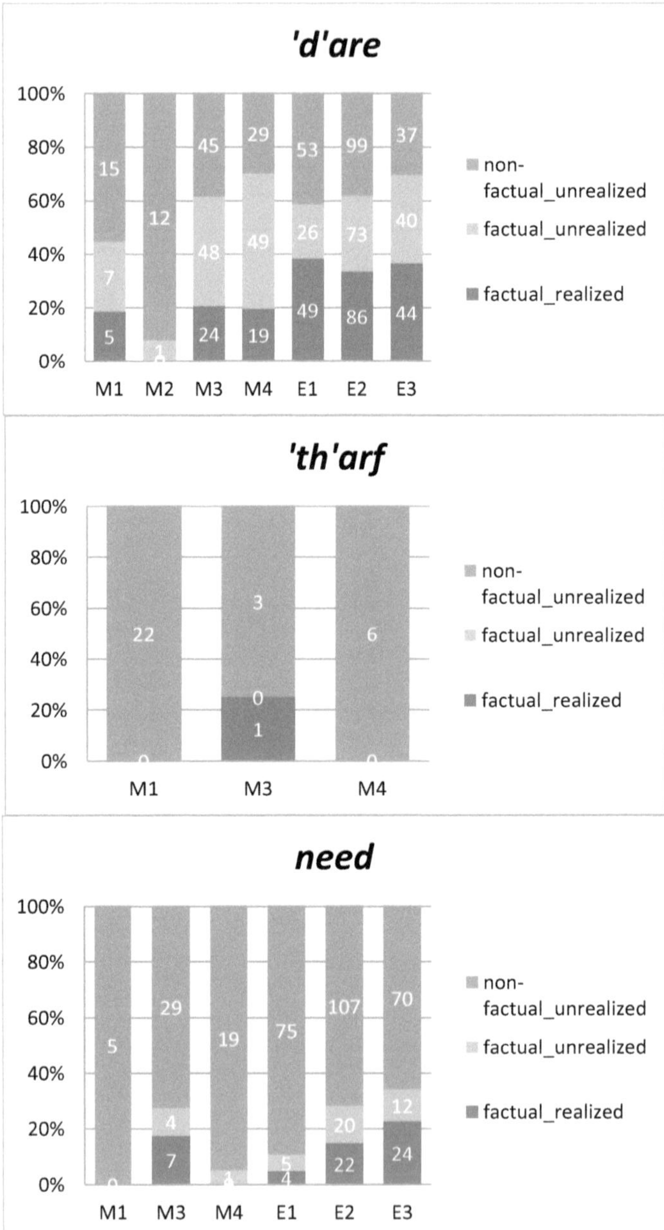

Figure 3: (non-)factual (un-)realised and *'d'are*, *'th'arf* and *need* plus infinitival complementation in ME and EModE (raw data)

(216) Yef it be ani þat dar noht drinke hir mesur, þai sal grace god and gruche noht. (PPCME2, CMBENRUL,28.957)
If it be any who dare not drink their measure, they shall grace god and complain not.
'If there is any who dare not drink their measure, they shall thank god and not complain.'

(217) And when the xij ġere were gone, þere bigon bituene ham a grete debate, so þat þai werrede strongely in-fere, and eueryche of ham dede oþere miche disese, ffor Morgan wolde haue hade alle þe lande fram biġende Humber, þat Conedag helde; but he come aġeynes him with a strong power, *so þat Morgan derst nouġt abide*, but fley awaye into Walys; (PPCME2, CMBRUT3,21.605)
And when the xii years were gone, there began between them a great debate so that they made-war strongly in fear, and everyone of them did other much disease, because Morgan would have had all the land from beginning Humber, that Conedag held; but he came against him with a strong power so that Morgan dared not wait, but flied away to Wales;
'Twelve years later, a great debate began among them so that they started a war based on fear and all of them did a lot of harm because Morgan would have had all the land from Humber onwards, which Conedag owned; but he would come against him with such a strong power that Morgan dared to wait, but he flied away to Wales.'

My data corroborate the restriction of *tharf* to non-factual unrealised contexts, except for one instance in a negative factual realised meaning (218). *Need* is also found more frequently with non-factual unrealised meanings, as in (219), in ME and in EModE. In the latter period, *need* is more frequent with factual realised and with factual unrealised meanings, but these only represent around 30 per cent of the data in E2 and E3 (see Figure 3).

(218) $and I am in a doute of swiche thinges $as ne han no felyng soules ne no naturel werkynges servynge to appetites as beestes han, whether thei han appetyt to duellen and to duren. "Certes," quod sche, "ne therof *thar the nat doute*. Now looke upon thise herbes and thise trees. (PPCME2, CMBOETH,435.C2.280)
And I am in a doubt of such things as not have no feeling souls not no natural workings serving to the appeites as beasts have, whether they have appetite to dwell and to last. "Certainly", quote she, "not therefore need you-obl.-exp. not doubt. Now look upon these herbs and these trees.

(219) And at this meting, y=e=lord Hasting, whose trouth towarde the king *no manne* doubted nor *neded to doubte*, perswaded the Lordes to belieue, that the Duke of Gloucester, was sure and fastlye faithfull to hys prince, and that the lorde Riuers and lord Richard with the other knightes wer for maters attempted by them against ye dukes of Gloucester & Buckingham, (PPCEME, MORERIC-E1-P1,23.45)

Criterion (vi) deals with the occurrence (and confusion) of *tharf* and *dare* in semantic contexts of necessity, possibility and volition (see MED s.v. *durren* 2, (a) and s.v. *thurven* 7. (a) and 8). '*Th'arf* is only found expressing volition in two examples, in (201) above from M3, and in (220) below from M1. The remaining 30 occurrences of *tharf* in my data convey necessity or obligation. In the case of *dare*, necessity and obligation are the most frequent meanings in M1, M4 and EModE, such senses being also attested in the two periods under study, as in (203) and (204) above and (221) below from E2 (see Table 7). Possibility interpretation is central in 15 occurrences from M3 onwards, as in (222), attested in M4. Finally, volition is the most frequent meaning in M2 and M3, and constitutes the main interpretation in 16 examples from M2 to E2, as in (223).

	M1	M2	M3	M4	E1	E2	E3	Total
Necessity/ Obligation	3 (2.45)	1 (1.64)	3 (0.89)	3 (1.14)	4 (1.22)	15 (2.47)	5 (1.3)	34 (11.13)
(Im) possibility	0	0	2 (0.59)	3 (1.14)	3 (0.91)	6 (0.99)	1 (0.26)	15 (3.9)
Volition	0	2 (3.28)	4 (1.19)	1 (0.38)	1 (0.3)	8 (1.31)	0	16 (6.47)
Total	3 (2.45)	3 (4.91)	9 (2.68)	7 (2.66)	8 (2.44)	29 (4.77)	6 (1.57)	65 (21.5)

Table 7: Semantics of '*d'are* from ME to EModE (raw and n.f./10,000 IP-MATs)

(220) Ðat seiđ sanctus Ieronimus: *Est autem penitere peccata ante acta deflere, et flenda non repetere*, "Swa scal," he seiđ, "mann his senne berewsen, đat he eft ne do đat *he* eft *đurue be-riwsin*." (PPCME2, CMVICES1, 121.1492)
That said Saint Jeronimus: ... "So shall", he said, "man his sin repent, which he afterwards not do what he afterwards wants to repent."
'That said Saint Jeronimus: "Est autem penitere peccata ante acta deflere, et flenda non repetere", "So shall", he said, "man repent his sin, which he afterwards does not do what he wants to repent."'

(221) Exit. T. S. what shift she'll make now with this peece of flesh In this strict time of Lent, I cannot imagine, Flesh *dare not peepe abroad* now, I haue knowne This Citie now aboue this seuen yeers, (PPCEME, MIDDLET-E2-H, 16.334)

(222) & do þer-to ambros, burnet & þe crispe malue &, if þer be bane broken & *þu dare* noghte serche it ġit, gyf hym þis to drynke (PPCME2, CMTHORN, 69.484)
and do thereto Ambrose, Burnet and the crisp mallow &, if there be bone broken & you dare not probe it yet, give him this to drink
'And do for this purpose Ambrose, Burnet and the crisp mallow and, if there be bone broken and you cannot probe it yet, give him this drink'

(223) but for sweats in his cloaths without any exercise abroad, you shall giue them either when the weather is so much vnseasonable, that you cannot go forth, or when your horse is so much in danger of lamenes, *that you dare not straine him*, (PPCEME, MARKHAM-E2-P2,1,82.48)

To sum up, the six criteria analysed above demonstrate that the diachronic evolution undergone by *dare* in ME and EModE is due not only to the phonological and orthographic confusion between it and *tharf*, but also to the competition between *tharf* and *need* from ME onwards and the influence of *need* on *dare*. In the last two subperiods of ME, *th*-spelling is found with courage meanings and *d*-spelling is attested with necessity meanings. The verb *need* starts to compete with *tharf* in M3, when the former conveys the meaning of force based on external, internal, general and logical factors (see Taeymans 2006 and Loureiro-Porto 2009). *Dare*, *tharf* and *need* express necessity when they select subordinate verbs denoting 'fear' and 'doubt', and, at least in the first periods of ME, they mainly occur in 'non-factual unrealised' contexts. However, whereas *tharf* and *need* can occur in Experiencer constructions, *dare* is only attested in personal constructions in my database (cf. MED s.v. *durren* 2 (b)). As a consequence of the relationship between *dare*, *tharf* and *need*, the first occurrences of *dare* selecting *to*-infinitive complement clauses and *need* governing BI clauses are attested in the M3 and M4 subperiods in my data. *Dare* also selects a *that*-clause as its complement in three instances in ME, two dating from M1 and one from M3:

(224) *And herby þis lady mente on curteys maner as* sche durste þat Iesu schulde helpe þis feeste of wyn by his miracle. (PPCME2, CMWYCSER,360.2377)

And hereby this lady mentioned on curtsy manners that she dared that Jesus should help this feast of wine by his miracle.
'Then this lady mentioned politely that she wished that Jesus should help this feast of wine with his miracle'

I hypothesise that *dare* temporarily adopts this selection, more typical of lexical verbs, as a result of the influence exerted by the homonymous noun *tharf*, which more frequently selects a *that*-clause:

(225) Him is ðearf ðæt hie geðencen hu micel menigu ðæra getreowfulra bið, ðe ægðer ge hi selfe clæne gehealdað, ge eac oðre of hira gedwolan ahwierf. (CP 403.20) (Molencki 2002: 376)

The obsolescence of *tharf*, which is not attested after M4 in my data, affects the distribution and polarity of *dare* and *need*. *Dare*, with higher frequency from M1 to M3, continues to increase until E2, whereas *need* reflects a significant rising tendency from M4 to E1. Both *dare* and *tharf* are more frequently attested in negative clauses from M1 to M3; in the case of *tharf*, the verb occurs almost categorically in negative contexts. In contrast, *need* is found more frequently in affirmative clauses in ME. The gradual increase of *dare* in affirmative clauses in ME drops off in E1, resulting in a levelling of its occurrence in affirmative and negative clauses. In the case of *need*, its occurrence in negative clauses rises significantly from M4 to E1.

3.3.3 Modal, lexical and blend constructions

As a result of the confusion with *tharf* and competition between *tharf* and *need*, in LME *dare* has, on the one hand, the features that it characteristically showed in OE (acceptance of coordination, VP-deletion, desemantisation and BI-complement selection), and, on the other hand, new features, such as *to*-infinitive complementation and other lexical-verb characteristics. *Need* shows lexical features such as inflections for second- and third-person singular in simple present and simple past *–ed*, non-finite forms and *to*-infinitive complementation, but starts to select BI complement clauses and to show inflectional forms which are not overtly marked.

Among the lexical features acquired by *dare* is the infinitive form *dur*, its earliest attestation recorded in 1325 (226) (MED s.v. *durren*,

1a (a)). In my data, three examples of the infinitive form are attested in M3 and all of them exhibit variation in spelling, as the form *dare* in (227), *dor* in (228) and *dar*. Examples (226) to (228) illustrate the co-occurrence of infinitive *dare* with the modals *chuld* (*should*) and *shall*, which was possible in OE and in ME.[21] The plausibility of the non-finite form *to dare* in (229) allows it to govern a clausal subject, an option which was not possible before.

(226) he a word ne *sal dur* speke. (a1400 (a 1325) *Cursor* (Vsp A.3) (MED s.v. *durren*, 1a (a))).

(227) Fynally assure your Grace I and all others here bee all aferde of one thing that he shall not *dare* abide us. (PCEEC, ORIGIN1,231.037.670)

(228) and he seyd nay, but seyd he that chuld do it chuld bettyr *dor* take it up-on hym than he chuld. (PCEEC, PASTON,I,34.011.192)

(229) *To* apere or *dore* schewe his hede. (c1425 (a1420) Lydg. *TB* (Aug A.4) 1.2491) (MED s.v. *durren*, 1a (a)).

The infinitive form *dur* can also be used as the past participle of a present perfect verbal group, as in (230) with the auxiliary *hath*. However, variation is at work here, as illustrated in (231), where *hadde* is followed by the simple past form *durst*, which functions as a past participle. The perfect construction with *dare* is attested in interrogative sentences from LME onwards, as in (232), but the past participle form of *dare* is not attested in my data, though. In example (232), *dare* exhibits lexical and modal features, since it is governed by an auxiliary verb which inverts with the subject to produce an interrogative clause, but at the same time *dare* selects a BI complement clause.

(230) þe Mayer *hath not dar* do right lawe ne execucon. (c1448 *Shillingford* 53) (MED s.v. *durren*, 1a (a)).
'The mayor has not dare do neither the right law nor the execution.'

(231) If I *hadde durst*, certeyn I wolde have karoled. (a1425 (?a1400) *RRose* (Htrn 409) 809) (MED s.v. *durren*, 1a (b)).
'If I had dare, certain I would have sung.'

21 The increasing reluctance of modals to co-occur with other auxiliaries is completed in the ModE period (see Loureiro-Porto 2009: 192).

(232) How *hast* thou *dorre be* so *hardi*? ((c1450) Malory Wks. (Win-C) 295/8) (MED s.v. *durren*, 1b (a)).
'How has you dare to be so bold?'

With the obsolescence of the equivalent verb *gedyrstlæcan*, other expressions and loan words were used as complements of *dare* in order to reinforce the latter's lexical meaning and to provide an external argument for this verb, as *hardy* 'bold' in (233) (see MED s.v. *durren*, 1 (b)).

(233) Þat feld is not so wel closed but þat men may entren at here owne list, But in þat cesoun þat the bawme is growynge men put þere to gode kepynge þat no man *dar ben hardy* to entre. (PPCME2, CMMANDEV,32.795)
That field is not so well closed, but that men may enter at their own desire. But, in that season when the balm is growing, men put thereto good keeping, so that no man dare be hardy to enter.
'That field is not so well closed, but men may enter at their own desire. But, in that season when the balm is growing, men put that thereto good keeping, so that no man dare be hardy to enter.'

The new form *dursted* for the simple past shows a combination of the old preterite-present form *durst* and the weak form of regular verbs ending in *–ed*, as in (234). However, one has to be cautious with this example since it is the only instance found in the MED for ME, with no occurrences recorded in the OED, Visser (1963–73) or my database. The most common past-tense forms are *durst* and its variants *dorste*, *dirst* and *darste* (OED s.v. *dare*, v.[1] 3). It is not until EModE that the first occurrences with the new simple past form *dared* are attested, as in (235) from E2.

(234) þai went be nyght, for þai ne *dursted* Be day (c1400 *St. Anne(1)* (Min-U Z.822.N81) 1415) (MED s.v. *durren*, 1b (b)).
'They went by night because they did not dare by day'

(235) The superscription to the Kings sacred Majesty. Dread Soverain your Majesty voutsafe to lett fall your princely eys uppon these few unworthy lynes, which *dared not appear* in your royall presence, proceeded they not from a loyall, and an unreprooveable hart, howsoever seeming crooked by misfortune, in your just, and all discerning judgment: (PCEEC, HOLLES,I,95.029.821)

The old form *durst* is found with *to*-infinitives in the following three examples in my data:

(236) And when pees was made oueral, þrouġ his noble knyġthode þat he hade, & also for his owen worþynesse, and no man, were he neuer so grete a lorde, *derst nouġt meve werre aġeynes him, noþer to arise and forto make* þe lande of Fraunce in quiete & pees, he wonede þere ix ġere, (PPCME2, CMBRUT3,80.2433)
'And when peace was made overall through his noble knighthood that he had and also for his own worthiness, and no man, were he never so great a lord, dared neither made war against him nor to arise so as to make the land of France in quiet and peace, he lived there nine years'

(237) KYng Arthure hade duellede in þe contre but a litil while, þat men ne tolde him þat þer was comen a grete Geaunt into Spayne, and hade rauesshede faire Elyne, þat was cosyn to Hoel of Britaigne, & hade brouġt here vppon an hull þat is clepede þe Mount of seynt Barnard; & þere was noman in þat contre so bolde, ne so hardy, *þat derst wiþ him to feiġt*, ne come neyġ þe place þere þe Geaunt duellede; (PPCME2, CMBRUT3,84.2536)
'King Arthure had dwelled in the country but a little while, that men hadn't told him that there had come a great Giant to Spain and had carried away the beautifyl Elyne, who was the cousing of Hoel of Britain, and had brought her upon a hill that is called the Mountain of Saint Barnard; and there was no man in that country so bold, not so hardy, that dared with him fight nor come closer to the place where the Giant dwelled;'

(238) And that they seyd they *durst not for to take vppon hem* for to be bonden, and as for money they had non for to pay at that tyme; and there-fore I kept stylle the bestys. (PCEEC, PASTON,I,301.099.2906)
'Hence, they said they dared not to take upon them to be bound, and as for money they had nothing to pay at that time; and therefore I will still keep the beasts.'

Example (236) is very revealing as regards the degree of variation attested at this time because the form *derst* selects the two types of the infinitive as its complements: BI *meve* and *to*-infinitive *to arise*. Distance may account for the insertion of the *to* complement in the second part of the coordination in (236) and also in the case of example (237), in the complement of *fight*, *wiþ him*, between *derst* and the infinitive clause. Finally, the *to*-infinitive clause is reinforced by the preposition *for* in (238). Visser (1963 [1973]) considers rhythm one of the reasons for the use of *durst* with the *to*-infinitive. However, the stress patterns of the examples above do not represent any critical context: the stressed monosyllable verb *meve* is overshadowed because it is immediately followed by its stressed argument *were* and *arise* is secondary-syllable stressed; *feiġt* is preceded by a pronoun, which is unstressed; and *take* is overshadowed because it is part of a phrasal verb and the stress pattern is unproblematic because it is preceded by a negative particle which functions as a stress-clash buffer (Schlüter, personal communication).

In the case of *need*, the BI clause is attested in 7 examples in my ME data: four examples in M3 and three in M4. In one instance, in (239), *need* does not show *–s* inflection for third-person singular. Example (239) could be classified as 'indeterminate' because it occurs in a context where both the subjunctive and the indicative mood are possible. Example (240) illustrates the use of *need* in a subjunctive context and the occurrence of a perfect construction in subordinate clause in the bare infinitive form, i.e. *a go*, which indicates that the verb *need* is undergoing desemantisation. *Need* is also attested with the BI clause in three examples in the Experiencer construction, as in (241), with a third-person singular form and an oblique Experiencer such as *me*.

(239) *If it need be*, adde therto abstynence and other manere turmentynge of thy flesshe, for truste it wel, (PPCME2, CMAELR4,11.290)
'If it need be, add abstinence there and other forms of tormenting your flesh, and trust it well,'

(240) My Lady Caltorp hath ben at Geppeswich on pilgry-mache, and came homward be my lady of Norffolk, and ther was moche cominicacion of your mater be-twix you and myn vncle, seyng to my Lady Caltorp *ye nede not a go* to London, ye myght haue had an ende at home, rememberyng to my seid Lady Caltorp of the mocion that he made towchyng the maner of Sporle, promyttyng to my lady to a-bide þat and to write and seale as largely as any man wol desire hym; and at hes departyng from my lady he was not mery, (PCEEC, PASTON,I,664.228.6854)
'My Lady Caltorp has been at Geppeswich on pilgrimage. She came homewards to my lady of Norffolk and there was much communication of the matter between you and my uncle, saying to my Lady Caltorp that you need not have gone to London, you might have had and end at home, remembering to my said Lady Caltorp of the motion that he made touching the manner of Sporle, promising to my lady to wait that and to write and seal as largely as any man would desire; and at his departing from my lady he was not merry,'

(241) Also it comeþ for many oþer causes of þe whiche *me nedeþ not telle* of nowþe. (PPCME2, CMHORSES,117.312)
Also it comes for many other causes of the which I-obl.-exp. needs not tell of now.
'Also it comes for many other reasons of which I need not tell about now.'

The modal and lexical features reflected by the examples of *dare* with a *to*-infinitive, in (236) to (238), and *need* with a BI clause, in (241), lead to what Denison (1998: 167–170) terms mixed usages. These are structures in which the verb shows both modal and lexical features, as in example (242). The selection of a bare infinitive complement clause in this example suggests that *dare* is a modal, whereas *do*-support indicates its status as a lexical verb.

(242) 'I *don't dare risk* meeting her. But I should like to talk to her very much.' (1992 Tartt, Secret history vi.425) (Denison 1998: 169)

Similarly, the occurrence of the old forms *derst* and *durst* with a *to*-infinitive clause gives *dare* blend features in (236) to (238). With *need*, the form *nediþ* with the *–þ* inflection for third-person singular present in (241) is a lexical feature, whereas the BI clauses *telle* and *go*, respectively, reflect the standard complementation for modal verbs. Example (243) is an instance of Schlüter's (2010: 299) 'ambiguous uses', i.e. cases in which the verb does not display any sign of being either an auxiliary or a lexical verb. These are finite uses of *dare* and *need* other than third-person singular, as in (243), and of the finite form *darest/needest* in second-person singular, as in (244).

(243) As towchyng the preferment of Mr Yng, I nede nat wryt on to yow; for I $suppose he hath aduertysyd yowr lordshyp at the leyngth in that behalf, $and also desyryd yowr cownsell, now that the Kyng hath shewyd hym $hys pleasure how for the exspedicion of hys matter he $shall $be $ferther orderyd and demeanyd. (PCEEC, FOX,55.007.157)

(244) ...but *thou Rosader the youngest in yeares, but the eldest in valout,* art a man of strength and *darest doo what honour allowes thee;* ... (T.Lodge: Rosalynde 1590; EEPF) (Schlüter 2010: 299)

The development of *dare* and *need* in ME is characterised by variation and innovation since their modal and lexical features are not typical of either ME main verbs or ME pre-modals. The coexistence of modal forms with lexical forms is referred to as 'layering' (Heine 1993).

3.4 Complementation choices over time: Qualitative and multivariate analysis of *dare* and *need*

The aim of this study is to examine infinitival alternation with *dare* and *need* both diachronically, from EModE to PDE, and synchronically, in the American and British English regional varieties. As discussed in Chapter 2, the analysis of the data using the 'glm' function in R is divided into three models comprising the periods of time and dialects under study: *Model 1* contains the British data for EModE; *Model 2* contains American and British data for LModE, and *Model 3* includes PDE data for both varieties. The fact that *need* is attested with a *to*-infinitive clause in only 6 examples in the British data for LModE makes it impossible to run any reliable statistical method with 6 or 7 predictors. Similarly, my British data for *dare* plus the *to*-infinitive clause contain only 18 examples. The analysis of *need* and *dare* in LModE is therefore restricted to data for American English, and the exploration of *dare* with infinitival complementation in American PDE is necessarily qualitative.

Following the methodology explained in Chapter 2, seven predictors were included in *STEP 1* for the analysis of *dare* and *need*:

1. presence/absence of explicit morphology in the main verbal form
2. syntactic construction in which *dare*/*need* and infinitival complementation occur, i.e. adverbial, dependent or main clause
3. polarity of the construction, i.e. positive vs negative
4. use of *do*-support in negative, interrogative and emphatic affirmative sentences
5. Principle of Rhythmic Alternation
6. animacy of the subject
7. notional characterisation of *dare*/*need* and the infinitival clause

STEP 2 adds to *STEP 1* the following variables:

1. 'fear' verbs, e.g. *to be afraid*/*ashamed*/*frightened*, *fear*, *doubt*, *seek*, *search*, *grieve*, etc. (MED s.v. *durren* 2a.(a))

2. passivisation of the main clause and/or of the infinitive complementation
3. presence/absence of a relative clause as the subject/object of the construction
4. presence/absence of a perfect construction in the infinitive complement clause
5. valency of the subordinate infinitive verb, i.e. intransitive, transitive or coordinated
6. distance between the main verb *dare* or *need* and the *to*-infinitive/BI clause
7. syntactic category of the subject, i.e. basic or non-basic.

The study of two interactions – RHYTHMIC ALTERNATION and POLARITY and NOTIONAL CHARACTERISATION and POLARITY – using a multivariate analysis was not possible because of the scarcity of data for the dependent variables per period and/or per regional variant. A univariate analysis of these factors was carried out to identify possible trends.

As mentioned in the previous section, *dare* and *need* start to show variation between *to*-infinitive and BI complementation in LME and particularly from EModE onwards as a result of morphosyntactic and semantic changes. My decision to restrict the analysis of the distribution of *dare* and *need* and infinitival alternation to the four main periods of English, i.e. from ME to PDE, is justified by the low number of examples per subperiod of time.[22] As Table 8 indicates, *dare* is attested with BI complementation more frequently than with *to*-infinitive complement clauses in all four periods under study. The incidence of *dare* and the *to*-infinitive varies significantly across time, however, increasing significantly from EModE to LModE ($\chi^2(1)=36.4$, $P=<.0001$) and remaining unchanged from LModE to PDE ($\chi^2(1)=0.06$, $P=0.6714$) in the British English regional variant. In the American variant, the incidence of *dare* with respect to *to*-infinitive/BI alternation remains

22 In line with Section 3.2, examples in which *dare* and *need* show VP-deletion, have parenthetical uses or occur in fixed expressions are not included in the statistical analysis presented in these sections. In addition, examples extracted from the Bible are not considered here because this genre contains many archaic uses which may not be representative of the English language at the time.

stable from LModE to PDE ($\chi^2(1)=1.76$, P=0.116). As regards *need* with *to*-infinitive/BI complementation, the situation is slightly different. The frequency of *to*-infinitive clauses, which constitute the most common infinitival complementation choice in ME, decreases significantly in use in favour of BI clauses in EModE ($\chi^2(1)=37.1$, P=<.0001). The incidence of BI complementation also increases from EModE to LModE in the British variety ($\chi^2(1)=46.2$, P=<.0001), but undergoes a trend-reversal in PDE in favour of *to*-infinitive complementation ($\chi^2(1)=385.05$, P=<.0001). Similarly, the *to*-infinitive is a marginal complement in American LModE, but increases in use significantly in PDE ($\chi^2(1)=210.92$, P=<.0001).

As regards the effect of the regional variant, my data show that the incidence of *dare* plus infinitive complement is not connected with this factor either in LModE ($\chi^2(1)=0.02$, P=0.7642) or in PDE ($\chi^2(1)=1.16$, P=0.1834). However, the *to*-infinitive is more frequent with *need* in American than in British English in LModE ($\chi^2(1)=9.91$, P=0.0009). In contrast, *to*-infinitive/BI complementation has a similar distribution with *need* in both British and American PDE ($\chi^2(1)=1.46$, P=0.1859).

The following sections describe and analyse the factors and contexts with *to*-infinitive and BI complements. Section 3.4.1 presents the findings from the corpus study of *dare* and *need* with *to*-infinitive/BI complementation in EModE, and the results in American and British LModE are given in Section 3.4.2. Finally, Section 3.4.3 examines the complementation choices of *dare* and *need* in both regional varieties in PDE.

	ME		EModE		LModE				PDE			
	British		**British**		**British**		**American**		**British**		**American**	
	dare	*need*	*dare*	*need*	*dare*	*need*	*dare*	*need*	*dare*	*need*	*dare*	*need*
BI	250 (34.15)	7 (0.96)	488 (38.96)	195 (15.57)	44 (11.19)	91 (23.14)	187 (22.56)	150 (18.1)	63 (1.89)	116 (3.48)	11 (3.02)	20 (5.49)
TO	4 (0.55)	52 (7.1)	30 (2.39)	155 (12.37)	18 (4.58)	6 (1.53)	84 (10.14)	41 (4.95)	30 (0.90)	884 (26.54)	10 (2.74)	213 (58.44)
Total	254 (34.69)	59 (8.06)	518 (41.35)	350 (27.94)	62 (15.77)	97 (24.67)	271 (32.70)	191 (23.05)	93 (2.79)	1000 (30.03)	21 (5.76)	233 (63.93)

Table 8: Distribution of *dare* and *need* and *to*-infinitive/BI complementation from ME to PDE in British and American English (raw and n.f./10000 IP-MATs and <s> units)

3.4.1 Model 1: *Dare* and *need* and *to*/BI complementation in Early Modern English

This section analyses the distribution of infinitival complementation with *dare* and *need* and the factors responsible for infinitival variation in EModE. Occurrences of both *dare* and *need* with an infinitival clause increase in use from ME to EModE, probably influenced by the obsolescence of *tharf* (see Section 3.3.2, Table 1). The increase in use of *to*-infinitive complements with *dare* (30 examples out of 518) and BI clauses with *need* (195 out of 350) makes it possible to apply statistical measures using 'glm' on my EModE data set. Tables 134 and 135 in Appendix show the distribution of each predictor with *dare* and *need* and their infinitival complements. *Dare* and *need* show a similar distribution of '(non-)explicit' morphology ($\chi^2(1)$=0.03, P=0.8875) when they select infinitive clauses.

Dare and *need* behave differently with respect to the polarity of the main verbal group ($\chi^2(1)$=75.6, P=<.0001). While *dare* with an infinitive clausal complement shows a slightly higher preference for positive polarity (55.79 per cent of the total), *need* shows a 74.29 per cent preference for negative polarity. In terms of syntax, *dare* and *need* with infinitival complementation are found more frequently in main clauses, followed by dependent and adverbial clauses. However, their distribution differs significantly. With *need*, its incidence in main clauses is significantly higher and in adverbial clauses lower than in the case of *dare* ($\chi^2(1)$=13.65, P=0.0002 and $\chi^2(1)$=19.6, P=<.0001, respectively). However, the distribution of the two verbs with infinitival alternation in dependent clauses is similar ($\chi^2(1)$=0.01, P=0.8415); The chi-square tests compare each SYNTAX level for *dare* and *need* with the sum of the other two values of each verb.

With respect to the Principle of Rhythmic Alternation, the distribution of the two complementation options is similar in unproblematic and critical contexts with both verbs ($\chi^2(1)$=1.09, P=0.2617). In complex contexts, *dare* and *need* differ in the use of passive constructions and relative clauses. The incidence of passivisation is significantly higher with *need*, whereas *dare* is almost entirely restricted to active infinitive clauses ($\chi^2(1)$=11.28, P=0.0003). *Dare*, on the other hand, is more frequently attested in relative clauses than *need* ($\chi^2(1)$=4.1, P=0.0337). The proportion of these verbs with perfect infinitival complements is not significantly different ($\chi^2(1)=1.58$, P=0.1463), and no significant differences were found in the distribution of the three types of infinitival lower verbs either. The results of the chi-square tests are: $\chi^2(1)=0.13$, P=0.6315 for intransitive verbs; $\chi^2(1)=0$, P=0.9203 for transitive verbs and $\chi^2(1)=0.29$, P=0.4274 for coordinated lower verbs. Both *dare* and *need* are more frequently attested with transitive infinitive verbs, while intransitive lower verbs amount to around 10 per cent of the data and so-called coordinated examples are marginal. Distance is not shown to be a significant differentiating factor between *dare* and *need* when adjacency and the quantile are compared ($\chi^2(1)=0.55$, P=0.3897), adjacency between the main verb *dare* or *need* and infinitival clauses being the most common scenario. However, these constructions differ in the distribution of *need* and infinitival complementation with non-basic subjects, which is lower than that of the *dare* construction ($\chi^2(1)=8.9$, P=0.0017).

In relation to semantic/pragmatic predictors, *dare* and *need* do not behave alike. As mentioned in Section 3.2, *dare* only occurs in 3 examples with 'fear' verbs, whereas *need* is found in 67 instances with this semantic interpretation (19.14 per cent of the data). Both *dare* and *need* prefer animate subjects, but *need* is more frequently attested with non-animate subjects ($\chi^2(1)=6.96$, P=0.0054).[23] The distribution of these two verbs with respect to the three values of the notional characterisation factor varies significantly (P=<.0001 for all three levels). The occurrence of *need* in non-factual unrealised contexts is significantly higher than that of *dare*: 73.71 vs 37.64 per cent, respectively. In contrast, *dare* is distributed more evenly in the three contexts and shows similar distribution in non-factual unrealised and factual realised instances (37.64 and 35.52 per cent, respectively; see Section 3.2).

3.4.1.1 *Model 1:* Dare *and the infinitive clause in EModE*

In the *dare* data set, POLARITY, RHYTHMIC ALTERNATION, NOTIONAL CHARACTERISATION, SUBJECT COMPLEXITY and DISTANCE are the only predictors that show enough data in all of their levels to allow them to

23 The data selected for the chi-square test correspond to animate vs non-animate examples of *dare* and *need*.

be added to the model. The absence or scarcity of data in some of the levels of the other predictors only allow for a qualitative analysis of these aspects ((245), Table 9). I will deal with these less frequent variables first and then proceed to explain the predictors included in *Model 1* and their results.

The distribution of infinitival complementation with respect to morphology is dichotomous. Of the 30 examples with *to*-infinitive clauses, only one has non-explicit morphology, as illustrated in (245) (see Table 9). The subject of *dare* in this example is the relative clause *that*, whose antecedent is a third-person singular, i.e. *my presumtion.* The absence of *–s*/*–th* third-person singular inflection in this example gives it an indeterminate status, occurring variously as the old form *dare* with covert subject-verb agreement in the indicative mood, *dare* in the subjunctive mood, or the modal periphrastic construction in a subjunctive context replacing the subjunctive inflections.

	Explicit							**Non-explicit**		
	Dares	***Darest***	***Finite Dared/ durst (simple past)***	**To *dare***	**Bare *dare***	***Daring***	**Non-finite *dared/ durst***	**S/he/it *dare***	**You *dare***	**Other**
BI	24	6	143	1	3	1	3	37	16	254
TO	2	0	1	0	8	17	1	1	0	0

Table 9: Morphology and paradigm forms of *dare* plus *to*-infinitive/BI clause in EModE (raw and n.f./10,000 IP-MATs)

(245) Noble Cosin, My last letter was writen in such hast as indeed I know not well what it wase: I beseech you to excuse my presumtion *that dare to writ* to one that doth exselle in that. (PCEEC, OXINDE,I,233.143.2212)

Overt subject-verb agreement in third-person singular present is attested in two examples with *to*-infinitive, as in (246). BI complements are more frequent with non-explicit forms, as in (247), but they occur with the regularised *s*/*–th* inflection in 24 (out of 61 instances), as in (248) (see Table 9).

(246) Since my last, of the newes out of Itallie, we haue gathered a litle newe courage, that the hoape of a peace is not yett desperatt, for that the Pope hath underhand geiuen to understand to some of the Kinges seruants at Rome that *he dareth not as yett to p~ceade* in other demonstrations towardes the Kinge, untill he haue some better aduantage ouer his enemies, to beare him out against the greatnes of Spayne, and therefore aduising him to looke to the accomodating of his affaires. (PCEEC, EDMONDE,106.003.60)

(247) Calays for somoch excedith Bolen, for in Calays Master Mondey serveth diligently without any such protestacion. Master $Ager *dare not aventure* soo far at Bolen. A faulte there is, which I thinke Mastre Southwel wyl and canne disclose. (PCEEC, GARDIN,150.001.595)

(248) I must commend your courage, *that dares withstand* such mightie gyants. (PPCEME, DELONEY-E2-P2,36.138)

The second-person singular present is found in 6 examples with the explicit *–st* form, as in (249), always with BI complements. However, BI complements are attested in 16 instances with the non-explicit form, as in (250). The *to*-infinitive only occurs in one example, in (251), with the second-person singular present. This is an example of explicit morphology because *dare* is a non-finite form preceded by the negative operator *do*.

(249) Amaziah is forbidden to strengthen himself with the armyes of Israel, onely because Israel had offended God; if Amaziah might not ioyne the armyes of Israel with his armyes to strengthen him, *darest thou ioyne* the goods of the poore with thy goodes to inrich thee? (PPCEME, SMITH-E2-H,C2R.168)

(250) My only desire to be with you, if possibly I could, is to knowe what *you* must not or *dare not write*, for I misbode some greate matter. for I misbode some greate matter. (PCEEC, COSIN,I,89.025.924)

(251) I charge thee, therefore as thou wilt answer it to the great God, the Judge of all the Earth, that thou *do not dare to* waver one tittle from the Truth, upon any account or pretence whatsoever: For tho' it were to save thy Life, yet the value of thy precious and immortal Soul is much greater, than that thou should'st forfeit it for the saving of any the most precious outward Blessing thou dost enjoy; (PPCEME, LISLE-E3-P1,4,108.142)

Dare occurs with the two explicit forms for the simple past in my EModE data set, i.e. with regularised forms with weak *–d* inflection and the old form *durst*.[24] *Durst* is the most frequent form in the simple past. It occurs mainly with BI complementation (140 out of 143 examples), as in (252), and is also attested with a *to*-infinitive clause in one example (253) (see Table 9). Two principles may be at work in example (253): the Principle of Rhythmic Alternation favours the use of the *to*-infinitive as a stress-clash buffer between *nowe* and *shewe*, while the Complexity Principle selects the most explicit variant in a complex context such as this, with intervening material between *durst* and the infinitival clause headed by the verb *shewe*. The new form *dared* is attested in three instances and in all of them the complement is the BI, as in (254). No examples of *dared* plus *to*-infinitive are found in this period.

(252) I am deafe to commaundment and dumbe to Authority. I know hir Majesty excelleth hir sexe and all gods creatures in many Princely vertues whearof secresy is one and in hir brest *durst I repose* my life my honour what not if I had hir favour and promise. (PCEEC, STUART,174.012.446)

(253) He sayth that the subject of those Comissions was to p~fesse that albeitt he *durst* not nowe *to shewe* any affection towardes the Catholickes for feare to allyenne her maties fauor from him and because in his realme there is so stronge a p~tie against them, yett that hereafter uppon better comoditie he will make better demonstration towardes them. (PCEEC, EDMONDE,391.021.483)

(254) I thought to have sent a spider by him, which was brought mee out of the feilds, large & round & finely marked green, and even allmost as bigge as the figures inclosed drawne by your mother, for your sisters *dared not doe* it: it may bee seen in Moufetus, and I have had of them before & one drawne out in oyled colours upon an oyled paper. (PCEEC, BROWNE,159.028.554)

BI clauses are attested with all four non-finite forms: marked infinitive (255), unmarked infinitive (256), an *–ing* form (257), and the past participle (258). The three examples of *dare* in the past-participle form followed by a BI complement correspond to the old form *durst* in *as*-clauses, as in (258).

24 For the sake of simplicity, all the possible spelling forms/variants corresponding to the simple past are referred to as *durst* in EModE.

(255) And blushyng in youth, sayth Aristotle is nothyng els, but *feare* to do ill: which feare beyng once lustely fraid away from youth, then foloweth, *to dare do* any mischief, to contemne stoutly any goodnesse, to be busie in euery matter, to be skilfull in euery thyng, to acknowledge no ignorance at all. (PPCEME, ASCH-E1-P2,14V.103)

(256) Right deare brother, I find to true the Frenche adage, Qu'un mal ne vint jamais seul; for as the horrible and soudain murdar of my most faithful subiect and most vaillant baron was unto me a heartsore and grivous tidinges, so was it tenfold redoubled with knowelege that a Skot *shuld dare violate* his handes on any of our noble bloude, in a peacable concord, whan our frendship shuld haue sent out his hotest beames to the kindeling of the entier affection of bothe realmes; that any of that nation shuld ons dare haue had a thoght to maculate suche a contract of amitie. (PCEEC, ROYAL1,19.004.48)

(257) I shall nowe attend her majesties furder pleasure, *not daring wryte* to herselfe being thus offended, but will humbly desire your lordships good constructions of my doinges to hir highnes, yf you shall fynde the consideration worthie, with your honourable and frendly meanes in my behaulfe, being a man absent, but moste faythfull and loyall to my moste dread soveraigne mistres, (PCEEC, LEYCEST,98.029.1037)

(258) I understand nothing of itt; and I hugg my ignorance, and shuld hate any such bould thought, as *durst be* so iniurious both to you and mee. (PCEEC, TIXALL,51.018.358)

To-infinitive complements following non-finite forms are more frequent than BI complements. Most of the *to*-infinitive clauses follow main non-finite *–ing* forms, such as *daring* in (259), and unmarked infinitives, such as *dare* in (260) (see Table 9). The BI infinitive is found in 6 examples preceded by modal verbs and in two with *do*-support, as illustrated in the negative clause in (251) above and in (261) below with subject-auxiliary inversion. The lack of instances with non-finite marked infinitives may be due to the avoidance of such forms to be preceded by *to*-infinitives, as predicted by the *horror aequi* principle. Only one occurrence with the past participle is attested with *dare* and the *to*-infinitive: a perfect construction, in which the main verb takes the regularised *–ed* past-participle form (262).

(259) But at length it falling upon others in the towne 's neighborhood, none of my little children escaping it, we only tooke some cordialls at the begining *not daring any way to stop* what Nature though very violently drave forth;

which after 3 or 4 dayes abated though not quite gon in some till 9 or 10. (PCEEC, DUPPA,160.061.1015)

(260) And which troubles him, he hears that the gentlemen do give out that in two or three years a Tarpawlin *shall not* dare to look after being better then a Boatswain- which he is troubled at, and with good reason. (PPCEME, PEPYS-E3-H,7,410.27)

(261) Had I not had this ocation to send to your father, yet I had sent this boy vp to Loundoun; he is such a rogeisch boy that I dare not keepe him in my howes, and as littell *do I dare to let* him goo in this cuntry, least he ioyne with the company of vollentirs, or some other such crwe. (PCEEC, HARLEY,181.052.1490)

(262) noebody that has, will ere desyre to doe it againe, for theire owne sakes, as well as mine: O $'t $is a most dismall dresse, I *have not dared to looke* in the glasse since I wore it, and certainly if it did soe ill with Other People as it do's with mee, it would never bee worne. (PCEEC, OSBORNE,80.036.1873)

The remaining contexts are cases of non-explicit morphology with first-person singular, with plural subjects and finite *dare*. The 254 examples are restricted to BI complementation, as in (263).

(263) But now there be some, that haue great loue to learning, good lust to labor, be willing to learne of others, yet, either of a fonde shamefastnes, or else of a proud folie, *they dare not*, or will not, *go to learne* of an nother: And therfore doth Socrates wiselie adde the sixte note of a good witte in a childe for learning, (PPCEME, ASCH-E1-P1,9R.154)

Do-support is attested in two examples with *to*-infinitive clauses, in (251) and (261) above. In example (251), *do* is accompanied by the negator *not*, whereas in (261) *do* is required by subject-auxiliary inversion. *Do*-support in (261) may be justified by the Principle of Rhythmic Alternation, according to which the *to*-infinitive acts as a stress buffer in order to avoid a critical context between the two stressed monosyllabic words *dare* and *let*; or, by analogy, with the inversion of the subject and the auxiliary at the beginning of the clause: *Had I not had*. The absence of any instances of subject-*dare* inversion when the verb selects a *to*-infinitive clause reinforces the view that *do*-support with *to*-infinitive clauses is a new development. Direct *not*-negation and subject-verb inversion are the most frequent syntactic contexts with the two types of complements in this period.

As regards the variable SYNTAX, *dare* plus a BI clause is significantly more frequent in main clauses, as in (264), than in adverbial or dependent clauses ($P=5.75e^{-08}$ and P=0.029, respectively; see Table 10). The variation of the two infinitival complementation choices in adverbial and dependent clauses is also statistically significant ($\chi^2(1)=6.72$, P=0.0052): BI clauses are more frequently attested in dependent clauses, as in (265), whereas *to*-infinitive complements prefer adverbial contexts, as in (264). Example (264) contains both uses of *dare* and the infinitival construction: the BI clause *I durst not answear him* in the main clause, and the *to*-infinitive *not dar'ing to Justify myselfe* in the adverbial.

	Adverbial	Dependent	Main
BI	109 (8.7)	149 (11.89)	230 (18.36)
TO	19 (1.52)	8 (0.64)	3 (0.24)

Table 10: Syntactic dependency and *dare* plus *to*-infinitive/BI clause in EModE (raw and n.f./10,000 IP-MATs)

(264) I *durst not answear* him in a way of Argum=t=, but gave him thankes & the best satisfaction I could, thoughe I bitt my lipp for anger, *not dar'ing to Justify* myselfe in an honest cause. (PCEEC, KNYVETT,147.039.1559)

(265) Moreouer they *complayned, that* bycause of the euill slanders which their enimies had made of them, *they durst not personally appeare* in the Kings presence, vntill the Prelates & Barons had intreated for them, that they might be permitted to purge themselues before the King, and be lawfully iudged by their peeres, so that many that saw their letters, did praise their diligence, & extoll their fidelitie towards the common wealth. (PPCEME, STOW-E2-P1,554.72)

The data show no significant differences with respect to the complexity of the infinitival complement: both BI and *to*-infinitive clauses favour verbs that require an argument, as in (266), in which the verb *show* selects *his face*, more than intransitive verbs, as in (267), in which *see* behaves intransitively ($\chi^2(1)=2.57$, P=0.0551). As shown in Table 11, both types of complements are rare with coordinated lower verbs, as in (268), with BI clauses headed by *enter* and *come*. Fisher's Exact test demonstrates that correlation between coordination and *to*-infinitive/ BI complementation in intransitive/transitive lower constructions is not statistically significant (P=0.059 and P=0.273, respectively).

	Coordination	**Intransitive**	**Transitive**
BI	6 (0.48)	48 (3.83)	434 (34.65)
TO	2 (0.16)	6 (0.48)	22 (1.76)

Table 11: Valency and *dare* plus *to*-infinitive/BI clause in EModE (raw and n.f./ 10,000 IP-MATs)

(266) Sir Thomas Glover is come home from Constantinople, contrarie to expectation, for his comportement was geven out to be such there, that there was an opinion *he durst not have shewed his face*, but he makes offer to justifie himself in whatsoever can be laide to his charge. (PCEEC, CHAMBER,I,412.029.1221)

(267) Ande I do com to you to my heuy mastres I scholde renew her hewyn-esse and nat elles/ Ande also *I dare nat well be sen* in London/ I thanke God and the Keng I myght, but I wyll not, ande I may do oderwisse, put my percseon in ewre in London, for it scholde be a gret noysse theroff; (PCEEC, CELY,131.104.2317)

(268) Also in this Countrey are sundry sorts of wilde beasts, which my selfe and others of our Company going on shore of purpose haue seene, and percei-ued some of them to be very fierce and cruell: so that afterwards when we found their dens, we durst *not enter them, nor come very neere them*, lest they should be in them. (PCEEC, COVERTE-E2-P1,6.59)

Dare occurs categorically with BI complements when the infinitive is passive, as in (267) above, or is part of a perfect construction, as in (266) above (see Table 134 in Appendix). As regards relative clauses, no variation is attested with respect to infinitival complementation (P=0.097) (see Table 12). Of the three examples with 'fear' verbs, *dare* occurs in one instance with the *to*-infinitive, with *waver*, conveying doubt or indecision (251) above, and in the other two examples with a BI clause, with *doubt*, as in (269).

	Relative	Other
BI	84 (6.71)	404 (32.25)
TO	2 (0.16)	28 (2.24)

Table 12: Relativisation and *dare* plus *to*-infinitive/BI clause in EModE (raw and n.f./10,000 IP-MATs)

(269) Sir- I trust the same mercy which conducted me safely hither hath comfortably preserved you. If that confidence did not refresh me, this journey would be very sad; but I dare not *doubt* the tender compassions of our heavenly Father to you, because I have alwaies experienced your tenderness to me. (PCEEC, HARLEY,217.068.1810)

As regards ANIMACY, *dare* and both types of infinitive clause are more frequently found with animate subjects, but *to*-infinitive complements are favoured with non-animate subjects, as in (245) above (P=0.032; see Table 13).

	Animate	Non animate
BI	470 (37.52)	18 (1.44)
TO	26 (2.08)	4 (0.32)

Table 13: Animacy and *dare* plus *to*-infinitive/BI clause in EModE (raw and n.f./10,000 IP-MATs)

The factors with at least five or more examples in each of their levels are POLARITY, RHYTHMIC ALTERNATION, NOTIONAL CHARACTERISATION, SUBJECT COMPLEXITY and DISTANCE. Because of the lack of enough data for the *to*-infinitive clause, the three predictors of *STEP 1*, POLARITY, RHYTHMIC ALTERNATION and NOTIONAL CHARACTERISATION, were used for the multifactorial statistical analysis. The univariate analysis for SUBJECT COMPLEXITY reveals that the type of subject that *dare* selects affects the distribution of *to*-infinitive/BI clauses ($\chi^2(1)=76.16$, P=<.0001). As Table 14 illustrates, *to*-infinitive clauses are more frequently found with non-basic subjects than BI clauses. In fact, the 15 examples attested with non-basic subjects plus *to*-infinitive complements are adverbial constructions, including *daring* and unexpressed subjects, as in (270), where the subject of the main clause *we* acts as the subject of the *dare* plus *to*-infinitive construction. The form *daring* is frequently followed by *to*-infinitive clauses (17 out of 18 examples; see Table 9), always with adverbial uses and either non-basic unexpressed subjects, as in (270), or basic subjects (2 out of 17 instances), as illustrated in (271) with the NP *Three Caphala's*.

	Non-basic	**Basic**
BI	24 (1.83)	464 (35.47)
TO	15 (1.15)	15 (1.15)

Table 14: Subject complexity and *dare* plus *to*-infinitive/BI clause in EModE (raw and n.f./10,000 IP-MATs)

(270) But before I give you the story of this gallant slave, 'tis fit I tell you the manner of bringing them to these new colonies; those they make use of there, not being natives of the place: for those *we* live with in perfect amity, *without daring to command 'em*; (PPCEME, BEHN-E3-P1,148.12)

(271) The Day after, as soon as we heard the Waters were abated, we set forward, and found it true what had been reported *Three Caphala's not daring to pass* the Lake, where they had lain some Days, till we had led the way. (PPCEME, FRYER-E3-H,II,186.214)

The only example with the form *daring* plus BI is (272), in an adverbial syntactic structure with a non-basic unexpressed subject. The other 23 non-basic subject occurrences are distributed as follows: 11 in adverbial clauses, 12 in dependent clauses, as in (273), and only one in a main clause, in (274). *Dare* plus a BI clause is more frequent with basic subject, i.e. NP, as in (275), or pronouns.

(272) I shall nowe attend her majesties furder pleasure, *not daring wryte to herselfe* being thus offended, but will humbly desire your lordships good constructions of my doinges to hir highnes, yf you shall fynde the consideration worthie, with your honourable and frendly meanes in my behaulfe, being a man absent, (PCEEC, LEYCEST,98.029.1037)

(273) Thinketh he that I would sende hym hence, which neyther is in y=e=plight to sende out, and in what place coulde I recken him sure, if he be not sure in this the sentuarye whereof, was there neuer tiraunt yet *so deuelish, that durste presume* to breake. (PPCEME, MORERIC-E1-P1,38.195)

(274) *The King and the Queen* lay two nights upon Thames, and it is said *durst not lodge* in Whyte Hall. (PCEEC, COSIN,II,155.075.1929)

(275) And suerly syth I see he ys dryven to seke fermors becawse *every man dare not deale with yt* as his leters do mentyon, me thynke he shuld make a dyfferens betwene a frynde & a stranger but all ys a lyke to hym. (PCEEC, BACON,II,139.245.4334)

As regards the multivariate analysis, I first considered the factors of *STEP 1* which, according to the literature, play a role in the distribution of *dare* and infinitival alternation, i.e. POLARITY, RHYTHMIC ALTERNATION and NOTIONAL CHARACTERISATION. *Model 1, STEP 1* indicates that only NOTIONAL CHARACTERISATION is a determinant factor, whereas POLARITY and RHYTHMIC ALTERNATION show a similar distribution of *dare* plus the *to*-infinitive/BI clause in each of their levels (Pr(>|z|)=0.5808 and Pr(>|z|)=0.2463, respectively). The addition of the complexity factor DISTANCE, whose impact is not highly significant, improves the model (ANOVA: Pr(>Chi)=0.041). The BI clause is taken as the reference level because this is the variable with the highest number of examples; negative values in the estimate therefore point to a BI clause preference (see Table 15). Table 15 only contains the significant predictors after step backward is applied to *Model 1.*

Predictor	**Estimate**	**P-value**	**OR**
Intercept	-4.0167	3.01e-14***	1/0.01801243=55.5172
Notional characterisation	1.7951	0.00147**	6.02014678
(ref.: *Factual Realised*)	0.8041	0.15305	2.23461335
Factual Unrealised			
Non-Factual Unrealised			
Distance (Log_words_mv_inf)	-0.6500	0.05870.	1/0.52205630=1.9155

Table 15: *Model 1, STEP 2,* significant factors with *dare* plus *to*-infinitive/BI clause in EModE (step "backward" results)

The semantic/pragmatic context in which *dare* and the infinitival complement occur is the only significant factor in the multifactorial analysis for my EModE data. The chances of *to*-infinitive clause are 6.02 percentage points higher than the BI clause in factual unrealised contexts in comparison to factual realised ones (Pr(>|z|)=0.00147). Of the 15 examples found in factual unrealised contexts with *to*-infinitive, 13 correspond to the form *daring* and the contexts explained above. In the other two instances, *dare* and the *to*-infinitive occur in the third-person present, in (276), and in the perfect construction, in (277) (see Table 16). As Table 15 shows, the distribution of infinitival complementation in factual realised contexts is not significantly different when compared to non-factual unrealised ones (Pr(>|z|)=0.15305).

	Factual realised	**Factual unrealised**	**Non-factual unrealised**
BI	179 (13.68)	124 (9.48)	185 (14.14)
TO	5 (0.38)	15 (1.15)	10 (0.76)

Table 16: Notional characterisation of *dare* plus *to*-infinitive/BI clause in EModE (raw and n.f./10,000 IP-MATs)

(276) Since my last, of the newes out of Itallie, we haue gathered a litle newe courage, that the hoape of a peace is not yett desperatt, for that the Pope hath underhand geiuen to understand to some of the Kinges seruants at Rome that *he dareth not as yett to p~ceade* in other demonstrations towardes the Kinge, untill he haue some better aduantage ouer his enemies, to beare him out against the greatnes of Spayne, and therefore aduising him to looke to the accomodating of his affaires. (PCEEC, EDMONDE,106.003.60)

(277) *I have not dared to looke in* the glasse since I wore it, and certainly if it did soe ill with Other People as it do's with mee, it would never bee worne. (PCEEC, OSBORNE,80.036.1873)

Factual unrealised contexts differ significantly from the reference level of non-factual unrealised in *Model 1* (Pr(>|z|)=0.0261). The latter increases the odds of the BI infinitive clause, illustrated in (278), by 2.694 percentage points. The notional characterisation of the construction accounts for the distribution of *dare* and infinitival alternation in my data, since the BI clause is selected when the construction occurs in factual realised or in non-factual unrealised contexts, whereas the *to*-infinitive is used in factual unrealised ones.

(278) For he saide to my Lord of Oxford, as Ed: Boughen told me, that though I were a good scholer at my pen, and wrote well, yet he doubted not but att an argument he could plunge me. The man thincketh well of him self, yet if

K. James please *I dare looke him* in the face in his owne scholes. (PCEEC, COSIN,I,22.010.315)

The predictor DISTANCE reveals a trend in favour of the BI clause when there is an increase in one unit (Pr(>|z|)=0.0587). The restriction of direct negation and inversion with *dare* and the BI clause may also be responsible for this. Hence, the *to*-infinitive clause is therefore not found to be a strategy evincing a more complex context in my EModE data.

To sum up, this study of *dare* and infinitival alternation in EModE shows that the old variant is still the only type of complement attested with the passive voice and the perfect construction. The semantic/pragmatic predictor is the only significant factor in the distribution of the variants and the *to*-infinitive complement prefers factual unrealised contexts. The fact that an increase in the distance between *dare* and the infinitival clause does not favour the more explicit variant may be related to the conceptualisation of *dare to* as a unit. Morphology shows that the *to*-infinitive is almost absent with non-explicit forms. The BI clause is attested with all the regularised forms and also with the four non-finite forms of *dare*. However, the *to*-infinitive also shows a higher incidence with these non-finite forms, mainly with the form *daring* and the bare infinitive *dare*. The high proportion of *daring* with the *to*-infinitive clause also explains the stronger preference by the *to*-infinitive for adverbial clauses and non-basic main clause subjects in comparison to the BI clause. In this period, the construction still favours the old strategy for negation with the direct form; the only two occurrences attested with *do*-support are found with the new marked infinitive. Non-animate subjects tend to favour the *to*-infinitive clause and text-type predictors were not shown to be statistically significant.

3.4.1.2 *Model 1:* Need *and the infinitive clause in EModE*

As in the case of my *dare* data set, a number of predictors cannot be included in the analysis of *need* plus infinitive clause in *Model 1* because of the low number of examples in some of its levels. One of these factors is the variable DO-SUPPORT, owing to the lack of occurrences in interrogative and negative clauses in my EModE database. Subject-verb inversion and direct negation (illustrated below in (279) and (280)) are the only strategies available with *need* plus infinitival complement in my data.

(279) Then I, in some measure recovering my self, spoke thus to her: *Need my Sorrows then be repeated*; and do not the Severities acted by Fortune against me, appear enough of themselves, without these Admonitions? (PPCEME, BOETHPR-E3-P1,15.13)

(280) Yowr wourshipe *nede not to doweght* this his promyse for I know he shall thane be provydyd. (PCEEC, BACON,I,190.143.2540)

SUBJECT COMPLEXITY is not analysed in *Model 1* either because of the low number of instances of *need* and the BI clause with non-basic subjects. Both infinitival complements occur marginally with non-basic subjects (P=0.151; see Table 17): the BI clause is not found with unexpressed subjects and it is only attested in three examples with complex main verb subjects, as illustrated by *nor you nor I* in (281).

	Non-basic	**Basic**
BI	3 (0.24)	192 (15.33)
TO	6 (0.48)	149 (11.89)

Table 17: Subject complexity and *need* plus *to*-infinitive/BI clause in EModE (raw and n.f./10,000 IP-MATs)

(281) I knowe no man I can build upon in that Assembly, but *nor you nor I* need greatly feare them, for what have we don? (PCEEC, COSIN,I,141.031.1138)

The predictor VALENCY is not included in the multivariate analysis because of the low incidence of the construction with coordinated lower infinitival verbs, with either the BI clause, as in (282), with the lower verbs *look into* and *seek for*, or the *to*-infinitive clause, as in (283), with *stop* and *let*. The distribution of *need* and the infinitival construction is quite similar regardless of the valency of the lower verb (see Table 18). The univariate analysis indicates that the difference between intransitive and transitive lower infinitival clauses is not statistically significant ($\chi^2(1)$=2.21, P=0.0949)

	Intransitive	**Transitive**	**Coordination**
BI	14 (1.12)	178 (14.21)	3 (0.24)
TO	19 (1.52)	131 (10.46)	5 (0.4)

Table 18: Valency and *need* plus *to*-infinitive/BI clause in EModE (raw and n.f./ 10,000 IP-MATs)

(282) Sir, I know you ar no worshipper of images; or, if you wer, *you need not look into* the aire for them, *or seek for* them any where but in your self, where you may find a theater of God 's making, a soul not onely free from the vices of the time, but full of all good impressions. (PCEEC, DUPPA,14.009.181)

(283) Finally, the Kingis Grace caused me to write hym ferther that hit shold be provided that vppon his aduertisement fro tyme to tyme he shold haue money sent in tyme convenient so that *he shold not nede to stoppe or lett* therfore. (PCEEC, MORE,261.005.43)

Finally, owing to the categorical behaviour of *need* plus *to*-infinitive in some levels, the hypothesis of interaction between RHYTHMIC ALTERNATION and POLARITY cannot be corroborated. The remaining predictors contain at least 5 instances featuring both types of infinitive complementation, i.e. POLARITY, ANIMACY, RELATIVE, PERFECT INFINITIVAL CLAUSE, MORPHOLOGY, SYNTAX, RHYTHMIC ALTERNATION, NOTIONAL CHARACTERISATION, FEAR VERBS, PASSIVISATION and DISTANCE. The number of examples of *to*-infinitive complements (155 out of 350 occurrences) allows all these factors to be added to *Model 1* (see Levshina 2015: 257). Following the methodology used for *dare* in EModE, the BI clause has been used as the reference level because of its frequency. Table 19 displays the relevant variables after the step "backward" process, indicating that the variables POLARITY, RELATIVE, SYNTAX and FEAR VERBS do not determine the variation of infinitival complements with *need*.

Predictor	Estimate	P-value	OR
Intercept	0.05598	0.93760	1.05757646
Morphology (ref.: *Explicit*) Non-explicit	-2.81887	< 2e-16 ***	1/0.05967338= 16.7578
Rhythmic Alternation (ref.: *Critical*) Unproblematic	-0.94898	0.02980 *	1/0.38713692= 2.583
Notional characterisation (ref.: *Factual realised*) Factual Unrealised Non-Factual Unrealised	2.48905 2.14391	0.00129 ** 0.00127 **	12.04978304 8.53270180
Log_words_mv_inf	-0.37441	0.07830 .	1/0.68769170= 1.4541
Animacy (ref.: *Animate*) Non-Animate	-1.36612	0.02537 *	1/0.25509593= 3.92
Passivisation (ref.: *No*) Yes	2.70379	0.00095 ***	14.93623509
Perfect infinitive (ref.: *No*) Yes	1.68458	0.04187 *	5.39017333

Table 19: *Model 1, STEP 2*, significant factors with *need* plus *to*-infinitive/BI clause in EModE (step "backward" results)

The results indicate that the variable MORPHOLOGY exhibits the strongest effect (Pr(>|z|)=< $2e^{-16}$): non-explicit morphology is significantly more frequent with BI complementation (by 16.76 percentage points) than explicit morphology, showing that the *to*-infinitive is preferred when *need* shows explicit morphology (see Table 20).

	Explicit			Non-explicit			
	Needs	***Needest***	***Finite needed (simple past)***	**Non-finite *need***	**She/he/ it *need***	**You *need***	**Other**
BI	9 (0.72)	5 (0.40)	6 (0.48)	6 (0.48)	24 (1.92)	46 (3.67)	99 (7.90)
TO	10 (0.80)	2 (0.16)	16 (1.28)	85 (6.79)	9 (0.72)	13 (1.04)	20 (1.60)

Table 20: Morphology and paradigm forms of *need* plus *to*-infinitive/BI clause in EModE (raw and n.f./10,000 IP-MATs)

The most significant differences with respect to the various (non-) explicit morphological forms are the high incidence of the BI clause with 'other' forms, as in (284), and the high proportion of the *to*-infinitive with the non-finite explicit form *need*, as in (285) and (286). The only non-finite form attested in EModE is BI: *need* is preceded by a catenative verb in only one occurrence, in (286), whereas the other 90 instances correspond to modal verbs.

(284) if your counttes be redie it were good you sent them over that m=r=lambert may loucke them over at his lesur, ceping copis of them with your self, for *wee neede see* but wone yerse acounnte sinse you hade charge of the plase. (PCEEC, STOCKWE,II,7.052.1036)

(285) We sometimes beg of God, for a Wife or a Child, and he alone knows what the wife shall prove, and by what dispositions and manners, and into what fortune that child shall enter: but we *shall not need to fear* concerning the Event of it, if Religion, and fair Intentions, and Prudence manage, and conduct it all the way. (PPCEME, JETAYLOR-E3-H,12.89)

(286) And reason, sithe no man hath cause to haue it, but whose conscience of his own faut *maketh hym faine neede to require* it, what wil then hath yonder babe? (PPCEME, MORERIC-E1-P1,32.138)

The explicit form *needest* for second-person present is infrequent in EModE with either type of infinitive complementation (2 per cent of the total data), as in (287). The non-explicit form *need* is more frequent (16.85 per cent of the data) and prefers the BI clause, as in (288).

(287) Yf thou wilt fill the neede that Nature Requires, *thou needest not seeke* fortunes plenty. (PPCEME, BOETHEL-E2-P1,31.422)

(288) Dearest Heart, Tom will give you an account of his Journy to Moor Parke and I can only tell you that wee are all well hear and that *you need not presse* M=rs=Carter to come downe yet for my Aunt is of opinion as well as I that I shall not come soe soon. (PCEEC, OSBORNE,198.081.4270)

As Table 20 shows, the distribution of *need* forms with third-person singular present *need* marked for agreement with*–s*/*–th* inflection is quite similar with both types of complements (289)-(290). With covert agreement, *to*-infinitive is dispreferred (9 out of 33 instances), as in the selection of BI in (291).

(289) The plaine way is the best thoughe the furthest about, & *an honest cause needs seeke* no corners. (PCEEC, KNYVETT,164.044.1899)

(290) And i. busshel and an halfe of white or grene pees, wyll sowe as moche grounde, as two busshels of gray pees: and that is bycause they be so smal, and *the husband nedeth not to take* so great an handful. (PPCEME, FITZH-E1-P1,21.289)

(291) Hir majesty sayth, *he nede be* at no chardg ther, for he shall bot as a privat man attend on your lordship. (PCEEC, LEYCEST,45.013.370)

When *need* is inflected for past tense (*–ed*), the *to*-infinitive option is favoured, as in (292). The reason for this may be the distance between the inflected form *needed* and the infinitive complement. BI clauses are attested in 6 examples in simple past with the explicit form, as in (293), where the fact that *needed* and *would* are coordinated might justify the selection of the BI complement.

(292) "If I were a man, my lordes, that did not regarde an othe, *I neededнot*, as it is well knowen, in this place, at this tyme, nor in this case, *to standhere* as an accused person". (PPCEME, ROPER-E1-H,87.92)

(293) Yt when hee was well, ye receipts and payments were managed by other hands and yt this thing was of yt nature yt it neither *needed*, nor would I feared *stay for his recovery*. (PCEEC, ESSEX,105.025.681)

The factor NOTIONAL CHARACTERISATION is also significant in *Model 1* (see Table 19), especially as regards the difference between factual realised and factual unrealised semantic/pragmatic environments (Pr(>|z|=0.00129)). The odds of the BI clause significantly increase in factual realised contexts, as in (294), by 12.05 percentage points, with respect to factual unrealised ones, as in (295). The BI clause *make no Apology in behalf of my Father* in (294), convey realised contexts and the propositions including *need* are factual. In (295) the context that follows the construction, *known almost to every one*, confirms that the action of 'describing' is not performed and the proposition is a fact.

(294) But I must needs say, Sir Walter used me a little unkindly, to take the Book away without my Knowledge; nevertheless, *I need make no Apology in behalf of my Father*, considering how useful and necessary it is for Privy Counsellors, and those in his Place, to intercept and keep such kind of Writings; (PPCEME, RALEIGH-E2-H,I,214.C1.436)

(295) But whatever be the use of it, certain it is, that the structure of it is very admirable; what it appears to the naked eye, *I need not describe*, the thing being known almost to every one, but it appears through the Microscope, to consist of two parts, the one a sheath, without a chape or top, shap'd almost like the Holster of a Pistol, (PPCEME, HOOKE-E3-P2,163.140)

To-infinitive complementation prefers factual unrealised contexts, as in (296) vs (297), but the difference is not significantly different (Pr(>|z|=0.449319)). The proposition in example (296) is factual but unrealised. In (297), it is uncertain whether the subject *yowr wourshipe* has doubted about the promise or not. In contrast, as regards the dichotomy non-factual unrealised/factual realised, the incidence of *to*-infinitive clauses significantly increases by 8.53 percentage points with the former meaning (Pr(>|z|=0.00127)) (see also Table 21 for raw and normalised data).

	Factual realised	Factual unrealised	Non-factual unrealised
BI	42 (3.35)	28 (2.24)	125 (9.98)
TO	11 (0.88)	11 (0.88)	133 (10.62)

Table 21: Notional characterisation of *need* plus *to*-infinitive/BI clause in EModE (raw and n.f./10,000 IP-MATs)

(296) I will enquyr after this Daniell, that I may owne him for a knave, but *yow needed to have given* him no more then the waight, though he had brought it to Naples. (PPCEME, HOLLES,I,127.040.1001)

(297) Sur, I have delyveryd yowr letter to Mr Gosselyng, and thare uppone he have wryttene yow agayne that yowr monnye shall be payd yow at Norwyche the Frydaye before Mydsommer. *Yowr wourshipe nede not to doweght* this his promyse for I know he shall thane be provydyd. (PCEEC, BACON,I,190.143.2540)

Even though passive constructions are not frequent with *need* and infinitive clauses, PASSIVISATION is shown to be statistically significant (Pr(>|z|)=0.00095; see Table 19): passive main and lower clauses prefer *to*-infinitive complements by 14.93 percentage points, as in (298) (see Table 22).

	Passive	**Active**
BI	6 (0.48)	189 (15.09)
TO	12 (0.96)	143 (11.42)

Table 22: Passivisation and *need* plus *to*-infinitive/BI clause in EModE (raw and n.f./10,000 IP-MATs)

(298) Dan. If none can deny this, and he be the worker of the wrath and malice in the heart of the witch; then *what needeth he to be hyred*? (PPCEME, GIFFORD-E2-P1,D1R.190)

As regards the statistical contribution of perfect verbal forms in the lower clauses, the probability of *to*-infinitive is 5.39 percentage points higher than that of BI (Pr(>|z|)=0.04187). The perfect construction with a *to*-infinitive clause (*to have written to me*) is illustrated in (299) (see Table 23).

	Perfect	**Other**
BI	5 (0.4)	190 (15.17)
TO	10 (0.8)	145 (11.57)

Table 23: Perfect and *need* plus *to*-infinitive/BI clause in EModE (raw and n.f./10,000 IP-MATs)

(299) Good brother. I know well. you *needed not to haue written* to me at all: concerninge this bisnes. (PCEEC, KNYVETT)

With respect to ANIMACY, *Model 1* indicates that when *need* selects a non-animate subject the probability of BI clauses is 3.92 percentage points higher than with animate subjects. Example (300) illustrates this preference with the non-animate subject *an honest cause.* In contrast, animate subjects are slightly more frequent with the *to*-infinitive, as in *my cosyn Thyrland* in (301) (see Table 24).

	Animate	Non-animate
BI	177 (14.13)	18 (1.44)
TO	142 (11.34)	13 (1.04)

Table 24: Animacy and *need* plus *to*-infinitive/BI clause in EModE (raw and n.f./10,000 IP-MATs)

(300) And truly I thinke those Blinde guides doe but leade men into a further Laberinth' of troubles. The plaine way is the best thoughe the furthest about, & *an honest cause* needs seeke no corners. (PCEEC, KNYVETT)

(301) Therffore *my cosyn Thyrland* nede not too entrete master Hollys nor to be inhis da as my brother Hugh dothe write too me. (PCEEC, WILLOUG,78.032.285)

The results of *Model 1* confirm that the variable RHYTHMIC ALTERNATION is statistically significant (Pr(>|z|)=0.02980; see Table 19 and Table 25). BI clauses are more frequently attested in unproblematic contexts, whereas the *to*-infinitive is found in critical stress patterns (by 2.58 percentage points).

	Critical	Unproblematic
BI	25 (2)	170 (13.57)
TO	59 (4.71)	96 (7.66)

Table 25: Rhythmic Alternation and *need* plus *to*-infinitive/BI clause in EModE (raw and n.f./10,000 IP-MATs)

POLARITY does not affect infinitival alternation with *need* on its own but, when combined with RHYTHMIC ALTERNATION, it partly explains the results for the latter. As Figure 4 illustrates, the *to*-infinitive clause is the only complementation option attested in critical negative contexts.[25] In the 36 occurrences attested in these contexts, *need* is preceded by a modal verb which carries the negative particle, such as *should* in (302). Consequently, the *to*-infinitive functions as a

25 For this reason, the interaction of these two factors could not be included in *Model 1.*

stress-clash buffer between the base form *need* and the initially stressed infinitive verb. If the lightly stressed negative adverbial *never* has scope over *need*, it precedes the main verb, as in (303); the selection of a BI clause in an example such as (303) would lead to a stress clash between *need* and the infinitive verb *change*. The univariate analysis of affirmative and critical contexts reveals no significant differences with respect to infinitival alternation ($\chi^2(1)=0.15$, $P=0.5839$). The chi-square test was calculated by comparing the critical and affirmative examples of BI and *to*-infinitive with the total of the two other unproblematic contexts plus the critical-negative one.

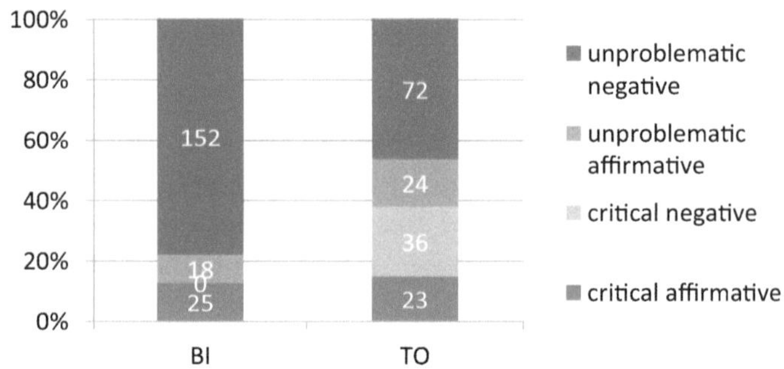

Figure 4: Rhythmic Alternation and polarity affecting *need* plus *to*-infinitive/BI clause in EModE (raw data)

(302) Then the Judge having spoken to the like effect also said to the Jury, That they *should not need to trouble* themselves to find him Guilty of the Felony, but only it was sufficient if they found him Guilty to be the Author of the Book: for, quoth he, it is already determined by all the Judges of the Land, that the Author of that Book was in the compass of the Statute of Felony; (PPCEME, JUDALL-E2-P2,1,176.346)

(303) If such copie books were finely printed, being graven by some cunning workman, and those of the most perfect and plaine formes of letters, that could possibly be procured, in a strong and very white paper, one Booke or two of them would serve a scholler neere all his time that he *should never need to change* his hand. (PPCEME, BRINSLEY-E2-P2,31.120)

DISTANCE is the last factor in my EModE data, but this is not significant ($Pr(>|z|)=0.037913$). However, the *to*-infinitive clause tends to decrease when one unit is attested between *need* and the infinitive lower verb.

To sum up, even though BI can be inflected for past and second- and third-singular present tense, it frequently has non-explicit morphology, mainly in the so-called 'other' contexts. When *need* exhibits explicit morphology, it favours *to*-infinitive complements, especially when preceded by a modal verb. The *to*-infinitive is also found in passive and perfect constructions more frequently than the BI. In critical stress patterns, the *to*-infinitive acts as a stress-clash buffer. Negation is also a significant factor in the distribution of *to*-infinitive/BI in these contexts: in critical contexts in which *need* is preceded by a modal verb, it carries negation and so the *to*-infinitive avoids a stress clash between the main and lower verbal monosyllabic form. The negation strategy used with the BI clause is direct negation and the negative particle is unstressed so it creates an unproblematic context. As regards distance, BI is attested when the number of intervening words between *need* and the infinitival clause increases. In my EModE data, the *to*-infinitive is still more frequently found in non-factual unrealised meanings. The distribution of this complement option is also higher in factual unrealised semantic/pragmatic contexts. Finally, non-animate subjects prefer BI clauses. In consequence, BI complementation can be argued to be favoured in semantic contexts typically related to modal verbs or more abstract entities.

3.4.2 Model 2: *Dare* and *need* and the *to*/BI complementation in Late Modern British and American English

In addition to the predictors investigated in EModE, in LModE I also consider regional variation between British and American English. As mentioned in Section 4, regional variation is not significant with *dare* in LModE, given that BI is attested in approximately 70 per cent of the instances in both British and American English ($\chi^2(1)=0.02$, $P=0.7642$; see Tables 134 and 135 in Appendix). In contrast, *need* selects BI more frequently in British English ($\chi^2(1)=10.46$, $P=0.0009$).

With *dare*, the British and the American data sets behave alike with respect to the following predictors: MORPHOLOGY, POLARITY,

SYNTAX, RELATIVE, SUBJECT COMPLEXITY and NOTIONAL CHARACTERISATION.[26] The distribution of explicit and non-explicit morphology is quite similar, even though explicit morphology is slightly higher ($\chi^2(1)=0.08$, P=0.6629). Both varieties show a higher incidence of *dare* plus infinitival complementation in affirmative clauses (69.37 per cent in the data for American English and 64.52 per cent for British English). Conversely, *need* occurs with non-explicit morphology in more than 80 per cent of the data and is more frequently found in negative clauses, approximately 60 per cent in both varieties.[27]

As regards the syntax of the sentence, *dare* and *need* plus infinitival complementation are more frequent in main clauses than in dependent and adverbial ones, *need* being more salient than *dare* in this respect in both varieties.[28] The *dare* construction is attested mostly with transitive lower infinitivals and in contexts of coordination in British English, whereas the American English data contain more transitive ($\chi^2(1)=5.06$, P=0.0089) and intransitive infinitival complements. In contrast to *dare*, *need* selects more intransitive lower verbs (20.94 in American English and 24.74 per cent in British English). *Need* has a similar behaviour in British and American English with respect to transitive and intransitive lower verbs ($\chi^2(1)=0.34$, P=0.4624) and its incidence with coordinated lower verbs is marginal.

In British English, the proportion of *dare* in critical stress patterns is significantly higher than it is for American ($\chi^2(1)=8.87$, P=0.0018). *Need*

26 The chi-square tests for *dare* in my American and British data are not significant with the following factors: Morphology ($\chi^2(1)=0.08$, P=0.6629); polarity ($\chi^2(1)=0.35$, P=0.4583); syntax, i.e. adverbial vs dependent ($\chi^2(1)=0.01$, P=0.9203), adverbial vs main ($\chi^2(1)=1.33$, P=0.1738) and dependent vs main ($\chi^2(1)=1.44$, P=0.167); relative clauses ($\chi^2(1)=0$, P=0.8065); subject complexity ($\chi^2(1)=0.2$, P=0.4708); notional characterisation, that is, factual realised vs factual unrealised ($\chi^2(1)=0$, P=0.8065), factual realised vs non-factual unrealised ($\chi^2(1)=1.25$, P=0.2017) and factual unrealised vs non-factual unrealised ($\chi^2(1)=0.29$, P=0.4543).

27 The results of the chi-square for *need* in American and British English with respect to morphology are $\chi^2(1)=2.85$, P=0.0614, and for polarity, $\chi^2(1)=0$, P=0.8415.

28 The difference in use of *need* and the infinitival clause in main vs dependent clauses is not statistically significant in either variety of English ($\chi^2(1)=1.88$, P=0.1261). Adverbial clauses are marginal in both varieties and occur only once in British English.

shows a similar distribution in both varieties and is commonly attested in unproblematic stress patterns ($\chi^2(1)=1.87$, P=0.1198). As regards complexity factors, only one occurrence of *dare* in attested in a passive construction in each regional variant, whereas around 18 per cent of the *need* examples co-occur with passive forms in both varieties. No instances of *dare* co-occurring with perfect-aspect verbs were attested in my LModE data and only two examples are attested with *need* in each variety. In relative clauses, *dare* is present in around 23 per cent of instances in both varieties, whereas *need* is found in 7.33 per cent of the data in American English and 10.31 per cent in British; this difference is not statistically significant, however ($\chi^2(1)=0.41$, P=0.3865). The incidence of *dare* with non-basic subjects is around 7 per cent. *Need* is also restricted to basic subjects in both American and British English, and its proportion with non-basic subjects is less than 11 per cent ($\chi^2(1)=0.66$, P=0.3055). With respect to distance, the quantile starts in one word for both *dare* and *need* in both varieties of English.

As far as animacy of the subject is concerned, *dare* is restricted to animate subjects in British English but it selects non-animate subjects in 5.9 per cent of the American English data. In contrast to *dare*, *need* shows a higher incidence of non-animate subjects (P=<.0001), with no regional differences ($\chi^2(1)=0.36$, P=0.4543).[29] No instances of 'fear' lower verbs are attested with *dare* in the British data and only two examples are registered in American English. *Need* occurs with 'fear' verbs in only 4.71 per cent of the American English examples, and in 7.22 per cent of the cases in British English, with no statistically significant difference between them ($\chi^2(1)=0.37$, P=0.3802). *Dare* plus infinitival complementation is distributed in a similar way in the three levels of my semantic/pragmatic characterisation in both varieties: the construction more frequently occurs in non-factual unrealised contexts, followed by factual unrealised. The preference for *need* with non-factual unrealised meanings is also significantly higher than *dare* in both varieties: the difference between *need* and *dare* in American English in non-factual unrealised vs factual unrealised meanings is $\chi^2(1)=24.18$, P=<.0001 and in non-factual unrealised vs factual realised

29 To calculate the difference between *need* and *dare*, the data for *dare* in American English were compared separately with the data for *need* in American and British English.

is $\chi^2(1)=8.87$, P=0.002; in the British variety, the results are $\chi^2(1)=4.38$, P=0.0186 for the first two meanings and $\chi^2(1)=10.29$, P=0.0007 for the second two. As for the difference between the two varieties of English, *need* shows a lower incidence of factual unrealised meanings in American than in British English in comparison with factual realised and non-factual unrealised contexts, i.e. $\chi^2(1)=4.76$, P=0.0126 and $\chi^2(1)=4.31$, P=0.0181, respectively. In contrast, factual realised and non-factual unrealised meanings show the same proportion in American and British English, i.e. $\chi^2(1)=0.25$, P=0.512.

3.4.2.1 Dare *and the infinitive clause in LModE*

This section provides a qualitative study of the most salient features of *dare* plus infinitival clausal complementation in the British LModE variety, together with a qualitative and multifactorial analysis of the data for American English. A multivariate analysis of the British LModE data was not possible because of the low number of examples, in particular of those with *to*-infinitive clause.

As in the case of the EModE data, *dare* more frequently shows non-explicit morphology when it selects BI in British LModE. In contrast, *dare* has explicit morphology with *to*-infinitive complementation. As Table 26 illustrates, the BI clause is restricted to other non-explicit morphology, as in (304), and to past tense, as in (305) and (306). When inflected for past tense, the BI clause follows regularised *–ed* inflected forms in two occurrences, as in (305), and the old form *durst* in 7 examples, as in (306).

	Explicit						Non-explicit	
	Dares	***Dared/ durst***	***To dare***	**Bare *dare***	***Daring***	**Non-finite *dared/ durst***	**S/he/it *dare***	**Other**
BI	1	9	0	0	0	2	2	29
TO	1	5	1	4	2	3	0	2

Table 26: Morphology and paradigm forms of *dare* plus *to*-infinitive/BI clause in British LModE (raw data)

(304) In the mean Time, let Love and Honour be your Guide: But ask me no more Questions; for I can only wish you knew what *I dare not tell* you. (PPCMBE, DAVYS-1716,39.514)

(305) Surely he don't contemplate matrimony himself? Herb. I'm almost inclined to think so. Ah! if I *dared approach* the subject of my painful though. (PPCMBE, BROUGHAM-1861,19.686)

(306) Indeed the Janizaries had no mercy on their poverty, killing all the poultry and sheep they could find, without asking to whom they belonged; while the wretched owners *durst not put* in their claim for fear of being beaten. (PPCMBE, MONTAGU-1718,103.307)

In contrast, *dare* displays all the morphological variants when it co-occurs with *to*-infinitive clauses, the past-tense form, as in (307), and the bare infinitive after a modal, as in (308), being the most frequent. *Dare* is in the weak past-tense form *dared* in the 5 occurrences with the *to*-infinitive clause. The 5 examples with the non-finite forms *dared/ durst* are all cases of the perfect construction and *dare* exhibits the inflected form *–ed* with *to*-infinitive, as in (309), and with BI, as in (310). The non-finite forms with *to*-infinitive and*–ing* are only attested with *to*-infinitive complementation, as in (311) and (312), respectively.

(307) For their peculiar vessels no coast was too shallow, no river too small; they *dared to ascend* the streams for eighty or an hundred miles, and if other plunder invited or danger pressed, they carried their vessels from one river to another, and thus escaped with facility from the most superior foe. (PPCMBE, TURNER1–1799,75.447)

(308) But what answer can we give? *Shall we dare to put* the words into His mouth?" Look to Me and follow Me; I have given you an example. (PPCMBE, TALBOT-1901,191.355)

(309) The present Bassa *has not dared to punish* the murder; on the contrary, he affected to applaud the actors of it, as brave fellows, that knew how to do themselves justice. (PPCMBE, MONTAGU-1718,90.162)

(310) That Uppingham was Uppingham because *I had dared take* my stand on new principles, and work them steadily out in opposition to the opinions of others. (PPCMBE, THRING-187X,238.725)

(311) He told him they were fully resolv'd to dye for their Country, and ready to fight it out to the last Man, if Occasion requir'd, at which Xerxes derided him, as he did before when he spake of the Valour of his Country-men; for he imagin'd they would be so scar'd at his Numbers, as *not to dare to give* him Battle. (PPCMBE, HIND-1707,310.144)

(312) He had no sooner recovered his Legs, than forth from the Bed, upon his Legs likewise, appeared - with Shame and Sorrow are we obliged to

proceed - our Heroe himself, who, with a menacing Voice, demanded of the Gentleman who he was, and what he meant *by daring to burst* open his Chamber in that outrageous Manner. (PPCMBE, FIELDING-1749,3,7.355)

Finally, the occurrence of *dare* in third-person simple present tense is infrequent in British LModE. With BI, *dare* has non-explicit morphology in two instances, as in (313), and the explicit form with–*s* inflection in one (314). Only one instance is found with *to*-infinitive with the third-person singular present tense *dares* (315).

(313) They cut off his hand, head and feet, and throw them before the palace gate, with all the respect in the world; while *the Sultan* to whom they all profess an unlimited adoration sits trembling in his apartment, and *dare neither defend nor revenge* his favorite. (PPCMBE, MONTAGU-1718,112.421)

(314) I would therefore have such as are very young, or of a tender constitution meet every morning at nine; especially in the winter-season, when *vigorous health dares scarcely look abroad.* (PPCMBE, BARCLAY-1743,38.275)

(315) Cha. Now, if you had only played your part half as well, you might have passed for a woman. Lady C. Passed for a woman! who *dares to say* I'm not one? Stamps her foot with rage. (PPCMBE, COLLIER-1835,20.671)

Dare is found in 6 interrogative clauses and it selects a BI clause with subject-verb inversion in half of them, as in (316). In the other three examples, *dare* selects a *to*-infinitive clause and co-occurs with an auxiliary, as in (308) above, or with a *wh*-interrogative subject pronoun, as in (315) above. As for *do*-support, this strategy is still infrequent at this stage: it is attested with a BI clause in the simple present tense in (317) and with the *to*-infinitive in two instances in the past tense, as in (319) (see Table 27). Direct *not* negation is the most frequent negative strategy with BI, as in (304) and (306) above, *to*-infinitive being attested in only example (311), where *not* is placed before *to dare.* A *to*-infinitive complement is also registered in the negative example in (309) above, but the negative particle is supported by the auxiliary form *has* here. The two other instances with auxiliary verbs are interrogative sentences with modal verbs, where *dare* selects *to*-infinitive, as in (308) above and (319) below.

	Do-support	*Not/Inversion*	Auxiliary
BI	1 (0.25)	20 (5.09)	0
TO	2 (0.51)	1 (0.25)	3 (0.76)

Table 27: Negation/inversion and *dare* plus *to*-infinitive/BI clause in British LModE (raw and n.f./10,000 IP-MATs)

(316) Edmund denied the charge against him with equal spirit and modesty - master Robert answered him sharply - *how dare you contradict* my cousins, do you mean to give them the lye? (PPCMBE, REEVE-1777,26.566)

(317) How I should like to be released from this joyless government if it was His will. But I *don't dare ask* it. I see so many signs that it is His will that it should be borne. (PPCMBE, THRING-187X,239.756)

(318) I immediately retired to my Father's House: but he *did not dare to receive* me. Nor did any one else; till at length Henry Parks took me in; (PPCMBE, WESLEY-174X,12.48)

(319) How then *shall we* be able to endure His looks, or *dare to appear* before Him, unless we have done all in our power to make ourselves such as He approves? (PPCMBE, FROUDE-1830,2,24.248)

Fisher's Exact test indicates that although POLARITY is not statistically significant (P=0.134) in this period, the distribution of *dare* in affirmative clauses is higher than in the negative with both types of complements (see Table 28). With respect to RHYTHMIC ALTERNATION, even though the BI clause is more frequent in unproblematic stress patterns and the *to*-infinitive in critical ones, the differences are not statistically significant ($\chi^2(1)=0.37$, P=0.3741) (see Table 29).

	Negative	Affirmative
BI	18 (4.58)	26 (6.61)
TO	4 (1.02)	40 (3.56)

Table 28: Polarity and *dare* plus *to*-infinitive/BI clause in British LModE (raw and n.f./10,000 IP-MATs)

	Critical	**Unproblematic**
BI	19 (4.83)	25 (6.36)
TO	10 (2.54)	8 (2.03)

Table 29: Rhythmic Alternation and *dare* plus *to*-infinitive/BI clause in British LModE (raw and n.f./10,000 IP-MATs)

In the only passive clause attested in the British LModE data (320), *dare* selects a BI clause. *Dare* is attested in RELATIVE clauses in very similar proportions with both types of infinitival complementation ($\chi^2(1)=0.92$, $P=0.1949$; see Table 30). As regards SUBJECT COMPLEXITY, *dare* occurs with a BI clause in two non-basic examples, as in (321), with the NP *no man* postmodified by the PP *of the common timid feelings of mankind*. With a *to*-infinitive clause, *dare* is found with unexpressed non-basic subjects in two examples, as in (311) and (312) above, whose referents are the pronoun *they* and the NP *the Gentleman*, respectively, and with complex non-basic subjects in two instances, as in (322) with the relative clause introduced by *who* modifying the NP *which philosophers*. In the majority of the cases *dare* selects basic subjects with either type of complementation, though.

(320) Miss. I know not what I shall have from his Hands, but I am sure I shall have nothing but Blows from my Mother's: I dare as well *be hang'd as go* Home. Bare. Oh Madam, now you are a Soldier's Lady you must despise Fear. (PPCMBE, DAVYS-1716,50.900)

	Relative	**Other**
BI	8 (2.03)	36 (9.15)
TO	6 (1.53)	12 (3.05)

Table 30: Relativisation and *dare* plus *to*-infinitive/BI clause in British LModE (raw and n.f./10,000 IP-MATs)

(321) I have heard Nelson used to say "never mind the justice, or impudence of any thing, let me but be successful." That is what *no man, of the common timid feelings of mankind*, would have dared say or feel, and what's the world's opinion of Nelson? (PPCMBE, HAYDON-1808,1,36.926)

(322) Such is the child of nature! Such the noble savage! Such the primitive condition of man, *which philosophers, who had never studied it*, have dared to hold up to our example! (PPCMBE, READE-1863,219.461)

With SYNTAX, the *dare* construction is more frequent with main clauses, but the variation is not significant in British LModE (see Table 31).[30]

	Adverbial	**Dependent**	**Main**
BI	9 (2.29)	10 (2.54)	25 (6.36)
TO	3 (0.76)	6 (1.53)	9 (2.29)

Table 31: Syntactic dependency and *dare* plus *to*-infinitive/BI clause in British LModE (raw and n.f./10,000 IP-MATs)

With respect to the NOTIONAL CHARACTERISATION predictor, *dare* plus *to*-infinitive is more frequent in non-factual unrealised instances, as in (323), than with BI (see Table 32). This difference, however, is not statistically significant in any of the three (non-)factual (un-)realised levels of this predictor.[31]

	Factual realised	**Factual unrealised**	**Non-factual unrealised**
BI	18 (4.58)	8 (2.03)	18 (4.58)
TO	5 (1.27)	3 (0.76)	10 (2.54)

Table 32: Notional characterisation of *dare* plus *to*-infinitive/BI clause in British LModE (raw and n.f./10,000 IP-MATs)

(323) Be pleased to state the nature of the objection. Cha. Caroline has bestowed her affections upon another. Frank. Aside. What is he driving at Sir G. The

30 The chi-square test is $\chi^2(1)=0.21$, P=0.4274 for the difference between main and dependent clauses. Fisher's Exact tests are P=0.388 for dependent vs adverbial and P=0.621 for main vs adverbial clauses.

31 The chi-square test indicates that infinitival complementation is not significant for factual realised vs non-factual unrealised contexts ($\chi2(1)=0.61$, P=0.2753). Likewise, the results of Fisher's Exact test are not significant for the factual unrealised contexts with either the factual realised or the non-factual unrealised ones, i.e. P=0.518 and P=0.457, respectively.

devil she has! d- it, I'll play the very devil with the jade if she *has dared to jilt* us. But, pray sir, when did you pick up this agreeable information? Frank. Aside. My master's in a mess, I've a notion. Cha. From my trusty servant. (PPCMBE, COLLIER-1835,10.222)

The American LModE data enable a statistical analysis of the *dare* construction if DO-SUPPORT, PASSIVISATION and VALENCY are discarded owing to insufficient data. As in British English, direct *not* negation and inversion are the most frequent syntactic patterns with *dare* plus *to*-infinitive/BI in American LModE (Table 33). With *do*-support, BI is preferred, but the difference with the *to*-infinitive is not statistically significant (P=0.131). Regarding the distribution of *do*-support and modal/auxiliary occurrence, the BI clause tends to occur with *do*-support, whereas the *to*-infinitive is usually accompanied by modal/auxiliary negation and inversion, but this difference is not statistically significant (P=0.055).

	***Do*-support**	***Not*/inversion**	**Auxiliaries**
BI	8 (0.97)	108 (13.03)	5 (0.6)
TO	3 (0.36)	13 (1.57)	10 (1.21)

Table 33: Negation/inversion and *dare* plus *to*-infinitive/BI clause in American LModE (raw and n.f./10,000 IP-MATs)

The difference is significant when direct negation/inversion is contrasted with auxiliary verbs ($\chi^2(1)=25.86$, $P=<.0001$): BI is preferred with direct-*not* and inversion, as in (324), and *to*-infinitive is favoured with auxiliaries. BI is attested in 21 (out of 108) examples showing subject inversion, as in (324), whereas only 3 (out of 13) examples of inversion contain *to*-infinitives, as in (325) (see Table 33).

(324) Marm. Lord Marmion I came prepared With friendly offers to redress those wrongs Of which as king of Scotland you complain'd: But as ally of France, sir, my commission Is silent on that head, nor *dare I hope* My master will accept of terms like these. (COHA, fic_1812_8551)

(325) Youth is tender and kind, but age hardens all things. And what *dare I to hope* from my brother, when my only son --? Be still! Hold thy peace poor mother! Think that thou hast dreamed it, and tell not thy feverish dreams. (COHA, fic_1815_9352)

The predictors PASSIVISATION and PERFECT are not included in *Model 2* because *dare* is only attested in one instance with a passive construction (326), where it selects a BI clause, and because of the lack of evidence of *to*-infinitive/BI complements in perfect constructions (see Section 3.4.1.1).

(326) Sir C. Sir Credulous Testy Attach me to no attachment, sir; you have a violent affection for her money, *I dare be sworn*. (COHA, fic_1817_8785)

As regards VALENCY, coordination is attested in one instance with the *to*-infinitive (327) with the subordinate verbs *profit* and *speak*, and in 5 examples with BI, as in (328) with *question* and *criticize* (see Table 34). Differences between BI vs *to*-infinitive clauses with intransitive/transitive lower verbs are not statistically significant ($\chi^2(1)=0.25$, $P=0.4795$) since both infinitival complements are more frequent with transitive subordinate verbs.

	Coordination	Intransitive	Transitive
BI	5 (0.6)	23 (2.78)	159 (19.18)
TO	1 (0.12)	8 (0.97)	75 (9.05)

Table 34: Valency and *dare* plus *to*-infinitive/BI clause in American LModE (raw and n.f./10,000 IP-MATs)

(327) Mail. Vicomte de Maillac If I dared *to profit* by this happy moment, *and speak* of my love -- Ad. Adelaide No, no! -- Do you not hear that I wish to be entertained? (COHA, fic_1815_9352)

(328) Oh, for the inconsistency of respectability, that needs the marriage vow to turn something which is filthy into the purest and most sacred arrangement that none dare *question or criticize*. (COHA, nf_1911_767566)

Model 2 for *dare* in American LModE includes the *STEP 1* predictors MORPHOLOGY, POLARITY, SYNTAX, RHYTHMIC ALTERNATION, SUBJECT ANIMACY and NOTIONAL CHARACTERISATION and the *STEP 2* factors RELATIVE and SUBJECT COMPLEXITY. Provided the quantile of the *STEP 2* factor DISTANCE is 1 word, RHYTHMIC ALTERNATION and DISTANCE will be run separately because the critical level of RHYTHMIC ALTERNATION corresponds to 0 words of DISTANCE and the unproblematic level corresponds to at least one word. Table 35 reflects the significant predictors of *dare* and the *to*-infinitive/BI complementation in American LModE and their relative strength after the application of the step "backward" function.

Predictor	Estimate	P-value	OR
Intercept	0.7383	0.008916 **	2.0923677
Morphology (ref.: *Explicit*) Non-explicit	-2.0928	6.34e-10 ***	1/0.1233376= 8.1078
Polarity (ref.: *Affirmative*) Negative	-1.4979	0.000245 ***	1/0.2235904= 4.4724
Rhythmic Alternation (ref.: *Critical*) Unproblematic	-0.7027	0.030235 *	1/0.4952221=2.0192
Subject complexity (ref.: *Basic*) Non-basic	1.2084	0.033114 *	3.3480514

Table 35: *Model 2, STEP 2*, significant factors with *dare* and *to*-infinitive/BI clause in American LModE (step "backward" results)

MORPHOLOGY is shown to be a significant factor in the distribution of *dare* and infinitival complementation alternation in my American LModE data ($Pr(>|z|)=6.34e^{-10}$). The chances of BI complements increase by 8.11 percentage points when *dare* shows non-explicit morphology, as in (329) and (330). No examples of the old *–st* inflection for second-person singular present are attested in American LModE. Consequently, instances such as (329) have been classified as non-explicit (see Table 36). (330) is an example with a third-person simple present tense form evincing covert agreement between the subject and *dare*. Only two instances (out of a total 17) are found without *–s* inflection for third-person present and a *to*-infinitive clause (see Table 36). The lack of inflection in example (331) may be explained by the type of construction in which *dare* and the *to*-infinitive occur, i.e. the protasis of a conditional sentence, which allows both indicative and subjunctive mood. In contrast, (332) is a clear indicative-mood example where the *–s*/*–th* would be expected, covert agreement here evincing either the reluctance of *dare* to regularise or the modal properties of the construction. The analysis of the notional characterisation of *dare* and the *to*-infinitive/BI clause may shed light on this issue.

	Explicit						Non-explicit	
	Dares	***Finite dared/ durst (simple past)***	***To dare***	**Bare *dare***	***Daring***	**Non-finite *dared/ durst***	**S/he/it *dare***	**Other**
BI	19	21	0	26	0	2	15	104
TO	6	11	1	31	11	8	2	14

Table 36: Morphology and paradigm forms of *dare* plus *to*-infinitive/BI clause in American LModE (raw data)

(329) And who are you *that dare make* that presumptuous supposition? (COHA, fic_1817_8550)

(330) -- I love your daughter, With such a holy, pure, emblemish'd passion, (She could inspire no other!) -- that such base designs I never dreampt of. -- Sir, I pledge my word, (And I would reach his life *who dare dispute it*) 'T was chance that brought me to her dearest presence, Where, for the first time I declar'd that love, She had inspir'd me with. (COHA, fic_1810_8694)

(331) And if ever *a man dare to insult* your gray wig, I vow, by Saint Peter, I'll hit him a dig. (COHA, fic_1812_8872)

(332) High Priest. High Preist And who are you, *Who dare to judge* the manners of my country; And seek to change the customs of old times!! (COHA, fic_1815_8716)

The BI complement is more frequent with the two types of non-explicit forms: other morphology and without an –*s*-inflected third-person singular form. In the explicit forms (third-person singular present *dares*, in (333) and (334), and finite past tense, in (335) and (336)), the variation between BI and *to*-infinitive is not statistically significant ($\chi^2(1)=0.31$, $P=0.3961$). The old form *durst* in the simple past is attested on two occasions (out of 32): in one instance with BI (337), and in one example with *to*-infinitive (338).

(333) It is content to relish what *it dares not rival*. (COHA, mag_1816_552808)

(334) -- Widow. Lanissa "A foreign hero"! -- why he succour me? For what should he attempt to save my life? What is this gen'rous hero then -- so kind, -- Who, tho' he knows me not, still *dares to shield* me: --That my distresses should so nearly touch him! -- Have all the French the feelings of my lover? (COHA, fic_1815_8716)

(335) Giovanna. Giovanna Said I not all was well? Unfix your eyes, and smooth your brow, my father. You look upon me with such searching gaze As though you waited news of death of life, And *dared not ask*, because, you feared the worst. (COHA, fic_1819_9004)

(336) 'We wonder a little how *he dared to print* his book there, and should ask him if its ill success might not be ascribed to the malign influences of that city, had he not assured us, that it is unphilosophical to resort to extraordinary causes, when ordinary ones are adequate to explain a fact. (COHA, mag_1817_552906)

(337) Per. Percy Alas! What shall I say then? What will vouch my truth? -- *Durst I my name reveal* -- El. Elinor O, sir, forbear: Lest its dread potency unseat our towers. (COHA, fic_1819_8706)

(338) Dame. Dame Spindle Can't, I can't buoy; more than *I durst to do.* If squire Pinch should hear o n't, he 'd turn us out; as sure as I do speak it. (COHA, fic_1818_886)

The incidence of *to*-infinitive complementation is higher with explicit morphology, attested with all of the non-finite forms of *dare* and highly frequent in the data. *Dare* and *to*-infinitive is more frequent than BI in contexts with unmarked infinitive forms, as in (339) where *dare* is preceded by the modal *will*, and in (340), with the two constructions in the imperative form. The 10 past participle forms found illustrate that the new, regularised *–ed* form *dared* and BI complements are also attested with this form (2 examples), as in (341), but the proportion of *to*-infinitive with this morphological variant is higher (342). *To*-infinitives and *-ing* forms only co-occur with *to*-infinitive clauses, the former attested only once, in example (343).

(339) LADY WILDERING -- Oh, I 'll go through with it, and as I 'm to be Bruce 's partner, I *wo n't dare to play* badly. (COHA, fic_1919_13376)

(340) VALSIN picking up the warrant. *Dare to say* her mouth is wide? ELOISE cyclonic. *Dare to arrest* her! VALSIN It does seem a pity. He folds the warrant slowly and replaces it in his pocket. (COHA, fic_1912_14258)

(341) TSUMU By the King 's orders *no man has dared gaze* upon Her Majesty. They all fell prostrate before her. (COHA, fic_1915_14265)

(342) BARON. Baron. Baron Wildenhain He is a fine fellow. How anxious for his mother." A noble youth. What shall I do for her? foolish boy, untutored in the opinions of the world *he has dared to demand* that I should

marry her; yet I can not but applaud him for the spirited manner in which he called upon me to do what he thinks right in respect to his mother." (COHA, fic_1814_8642)

(343) In either supposition, it is certainly desirable, that the executive should be in a situation *to dare to act* his own opinion with vigor and decision. (COHA, nf_1817_747651)

The POLARITY of the clause also exerts a statistically significant influence on the selection of the infinitival complement (Pr(>|z|)=0.000245; Table 37). Affirmative clauses favour *dare* plus *to*-infinitive by 4.47 percentage points, as in (342) and (343) above and (344) below. In contrast, BI is preferred in negative clauses: in 67 (out of 73) negative clauses with direct negation, as in (345) (see Table 37), and in 6 examples with *do*-support. Direct negation is not attested with *to*-infinitive clauses, in which negative polarity is manifested through a negator preceding the main verb (3 out of 10 occurrences), as in (346), or associated with auxiliary verbs, for example, with *will* in (347) (see Table 37).

	Negative	**Affirmative**
BI	73 (8.81)	114 (13.76)
TO	10 (1.21)	74 (8.83)

Table 37: Polarity and *dare* plus *to*-infinitive/BI clause in American LModE (raw and n.f./10,000 IP-MATs)

(344) But in the Temple Jackson is standing too; and *I dare to say* that not Napoleon with brow and frontal scope moulded like the imperial globe; (COHA, mag_1917_430781)

(345) We are cheerful without cards, and conversable without calumny. *We dare not be ashamed to love* the oppressed, or fear to call him loudly rogue whose actions deserve the appellation. (COHA, fic_1815_9352)

(346) Wie. Mr. Wieland I took a walk on the meadow, *not daring* to think that I could be missed. Erl. Captain Erlach He was then the "somebody" whom you sought? (COHA, fic_1815_9352)

(347) Fortunately, that is impossible just now; and he *will not dare* to attempt it. (COHA, fic_1912_14258)

The analysis of the weight of the RHYTHMIC ALTERNATION factor reveals that the odds of the *to*-infinitive complement type are higher in critical stress patterns (by 2.02 percentage points), as in (344) above. In example (344), the *to*-infinitive acts as a stress-clash buffer between the two monosyllabic verbs *dare* and *say*. BI is more frequently attested in unproblematic contexts, such as (348), with the stressed monosyllabic form *dare* followed by the first unstressed disyllabic verb *refuse* (see Table 38).

	Critical	**Unproblematic**
BI	48 (5.79)	139 (16.77)
TO	39 (4.71)	45 (5.43)

Table 38: Rhythmic Alternation and *dare* plus *to*-infinitive/BI clause in American LModE (raw and n.f./10,000 IP-MATs)

(348) Would they *dare refuse* a plan advantageous to the men who held them in the hollow of their hands? (COHA, mag_1912_486100)

Although the interaction of RHYTHMIC ALTERNATION and POLARITY cannot be corroborated by the model, the univariate analysis reveals a number of trends. The distribution of the two complementation options in negative and affirmative clauses in so-called unproblematic stress patterns is statistically significant ($\chi^2(1)=17.09$, P=<.0001): BI clauses are more frequent in negative unproblematic contexts whereas the *to*-infinitive is favoured in the affirmative variant. This conclusion is related to the proportion of *dare* plus BI with direct *not* negation (91.78 per cent of the data set, in 67 out of 73 examples; see Table 37), where *not* is placed between *dare* and the BI clause in 66 (out of 69) examples, thus leading to well-formed stress patterns, as in (349) (see Table 39). The negative element makes *dare* invert with the subject in only one instance (350), which results in a stress pattern such as that observed in (349). The two other examples of BI with negative polarity in unproblematic contexts correspond to instances of *do*-support, as in (351): both occurrences are unproblematic because the lower infinitival verbs are phrasal, so stress lies on the particles and the verbs become overshadowed, as in *run away* in (351).

	Critical		Unproblematic	
	Affirmative	**Negative**	**Affirmative**	**Negative**
BI	44	4	70	69
TO	35	4	39	6

Table 39: Rhythmic Alternation and polarity affecting *dare* plus *to*-infinitive/BI clause in American LModE (raw data)

(349) But it was obvious that, even if he would, he could not come with us, and we certainly *dared not confide* in him. (COHA, mag_1919_467032)

(350) Marm. Lord Marmion I came prepared With friendly offers to redress those wrongs Of which as king of Scotland you complain 'd: But as ally of France, sir, my commission Is silent on that head, nor *dare I hope* My master will accept of terms like these. (COHA, fic_1812_8551)

(351) Still, I *did not* dare *run away*, and so I timidly rang the bell. (COHA, mag_1917_434821)

In critical contexts, the *to*-infinitive is preferred in affirmative sentences (vs negative unproblematic; $\chi^2(1)=24.13$, P=<.0001) to avoid a stress clash, as in (344) between the two monosyllabic stressed verbs *dare* and *say*. The incidence of *to*-infinitive clauses in negative critical contexts, as in (352), is also significantly higher than that of BI, as in (353), in comparison with negative and unproblematic contexts (P=0.006).[32] In the four occurrences with *dare* plus BI in negative critical contexts, *do*-support materialises negation, resulting in a stress clash between the two stressed monosyllabic words, as in (353) between *dare* and *stay*. Negation is associated with auxiliaries when *dare* selects *to*-infinitive clauses, as in (352) with *do*-support, and in (347) above with a modal verb *will*. Example (354) is the only instance in which the negative element is the coordinating conjunction *nor*, placed before *dare* and the

32 The results of the chi-square test for affirmative clauses in critical and unproblematic rhythmic stress patterns are $\chi^2(1)=1.06$, P=0.2384. Fisher's Exact test indicates no significant difference between negative and affirmative critical rhythmic alternation patterns (P=0.52). Finally, negative critical contexts do not differ from affirmative unproblematic contexts with respect to distribution of infinitival alternation (P=0.327).

to-infinitive. In these negative critical contexts, the *to*-infinitive acts a stress-clash buffer.

(352) *I did not dare to hope* that you would ever forgive me -- and he was certain you would think only of revenge. (COHA, fic_1913_13915)

(353) "She insulted me!" Mrs. Ladybug screamed, as soon as she was able to speak. "She insulted me. And then she hurried off because she *did n't dare stay*! (COHA, fic_1918_3632)

(354) Capt. Dor. Captain Dorriville Is this the rich reward for all my services? but hold, *nor dare to reprobate* my country's laws, because a villain has abused them! (COHA, fic_1815_8719)

DISTANCE also affects complementation alternation and favours the use of BI clauses (Pr(>|z|)=0.01326).[33] An increase in one unit between *dare* and the infinitival clause decreases the use of the *to*-infinitive by 1.84 percentage points. These results can be related to those obtained with the RHYTHMIC ALTERNATION predictor and, to some extent, to POLARITY: preference for the *to*-infinitive clause is significant when distance is null (0 words), i.e. in affirmative and negative clauses in critical contexts, because the *to*-infinitive acts as a stress-clash buffer in these negative examples, as the use of *do*-support would create a critical pattern. The odds of the BI clause increase when DISTANCE varies from 0 to 16 words, as in the unproblematic stress patterns in (355) with the two intervening words *the Council*, which create a stress lapse between the two monosyllabic stressed words *dare* and *offer*.

(355) "What excuse," asks the Transcript," has the Governor for his action in the Hall case, and what defence *dare the Council offer* for thus mocking justice in Massachusetts and making of it a commonwealth where the rich thief may rob the poor without fear of paying the penCourt for committing acts in restraint of their trade. (COHA, mag_1914_487170)

SUBJECT COMPLEXITY favours the *to*-infinitive with *dare* when the latter agrees with non-basic subjects (Pr(>|z|)=0.033114). All of the examples of non-basic subjects with *dare* plus *to*-infinitive are unexpressed.

---

33 These results are obtained by replacing the predictor RHYTHMIC ALTERNATION with DISTANCE and applying the step "backward" function.

Ten (out of 12) examples of this type contain *–ing* forms, as in (356), and two have (un-)marked infinitives, as in (343) above. The 7 examples with a BI clause and a non-basic subject are complex constructions such as (357), in which *the officer* is postmodified by the PP *on the quay* (see Table 40).

	Non-basic	**Basic**
BI	7 (0.84)	180 (21.72)
TO	12 (1.45)	72 (8.69)

Table 40: Subject complexity and *dare* plus *to*-infinitive/BI clause in American LModE (raw and n.f./10,000 IP-MATs)

(356) *Italy, by daring to declare* war against Turkey in 1911, at a moment when a wave of pacifism, regardless of the causes at issue, was sweeping over the world, gave the first blow to the German domination of the universe. (COHA, news_1917_682980)

(357) All France knows the Citizeness Eloise d'Anville. Do you suppose *the officer on the quay* would dare oppose -- LOUIS with a gesture of resignation. I know you think it. (COHA, fic_1912_14258)

Model 2 has determined that morphology is a strong predictor of complementation choice in American LModE: *to*-infinitive clauses are more frequent with morphologically explicit forms and BI clauses usually co-occur with non-explicit forms. The British English data show the same tendency, but the proportion of the explicit form *dares* is marginal with both types of complements. In British English, the BI clause is mainly restricted to the other non-explicit forms and to the simple past explicit form, whereas the *to*-infinitive occurs more frequently with the simple past and the unmarked infinitive form. As regards the simple past tense forms of *dare*, in my British English data the old form *durst* is still attested in half of the occurrences and in all of them *durst* selects a BI clause, whereas the weak regularised form *dared* is associated with the *to*-infinitive. In American English, *dared* is the most frequent form for the simple past and the old form *durst* is restricted to two instances, illustrating each of the two complement options. With respect to past participles, *dared* is the only form attested in both varieties and the perfect construction is the type of structure in which it occurs.

In American English, POLARITY and RHYTHMIC ALTERNATION are significant in *Model 2*. Negative polarity favours the BI clause and affirmative polarity prefers the *to*-infinitive complements. As regards, RHYTHMIC ALTERNATION, the *to*-infinitive acts as a stress-clash buffer in critical stress patterns. The univariate analysis of these two factors shows that the type of negative strategy associated with each complementation choice is related to the type of stress patterns. The *to*-infinitive clause is preferred in critical contexts and in negative clauses in order to avoid a stress clash when *do*-support or an auxiliary verb carries the negation, and the infinitival verb is monosyllabic or stressed on the first syllable. In contrast, the BI clause is associated with unstressed direct *not* negation, which creates an unproblematic context. *Do*-support is quite infrequent with *dare* plus infinitival complementation in both varieties of English; in the American data, *do*-support occurs with both types of complementation in negative clauses. Direct negation and inversion are the most frequent strategies with both types of complements.

The predictors DISTANCE and RHYTHMIC ALTERNATION are collinear so the results obtained in *Model 2* for the former, which favours BI with the increase in one unit, are in line with the preference for this complement in unproblematic stress patterns. In the British variety, the low number of examples does not allow for their statistical analysis.

Model 2 also reveals that *to*-infinitive clauses are preferred with non-basic, mainly unexpressed SUBJECTS, whereas the BI clause is slightly preferred with basic subjects. As in EModE, the preference of the *to*-infinitive for non-basic subjects is manifested in instances with the *–ing* form *daring* (in 10 out of 12 examples) in adverbial clauses (9 out of 10 cases). Likewise, the *to*-infinitive clause is associated with non-basic subjects, according to the univariate analysis of British English. Of the factors that measure complexity, the predictor VALENCY could not be added to *Model 2* because of the small number of examples in the coordination level in American English, as in the case of intransitive verbs in the British English data. In the American English data set, *dare* and the infinitival construction occur more frequently with transitive lower verbs, but the univariate analysis indicates that this trend is not statistically significant. SYNTAX and RELATIVE do not explain infinitival alternation either, and PASSIVISATION is attested in one example in each regional variety, in which *dare* governs a BI complement, as in the EModE data set. Regarding ANIMACY, though not a statistically significant factor, both complementation types seem to prefer animate subjects in British and in American English. The NOTIONAL CHARACTERISATION predictor is not decisive either; in general, both types of infinitival complements occur more frequently in contexts conveying non-factual unrealised meanings.

3.4.2.2 Need *and the infinitive clause in LModE*

The low number of occurrences of *need* plus infinitival complementation attested in my British LModE data set only allows a qualitative analysis and a univariate analysis with a small number of factors. Although *need* selects mainly BI complements, the 6 examples of *need* plus a *to*-infinitive clause reveal certain trends. Morphologically, *need* in most of these examples occurs with non-explicit forms (see Table 41): with other forms, as in (358), or with the third-person singular and covert agreement, as in (359). When *need* selects a *to*-infinitive clause, it takes an explicit form, a non-explicit form being attested in only example (360).

	Explicit			Non-explicit		
	Needs	***Finite needed (simple past)***	***Non-finite need***	***Needing***	***S/he/it need***	***Other***
BI	1	1	1	0	19	89
TO	3	1	0	1	0	1

Table 41: Morphology and paradigm forms of *need* plus *to*-infinitive/BI clause in British LModE (raw and n.f./10,000 IP-MATs)

(358) As to the Working Bees, they being so well known, *I need say* nothing about them; (PPCMBE, MAXWELL-1747,15.92)

(359) I had sent an express to my father in the morning that *he need not come*, and I had a very kindly answer. (PPCMBE, BOSWELL-1776,50.500)

(360) With regard to these and all our worship, I have sometimes thought that the twofold meaning in English of the word "familiar" expresses what *we need to secure*. (PPCMBE, TALBOT-1901,103.198)

Of the 23 examples with third-person singular present tense, *need* exhibits covert agreement in 19 instances, in which the complement is always a BI clause (see Table 41). Only 4 instances take overt forms, of which the *to*-infinitive is attested in three, as in (361). Simple past *needed* is attested with each of the variants, as in (362) with a *to*-infinitive. As in the case of *dare*, the *–ing* form is still associated with *to*-infinitive complementation, as in (363).

(361) True life *needs to be drawn out*, and all the false striving, though it must be represeed, seldom turns into healthy action. (PPCMBE, THRING-187X,240.779)

(362) 'Happy were the Latins,' he says, 'who *needed* only *to learn* Greek, and that not by school-teaching, but by intercourse with living Greeks. (PPCMBE, BAIN-1878,361.30)

(363) Now, the elder brother was kind almost to patronizing, though evidently persuaded that Colin was a gay careless youth, with no harm in him, but *needing to be looked after*; (PPCMBE, YONGE-1865,184.628)

POLARITY also helps to account for infinitival complementation with *need* in British LModE. As shown in Table 42, the 6 examples of *need* and the *to*-infinitive clause are affirmative clauses, as in (360) to (363). Conversely, the proportion of *need* plus BI clauses is higher in negative clauses, the negative strategy being direct negation, as in (359), except in (364) in which *shall* carries the negative particle *not*.

	Negative	**Affirmative**
BI	58 (14.75)	33 (8.39)
TO	0	6 (1.53)

Table 42: Polarity and *need* plus *to*-infinitive/BI clause in British LModE (raw and n.f./10,000 IP-MATs)

(364) There is another particular Account of a Gang of French and English Pirates roving in the South Sea, at several Times, from the Year 1684 'till 1689, which *we shall not need take Notice of*, as being the same which will be mention'd in speaking of Capt. Dampier; (PPCMBE, COOKE-1712,1,440.318)

As regards RHYTHMIC ALTERNATION, *need* occurs mainly in unproblematic stress patterns. However, the effect of this principle is not corroborated by the British LModE data because *need* selects a BI clause in the 8 examples in critical contexts, as in (365). The proportion of passive constructions is even higher with a *to*-infinitive clause (P=0.008; see Figure 5). In contrast, BI clauses are attested in the two examples with the perfect construction in my database, as in (366). The BI clause is also the only type of infinitival complementation in the 7 occurrences with 'fear' lower infinitival verbs (367).

(365) And as the Advantage will be great in forbearing to give them Battle, so, on the other side, the Danger will be more said she than we *need venture*, and the Loss, in case it fall upon us, greater than the Advantage of the Victory, if we should obtain it. (PPCMBE, HIND-1707,319.244)

(366) As I find on looking into my affairs, that instead of being very rich I am likely to be very poor, I cannot afford more than ten shillings for Sackree; but as we are to meet in Canterbury I need not *have mentioned* this. (PPCMBE, AUSTEN-180X,163.79)

(367) "So you must be very good to her, Violetta, and you shall help me make her clothes; but you need not *be afraid* I ever could love any one half or one quarter as much as you, my own dear child, not if she were ten times as beautiful, (PPCMBE, YONGE-1865,166.185)

Figure 5: Passivisation and *need* plus *to*-infinitive/BI clause in British LModE (raw and n.f./10,000 IP-MATs)

As regards NOTIONAL CHARACTERISATION, *need* plus *to*-infinitive is mostly restricted to non-factual unrealised meanings (see Table 43). Although *need* plus BI is more frequently attested in non-factual unrealised contexts, this pattern is also attested with factual realised and factual unrealised meanings.

	Factual realised	Factual unrealised	Non-factual unrealised
BI	15 (3.81)	9 (2.29)	67 (17.04)
TO	1 (0.25)	0	5 (1.27)

Table 43: Notional characterisation of *need* plus *to*-infinitive/BI clause in British LModE (raw and n.f./10,000 IP-MATs)

The number of examples of *need* plus *to*-infinitive/BI clauses in my American LModE database permits a multifactorial analysis with four factors. Following the methodology adopted in previous sections, I will first explore the predictors which cannot be analysed in *Model 3* for *need* in American English. MORPHOLOGY clearly explains the distribution of *to*-infinitive/BI clauses governed by *need* (see Table 44). *Need* prefers non-explicit forms when it selects a BI clause, as in (368); explicit morphology is only attested in two examples with this type of complementation, as in (369) with overt subject-verb agreement in third-person singular simple present, and in (370) in simple past with *do*-support. Explicit forms are more frequent with the *to*-infinitive clause, as in (371) with non-finite base verb *need.*

	Explicit			Non-explicit	
	Needs	**Finite *needed (simple past)***	**Non-finite *need***	**S/he/it *need***	**Other**
BI	1	1	0	47	100
TO	9	8	12	1	12

Table 44: Morphology and paradigm forms of *need* plus *to*-infinitive/BI clause in American LModE (raw data)

(368) *I need not look for* a proof beyond the case before us. What is the reason on which this proverbial observation is founded? (COHA, nf_1817_747651)

(369) Altorf. Eberard de Altorf To wed her? Why, know'st thou not I 'm wedded to another? Rossberg. Rosina de Rossberg To one thou lov'st? Altorf. Eberard de Altorf It *needs not answer* that. (COHA, fic_1819_9004)

(370) However, a person as charming as Betsy Butterfly *did not need worry* about her name. (COHA, fic_1918_3632.txt)

(371) Each day brings closer the time when large amounts of crude *will need to be treated* to supply liquid fuel foe marine service. (COHA, news_1919_684747)

The *to*-infinitive is almost categorically found with third-person present *–s* inflection, whereas BI is strongly associated with covert forms, as in (372). Only one explicit form with third-person agreement selects a BI complement (369), and one non-explicit form co-occurs with a *to*-infinitive clause (373). The simple past form is mainly attested with the *to*-infinitive complement (374), BI being attested only in (370). Finally, no examples of BI have explicit non-finite base forms of *need*: of the 12 examples with *to*-infinitive clauses, only 2 have modal verbs preceding *need*, and the other 10 are instances of *do*-support, as in (375).

(372) Pac. Pacomo (aside) O you old Jezebel! Alm. Count Almeyda Their offence is the same: the 'squire's fate must therefore depend upon that of the knight. Pac. Pacomo O! if that 's all, *your lordship need give* yourself no further trouble. (COHA, fic_1912_14258)

(373) El. Elinor What *need to search* my heart? Thou know'st it thine. (COHA, fic_1819_8706)

(374) But Betsy thought the whole affair was only a joke. So she merely laughed -- and sent Freddie no answer at all; for she hardly believed that *she needed to explain* to him that nothing could induce her to stir out after sunset. (COHA, fic_1918_3632)

(375) You *do n't need to go away* to make me know you 're better than all the rest. (COHA, fic_1916_13334)

The type of negation and interrogation strategy also helps to explain the variation (see Table 45). BI complementation is found with direct negation (in 95 out of 107 examples), as in (376), and in contexts of subject-verb inversion, in (377). Inversion in example (377) is triggered by clause-initial negative *nor*. *Do*-support is first found with *need* plus infinitival clause in my data in the American LModE period. Unlike in

(377), *do*-support is used in inversion in the only example of negative fronting and a *to*-infinitive clause, in (378), in fact the only occurrence with direct negation and a *to*-infinitive clause in my data. No instances have been registered with other auxiliaries in negative or interrogative clauses.

	***Do*-support**	***Not*/Inversion**
BI	1 (0.12)	107 (12.91)
TO	15 (1.81)	1 (0.12)

Table 45: Negation/inversion and *need* plus *to*-infinitive/BI clause in American LModE (raw and n.f./10,000 IP-MATs)

(376) But *we need not resort* to foreign experience on this subject. (COHA, nf_1817_747651)

(377) Environment is more responsiblethan heredity. *Nor need we trouble* ourselves about predestina-tion and election. (COHA, nf_1916_773813)

(378) But Christ can be all the more surely our model of inspiration if we can think of him as facing life with only such resources and faculties as other men have, and yet making out of them so sublime a life. Nor *do we need to consider* him as altogether unique in his divineness; (COHA, nf_1916_773813)

(379) Mount. Mountfort 113 By the gods, Tho' fourscore stiff'ning winters gripe my limbs, And dim these eyeballs, with a cripple's crutch, I'd beard the Tyrant! Bard. Bardolph Persuasion *it needs not* my heart *to stir.* (COHA, fic_1819_8706)

In contexts with PERFECT verbal forms, my American LModE data contain only two occurrences, both with BI complements, as in (380).

(380) This would have been completely averted if Mr. Hughes had, at the very outset of his campaign, done what he easily might have done to bring about that result. He need not *have said* a word to hamper his freedom in the event of election; (COHA, mag_1916_486336)

The predictor SYNTAX is excluded from *Model 2* because of the low incidence of *to*-infinitive complementation in adverbial clauses (see Table 46). That said, the difference between *to*-infinitive/BI complements in adverbial vs dependent/main clauses is not statistically significant (P=0.478 and P=0.132, respectively). BI clauses are significantly preferred in main clauses, as in (381), and the *to*-infinitive in dependent clauses, as in (382) ($\chi2(1)=15.62$, P=0.0001). Finally, the only example of coordination is attested in (382), where a *to*-infinitive complement is selected.

	Adverbial	**Dependent**	**Main**
BI	5 (0.6)	15 (1.81)	129 (15.57)
TO	3 (0.36)	15 (1.81)	24 (2.9)

Table 46: Syntactic dependency and *need* plus *to*-infinitive/BI clause in American LModE (raw and n.f./10,000 IP-MATs)

(381) The nightmare of disease germs everywhere, in books and brooks, and through all the ambient air, *need plague* us no more. (COHA, mag_1912_465817)

(382) The tariff they have just enacted shows that they have learned nothing about the tariff since MCKINLEY died, leaving as his legacy *the declaration that* the period of exclusiveness was past, and *that the Americans needed to allow themselves access to the world 's trade.* (COHA, news_1910_678947)

As regards VALENCY of the infinitival verb, coordination is attested in one example with BI, in (383), and elsewhere with the *to*-infinitive, illustrated in (384). The coordinated infinitive lower verbs are *spend* and *dwell on* in (383) and the two instances of *have* in (384) (see Table 47). The variation between transitive and intransitive subordinate verbs is not statistically significant ($\chi2(1)=0.01$, P=0.7642).

(383) Abbess. Abbess Thank heaven, I *need not spend* these precious moments In tedious tales, *nor dwell on* worldly love -- Too vain a topic for a saint like thee. (COHA, fic_1812_8551)

(384) While we can see real benefit in bringing God and Christ as familiar friends to tile man or woman to whom? lie has seemed afar off, this age surely *needs to have* its sense of reverence strengthened. not weakened, *and to have* a God too much occupied with great events to learn modern slang. (COHA, news_1917_683168)

	Coordination	Intransitive	Transitive
BI	1 (0.12)	32 (3.86)	116 (14)
TO	1 (0.12)	8 (0.97)	33 (3.98)

Table 47: Valency and *need* plus *to*-infinitive/BI clause in American LModE (raw and n.f./10,000 IP-MATs)

Concerning semantic/pragmatic factors, 'fear' verbs are attested with BI in 9 occurrences, as in (385), and in none with *to*-infinitive clauses. With respect to NOTIONAL CHARACTERISATION, neither of the two types of infinitival complementation is attested in factual unrealised contexts (see Table 48). When non-factual unrealised and factual realised meanings are compared, the *to*-infinitive option is significantly preferred (P=0.037) in the former, as in (386), which conveys uncertainty about whether or not the *farmers* end up learning, whereas BI is more frequent in factual realised meanings, as in (387), where the complement of the verb *repeat* (*that the well educated lawyers form but a small part of the whole number*) is expressed, so the action of repeating is performed and the proposition is a fact.

	Factual realised	Factual unrealised	Non-factual unrealised
BI	36 (4.34)	3 (0.36)	109 (13.15)
TO	4 (0.48)	2 (0.24)	36 (4.34)

Table 48: Notional characterisation of *need* plus *to*-infinitive/BI clause in American LModE (raw and n.f./10,000 IP-MATs)

(385) He can afford to improve his lot and advance. Koreans *need no longer fear* to be economically ambitious. This new security and new ambition of the Korean are illustrated by his changed attitude toward saving. (COHA, mag_1919_466954)

(386) These essentials should receive the greatest of attention at all times. Farmers need to *learn the merits of rape*, carrots, Canada peas and alfalfa or clover. Hogs can be brought along nicely for the first six months without much corn if they can have a nice patch of forage such as alfalfa or rape. (COHA, nf_1913_773672)

(387) We *need not repeat* what we stated so explicitly in the first division of our subject, that the well educated lawyers form but a small part of the whole number; (COHA, mag_1819_553205)

Model 2 includes the *STEP 1* factors with enough data in their levels: POLARITY, RHYTHMIC ALTERNATION and SUBJECT ANIMACY. The factors in *STEP 2* are not analysed by means of 'glm' in an attempt to avoid overfittedness, but will be described after the significant predictors of *Model 2*. The step "backward" function indicates that only POLARITY and RHYTHMIC ALTERNATION help to account for the variation between *to*-infinitive/BI clauses in *Model 2, STEP 1* (see Table 49).

Predictor	**Estimate**	**P-value**	**OR**
Intercept	0.0601	0.8788	1.06193
Polarity (ref.: *Affirmative*)	-0.8505	0.0248*	1/0.4272076=2.3407
Negation			
Rhythmic Alternation (ref.: *Critical*)	-1.0967	0.0151*	1/0.3339674=2.9943
Unproblematic			

Table 49: *Model 2, STEP 1*, significant factors with *need* and *to*-infinitive/BI clause in American LModE (step "backward" results)

POLARITY indicates that the odds of BI clause significantly increase in negative clauses (by 2.34 percentage points), as in (387) above. In contrast, the distribution of the *to*-infinitive option is higher in affirmative clauses, as in (386) above (see Table 50).

	Negative	**Affirmative**
BI	96 (11.58)	53 (6.39)
TO	16 (1.93)	26 (3.14)

Table 50: Polarity and *need* plus *to*-infinitive/BI clause in American LModE (raw and n.f./10,000 IP-MATs)

A cross-tabulation of the factors POLARITY and NOTIONAL CHARACTERISATION confirms the results of *Model 1* for EModE and the univariate analysis of NOTIONAL CHARACTERISATION described above. Figure 6 reveals that POLARITY explains the variation in non-factual unrealised contexts: BI is more frequent with negative and non-factual unrealised meanings, and *to*-infinitive complements are favoured with affirmative meanings ($\chi^2(1)=9.76$, $P=0.0009$). BI is the only option in factual realised semantic/pragmatic affirmative contexts, as in (388). The incidence of negative and factual realised vs affirmative and non-factual unrealised meanings is also significantly higher with BI ($P=0.0107$), but not with respect to negative non-factual unrealised ones ($P=0.612$). Example (389) contains two instances of negative factual realised meaning, in which the main verb *need* is negated and the proposition asserts that the addressee is *paltry* and *huffy*.

(388) A fortnight ago you published an editorial headed "The Social Evil". Concerning the substance of the editorial, I need only *say that it has my hearty approval.* (COHA, mag_1911_487095)

(389) Doo. Doolittle No harm, I hope, if the strangers be all mad. So *you need n't be* so paltry techy! I did n't say you was mad, Mister! And so as I had a rational curosity, I only wished to ax.
Mas. Hot. Master of the Hotel (Angrily) Wished to ax? Doo. Doolittle Yes *You need n't be* quite so huffy, Mister! Can't you answer a civil question, civilly? (COHA, fic_1815_8717)

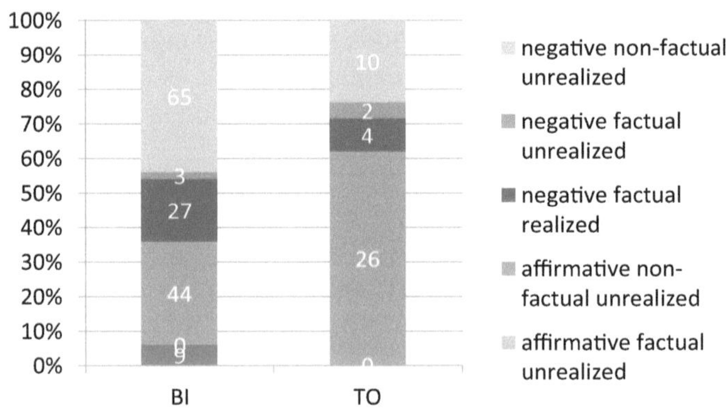

Figure 6: Notional characterisation and polarity affecting *need* plus *to*-infinitive/BI clause in American LModE (raw data)

The predictor RHYTHMIC ALTERNATION is also statistically significant in the model (Pr(>|z|)=0.0151). The chances of *to*-infinitive increase by 2.99 in critical contexts in comparison to unproblematic stress patterns. The *to*-infinitive acts as a stress-clash buffer in critical contexts, as in example (390), in which the marked infinitive is inserted between the stressed monosyllabic verbs *need* and *look* to achieve this effect. In contrast, BI is favoured in unproblematic examples such as (391), in which *only* avoids two stressed monosyllabic verbs in the immediate context (see Table 51).

	Critical	**Unproblematic**
BI	15 (1.81)	134 (16.17)
TO	13 (1.57)	29 (3.5)

Table 51: Rhythmic Alternation and *need* plus *to*-infinitive/BI clause in American LModE (raw and n.f./10,000 IP-MATs)

(390) Those building wooden silos *need to look* well to the foundations also. (COHA, nf_1913_773672)

(391) Of the smaller textile industries, linen and hemp, and jute, I *need only add* that of the former four fifths of the material has hitherto come from abroad and more than three quarters from Russia; (COHA, mag_1915_435396)

These results are influenced by POLARITY. In critical stress patterns and affirmative clauses, the *to*-infinitive is preferred to avoid a stress clash, as in (390) above. Similarly, the *to*-infinitive acts as a stress buffer in negative and critical stress patterns because *do*-support carries negation in these contexts, as illustrated in (392) (see Figure 7). BI is avoided in this context because it leads to a stress clash, as in (370) above with the stressed monosyllabic verbs *need* and *worry.* In the unproblematic stress patterns, the *to*-infinitive is preferred in affirmative clauses, whereas BI is more frequent in negative examples.

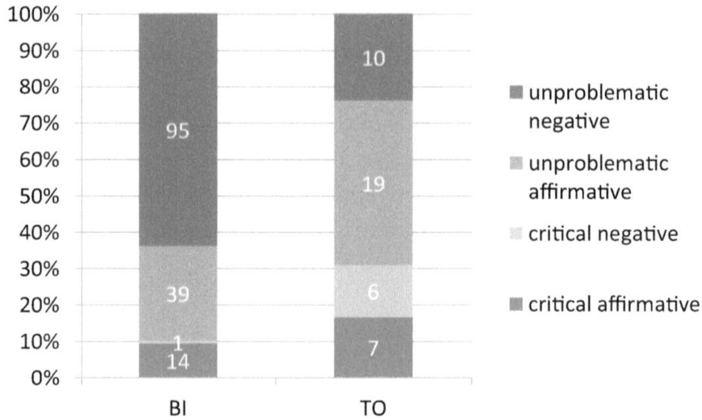

Figure 7: Rhythmic Alternation and polarity affecting *need* plus infinitival complementation in American LModE (raw and n.f./10,000 IP-MATs)

(392) "And do n't forget to invite Joseph Bumble!" Daddy cautioned him." Oh! we *do n't need to ask* him, said Chirpy Cricket. "He'll come without being invited, unless I 'm greatly mistaken." (COHA, fic_1918_3632)

Of the three *STEP 2* factors which cannot be added to *Model 2* (PASSIVISATION, RELATIVE and SUBJECT COMPLEXITY), only RELATIVE is significant. The incidence of *need* plus *to*-infinitive clause is higher in relative clauses ($\chi^2(1)=5.26$, P=0.0086) (see Table 52). In example (393), *need* selects as its arguments the *to*-infinitive clause and the relativiser *who*, whose antecedent is *those*. Finally, neither PASSIVISATION nor SUBJECT COMPLEXITY explains infinitival alternation in a statistically significant way ($\chi^2(1)=2.56$, P=0.068 and $\chi^2(1)=0$, P=0.8231, respectively; see Tables 53 and 54). The construction is more frequent in the active voice and with basic subjects.

	Relative	**Other**
BI	7 (0.84)	142 (17.13)
TO	7 (0.84)	35 (4.22)

Table 52: Relativisation and *need* plus *to*-infinitive/BI clause in American LModE (raw and n.f./10,000 IP-MATs)

(393) The former type is that of those who attain the new level of life by an agony of struggle and sweat and constantly renewed consecration, *who need to retain* the militant attitude toward sin. (COHA, nf_1916_773813)

	Passive	**Active**
BI	24 (2.90)	125 (15.08)
TO	12 (1.45)	30 (3.62)

Table 53: Passivisation and *need* plus *to*-infinitive/BI clause in American LModE (raw and n.f./10,000 IP-MATs)

	Non-basic	**Basic**
BI	16 (1.93)	133 (16.05)
TO	5 (0.60)	37 (4.46)

Table 54: Subject complexity and *need* plus *to*-infinitive/BI clause in American LModE (raw and n.f./10,000 IP-MATs)

In summary, *need* shows the same trends with respect to morphology in both American and British English: the *to*-infinitive is attested with explicit forms and BI with non-explicit ones. Overtly marked third-person present *need* prefers a *to*-infinitive clause, whereas the covert and other non-explicit forms tend to contain BI clauses. Direct *not* negation and inversion are the strategies found with the construction in the British variety, except in one instance of *need* plus BI clause preceded by a modal verb evincing negation. In American English, *do*-support mainly occurs with *need* plus *to*-infinitive. In both varieties, *need* selects BI in the few examples with perfect verbal form in the lower clause and in those with 'fear' lower infinitives. PASSIVISATION is only statistically significant in the British variety whereas relative clauses explain the variation in American English; both factors favour the *to*-infinitive option. SYNTAX can only be modelled statistically in American English, where the *to*-infinitive is more frequent in dependent clauses and BI in main clauses. Factual unrealised meanings are rare in American English (2.63 per cent of the data) and more frequent in the British variety (9.28 per cent of the data), *need* opting for BI complementation in the latter. As for the two other contexts, non-factual unrealised meanings favour *to*-infinitive and factual realised meanings favour BI in both varieties. POLARITY, as predicted by the univariate analysis for British English and *Model 2* for American English, reveals that the *to*-infinitive is found in affirmative clauses and BI is preferred in negative ones. This trend is also confirmed with examples of non-factual unrealised meaning, whereas with factual realised meanings, where *need* prefers BI clauses, polarity is not significant. RHYTHMIC ALTERNATION accounts for the variation in American English, where the *to*-infinitive acts as a stress-clash buffer between two critical syllables (see *Model 2*). This is related to the strategy of negation and inversion: the *to*-infinitive selects an auxiliary and hence it occurs in critical contexts to avoid the stress clash, whereas BI is associated with direct negation or inversion and is thus more frequent in unproblematic contexts. The univariate analysis indicates that RHYTHMIC ALTERNATION is not determining in the British data because BI clauses are the only variant attested in critical contexts.

3.4.3 Model 3: Dare and *need* plus *to*/BI complementation in Present Day English

This section analyses the frequencies of *dare* and *need* plus infinitival complementation and attempts to model the distribution of the construction based on the morphosyntactic, semantic and textual factors present in the American and British English diachronic data. As observed in Section 3.4, *dare* is more frequent with BI clauses in both American and British English (54.55 and 67.74 per cent, respectively; $\chi^2(1)=0.85$, P=0.2418), whereas *need* mainly selects *to*-infinitive complements in both cases (91.42 per cent in American English and 88.4 per cent in British English; $\chi^2(1)=1.46$, P=0.1859; see Tables 134 and Table 135 in Appendix).

As regards MORPHOLOGY, *dare* exhibits explicit forms in approximately 80 per cent of instances in both varieties (P=0.493), whereas *need* shows a similar frequency with explicit and non-explicit forms in both varieties ($\chi^2(1)=1.31$, P=0.2238). The construction with *dare* is more frequent in affirmative clauses in American English (68.18 per cent of the data), and marginally more so in negative clauses in British English (51.61 per cent), though this difference is not statistically significant ($\chi^2(1)=2.06$, P=0.0949). The construction with *need* is mostly restricted to affirmative clauses in American and British English, in significant contrast to *dare*, which is more frequent in negative sentences in both varieties ($\chi^2(1)$=6.82, P=0.0031 and $\chi^2(1)$=56.21, P=<.0001, respectively).

Dare and the infinitive have a statistically similar behaviour in all three levels of SYNTAX in both varieties, main clauses being the most frequent (see Tables 134 and 135 in Appendix).[34] *Need* is also more frequently attested in main clauses, followed by dependent and adverbial clauses, with a practically identical distribution in both varieties.[35] The infinitival argument that *dare* selects in British English are mainly transitive (81.72 per cent), with no occurrences of coordinated subordinate verbs attested. My American English data contain three examples of *dare* governing coordinated lower verbs; the distribution of intransitive and transitive subordinate verbs is very similar, with transitive verbs representing 54.55 per cent of the data. However, variation between transitive and intransitive lower verbs is not statistically significant in American or British English ($\chi^2(1)$=2.22, P=0.0723). No significant differences are attested as regards the distribution of *need* plus infinitive clause in American and British English either: *need* selects transitive lower verbs more frequently (around 75 per cent), whereas intransitive verbs amount to 18–20.3 per cent of the data, coordination being statistically marginal.[36] As regards RHYTHMIC ALTERNATION, the distribution of *dare* plus infinitive clause in unproblematic contexts is higher in American than in British English, but the difference is not statistically significant ($\chi^2(1)$=2.32, P=0.0783). *Need* is also more frequent in unproblematic than in critical stress patterns ($\chi^2(1)$=0.05, P=0.7518). No PASSIVE or PERFECT constructions are attested with *dare* in my data set; the distribution of *need*, on the other hand, is higher than 15 per

34 The results of Fisher's Exact test and chi-square test are as follows: Adverbial vs dependent, P=0.089; dependent vs main, $\chi^2(1)$=1.31, P=0.1542; main vs adverbial, P=0.3409.

35 Differences are not statistically significant at any of the levels of the predictor SYNTAX: Adverbial vs dependent, $\chi^2(1)$=0.04, P=0.729; adverbial vs main, $\chi^2(1)$=0.05, P=0.7083; main vs dependent, $\chi^2(1)$=0.01, P=1.

36 The results of the chi-square tests for the predictor VALENCY are: Intransitive vs transitive, $\chi^2(1)$=0.12, P=0.6547; intransitive vs coordination, $\chi^2(1)$=2.67, P=0.0689; transitive vs coordination, $\chi^2(1)$=2.46, P=0.0817.

cent in passive sentences in both varieties ($\chi^2(1)=0.2$, P=0.5839), and accounts for only 1.1 per cent of the data with perfect verbal forms in British English. *Dare* occurs significantly more frequently with relative clauses in American English (31.82 per cent; $\chi^2(1)=5.55$, P=0.007), whereas the distribution of *need* in this syntactic context is similar in both varieties (10–10.9 per cent of the data; $\chi^2(1)=0.02$, P=0.7913). In terms of SUBJECT COMPLEXITY, both *dare* and *need* prefer basic subjects in both varieties (P=0.3688 and $\chi^2(1)=0$, P=0.8625, respectively). Non-basic subjects account for no more than 15.05 per cent of the data with *dare* and 10.3 per cent with *need*.

Differences with respect to SUBJECT ANIMACY are significant: *dare* only co-occurs with animate subjects in American English, whereas non-animate subjects, though not very frequent, are attested in 5.38 per cent of the data in British English. *Need* also prefers animate subjects in both varieties of English ($\chi^2(1)=0.35$, P=0.4976). The difference between *need* and *dare* is evident in the American data and very significant with respect to the British data ($\chi^2(1)=17.1$, P=<.0001). The quantiles of DISTANCE are 0 for *dare* and 0.5 for *need* in both varieties. This shows that infinitive clauses are directly attached to *dare* and *need* in most of the examples in my data; for this reason, DISTANCE is not included in *Model 3* for PDE. The distribution of *dare* plus infinitive clause is affected by the semantic/pragmatic context in both varieties of English. In American English, the construction is more frequent when it conveys factual realised meanings, and in non-factual unrealised contexts in British English ($\chi^2(1)=7.85$, P=0.002). The distribution of *dare* in factual unrealised contexts is not higher than 22.73 per cent in either variety. The incidence of *need* with non-factual unrealised meanings is higher than that of *dare* when compared with factual realised plus factual unrealised meanings ($\chi^2(1)=47.73$, P=<.0001 for American English and $\chi^2(1)=84.74$, P=<.0001 for British English). In both varieties, *need* is mainly restricted to non-factual unrealised contexts, with a distribution of less than 7.4 per cent in factual realised and factual unrealised contexts.[37]

37 The variation of *need* in relation to semantic/pragmatic context is not significantly different in either American or British English: Factual realised vs factual unrealised, $\chi^2=0.29$, P=0.4424; factual realised vs non-factual unrealised, $\chi^2=0.52$, P=0.3833; non-factual realised vs factual unrealised, $\chi^2=2.07$, P=0.0991.

3.4.3.1 Dare *in Present Day English*

Dare-governed infinitival alternation has been in decline since the EModE period, reaching its lowest incidence in PDE, with 2.8 words per 10,000 s-units in my British English data and 5.8 words per 10,000 IP-MATs in American English. The occurrence of *dare* in American English in only 11 examples with BI clauses and in 10 with *to*-infinitive complements justifies the univariate descriptive approach used for this regional variety. Although the number of occurrences in the British data is also low, the frequency (30 occurrences) of the less frequent variant, i.e. *to*-infinitive complementation, allows for a multifactorial analysis with three levels. The analysis in this section consists of three parts: an examination of the British English data for *dare* and the factors that cannot be included in a multifactorial analysis using univariate analyses whenever possible, a summary of the results obtained from *Model 3* for *dare* in British PDE, and the comparison of the strongest predictors of the American data with those explaining the British data set.

The results for the distribution of the factor MORPHOLOGY in British PDE contrasts with those revealed by the diachronic data: both complementation options are more frequent with explicit morphology, as in example (394), with the non-finite base form *dare* and a BI clause, and in (395), with the *–ing* form *daring* and *to*-infinitive complementation (see Table 55). However, the distribution of *dare* plus BI with non-explicit morphology is higher than that of *dare* with *to*-infinitive clauses. Example (396) is the only instance of *dare* with non-explicit morphology and *to*-infinitive complementation.

	Explicit					Non-explicit	
	Dares	**Finite *dared* (simple past)**	**Non-finite *Dare***	***Daring***	**Non-finite *dared***	**S/he/it *dare***	**Other**
BI	0	14	26	0	5	5	13
TO	3	7	7	8	4	0	1

Table 55: Morphology and paradigm forms of *dare* plus *to*-infinitive/BI clause in British PDE (raw data)

(394) This desire that cannot find its name (though *it would dare speak it*, if it could) is pleasurable. (BNC Baby, A3C)

(395) It also has rather unfortunate connotations of self-styled guerrilla activists prowling the Dales ready to plunge daggers into the tyres of quarry wagons at night or to fire catapults at drivers *daring enough to run* their gauntlet during daylight hours. (BNC Baby, K4Y)

(396) The only two Hong Kong *legislators who* consistently *dare to speak out*, Mr Martin Lee and Mr Szeto Wah, have been threatened with expulsion from the committee now drafting China's post-1997 Basic Law. (BNC Baby, A7W)

Even though the third-person singular simple present form is quite infrequent in PDE, it explains the choice of complementation options: the explicit form of *dare* is only found with the *to*-infinitive complements, as in (397), and the non-explicit form is only attested with BI clauses, in (398) (see Table 55). Two (out of five) occurrences with BI clauses have the cliticised form *n't*, as in (399), which leads to the classification of these forms as non-explicit.

(397) "You are brave, Master Clerk," she murmured. "No one else *dares to speak* to the Lady Prioress like that". (BNC Baby, h9c)

(398) Alan: Oh that's <pause> get his permission for nothing! Barry: Well he won't know <pause> I don't <pause> I don't think <-|-> *he dare show* <-|-> Hugh: <-|->At the moment. Barry: his face at moment, he hadn't been anywhere round to, since all this <-|-> happened before Christmas. (BNC Baby, KBD)

(399) "All right," Lorton said irritably. "And he'll think I'm the most likely person. But he can't prove it. He *daren't* even try." (BNC Baby, GUU)

The simple past form *dared* selects both BI, as in (400), and *to*-infinitive complements with the same distribution ($\chi^2(1)=0.15$, P=0.5169). As regards non-finite forms, the distribution of *–ed* past participle is similar with both types of complements (P=0.499), as in (401) with the *to*-infinitive clause and in (402) with the BI. However, when *dare* exhibits a non-finite base form, it significantly prefers BI, as in (394) above ($\chi^2(1)=6.77$, P=0.0045).[38] Finally, the non-finite *–ing* form is only attested with a *to*-infinitive clause, as in (403).

38 These results are obtained by comparing explicit vs the addition of the other explicit forms.

(400) No supporter of the Latics *dared dream* it, but suddenly the improbable was a throbbing, joyous reality. (BNC Baby, A8N)

(401) She *had dared to step* inside Mr Brady's photographic establishment to view the wonderful daguerreotypes and portraits he had taken. (BNC Baby, CB5)

(402) You know? I *hadn't even dared go* near Furnival Gardens since I saw my old man for the second rime. (BNC Baby, HR9)

(403) He stood still, *not daring to move*, unable to break away. (BNC Baby, G0L)

Do-support is almost categorically found with BI, as in (404), with only one instance containing a *to*-infinitive complement (405) (see Table 56). In 7 (out of 11) examples with a BI clause, *do*-support occurs in imperative clauses and takes the negative particle, as in (406). The number of examples with direct *not* or inversion is higher with BI but is not statistically significant if compared to examples of *do*-support plus auxiliaries (P=0.322). The form *daring* is preceded by negative particles in 3 (out of 4) examples with the *to*-infinitive and direct negation, as in (407); the fourth example is part of a negative coordination (408).

	***Do*-support**	***Not*/Inversion**	**Auxiliaries**
BI	11 (0.33)	21 (0.63)	10 (0.3)
TO	1 (0.03)	4 (0.12)	6 (0.18)

Table 56: Negation/inversion and *dare* plus *to*-infinitive/BI clause in British PDE (raw and n.f./10,000 <-s> units)

(404) You have quite a catch there, little sister. She *did not dare look at* them for too long for fear of missing her footing or forgetting a move but the look on Edward's face added another notch to her enjoyment. (BNC Baby, BMW)

(405) She did not count this as a master and servant situation, yet she *didn't dare to presume* too far. (BNC Baby, CB5)

(406) "If Mum finds out I've been smoking she'll kill me. *Don't you dare tell* her either, Sally, or I'llkill you!" (BNC Baby, BMW)

(407) Ranulf and Maltote objected vociferously. "Why this?" Ranulf shouted. Maltote looked away, *not daring to confront* this dour but very important royal clerk. (BNC Baby, H9C)

(408) They neither cared *nor dared explicitly to challenge* this picture, as the pro-imperialists among the Germans had done. (BNC Baby, EA7)

Relative, which accounts for 9.68 per cent of the data, does not explain the distribution of *dare* plus infinitival complementation in my British PDE data (P=0.317) (see Table 57).

	Relative	**Other**
BI	5 (0.15)	58 (1.74)
TO	4 (0.12)	26 (0.78)

Table 57: Relativisation and *dare* plus *to*-infinitive/BI clause in British PDE (raw and n.f./10,000 <-s> units)

With respect to subject animacy (P=0.479; Table 58), *dare* plus *to*-infinitive is basically restricted to animate subjects, with only one example of a non-animate subject attested in my data (409), in which non-animate *it* refers to *the Commission's view*. Of the BI examples, 4 instances (out of 5) with non-animate subjects have BI clauses.

	Animate	**Non animate**
BI	59 (1.77)	4 (0.12)
TO	29 (0.87)	1 (0.03)

Table 58: Animacy and *dare* plus *to*-infinitive/BI clause in British PDE (raw and n.f./10,000 <-s> units)

(409) Focusing on economic decline, physical decay, and social disintegration as distinctive features of contemporary urban poverty, the report stressed *the Commission's view* – quite different from that of the Government, the Audit Commission, or even the CBI – that "the inner city and the peripheral estates are creatures of the whole society, not simply of their inhabitants". *It dared to question* the assumption that the creation of wealth, at whatever social cost, was necessarily the first priority of an economic system. (BNC Baby, AS6)

Only three factors can be included in the multifactorial analysis of *Model 3* because of the low number of instances of *dare* plus *to*-infinitive clause (30 occurrences). The predictors selected for *Model 3* are SYNTAX, POLARITY and NOTIONAL CHARACTERISATION because the diachronic analysis (see Sections 3.4.1.1 and 3.4.2.1) specifically evinces their relevance and also because they were found to explain the variation in the *need* data set. Before undertaking the multifactorial analysis, let us first look at results of the univariate study of the factors not included in *Model 3*: SUBJECT COMPLEXITY, RHYTHMIC ALTERNATION and VALENCY. SUBJECT COMPLEXITY has a significant determining effect on distribution ($\chi^2(1)=6.11$, P=0.0054): *to*-infinitive is more frequent with 'non-basic' subjects (see Table 59); unexpressed subjects account for 7 (out of 9) examples with the *to*-infinitive complementation choice and in all these instances *dare* exhibits the *–ing* form, as in (407) above; the subject is complex in the other two instances, as in (410), with the genitive construction *of Lincoln* postmodifying the NP *St Hugh*; and finally, the 5 examples with *dare* plus BI clause have 'complex non-basic' subjects.

	Non-basic	Basic
BI	5 (0.15)	58 (1.74)
TO	9 (0.27)	21 (0.63)

Table 59: Subject complexity and *dare* plus *to*-infinitive/BI clause in British PDE (raw and n.f./10,000 <-s> units)

(410) As late as the 1180s, *St Hugh of Lincoln dared to tease* Henry II of England about the tanner's blood in his veins. (BNC Baby, EA7)

The univariate analysis of RHYTHMIC ALTERNATION indicates that *dare* is found in critical and unproblematic contexts ($\chi^2(1)=0.02$, P=0.7184; see Table 60). The construction does not reflect significant differences in use with respect to the valencies intransitive and transitive ($\chi^2(1)=1.34$, P=0.1483), and is not attested with coordinated lower infinitive clauses with either type of infinitival complementation (see Table 61).

	Critical	Unproblematic
BI	34 (1.02)	29 (0.87)
TO	15 (0.45)	15 (0.45)

Table 60: Rhythmic Alternation and *dare* plus *to*-infinitive/BI clause in British PDE (raw and n.f./10,000 <-s> units)

	Intransitive	Transitive
BI	9 (0.27)	54 (1.62)
TO	8 (0.24)	22 (0.66)

Table 61: Valency and *dare* plus *to*-infinitive/BI clause in British PDE (raw and n.f./10,000 <-s> units)

The results of the multifactorial analysis for *dare* in British PDE with the predictors SYNTAX, POLARITY and NOTIONAL CHARACTERISATION indicate that POLARITY is not a significant factor. In fact, POLARITY does not improve *Model 3* or even point towards a tendency, as reflected in the step "backward" reduction (see Table 62).

Predictor	Estimate	P-value	OR
Intercept	1.4229	0.03699*	4.14931
Syntax	-0.9288	0.21517	1/0.3950411=2.5313
(ref.: *Adverbial*)	-1.6290	0.00776**	1/0.1961229=5.0988
Dependent			
Main			
Notional characterisation	-0.5905	0.40034	1/0.5540268=1.8049
(ref.: *Factual Realised*)	-1.6810	0.00532**	1/0.1861836=5.3710
Factual Unrealised			
Non-Factual Unrealised			

Table 62: *Model 3*, *STEP 1*, significant factors with *dare* and *to*-infinitive/BI clause in British PDE (step "backward" results)

If we consider POLARITY and RHYTHMIC ALTERNATION together, the distribution of the *to*-infinitive/BI is not shown to be statistically significant in either affirmative or negative critical contexts ($\chi^2(1)=0.15$,

P=0.4795; see Figure 8). The strategies for conveying negation with *dare* plus BI in negative critical contexts are cliticisation with *n't*, as in (411), and the use of auxiliary verbs, as in (412), which leads to stress clashes between *daren't* and *buy* in (411) and between *dare* and *pull* in (412). In contrast, the *to*-infinitive option is significantly more frequent in affirmative unproblematic stressed contexts versus negative unproblematic ones ($\chi^2(1)=4.05$, P=0.0191).[39] The results indicate, therefore, that RHYTHMIC ALTERNATION does not have an effect on the construction either on its own or in combination with POLARITY.

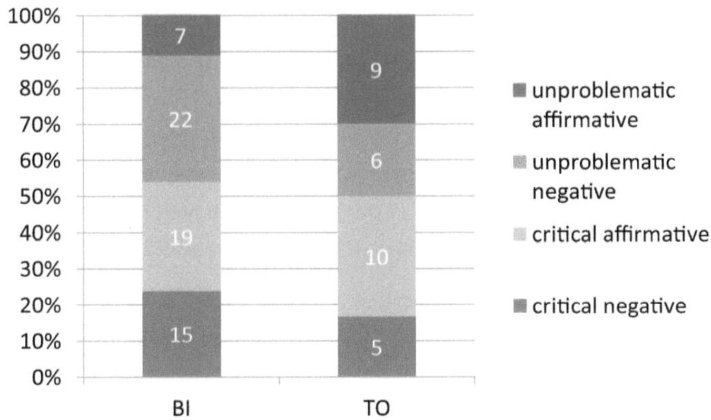

Figure 8: Rhythmic Alternation and Polarity affecting *dare* plus *to*-infinitive/BI clause in British PDE (raw data)

(411) Shelly: Oh yeah! One sixty <unclear>. Gary: <unclear>. Julie: Nine. One, two, three, four, five, six, seven, eight, nine. Shelly: Ain't it gone quiet! Gary: *She daren't buy it you see*! Julie: Right. Phil: I've had no money yet! (BNC Baby, KCU)

(412) The gun's threat had not stopped my advance. I was calling Sweetman's bluff, confident he *would not dare pull* the trigger, and equally confident

39 The chi-square test indicates that the following variations are not significant: Negative critical vs negative unproblematic ($\chi^2(1)=0$, P=0.7773), affirmative critical vs affirmative unproblematic ($\chi^2(1)=1.21$, P=0.1573), negative critical vs affirmative unproblematic ($\chi^2(1)=2.46$, P=0.0561) and affirmative critical vs negative unproblematic ($\chi^2(1)=0.64$, P=0.2733).

that my marine training would let me turn him into mincemeat. (BNC Baby, CCW)

Model 3 reveals that SYNTAX has a significant effect on the alternation between *to*-infinitive/BI clauses. The chances of BI complementation significantly increase by 5.09 percentage points when the construction is in a main clause, as in (413), in comparison with adverbial clauses (Pr(>|z|)=0.00776). *To*-infinitive complementation is more frequently found in adverbial clauses and, as indicated in the diachronic data, co-occurs especially with the form *daring*, which introduces suppletive constructions in 7 (out of 11) examples, as in (407) above and (414) below (see Bouzada-Jabois and Pérez-Guerra 2016). The difference is not significant in comparisons between adverbial and dependent clauses and main and dependent (Pr(>|z|)=0.21517 and Pr(>|z|)=0.27692, respectively). Infinitive complements may, therefore, be found in both dependent clauses with *to*-infinitive clauses, as in (415) and with BI clauses, as in (416) (see also Table 63). The *dare*-construction is part of the relative clause introduced by *who* in (415), and is part of the adverbial phrase headed by *more* in (416).

(413) "But who *would dare approach* the aloof Lady Eleanor? The Lady Prioress was in church, the other nuns preparing for Compline, and it was only a short walk. (BNC Baby, H9C)

(414) Corbett blushed and, tongue-tied, went back to eating, *not daring to raise* his head until he heard Dame Agatha's soft footfalls and the chamber door close behind her. (BNC Baby, H9C)

(415) The only two Hong Kong legislators *who consistently dare to speak out*, Mr Martin Lee and Mr Szeto Wah, have been threatened with expulsion from the committee now drafting China's post-1997 Basic Law. (BNC Baby, A7W)

(416) Shakily, Martin Grant raised the flare gun and fired. Two assault boats were *more than Delaney had dared hope for*. (BNC Baby, BPA)

	Adverbial	Dependent	Main
BI	7 (0.21)	12 (0.36)	44 (1.32)
TO	11 (0.33)	6 (0.18)	13 (0.39)

Table 63: Syntactic dependency and *dare* plus *to*-infinitive/BI clause in British PDE (raw and n.f./10,000 <-s> units)

NOTIONAL CHARACTERISATION is also significant as regards the distribution of the levels of the response variable (see Table 62). *Dare* plus *to*-infinitive complementation decreases significantly in non-factual unrealised meanings (5.37 percentage points) in comparison to factual realised contexts (Pr(>|z|)=0.00532). The difference between the variants is not significant when factual realised and factual unrealised meanings are compared (Pr(>|z|)=0.40034). *Model 3* indicates that *dare* tends to select the *to*-infinitive complement when the construction occurs in factual unrealised (417) vs non-factual unrealised contexts, but this difference is not statistically significant (Pr(>|z|)=0.07950). BI is therefore more frequent in non-factual unrealised contexts, as in (418), whereas the *to*-infinitive alternative is preferred in contexts expressing factual realised meanings, as in (419), and is slightly favoured in factual unrealised contexts, as in (417) (see Table 64). Note that (418) is not factual and it is uncertain whether *they all* carry out the act of dreaming; the proposition in (419) is factual and the predicate governed by *to observe* has been performed.

	Factual realised	**Factual unrealised**	**Non-factual unrealised**
BI	8 (0.24)	11 (0.33)	44 (1.32)
TO	11 (0.33)	8 (0.24)	11 (0.33)

Table 64: Notional characterisation of *dare* plus *to*-infinitive/BI clause in British PDE (raw and n.f./10,000 <-s> units)

(417) At the Mas Rose she hoped every day to see them riding down the white stony hillside track. Frederica *had wanted*, but *not dared, to ask* Alexander how his writing was going. It was not going well. (BNC Baby, FET)

(418) He was his own real self again, the own real self they all were. Those hypocrite clergymen, leader writers, Members of Parliament, East End missionaries. Stuffed shirts and waxen women. He was the fellow they *all hardly dared Dream* they were. He exulted in the communion of blood and water. (BNC Baby, GVL)

(419) He confronted the evidence on inner cities and, being a black social democratic scholar, *dared to observe* the clustering in 'ghetto' neighbourhoods of 'socially isolated' blacks and Hispanics. (BNC Baby, AS6)

As part of the descriptive and univariate descriptive analysis of the American PDE data, I first consider the factor MORPHOLOGY. *To*-infinitive complements are not found with non-explicit forms of *dare*, and BI clauses are only attested in two instances, both with third-person *dare* forms that show covert subject-verb agreement, as illustrated in (420) (see Table 65). *To*-infinitive complementation is attested in 2 (out of the 5) examples with third-person singular present forms, as in (421). The distribution of the explicit non-finite form *dare* and the simple past form *dared* is similar (P=0.563) when these two contexts are compared.

	Explicit			Non-explicit
	Dares	**Finite *dared* (simple past)**	**Non-finite *dare***	**S/he/it *dare***
BI	1	6	3	2
TO	2	6	2	0

Table 65: Morphology and paradigm forms of *dare* plus *to*-infinitive/BI clause in American PDE (raw and n.f./10,000 IP-MATs)

(420) Her pulse raced. She knew it was St. August without looking in the mirror. *How dare he risk* both their lives like this? (COHA, fic_1996_54389)

(421) It is the shaman in me *that dares to look into* the eyes of the deer, to listen to the raven's cry, and to dance toward my Wolf in order to take the journey toward healing the pain found in my ancestral line. (COHA, fic_1999_45341)

As shown in the diachronic and the synchronic data, *dare* plus BI is specifically associated with strategies of direct negation and inversion, as in (420) above. In contrast, neither of these strategies is attested with *to*-infinitive clauses (see Table 66). The *to*-infinitive type is found in two negative clauses, where negation is manifested in the auxiliaries: through *do*-support in (422) and the modal verb *could* in (423).

	Do-support	*Not*/Inversion	Auxiliaries
BI	2 (0.55)	6 (1.65)	2 (0.55)
TO	1 (0.27)	0	1 (0.27)

Table 66: Negation/inversion and *dare* plus *to*-infinitive/BI clause in American PDE (raw and n.f./10,000 IP-MATs)

(422) I know so many gifted writers who do n't publish a word; singers who do n't sing; born preachers who never claim their vocation; couples with a genius for children *who don't dare to have* them. (COHA, news_1995_631311)

(423) And he would speak so kindly that it was difficult for me to contradict; he stated his beliefs so humbly *that I could not dare to refute.* (COHA, fic_1998_44210)

POLARITY is not a significant factor in the distribution of the variants (P=0.2678). *Dare* plus infinitive complementation is simply more frequent in affirmative sentences (see Table 67). The factor RHYTHMIC ALTERNATION does not have a bearing on the construction, as reflected by the few examples of American PDE (P=0.616): the construction is attested in 15 (out of 22) examples in unproblematic contexts (see Table 68). As regards negation/inversion, the use of an auxiliary in these contexts creates a critical stress pattern in 3 (out of the 4) examples when *dare* is followed by an initially stressed syllable and the complement is a BI clause, as in (424).

	Negative	Affirmative
BI	7 (1.92)	5 (1.37)
TO	8 (2.19)	2 (0.55)

Table 67: Polarity and *dare* plus *to*-infinitive/BI clause in American PDE (raw and n.f./10,000 IP-MATs)

	Critical	Unproblematic
BI	4 (1.10)	8 (2.19)
TO	3 (0.82)	7 (1.92)

Table 68: Rhythmic Alternation and *dare* plus *to*-infinitive/BI clause in American PDE (raw and n.f./10,000 IP-MATs)

(424) But does a mere serpent have reflections and intentions? *Can one dare speak of the mind of a snake*? (COHA, nf_1997_776923)

SYNTAX is shown to be significant in American PDE, as it was in the data for British PDE (see Figure 9). *To*-infinitive is preferred in dependent clauses, as in (422) and (423) above, whereas BI is more frequent in main clauses, as in (424).

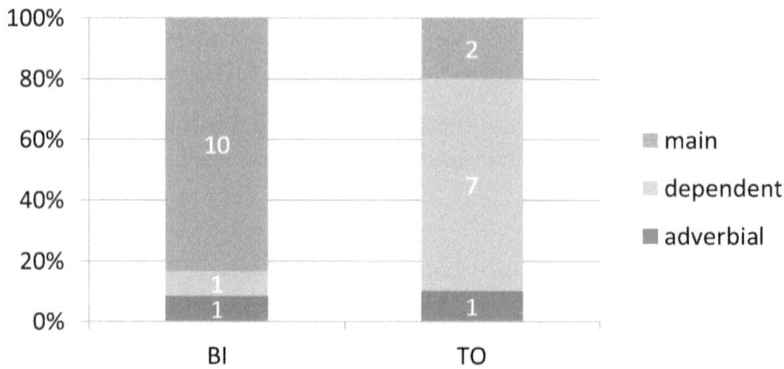

Figure 9: Syntactic dependency and *dare* plus *to*-infinitive/BI clause in American PDE (raw data)

In contrast to the synchronic British data, the semantic/pragmatic status of the American English examples does not indicate any difference in the distribution of the two infinitival complementation options.[40] *Dare* plus *to*-infinitive/BI is more frequent with factual realised meanings, as in (425) (see Table 69).

	Factual realised	Factual unrealised	Non-factual unrealised
BI	5 (1.37)	4 (1.1)	3 (0.82)
TO	6 (1.65)	1 (0.27)	3 (0.82)

Table 69: Notional characterisation of *dare* plus *to*-infinitive/BI clause in American PDE (raw and n.f./10,000 IP-MATs)

40 Fisher's Exact test reveals no significant differences for any of the levels of the NOTIONAL CHARACTERISATION predictor: Factual realised vs non-factual unrealised, P=0.6266; factual realised vs factual unrealised, P=0.2307; factual unrealised vs non-factual unrealised, P=0.3484.

(425) Even female singers, traditionally dainty types, got the message. Does n't Alanis Morissette sound as if she's performing at riflepoint in a gulag? *Nanci Griffith, prom princess of the country-folk school, dares to suggest* that life is something we can get through -- and get through more easily with a rousing or sweet-souled tune. (COHA, mag_1997_356703)

The analysis of the data shows that the BI clause is still the most frequent complement type in both varieties of English in PDE. The data show that infinitival complementation is favoured with explicit morphological forms in both varieties (approximately 80 per cent of the data), which are particularly associated with the *to*-infinitive alternative; in contrast, BI is often found with non-explicit forms. In British English, the distribution is similar with simple past and past participles but the forms *dares* and *daring* attract *to*-infinitive clauses whereas the covert form *dare* for third-person present is only found with BI clauses in my data. BI is also significantly favoured with other non-explicit and non-finite explicit *dare* forms. The American English data show the same distribution of simple past *dared* and non-finite explicit *dare* with both complementation options, whereas third-person present forms behave as in British English.

Regarding negation and inversion, both complementation types are attested in the British English variety in contexts of *do*-support, other auxiliaries and direct negation and/or inversion. However, *do*-support is more frequent with BI, with only one instance of a *to*-infinitive clause attested in this variety. In my American English data set, the *to*-infinitive is not attested with direct negation and/or inversion, but the BI clause is found with all of the strategies mentioned.

The results for POLARITY are not statistically significant in either the multifactorial analysis of *Model 3* for British English or the univariate analysis applied to the American data. The construction is found in affirmative sentences in a higher distribution in American English, but this difference is not significant with respect to the British English data, which show similar percentages in affirmative and negative sentences. The univariate analysis of RHYTHMIC ALTERNATION is not significant either. Since *to*-infinitive and BI clauses are both found with critical stress patterns, the Principle of Rhythmic Alternation cannot affect alternation in either variety. The predominance of *do*-support and auxiliaries with *to*-infinitive clauses in critical negative contexts is no longer observed in the PDE data.

Infinitival complementation is shown to be more frequent in main clauses. *Model 3* for British English shows that the odds of the BI clause are higher in main clauses and that the odds of the *to*-infinitive are higher in adverbial clauses, with dependent clauses showing a similar distribution for both variants. The univariate analysis of the American data indicates that BI is still significantly more frequent in main clauses, the *to*-infinitive is preferred in dependent ones, and only one adverbial clause is attested with each complementation type.

Dare plus *to*-infinitive/BI occurs significantly more frequently with factual realised semantic/pragmatic meanings in American English, and in non-factual unrealised contexts in the British variety. The predictor NOTIONAL CHARACTERISATION does not affect the distribution of the infinitival variants in American English. In contrast, *Model 3* reveals that factual realised contexts significantly favour *to*-infinitive complementation and that *dare* tends to select this complementation option in factual unrealised meanings, with BI clauses preferred in non-factual unrealised contexts.

Regarding ANIMACY, the construction always co-occurs with animate subjects in American English, and with both animate and non-animate subjects in the British variety, with no significant differences as regards complementation preference. Finally, the factors VALENCY, RELATIVE and SUBJECT COMPLEXITY are not shown to have a significant effect on infinitival alternation. Transitive lower verbs with basic subjects seem to be preferred, while non-basic subjects behave differently with both types of infinitival complement: as in the diachronic data, *to*-infinitive is more frequent with unexpressed subjects and BI is more productive with complex subjects. The instances of *to*-infinitive clauses with unexpressed subjects correspond to adverbial clauses with *–ing* forms.

3.4.3.2 Need *in Present Day English*

The British data are analysed first in the case of *need* plus infinitival complementation to provide a point of reference from which to select the predictors to be analysed in *Model 3* for American English. The American database contains only 20 examples with *need* plus BI clause, which allows for only two predictors in the multivariate analysis. Following the methodology used in the previous sections, I first focus on the predictors that reflect a categorical or semi-categorical distribution and then perform a multivariate analysis of the British PDE data.

The distribution of infinitival complementation options is clear with respect to MORPHOLOGY ($P=2.333e^{-27}$; see Table 70). *To*-infinitive clauses are found in half of the examples with explicit morphology, as in (426), with *need* showing–*s* inflection for third-person singular present tense, and in the other half with non-explicit forms, as in (427), with *need* showing the third-person plural present form. BI clauses are mainly attested with non-explicit forms of *need*, as in (428), with explicit forms occurring in only 4 examples, as in (429).

	Explicit					Non-explicit	
	Needs	**Finite *needed* (simple past)**	**Non-finite *need***	***Needing***	**Non-finite *needed***	**S/he/it *need***	**Other**
BI	1	2	1	0	0	59	53
TO	152	95	191	5	11	2	428

Table 70: Morphology and paradigm forms of *need* plus *to*-infinitive/BI clause in British PDE (raw data)

(426) *Virginia creeper needs to be clipped back* from windows and hauled out of gutters. (BNC Baby, A3E)

(427) These are concerns shared by substantial numbers of feminists. However, it is clear from these three papers that *the Continental traditions themselves need to be subjected to* feminist scrutiny. (BNC Baby, ECV)

(428) Terence: Now, you can give the answer in this form <pause> *you needn't write it out* in full. (BNC Baby, KE2)

(429) Suppose X is talking to Y, standing on the blue border of the carpet in X's office, in a given street, in Manchester, in England, in Britain, in Western Europe... Y might produce any of the following utterances: (21) a. There's another worn section *which needs repair* here. b. You've got a very nice room here. c. It's a really nasty day here. d. You have a comparatively mild climate here. (BNC Baby, F9V)

The distribution of the other non-explicit forms is quite similar with both types of complementation ($\chi2(1)=0.21$, $P=0.5777$) with respect to explicit plus non-explicit forms. In contrast, overt vs covert agreement in the third-person singular simple present tense seems to accord with the selection of either *to*-infinitive or BI. Example (429) above is the only instance with BI co-occurring with explicitly inflected third-person singular present *needs*. *Need* exhibits covert subject agreement in the remaining 59 examples with BI. Likewise, the *to*-infinitive alternative is associated with *–s* inflection, as in (426), except for two instances, as in example (430). It should be noted that the absence of*–s* inflection may be a performance error since example (430) belongs to an oral-speech text.

(430) None: I wo-- oh, I mean I <pause>with Chris <unclear> <pause>if I tell her where to go <pause>I mean
Ann: Think *she need to hit* the bloody ball <-|->at first!
None: <-|->She said <-|->I'll go one then and she will go and er give us a shout, because<unclear>
Ann: Could I? <pause>Gotta a hit the ball! <laugh> (BNC Baby, KB7)

Simple past *–ed* inflection is mainly attested with *to*-infinitive complements, as in (431). Only two instances of simple past *need* are found with BI clauses, as in (432). The *–ed* past participle form is registered only with *to*-infinitive clauses, as in (433)–(435). The past participle *–ed* form is only attested in perfect constructions in my diachronic database, whereas in PDE it is also registered in passive constructions (434) and non-finite modifiers (435).

(431) John McLeish was in his office, Saturday or no Saturday, telling himself *he needed to catch up* on the paperwork. (BNC Baby, AB9)

(432) And though some knights might be supplied free by feudal service, household ones had to be maintained by their lords, *mercenary ones needed pay*, and those with money-fiefs constituted a regular charge on the treasury. (BNC Baby, EA7)

(433) Heading west on the return flight path, the instructor said, 'This is the first time I've flown with a pupil and *haven't once needed to touch* the controls.' (BNC Baby, FPB)

(434) Although probably unlucky not to salvage a draw, Alton need to find more flair if *they are needed to finish* in the upper half of the table. (BNC Baby, BM4)

(435) *The details of amendments to the Bill needed to press* these points were sent to each Unionist MP, from Central Office not from the official Whips, and a special committee of agents and National Union leaders was set up to give MPs professional advice. (BNC Baby, EW1)

Non-finite forms co-occur mainly with *to*-infinitive complements, as in (435) above with an *–ed* form, in (436) with an *–ing* form and (437) with a base non-finite form. My data contain only one example, in (438), of the *to*-infinitive co-occurring with the non-finite base form *need* plus BI complementation. In this example from oral-speech, the speaker uses *might needn't* as a concatenation of modal verbs in which the second verb takes the clitic *n't* (see Nagle 2003).[41] As illustrated in Figure 10, non-finite forms are not frequent with either type of complement, with the exception of the non-finite base form, which accounts for 21.6 per cent of the *to*-infinitive data.

(436) *Needing to borrow* £50,000 million this year, Mr Lamont had to promise his creditors that he would put his accounts in order as soon as possible. (BNC Baby, E9S)

(437) How many roadside interview sheets do you think *we're going to need to order*? (BNC Baby, KD8)

(438) Richard: [. . .] as what Helen does so Helen says that they're gonna sort of go to the different colleges and compare notes when they come back from it so she *might needn't want to go* to Leicester
Margaret: Mm
Richard: erm, so I just, I just don't know, erm, so we just
Group of unknown speakers: <-|-> <unclear> <-|->
Margaret: <-|->Daniel <-|-> was saying hasn't she heard from any of her (BNC Baby, KE2)

41 Nagle (2003) studies double modals in southern United States. These constructions are typically a combination of the core modals *may*, *might* and *must* + (*not*) followed by *can*, *could*, *should*, *will*, *would*, *did* or *had* + (*not*). He concludes that "[i]t may be that for some speakers there are lexicalized pairs of double modals such as *might could* or an adverbialized *might*".

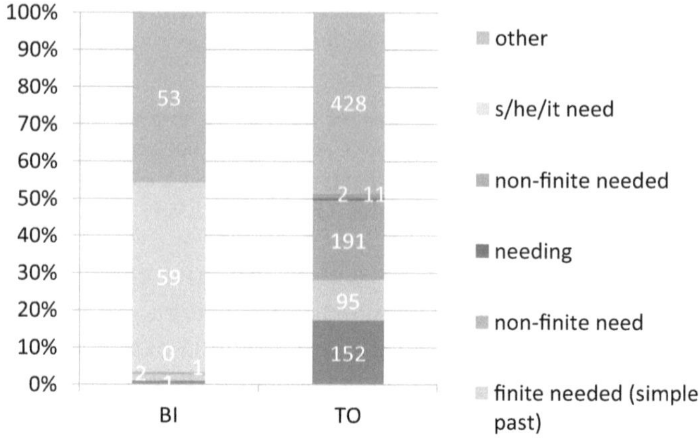

Figure 10: Paradigm forms of *need* plus *to*-infinitive/BI clause in British PDE (raw data)

The strategy used by *need* in negative and subject-inversion clauses has a determining effect on the distribution of *to*-infinitive/BI complementation (see Table 71). *Do*-support and other auxiliary verbs are only attested with *to*-infinitive clauses, except in example (438), as described above. The use of *do*-support with emphatic polarity is attested for the first time in my PDE data, occurring in 5 (out of 118) instances, as in (439) (see Huddleston and Pullum 2002: 97–98). BI complementation is only observed in contexts of subject inversion (440) and direct negation. Only one instance of *need* plus *to*-infinitive shows direct negation, *never* being the negative particle which precedes *need* (441).

	***Do*-support**	***Not*/Inversion**	**Auxiliaries**
BI	0	82 (2.46)	1 (0.03)
TO	118 (3.54)	1 (0.03)	17 (0.51)

Table 71: Negation/inversion and *need* plus *to*-infinitive/BI clause in British PDE (raw and n.f./10,000 <-s> units)

(439) He considered his notes; what he needed from this interview was to confirm that Angela Morgan had not been in the office on Saturday, and a statement of Peter Yeo's movements over the period within which Angela

Morgan had probably been killed. He also *did need to understand* the financial side. (BNC Baby, Ab9)

(440) Would Dick, even if she wished it, still want to marry her? And what about Grandfather? *Need she tell* Grandfather the truth – it would break his heart. (BNC Baby, CB5)

(441) He was so much a part of her that she *never needed* nor wanted *to examine* too closely the nature of her feeling for him. (BNC Baby, C8T)

As regards VALENCY, the distribution of the infinitive clauses is quite similar with all three types of subordinate verbs.[42] Transitive lower verbs are the most frequent, accounting for approximately 76 per cent of the data with both types of complementation, as in (439) and (441) above (see Table 72). Intransitive constructions have infinitival clauses in only 21.55 per cent of the examples, as in (442), while coordination, illustrated in (443) with *to*-infinitive, is very infrequent in my data.

	Coordination	**Intransitive**	**Transitive**
BI	2 (0.06)	25 (0.75)	89 (2.67)
TO	39 (1.17)	178 (5.34)	667 (20.03)

Table 72: Valency and *need* plus *to*-infinitive/BI clause in British PDE (raw and n.f./ 10,000 <-s> units)

(442) We sometimes get the feeling that not all the bodies that come down to us need *have done*. 'You think so? 'Sure of it. 'It's important to pick up this one,' said Mahmoud. (BNC Baby, J10)

(443) 'We then need *to reach in* to that inner child and *supply* what it did not have, and heal it.' (BNC Baby, E9S)

PERFECT constructions contain infinitive clauses in only a few instances: eight with BI, as in (444), and three with *to*-infinitive, as in (445), the occurrence of the perfect construction with BI being significantly higher than with *to*-infinitive (P=0.000003) (see Table 73).

42 The results provided by the chi-square test for intransitive vs transitive are $\chi^2(1)=0.01$, P=0.8231. The results of Fisher's Exact tests are P=0.129 for coordination vs intransitive and P=0.131 for coordination vs transitive.

In my British PDE data, a new construction is found with *need* plus infinitive clause, namely the progressive infinitive, as in (446). Only four instances of this pattern are attested in my data and the type of complementation is always the *to*-infinitive one. As for the occurrence of 'fear' verbs in infinitive clauses, only two instances are found, one per variant: in (447) with a BI clause and in (448) with a *to*-infinitive complement.

	Other	Perfect construction
BI	108 (3.24)	8 (0.24)
TO	881 (26.45)	3 (0.09)

Table 73: Perfect and *need* plus *to*-infinitive/BI clause in British PDE (raw and n.f./ 10,000 <-s> units)

(444) Disappointed, Clare wondered what had gone wrong. After all, he needn't *have visited her*. (BNC Baby, FPB)

(445) A more elaborate checklist is provided by the philosopher Lewis (1972), specifically to provide an index of those co-ordinates which a hearer would need *to have specified* in order that he could determine the truth of a sentence. (BNC Baby, F9V)

(446) Patrick: Because she said to me <pause> is your brother called Anthony? And I goes <pause> and I goes, yeah. And she goes, well your brother needs *to be swimming* more.
Anthony: Yeah I know. So what? Don't bother me. (BNC Baby, KSN)

(447) And, looking down at the still-outstretched arm, the glazed and open eyes, the great scarlet pool soaking into the earth, she knew that it was a body, that he had gone for ever, that there was nothing *she need fear from him ever again*. (BNC Baby, C8T)

(448) But recently, fancying an off-the-peg suit for her 40th wedding anniversary party, Barbara realised that she would be so confused by clothes shopping that she would need *to seek advice*. (BNC Baby, K3A)

The predictor NOTIONAL CHARACTERISATION is not included in *Model 3* because of the low number of occurrences with factual unrealised meanings (see Table 74), which are mainly attested with BI clauses, as in (449), in which it is clear that the proposition conveyed by the predicate 'repeat the argument here' did not take place. However, the difference between the frequencies of *need* plus *to*-infinitive/BI complementation in factual unrealised meanings is not statistically significant in comparison with non-factual unrealised or factual realised meanings (P=0.583 and P=0.2338, respectively). Examples conveying non-factual unrealised meaning are more frequent, representing 86.95 per cent of the data with BI clauses and 92 per cent with *to*-infinitive complements, the latter variant being significantly more productive in these contexts, as in (450), and the BI alternative being more frequent with factual realised meanings, as in (451) ($\chi^2(1)$=3.91, P=0.0286). Example (450) expresses the unknown event of whether 'the Soviet engineer will finally catch up with Hebrew', and (451) is factual and realised because the speaker knows that the defendant had asserted some right.

	Factual	**Factual unrealised**	**Non-factual unrealised**
BI	12 (0.36)	3 (0.09)	100 (3.00)
TO	47 (1.41)	24 (0.72)	813 (24.41)

Table 74: Notional characterisation of *need* plus *to*-infinitive/BI clause in British PDE (raw and n.f./10,000 <-s> units)

(449) We spent quite a long time sorting out this problem in the electrostatic case, and *we need not repeat* the argument here. Just by analogy with eqn (2.45) we obtain [formula]. (BNC Baby, FEF)

(450) Hebrew is a priority for all, and places in the famous ulpan system are available at once. But even after six months of intensive study many other problems remain. A Soviet engineer who lost his job a decade ago after applying to emigrate *needs to catch up.* (BNC Baby, A8P)

(451) Trespass was (and still is) essentially a wrong to possession and *the defendant need not have asserted* any right to deal with the goods or indulged in any 'appropriation' of them. (BNC Baby, FSS)

The other predictors show enough data in their levels with *to*-infinitive/BI to be included in the model, together with the predictors of *STEP1* and *STEP2*. The complete list of predictors analysed by *Model 3* is as follows: POLARITY, SYNTAX, RHYTHMIC ALTERNATION, PASSIVISATION, RELATIVE, SUBJECT COMPLEXITY, and SUBJECT ANIMACY. The *to*-infinitive option is taken as the reference level because it is more frequent than

BI in the British PDE data, so negative values in the estimate reflect a preference for the former. The step "backward" function reveals that POLARITY, RHYTHMIC ALTERNATION, PASSIVISATION and SUBJECT ANIMACY, have a significant determining effect on the distribution of infinitival complements in the data (see Table 75).

Predictor	**Estimate**	**P-value**	**OR**
Intercept	-4.7547	< 2e-16 ***	1/0.008610818=116.133
Polarity (ref.: *Affirmative*) Negative	2.8240	< 2e-16 ***	16.8433
Rhythmic Alternation (ref.: *Critical*) Unproblematic	2.0837	9.42e-09 ***	8.0344
Passivisation (ref.: *Active*) Passive	-1.2989	0.0013 **	1/0.272821099=3.6654
Animacy (ref.: *Animate*) Non-animate	0.9702	0.0011 **	2.6384

Table 75: *Model 3*, *STEP2*, significant factors with *need* and *to*-infinitive/BI clause in British PDE (step "backward" results)

POLARITY is the strongest predictor ($Pr(>|z|)=< 2e^{-16}$) (see Table 75) since the chances of BI increase by 16.84 percentage points when the construction occurs in a negative clause, as in (452). In contrast, *need* plus *to*-infinitive is found predominantly in affirmative sentences (see Table 76). The coordinated infinitival clauses in example (453) show this distribution of the variants with respect to polarity: the *to*-infinitive clause *to work slowly* is affirmative, whereas the BI clause *be pushed* is negated.

	Negative	**Affirmative**
BI	80 (2.40)	36 (1.08)
TO	98 (2.94)	786 (23.6)

Table 76: Polarity and *need* plus *to*-infinitive/BI clause in British PDE (raw and n.f./10,000 <-s> units)

(452) Nor is it good news for the majority of people who already own-especially those who became first-time buyers over the past four years and whose

complete capital has been wiped out: more than a million such people are probably technically bankrupt but *need not admit* it so long as they keep paying their mortgage. Such people are effectively under house arrest. (BNC Baby, AHB)

(453) He felt that Balbinder *needed* to work slowly and *not be pushed* - he needed more time and specific help to speak in sentences. (BNC Baby, CRS)

The effect of POLARITY and NOTIONAL CHARACTERISATION on complementation choice is statistically significant ($\chi^2(1)$=237.77, P=<.0001). As observed in the case of the American LModE data, the *to*-infinitive option is favoured in affirmative non-factual unrealised contexts and BI in negative non-factual unrealised ones (see Figure 11). Likewise, BI clauses with negative factual realised meanings are also significantly more frequent than *to*-infinitive clauses ($\chi^2(1)$=19.96, P=<.0001, when compared with the rest of the data). In affirmative factual realised and negative factual unrealised contexts, *to*-infinitive and BI show a similar distribution (P=0.435 and P=0.4740, respectively).

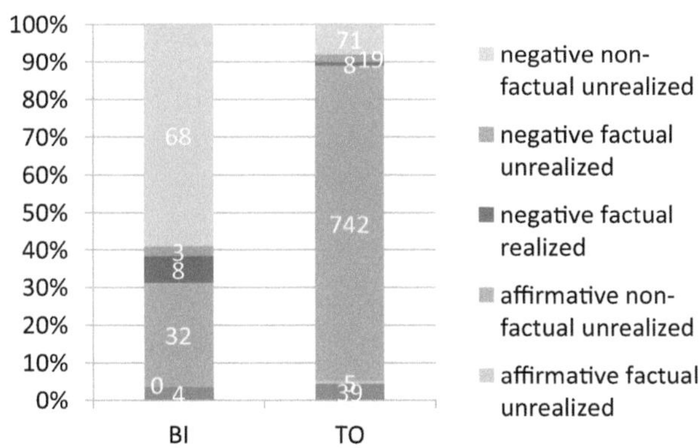

Figure 11: Notional characterisation and polarity affecting *need* plus *to*-infinitive/ BI clause in British PDE (raw data)

The predictor RHYTHMIC ALTERNATION is also shown to be very significant (Pr(>|z|)=9.42e^{-09}). Critical stress patterns favour *to*-infinitive by 8.03 percentage points, as in (454), whereas BI is frequently attested in unproblematic contexts, as in (452) above (also see Table 77). The *to*-infinitive clause functions as a stress-clash buffer between the stressed words *need* and *find* in (454).

	Critical	Unproblematic
BI	10 (0.30)	106 (3.18)
TO	370 (11.11)	514 (15.43)

Table 77: Rhythmic Alternation and *need* plus *to*-infinitive/BI clause in British PDE (raw and n.f./10,000 <-s> units)

(454) FINDING MORE TO READ Besides these almost standard reference sources, you will *need to find* more specific – and more specialised – ideas about what to read. (BNC Baby, HXH)

As observed in the diachronic data, *need* plus infinitival complementation is influenced by negative clauses and the Principle of Rhythmic Alternation. As illustrated in Figure 12, direct negation is frequent with BI, where *not* acts as a stress-clash buffer between the main verb *need* and a monosyllabic or initially stressed infinitive verb to create an unproblematic context. In contrast, when an auxiliary verb precedes *need* in a negative sentence, the auxiliary carries negation and, consequently, a critical context may arise if the infinitival verb is initially stressed or monosyllabic. In this case, the *to*-infinitive clause is selected to avoid stress clash, as in (455). No instances of BI in negative or critical contexts are registered in my British PDE database.

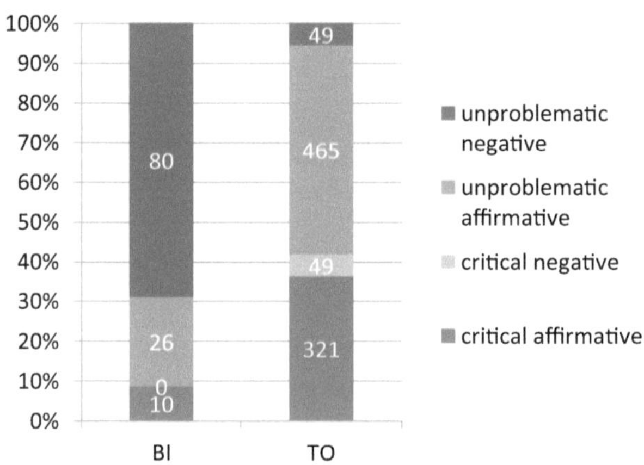

Figure 12: Rhythmic Alternation and polarity affecting *need* plus *to*-infinitive/BI clause in British PDE (raw data)

(455) She *did not need to ring.* (BNC Baby, C8T)

The frequency of *need* plus infinitival complementation in active/passive contexts also has a significant influence on the preference for *to*-infinitive/BI (Pr(>|z|)=0.0013). The odds of the *to*-infinitive alternative increase by 3.66 percentage points with the passive construction, as in (456), with a passive lower clause. Of the 165 passive constructions in my data, passivisation affects the main clause in only two cases, as in (434) above, both of which select *to*-infinitive complements. BI is preferred with active voice verbs (see Table 78).

	Passive	**Active**
BI	11 (0.33)	105 (3.15)
TO	154 (4.62)	730 (21.92)

Table 78: Passivisation and *need* plus *to*-infinitive/BI clause in British PDE (raw and n.f./10,000 <-s> units)

(456) Dougal sighed. He had taken it for granted that the other reasons didn't need *to be spelled out.* 'I want you to. I love you. 'Maybe I will. One day.' (BNC Baby, GUU)

With respect to SUBJECT ANIMACY, non-animate subjects are significantly more frequent with *need* plus BI (Pr(>|z|)=0.0011), as in (457). The odds of the *to*-infinitive clause with non-animate subjects decrease by 2.63 percentage points (see Tables 75 and 79).

	Animate	**Non-Animate**
BI	76 (2.28)	40 (1.2)
TO	675 (20.27)	209 (6.28)

Table 79: Animacy and *need* plus *to*-infinitive/BI clause in British PDE (raw and n.f./10,000 <-s> units)

(457) More interestingly, *the items which provide the focus to the concordance* need not be dictionary headings or even vocabulary words at all. (BNC Baby, F98)

Only 20 examples of *need* plus BI are attested in my American PDE database, so *Model 3* contains only two predictors. Most of the other factors are analysed using a univariate test.

As observed in the diachronic and synchronic studies, the explicit morphological form of *need* is associated with the *to*-infinitive alternative, as in (458), more than with the BI option (P=0.00059; see Figure 13).

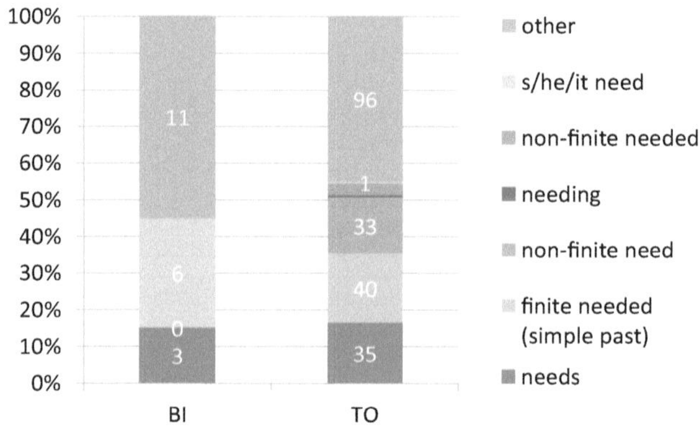

Figure 13: Morphology and paradigm forms of *need* and *to*-infinitive/BI clause in American PDE (raw and n.f./10,000 IP-MATs)

(458) "I been hearing a long time," he said, "how you're one of the real smart ones, Torres. I think maybe you got yourself a good question there. Japanese sure as hell *don't need to defend* against their own shit, huh?" (COHA, mag_1999_407884)

The analysis of the (non-)explicit morphological forms reveals that the two types of infinitive complementation behave similarly with other non-explicit morphology ($\chi^2(1)$=0.38, P=0.3929; see Figure 13). The main difference is attested with third-person singular present forms, which tend to co-occur with *to*-infinitive complements if the verbal forms shows *–s* inflection and BI complements when inflection is not overt. Since the only example of covert agreement with *need* and a *to*-infinitive complement is part of a direct quotation in a magazine text (459), the possibility that this may be a performance error cannot be discarded. The *to*-infinitive alternative is categorical when *need* is in the simple past form, as in (460), or in non-finite forms, such as the past participle form in (461). Four (out of seven) examples with non-finite *need* involve main-verb passivisation, as in (461). Non-finite forms are not frequent, except non-finite *need*, which occurs in 15.49 per cent of the data.

(459) But, says Youngs, "*visiting children need to abide* by the house rules. (COHA, mag_1997_398785)

(460) I was sweating, and I felt like I *needed to run*. I *needed to get out of* there. (COHA, fic_1997_54799)

(461) Computer engineers and automation experts *will be needed to design* these machines. (COHA, mag_1996_428685)

The distribution of *need* plus infinitive clause is quite similar in negative and interrogative clauses in both varieties of English. As in British English, *to*-infinitive is preferred in the American data when *need* is *do*-supported and when it is accompanied by auxiliaries (see Table 80). *Do*-support is attested in contexts reflecting emphatic polarity and clause-initial negative triggers, as in (462) and (463), respectively. BI complements are restricted to direct *not* negation and subject-*need* inversion.

	***Do*-support**	***Not*/Inversion**	**Auxiliaries**
BI	0	11 (3.02)	0
TO	17 (4.66)	0	2 (0.55)

Table 80: Negation/inversion and *need* plus *to*-infinitive/BI clause in American PDE (raw and n.f./10,000 IP-MATs)

(462) You don't need to send them when you file electronically, but you *do need to keep* them in case you are audited. (COHA, news_2000_622006)

(463) OBVIOUSLY the "literal repetition" of baptismal formulas and confessional documents and creeds is no substitute for faith, but neither *does faith need* to proceed altogether without them. (COHA, mag_1995_397043)

The choice of infinitival complementation is also influenced by syntactic context (see Table 81). The distribution of *to*-infinitive/BI is very similar in main clauses: 69.01 and 70 per cent, respectively. In contrast, *need* plus *to*-infinitive, as in (464), is significantly higher in dependent clauses, while BI complementation increases in adverbial clauses, as in (465) (P=0.024878).[43] The complements are the object of *mean* in (464) and part of an adverbial clause in (465).

	Adverbial	**Dependent**	**Main**
BI	4 (1.10)	2 (0.55)	14 (3.84)
TO	13 (3.57)	53 (14.54)	147 (40.33)

Table 81: Syntactic dependency and *need* plus *to*-infinitive/BI clause in American PDE (raw and n.f./10,000 IP-MATs)

(464) John is classified as parasympathetic dominant which *means he needs to be* on an animal protein diet to balance his system. (COHA, mag_2000_413242)

(465) It's a Hanks movie, directed by Robert Zemeckis (Back to the Future, Forrest Gump, What Lies Beneath), with a script by Texan Bill Broyles (Apollo 13), so *they probably needn't worry*. (COHA, news_2000_627648)

As in the case of the synchronic study on British English data, the Principle of Rhythmic Alternation is once again shown to be a significant predictor (P=0.0253; see Table 82): with critical stress patterns, *need* selects *to*-infinitive clauses, as in (466), while unproblematic contexts favour BI, as in (465) above, where the initial-syllable stress on the disyllabic forms *needn't* and *worry* leads to a stressed-unstressed-stressed-unstressed sequence.

	Critical	**Unproblematic**
BI	3 (0.82)	17 (4.66)
TO	83 (22.77)	130 (35.67)

Table 82: Rhythmic Alternation and *need* plus *to*-infinitive/BI clause in American PDE (raw and n.f./10,000 IP-MATs)

43 Fisher's Exact test shows that the difference between adverbial vs main and dependent vs main are not statistically significant (P=0.0752 and P=0.175439, respectively).

(466) You may *need to roughen* the surface of the plastic with sandpaper before applying the cement (see the manufacturer's instructions). (COHA, mag_1995_394838)

As regards NOTIONAL CHARACTERISATION, both types of complementation are shown to be more frequent with non-factual unrealised meanings. However, the incidence of the BI alternative is significantly lower in non-factual unrealised and higher in factual realised contexts (P=0.167). The distribution of each complement type in factual unrealised contexts is not statistically significant with respect to the other two meanings (P=0.4815) in comparison to factual realised and P=0.6031 in comparison to non-factual unrealised (see Table 83).

	Factual realised	Factual unrealised	Non-factual unrealised
BI	3 (0.82)	1 (0.27)	16 (4.39)
TO	14 (3.84)	10 (2.74)	189 (51.86)

Table 83: Notional characterisation of *need* plus *to*-infinitive/BI clause in American PDE (raw and n.f./10,000 IP-MATs)

With respect to the factors that measure complexity, *need* plus BI is not attested in contexts of relativisation. In passive constructions, only 2 instances have BI clauses and 33 have *to*-infinitive complements (see Table 84), with distribution proving statistically insignificant (P=0.394). As regards the progressive aspect level, in the only example attested, the complement is a *to*-infinitive (467).

	Passive	Active
BI	2 (0.55)	18 (4.94)
TO	33 (9.05)	180 (49.39)

Table 84: Passivisation and *need* plus *to*-infinitive/BI clause in American PDE (raw and n.f./10,000 IP-MATs)

(467) But he has avoided letting any of the girls, even the youngest ones, see him undressed, and he said that "once they reach 8 or 10 *none of the kids needs to be seeing* the opposite sex naked." (COHA, news_1998_626773)

With respect to VALENCY, one example of coordination contains a *to*-infinitive clause, in (468), no examples of coordination show BI clauses, and the difference between intransitive vs transitive subordinate verbs is not shown to be statistically significant ($\chi^2(1)=0.82$, P=0.2301) (see Table 85).

	Coordination	Intransitive	Transitive
BI	0	6 (1.65)	14 (3.84)
TO	16 (4.39)	37 (10.15)	160 (43.90)

Table 85: Valency and *need* plus *to*-infinitive/BI clause in American PDE (raw and n.f./10,000 IP-MATs)

(468) I needed *to get* in the car and *drive*. (COHA, fic_1997_54799)

SUBJECT COMPLEXITY is shown to be a determining predictor ($\chi^2(1)=7$, P=0.0024; see Table 86). BI is more frequent with non-basic subjects, as in (469), in which *anyone* is postmodified by *interested in tracking the sound a little closer to its source*. The proportion of *to*-infinitive clauses is higher when the subjects of *need* are basic, as in (466) above.

	Non-basic	Basic
BI	6 (1.65)	14 (3.84)
TO	18 (4.94)	195 (53.5)

Table 86: Subject complexity and *need* plus *to*-infinitive/BI clause in American PDE (raw and n.f./10,000 IP-MATs)

(469) *Anyone interested in tracking the sound a little closer to its source* need only travel to the southwestern Virginia town of Floyd. (COHA, news_1997_610601)

POLARITY and SUBJECT ANIMACY are the statistically significant predictors according to *Model 3* for British English with enough instances in all of their levels in my American database. The results of *Model 3* indicate that SUBJECT ANIMACY does not significantly affect the distribution of the variants (Pr(>|z|)=0.227; see Table 87).

Predictor	Estimate	P-value	OR
Intercept	-3.0869	< 2e-16***	1/0.04564335=21.909
Polarity (ref.: *Affirmative*) Negative	2.3009	1.1e-05***	9.9829
Animacy (ref.: *Animate*) Non-animate	0.6250	0.227	1.8681

Table 87: *Model 3, STEP*, significant factors with *need* plus *to*-infinitive/BI clause in American PDE

In contrast, POLARITY is shown to be a significant determinant of *to*-infinitive/BI alternation ($Pr(>|z|)=1.1e^{-05}$; see Table 87). The odds of the BI clause increase in negative clauses by 9.98 percentage points in comparison to *to*-infinitive complementation (see Table 88 for the raw and normalised frequencies).

	Negative	Affirmative
BI	9 (2.47)	11 (3.02)
TO	16 (4.39)	197 (54.05)

Table 88: Polarity and *need* plus *to*-infinitive/BI clause in American PDE (raw and n.f./10,000 IP-MATs)

The distribution of the examples with respect to polarity and the semantic/pragmatic contexts in my American PDE data is similar to that observed in British English (see Figure 14). *Need* selects the *to*-infinitive alternative in affirmative non-factual unrealised contexts and BI in negative non-factual unrealised ones ($\chi^2(1)=21.97$, P=<.0001). The occurrence of infinitival complementation in relation to affirmative factual realised meaning is not statistically significant (P=0.408), and the construction is hardly attested in the other contexts.

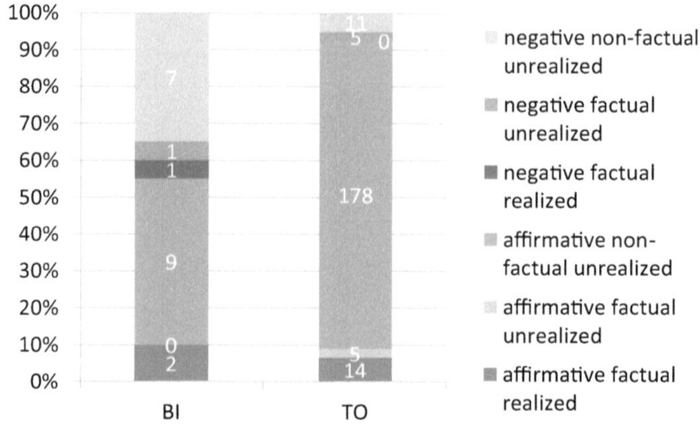

Figure 14: Notional characterisation and polarity affecting *need* plus *to*-infinitive/BI clause in American PDE (raw data)

As in British English, POLARITY has an effect on the Principle of Rhythmic Alternation (see Figure 15). In critical negative contexts, *need* selects the *to*-infinitive clauses to avoid the stress clash between *need* and the infinitive subordinate verb when an auxiliary carries negation, as in (470). The BI option is not attested in critical negative contexts, and is only observed in three examples of critical affirmative ones, as in (471), where *needs* and *be* are both stressed.

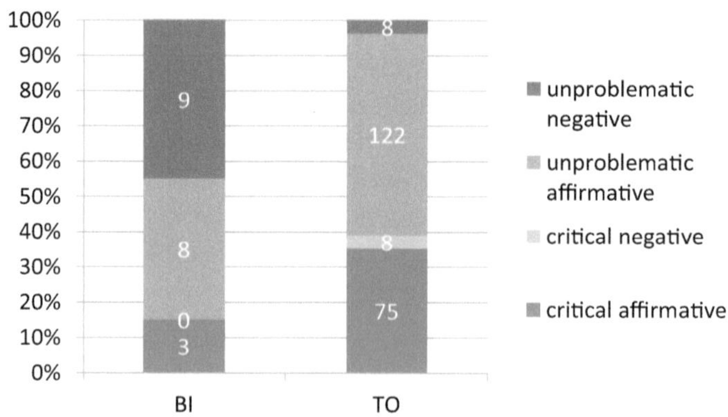

Figure 15: Rhythmic Alternation and polarity affecting *need* plus *to*-infinitive/BI clause in American PDE (raw and n.f./10,000 IP-MATs)

(470) 1. Place rack in upper third of oven. Place beans on large (preferably non-stick) jelly-roll pan (*they don't need to fit* in single layer). Drizzle with oils, season generously with salt and toss to coat. (COHA, news_2000_633204)

(471) It is an ideal which I hope to live for and to achieve. But if *needs be*, it is an ideal for which I am prepared to die. (COHA, nf_1997_776914)

The results confirm that a contrastive analysis of the data for American and British English using a multivariate analysis is only feasible with the predictors POLARITY and ANIMACY. In American English, ANIMACY does not explain the alternation in *need*, but in British English it indicates a significant preference for BI clause with non-animate subjects. *Model 3* shows no statistically significant differences in my American and British English data in relation to POLARITY: the *to*-infinitive is significantly favoured in affirmative clauses and the BI clause in negative ones.

The scarcity of data in the American English database precludes a multivariate analysis with more predictors, so only a few trends may be inferred from the results of the significant predictors in *Model 3* for British English and of the univariate predictors for American. As regards MORPHOLOGY, the *to*-infinitive alternative is found with explicit *need* forms and BI is more frequent with non-explicit forms. Although the variation is not significant with other non-explicit forms, BI clauses co-occur with covert third-person singular present forms. Finally, the *to*-infinitive alternative is favoured with the explicit forms *needs* and simple past *needed*, and non-finite forms.

To-infinitive complementation is categorically attested with *do*-support and with auxiliaries in negative and interrogative clauses in American and British English. In PDE, *do*-support is also used in contexts of emphatic polarity. *Need* plus BI continues to be preferred in contexts of subject-inversion and direct negation.

American and British English show similar results with respect to RHYTHMIC ALTERNATION. In both variants, *need* selects the *to*-infinitive as a stress-clash buffer in critical stress patterns. In contrast, BI is more frequent in unproblematic contexts. In negative contexts, BI is more frequent with unproblematic stress patterns, since direct *not* negation avoids the stress clash between *need* and infinitive verbal forms where stress falls on the first syllable. This is also the function fulfilled by the *to*-infinitive in negative critical contexts, in which an auxiliary carries a negative particle and the stressed form of *need* is followed by a stressed syllable.

PASSIVISATION is the third strongest predictor in *Model 3* for British English, where the odds of the *to*-infinitive are significantly higher than the BI clause in passive constructions. In contrast, the univariate analysis of the American English data indicates that passivisation is not significant. Similarly, while *Model 3* does not show SYNTAX, RELATIVE and SUBJECT COMPLEXITY to be significant predictors of infinitival complement choice in British English, the American data reveal a number of trends. As regards SYNTAX, both infinitival alternatives show a similar distribution in main clauses, and differ in dependent and adverbial clauses: the *to*-infinitive is preferred in the former and BI in the latter. As regards SUBJECT COMPLEXITY, *need* significantly prefers BI when subjects are non-basic and the *to*-infinitive with basic subjects. No examples of BI clauses are found when *need* occurs in contexts of relativisation.

VALENCY does not explain the alternation in either regional variety. Examples of PERFECT infinitive constructions are only attested in the British data, where BI clauses are more frequent. Likewise, 'fear' verbs are only found in British English, with one example of each complement type.

American and British English behave similarly with respect to the semantic/pragmatic variables. The infinitival complement construction conveys non-factual unrealised meanings more frequently. *Need* significantly selects the *to*-infinitive clause with non-factual unrealised meanings and BI with factual realised ones. The construction is barely attested in contexts expressing factual unrealised meanings in either variety, and *to*-infinitive vs BI variation is not significantly different. POLARITY has a statistical bearing on complementation choice with respect to the notional characterisation of the construction: when a BI clause is selected with a non-factual unrealised meaning, the construction tends to exhibit negative polarity, whereas *to*-infinitives attested with a non-factual unrealised meaning are found in affirmative clauses.

3.4.4 Infinitival complementation governed by *dare* and *need*: A diachronic and synchronic analysis

3.4.4.1 Dare

Infinitival complementation alternation in *dare* clauses has undergone a process of regularisation from Late Modern English to PDE. Morphologically, with infinitival complements *dare* exhibits non-explicit forms more frequently in EModE and British LModE ($\chi^2(1)$=0.65, P=0.3455; see Table 134 in Appendix), and a dramatic rise in explicit forms from British LModE to British PDE ($\chi^2(1)$=16.51, P=<.0001). In the American data the distribution of (non-)explicit forms is similar to British English in LModE and PDE ($\chi^2(1)$=0.08, P=0.6629 and P=0.1775, respectively).

Another regularisation feature is the introduction of *do*-support. This strategy is attested in two examples in my EModE data, with *to*-infinitive complements (see Figure 16). In this period, direct negation and subject inversion are the most frequent strategies with both types of complements. *Dare* reluctantly adopts *do*-support in British LModE: two examples with *to*-infinitive clauses and one with BI are attested in my database. In British PDE, direct negation and subject inversion are also the most frequent strategies in contexts of *do*-support, which, in the *dare* examples, is practically associated with the BI alternative (11 out of 12 examples). In LModE American English, *dare* occurs with both BI and *to*-infinitive clauses in clauses exhibiting either *do*-support or direct negation or inversion, whereas the *to*-infinitive option is significantly more frequent with auxiliary negation, which seems to set a new trend as far as *dare* complementation is concerned. Only two instances with *to*-infinitive complementation are registered in American PDE in this context, with an auxiliary and *do*-support, respectively. The remaining examples contain BI clauses. Direct negation and inversion are still the most frequent strategies in PDE in this respect, but their distribution significantly decreases from LModE to PDE with respect to the auxiliary solution in British English (P=0.028) and with *do*-support in American English (P=0.045).

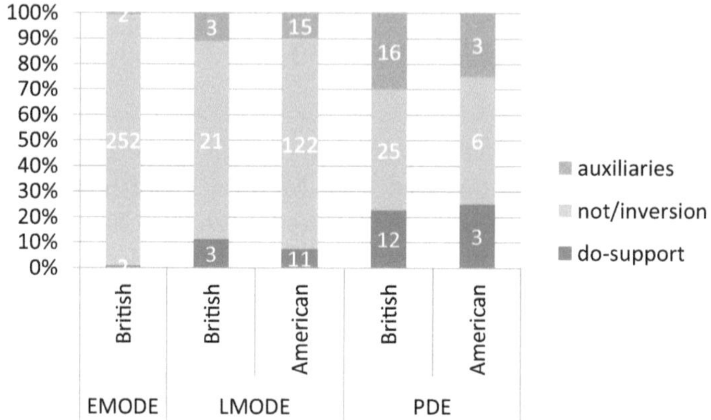

Figure 16: Negation/inversion and *dare* plus infinitival complementation in British and American English diachronically (raw data)

Diachronically, *dare* plus infinitival alternation is more frequent in affirmative POLARITY sentences. Where variation between EModE and British LModE is not statistically significant ($\chi^2(1)$=1.38, P=0.1897), from LModE to PDE the construction shows a significant increase in negative clauses ($\chi^2(1)$=3.28, P=0.048; see Table 134 in Appendix). No significant differences with respect to POLARITY are attested from LModE to PDE in the American data ($\chi^2(1)$=0.02, P=0.9203) or between the two regional varieties ($\chi^2(1)$=0.35, P=0.4583 for LModE; $\chi^2(1)$=2.06, P=0.0949 for PDE).

As for the RHYTHMIC ALTERNATION factor, *dare* plus infinitival complementation is more productive in critical contexts in the British variety from EModE to LModE ($\chi^2(1)$=16.31, P=<.0001) and onwards (LModE vs PDE: $\chi^2(1)$=0.01, P=1). The distribution of the construction in critical and unproblematic stress patterns in American LModE is similar to that observed for EModE ($\chi^2(1)$=1.68, P=0.1681) onwards (LModE vs PDE: $\chi^2(1)$=0.04, P=1). When compared with British LModE, the American English data show a significantly higher incidence of the construction in unproblematic contexts in this period (see Section 3.4.2.1).

SYNTAX has proved to be a significant factor of the distribution of the *to*-infinitive/BI variants. However, with respect to the use of *dare* plus infinitival alternation no significant differences are attested either diachronically or synchronically.[44] The construction occurs more frequently in main clauses, followed by dependent clauses. Adverbial clauses do not represent more than the 25 per cent of the data (see Table 134 in Appendix).

The contexts of the positive levels of the variables PASSIVISATION and PERFECT INFINITIVE categorically contain BI clause in EModE. No instances of the perfect construction are attested with *dare* plus the infinitival clause from this period onwards. Only two passivisation contexts are attested in LModE and they contain BI complements. No occurrences are attested in PDE. Neither VALENCY nor RELATIVE is a relevant factor either. As regards the predictor FEAR, the data contain almost no examples with these type of lower verbs, in which the factor is not significant. Non-animate subjects are not frequent, either diachronically or synchronically, with *dare* plus infinitive complementation.

As regards semantic/pragmatic contexts, *dare* plus infinitival complementation has approximately the same distribution with the three (non-)factual (un)realised meanings in EModE. This distribution of the data remains unchanged in British LModE.[45] This period only evinces a slight increase in infinitival complementation with non-factual unrealised meanings, which shows a significant difference from factual

44 *Dare* plus infinitival alternation shows similar proportions of the three levels of the variable SYNTAX IN British EModE and British LModE (adverbial vs dependent, $\chi^2(1)=0$, P=0.841; dependent vs main, $\chi^2(1)=0.94$, P=0.259; main vs adverbial $\chi^2(1)=1.2$, P=0.207). This is also the situation for British LModE vs British PDE (adverbial vs dependent, $\chi^2(1)=0.1$, P=0.571; dependent vs main, $\chi^2(1)=0.61$, P=0.325; main vs adverbial $\chi^2(1)=0$, P=0.791). No significant changes are attested between American LModE vs PDE (adverbial vs dependent, P=0.16; dependent vs main, $\chi^2(1)=2.13$, P=0.083; main vs adverbial, P=0.269). Finally, when contrast is made between American vs British, no significant differences are found neither in LModE (adverbial vs dependent, $\chi^2(1)=0.01$, P=0.92; dependent vs main, $\chi^2(1)=1.44$, P=0.167; main vs adverbial $\chi^2(1)=1.33$, P=0.173) nor in PDE (adverbial vs dependent, P=0.089; dependent vs main, $\chi^2(1)=1.31$, P=0.154; main vs adverbial P=0.341).

45 Differences in semantic/pragmatic meaning are not statistically significant between EModE and LModE: Non-factual unrealised vs factual realised, $\chi^2(1)=0.1$, P=0.6468; factual realised vs factual unrealised, $\chi^2(1)=1.04$, P=0.2301; non-factual unrealised vs factual unrealised, $\chi^2(1)=2.08$, P=0.1062.

realised meaning in the British PDE variety ($\chi^2(1)=4.27$, P=0.0239). As Table 134 in Appendix displays, instances with non-factual unrealised meanings are more frequent in British PDE than in British LModE, whereas the proportion of registers with factual realised meanings decreases. *Dare* plus infinitive complementation with factual unrealised meanings remains stable.[46] As mentioned in Sections 3.4.2.1 and 3.4.3.1, the distribution of the various NOTIONAL CHARACTERISATION levels in American and British English is similar in LModE, but the American variety shows a trend reversal for PDE in favour of the factual realised semantic context. When the American LModE data are compared with those in PDE, the distribution of the construction decreases significantly with non-factual unrealised vs factual realised meanings ($\chi^2(1)=4.57$, P=0.0166). The differences between non-factual unrealised and factual unrealised meanings and between factual realised and factual unrealised are not statistically significant in LModE vs PDE ($\chi^2(1)=1.86$, P=0.0843 and $\chi^2(1)=0$, P=0.7913, respectively).

3.4.4.2 Need

The MORPHOLOGY predictor reveals that *need* in examples of infinitival complementation is more frequent when it adopts a non-explicit form in EModE (see Table 135 in Appendix). In British LModE the proportion of explicit *need* forms decreases with respect to EModE ($\chi^2(1)=32.66$, P=<.0001), and grows significantly in PDE ($\chi^2(1)=49.51$, P=<.0001). The construction has a similar distribution of (non-)explicit forms in the British and the American LModE and PDE data ($\chi^2(1)=2.85$, P=0.0614 and $\chi^2(1)=1.9$, P=0.1463).

The first occurrences of *do*-support in my data, semi-categorically attested with the *to*-infinitive clauses, are attested in American LModE. In PDE, the *to*-infinitive clause is the alternative in contexts of *do*-support, including emphatic polarity, and with auxiliary verbs. Subject inversion and direct *not* negation are the two strategies associated with *need* plus BI.

46 Variation between factual unrealised meanings and factual realised and non-factual unrealised semantic contexts is not statistically significant ($\chi^2(1)=1.63$, P=0.1294 and $\chi^2(1)=0$, P=0.7773, respectively).

Need plus infinitival complement mainly occurs in negative clauses in EModE. In British LModE, the construction is still more frequent in negative clauses but its incidence in affirmative clauses significantly increases with respect to EModE ($\chi2(1)=7.08$, P=0.0053; see Table 135 in Appendix). This increase in the affirmative clauses is even more significant when the British data for the LModE and PDE periods are compared ($\chi^2(1)=89.88$, P=<.0001). My American LModE data do not differ from the British figures ($\chi^2(1)=0$, P=0.8415), but the construction shows a higher incidence in affirmative clauses in American PDE than in British ($\chi^2(1)=6.36$, P=0.0088).

As regards RHYTHMIC ALTERNATION, Table 135 in Appendix displays that *need* plus *to*-infinitive/BI complementation is more frequent in so-called unproblematic contexts in the periods under study, but its statistical incidence changes significantly over time. The distribution in unproblematic stress patterns is higher in British LModE than in EModE ($\chi^2(1)=10.59$, P=0.0007). In British PDE there is a trend reversal because of the significant increase of critical contexts ($\chi^2(1)=32.95$, P=<.0001 compared to British LModE). This is also the trend observed in the American English data for LModE and PDE ($\chi^2(1)=25.31$, P=<.0001). The distribution of critical and unproblematic stress patterns does not differ per regional variant in either LModE ($\chi^2(1)=1.87$, P=0.1198) or PDE ($\chi^2(1)=0.05$, P=0.7518).

In relation to SYNTAX, the construction is more productive in main clauses in my study. Given that adverbial clauses are not very frequent, the study focuses on *need* plus infinitival complementation in main and dependent clauses, evincing that the distribution does not vary either diachronically or diatopically (see Table 135 in Appendix).[47] *Need* plus infinitival complementation in passive voice contexts increases from EModE to LModE in British and in American English ($\chi^2(1)=15.59$, P=<.0001 and $\chi^2(1)= 25.81$, P=<.0001, respectively). This proportion remains unchanged over time in both varieties from LModE to PDE

47 The variation is not statistically significant between British EModE vs British LModE ($\chi^2(1)=2.89$, P=0.068), British LModE vs British PDE ($\chi^2(1)=0.04$, P=0.7401), American vs British LModE ($\chi^2(1)=1.88$, P=0.1261) and American vs British PDE ($\chi^2(1)=0.04$, P=0.729).

(see Table 135 in Appendix).[48] The statistical incidence of PERFECT tense forms in infinitive clauses is diachronically and synchronically low. VALENCY is not a strong determiner of variation in infinitival complementation. *Need* plus infinitival complementation is more frequent with transitive lower verbs than with intransitive ones, coordination being scarce. Co-occurrence with RELATIVE clauses does not exert any statistically significant influence on alternation in British English, in the American variety the *to*-infinitive option is preferred in this context in LModE, and in PDE BI is not an option with *need* in relative clause contexts. The predictor FEAR does not affect variation in EModE. In LModE the few examples of this type contain BI clauses in both regional varieties. 'Fear' verbs are attested in only two examples in the British PDE data, each with a different complementation option; no instances are attested in American PDE.

Need plus infinitive complement clause is diachronically more frequent with animate subjects (see Table 135 in Appendix). However, the number of non-animate subjects is significantly higher in LModE in comparison to EModE ($\chi^2(1)=10.88$, $P=0.0005$) in the British variety. This proportion remains stable from LModE to PDE in both the synchronic and the diachronic data (British LModE vs PDE: $\chi^2(1)=0.34$, $P=0.4795$; American LModE vs PDE: $\chi^2(1)=0.04$, $P=0.7518$; British vs American English data for LModE and PDE: $\chi^2(1)=0.36$, $P=0.4543$ and $\chi^2(1)=0.35$, $P=0.4976$, respectively).

The semantic/pragmatic characteristics of the examples do not exert a strong influence on the distribution of the infinitival variants from EModE to British LModE (see Table 135 in Appendix),[49] but do have a significant determining effect from British LModE to PDE: in PDE, examples with non-factual unrealised meaning increase at the expense of those conveying factual unrealised and factual realised

48 The variation is not statistically significant in British LModE vs PDE ($\chi^2(1)=0.01$, $P=0.7913$), British vs American LModE ($\chi^2(1)=0.01$, $P=0.7913$) or British vs American PDE ($\chi^2(1)=0.2$, $P=0.5839$).

49 The results of the chi-square test are as follows: Non-factual unrealised vs factual unrealised ($\chi^2(1)=0.09$, $P=0.6315$), non-factual unrealised vs factual realised ($\chi^2(1)=0.01$, $P=0.8065$), factual unrealised vs factual realised ($\chi^2(1)=0.12$, $P=0.5657$).

meaning ($\chi^2(1)=12.56$, $P=0.0001$ and $\chi^2(1)=16.21$, $P=<.0001$, respectively), the difference between factual unrealised and factual realised meanings not being statistically significant ($\chi^2(1)=0.04$, $P=0.6629$). As mentioned in Section 3.4.2, the distribution in non-factual unrealised contexts in both varieties of the LModE period is quite similar, but the number of examples with factual unrealised meanings decreases in the American English data with respect to the other two semantic/pragmatic contexts of the British variety (see Table 135 in Appendix). The distribution of infinitival complements remains unchanged with respect to the three levels in the American and British PDE data (see Section 3.4.3). In contrast to American LModE, the frequency of the construction increases with non-factual unrealised meanings in American PDE only when compared with the frequency of factual realised contexts ($\chi^2(1)=15.2$, $P=<.0001$),[50] while the proportion of factual realised contexts decreases in comparison with factual unrealised ($\chi^2(1)=6.44$, $P=0.0047$).

3.5 *Dare* and *need*

The most significant features of the evolution of *dare* and *need* at the end of ME and the beginning of EModE are the phonological/orthographic confusion between *dare* and *tharf*, and the relationship/competition between *tharf* and *need*. As a consequence of the former, *d-* forms increase at the expense of *th-/þ*-forms from the M1 to the M4 subperiods of ME. Both *d'are* and *th'arf* are attested expressing necessity, possibility and volition in ME. In contrast, *need* starts to express force meanings based on external, internal, general and logical factors in M3 and to select 'fear' verbs in the lower infinitive complements (see also Taeymans 2006 and Loureiro-Porto 2009). The occurrence of *th'arf* in sentences with subordinate verbs expressing fear, blame or doubt is worth mentioning. Despite the low frequency, *d'are* is found

50 The difference between non-factual unrealised and factual unrealised is not statistically significant ($\chi^2(1)=0.3$, $P=0.4166$).

with these types of verbs from ME to EModE. In addition to these semantic contexts, *need* and *th'arf* are attested in Experiencer and personal constructions. *D'are* is not found in the Experiencer construction in my data, but some examples are given in the MED (s.v. *durren*, 2 (b)). The syntactic and semantic features that *need* starts to show from M3 onwards make it compete with the verb *th'arf*. Unlike *th'arf*, *d'are* is found in contexts expressing fear in ME and EModE; *need* is attested in this context from M4 onwards.

Polarity and the notional characterisation of the constructions also affect the distribution of the three verbs. *Tharf* is restricted to negative clauses and non-factual unrealised contexts in my data. *D'are* is found mainly in sentences with negative polarity and expressing non-factual unrealised meanings in M1 and M2. *Need* is also attested expressing non-factual unrealised meanings in ME and EModE, but occurs in affirmative clauses from M1 to M4. The gradual increase of *d'are* in affirmative clauses, mainly in M3 and M4, may be influenced by the verb *need*. *D'are* is found in more factual unrealised contexts in M4 in comparison with the M1 and the M2 subperiods.

Both *dare* and *need* undergo a number of changes in M3 and M4. *To*-infinitive complementation is first attested with *dare* in my data in three examples in M3, in which *dare* exhibits the old past forms, occur in negative clauses and express non-factual unrealised meaning. Also in M3, *need* starts to select BI clauses and is attested in Experiencer construction (3 out of 4 instances) and negative clauses. *Dare* develops explicit (non-)finite forms, whereas *need* shows non-explicit forms for both the third- and second-person singular simple present tenses.

The obsolescence of *th'arf* by the end of ME has consequences for the polarity, semantic/pragmatic context and distribution of *need* and *dare*. Both verbs significantly increase their use in negative clauses. *D'are* is distributed evenly between affirmative and negative clauses, whereas *need* prefers negative clauses. The incidence of *d'are* in non-factual unrealised contexts, which decreases in M3 and M4, is higher in E1. Finally, the frequencies of both *d'are* and *need* increase significantly from M4 to E1.

From ME onwards, *dare* and *need* alternate between *to*-infinitive vs BI complementation in British and American English. This study has shown that this alternation has been influenced in varying degrees, both diachronically and synchronically, by morphosyntactic, semantic/pragmatic and textual features, as well as the Principle of Rhythmic Alternation and the Complexity Principle.

Morphosyntactically, the *to*-infinitive complementation alternative is frequent with explicit verbal forms and with contexts illustrating *do*-support in the EModE and LModE periods, whereas the BI option is preferred with non-explicit forms, direct *not* negation and subject inversion. The non-finite form *daring* is mostly confined to examples with *to*-infinitive clausal complements, while the covert third-person singular and other non-explicit forms of *dare* co-occur with BI clauses. The correlation between *to*-infinitive, on the one hand, and explicit morphology, and between BI clause and non-explicit forms, on the other, is stronger with *need* than with *dare*. *Dare* plus BI is more frequent with explicit forms, leading to blend constructions (see Duffley 1994, Denison 1998: 170, Beths 1999, Taeymans 2004 a,b, Schlüter 2010 and Bemposta-Rivas 2016). *Do*-support is first attested with *dare* in EModE and with *need* in American LModE, mostly with *to*-infinitive complementation. Both verbs are reluctant to adopt *do*-support and prefer direct negation or inversion. In the case of *dare*, even though *do*-support increases in use in PDE, the older strategies remain the most frequent. However, this tendency is no longer the case in PDE, where the BI alternative is the preferred type of complementation with *dare*. In the case of *need*, *do*-support is the predominant strategy used in PDE, where it is even attested with an emphatic polarity function; the few examples with BI clauses illustrate the persistence of older strategies.

The Principle of Rhythmic Alternation is confirmed in all periods in the case of *need* with the exception of British LModE, probably owing to the scarcity of examples. *Need* selects *to*-infinitive clauses in critical stress patterns and BI in unproblematic ones. Polarity is shown to influence this distribution: BI is more frequent in negative unproblematic contexts because it co-occurs with the unstressed direct *not* negator and in inversion with unstressed pronoun subjects, while *to*-infinitive complements are used in affirmative critical contexts to avoid a stress clash between the stressed forms of *need* and the infinitival verbs. A similar trend is observed for *dare* in American LModE. Complementation alternation is not affected by this factor in the rest of the data.

A number of factors have been analysed to ascertain the influence of the Complexity Principle on complementation choice: syntax, passivisation, the perfect construction, relativisation and valency. The hypothesis is that *to*-infinitive complements are selected in adverbial and dependent clauses, in passive and perfect constructions, and with relative clauses, and are more frequent with transitive and coordinated verbs.

Most of the examples of *dare/need* plus infinitive complementation are attested in main clauses. *Need* tends to select BI complementation in main clauses and *to*-infinitive clauses in dependent ones in LModE, regardless of the regional variant. In PDE, only the univariate analysis of the American English data yields significant results: the *to*-infinitive alternative is shown to be more frequent in dependent clauses, and BI in adverbial ones, while *need* occurs with both types of complements in main clauses. In the case of *dare*, syntax has a significant influence on the diachronic distribution of the variants, with the *to*-infinitive solution occurring more frequently in adverbial clauses and BI in main clauses, and the incidence of the *to*-infinitive/BI clause shown to fluctuate in dependent syntactic constructions.

Dare and *need* differ with respect to co-occurrence with passive verbs: the few examples of *dare* in EModE and LModE have BI complements. The incidence of *need* in passive constructions increases from EModE to LModE, and in the British data this factor explains the distribution of *to*-infinitive vs BI complementation: active clauses favour BI and passive clauses opt for the more explicit *to*-infinitive option.

Perfect verbal forms co-occur with *dare* in EModE only and with *need* in all the periods analysed. The old variants are attested when the infinitive verbs are marked for perfect aspect in EModE: BI clauses with *dare* and *to*-infinitives in the case of *need*. From LModE onwards, *need* selects BI clauses in this context.

Valency and relative clauses do not explain the *dare* examples. Relativisation is only statistically significant with *need* in the American LModE period and categorically in PDE when the construction selects the *to*-infinitive alternative. Subject complexity does not exert any influence on the diachronic distribution of the variants in the case of *need*. It is only in the American PDE data that the *to*-infinitive option is more frequent with basic subjects and BI complementation with non-basic ones. The Complexity Principle does not affect alternation in the case of *need*, therefore, but does have an influence in the case of *dare*: basic and non-basic subjects show a significant rise in co-occurrence with BI and the *to*-infinitive alternative, respectively, between EModE and PDE.

Of the three semantic/pragmatic factors analysed, 'fear' subordinate verbs are virtually unattested with the verb *dare*, and does not explain the variation. Neither does it explain *to*-infinitive/BI complementation with *need* in EModE. In LModE *need* only selects the BI alternative when 'fear' verbs are used in lower clauses. As regards animacy, non-animate subjects are diachronically infrequent in both constructions, but increase significantly with *need* in LModE. The new complement type is the one which selects non-animate subjects in both EModE and PDE: *to*-infinitive is favoured by *dare* with non-animate subjects in EModE, the new BI alternative in EModE, and the *to*-infinitive by *need* in this context in PDE.

The study of the notional characterisation of the construction shows that the frequency of *dare* and *need* plus *to*-infinitive/BI complementation is higher with non-factual unrealised meanings, mainly from LModE to PDE and at the expense of the factual realised contexts. *Dare* in American PDE shows a trend reversal: the few examples of the construction tend to convey factual realised rather than non-factual unrealised or factual unrealised meanings. Semantic/pragmatic issues do not have a bearing on the alternation in American PDE. Overall, the data indicate that the old variants seem to be favoured with non-factual unrealised meanings both diachronically and synchronically: *to*-infinitive with *need* from EModE to PDE, and BI with *dare*.

Finally, *need* and *dare* are attested in the so-called subject of infinitive construction in the periods studied but the frequencies here do not allow any quantitative treatment of the data (see Table 89), which justifies their description in this final section. Also, since the *to*-infinitive alternative is pervasive in the transitive data, alternation does not apply in the case of either *dare* or *need*. Table 89 shows that my data contain only one example of *need* in a subject of infinitive construction in EModE (472), and none of *dare*; the examples attested in LModE with *need* belong to the American variety (two examples in American English and one in the British variety in this period). The proportion of *need* + NP2 + *to*-infinitive grows steadily in American PDE, a pattern which is also attested in British PDE. The incidence of *dare* in this pattern also increases according to the normalised frequencies (0.24 in LModE and 0.82 in PDE) for the American variety. No occurrences of the *dare* transitive construction are attested in British PDE.

	EModE	LModE		PDE	
	need	***need***	***dare***	***need***	***dare***
American	0	12 (1.45)	2 (0.24)	9 (2.47)	3 (0.82)
British	1 (0.08)	0	1 (0.03)	17 (0.51)	0

Table 89: *Need* /*dare* + NP2 + *to*-infinitive clause in American and British English from EModE to PDE (raw and n.f./10,000 IP-MATs and <s> units)

(472) Another defect I note, wherin I shall *neede some Alchimist to helpe me*, who call vpon men to sell their Bookes, and to build Fornaces, quitting and forsaking Minerva, and the Muses, as barreyne virgines, and relying vpon Vulcan. (PPCEME, BACON-E2-H,2,4R.132)

As regards the morphology of *need* in this construction, the EModE example above (472) contains the non-finite bare infinitive form *need* since it is preceded by the modal *shall.* All the paradigmatic forms except non-finite *needed* are attested in the American data set. Finite *need* is the most frequent form in LModE and PDE and remains stable across both periods (P=0.4249). The second most frequent form is non-finite *need* in American LModE, not registered in my PDE data (see Table 90). British PDE also exhibits all the paradigm alternatives, finite *need* proving the most frequent again. The finite form of *dare* is the only one attested in both varieties in LModE, but is not found in the American PDE data set, which contains the explicit forms finite *dared*, *dares* and non-finite *daring* (see Table 90).

	LModE	PDE		
	Finite *dare*	**Finite *dared***	***dares***	***daring***
American	2	1	1	1
British	1	0	0	0

Table 90: Paradigm forms of *dare* + NP2 + *to*-infinitive clause in American and British English from EModE to PDE (raw data)

Table 91 illustrates that the subject of infinitive construction with *need* includes one or two words between *need* and the *to*-infinitive clause in both varieties in the periods studied, even though the normalised frequency of the examples with 4 intervening words in American PDE, as in (473), is similar to that of LModE. Most of the intervening phrases are pronominal in American English in both periods. In British PDE, the distribution of NP and pro is quite similar (9 and 8 examples, respectively). Complex NP2s are diachronically marginal (two examples in each period of American English, and none in the British data). The distance in the examples with *dare* is restricted to one-word, pronominal infinitival subjects in all three LModE examples. In American PDE, two of the instances also contain pro NP2s and one example includes the two-word pronominal *one another* (474).

	EModE	**LModE**				**PDE**		
	2w	**1w**	**2w**	**3w**	**5w**	**1w**	**2w**	**4w**
American	0	7 (0.84)	2 (0.24)	2 (0.24)	1 (0.12)	6 (1.65)	2 (0.55)	1 (0.27)
British	1 (0.08)	0	0	0	0	15 (0.45)	5 (0.15)	0

Table 91: Distance between *need* and the *to*-infinitive clause in American and British English from EModE to PDE (raw and n.f./10,000 IP-MATs and <s> units)

(473) In short, we are reminding ourselves that it matters for conduct what a person believes, and belief needs *some pattern, some substance*, to guide us. (COHA, mag_1995_397043)

(474) Kids dared *one another* to cross the white-and-blue Garda tape and grab a trophy from the wall, a stunt never repeated once the house had been shuttered and silenced and officially become inhabited by ghosts. (COHA, mag_1998_401840)

The EModE example with *need* has affirmative polarity. American LModE only contains 4 (out of 12) instances with negative polarity contexts, which indicates that *need* + NP2 + *to*-infinitive is associated with this polarity option. In three of the four examples with negative polarity, negation is operationalised via *do*-support, as in (475). In the fourth example, in (476), *not* occurs after the main verb *need* and before the infinitival clause, which may be indicative of transitive *need*'s reluctance to adopt the new negation strategy, as in the case of the intransitive. The few examples attested in the American PDE data set have affirmative polarity. In British PDE, 2 (out of 17) examples occur in negative clauses, where the auxiliaries mark negation. The 6 *dare* examples in the subject of infinitive construction also illustrate affirmative polarity.

(475) And after this we're going slow and going straight. And we *don't need you to tell* us how to do that. We want you to go away -- on a month's vacation. (COHA, fic_1914_3214)

(476) Fil. Filippo My lord, the nurse still lives -- Ridol. Ridolpho *We need not her To aid thy testimony*; for I remember There was a mark in semblance of a heart On my Cesario 's neck (COHA, fic_1819_8693)

As regards SYNTAX and VALENCY, the EModE example with *need*, in (472) above, occurs in a dependent clause and the infinitival predicate is transitive. In contrast, the American LModE data are mostly main clauses with transitive lower verbs, with only two examples occurring in the other levels of these factors. *Need* + NP2 + *to*-infinitive in adverbial and dependent clauses is not attested in my American PDE data. Although transitive infinitival verbs are still more frequent in PDE, the proportion of intransitive verbs is slightly higher in PDE than in LModE, as shown by the normalised frequencies: 0.12 and 0.82, respectively (see Table 92). In British PDE, the construction is mainly found in main clauses, with two examples attested in adverbial contexts. The distribution of valency levels is similar in British PDE and American LModE. As regards syntax, the two instances of *dare* in American LModE are main clauses, and the only British English example in this period occurs in a dependent clause (477). In PDE, *dare* is attested in two main clauses and in one adverbial one.

	LModE			**PDE**		
	Coordination	**Intransitive**	**Transitive**	**Coordination**	**Intransitive**	**Transitive**
American	1 (0.12)	1 (0.12)	10 (1.21)	0	3 (0.82)	6 (1.65)
British	0	0	0	3 (0.09)	2 (0.06)	12 (0.36)

Table 92: Valency and *need* + NP2 + *to*-infinitive clause in American and British English from LModE to PDE (raw and n.f./10,000 IP-MATs and <s> units)

(477) For this opinion I give the publick my reasons *which I here dare you to refute*. (PPCMBE, JOHNSON-1775,2,3.54)

The EModE example with *need* contains an animate NP2. Animate infinitival subjects are also slightly preferred in American LModE, but this tendency levels off by PDE (see Table 93). British PDE differs from American PDE in that the former favours animate NP2s. As for main-clause subject animacy, *need* prefers animate subjects both diachronically and synchronically. The variation between American LModE and PDE in this respect is not statistically significant (P=0.58) in either American or British PDE (P=0.431) (see Table 94). All occurrences with *dare* contain animate infinitival and main-clause subjects.

	EModE	**LModE**		**PDE**	
	Animate	**Animate**	**Non-animate**	**Animate**	**Non animate**
American	0	7	5	4	5
British	1	0	0	15	2

Table 93: Object animacy and *need* + NP2 + *to*-infinitive clause in American and British English from EModE to PDE (raw data)

	EModE	**LModE**		**PDE**	
	Animate	**Animate**	**Non-animate**	**Animate**	**Non-animate**
American	0	10	2	7	2
British	1	0	0	15	2

Table 94: Subject animacy and *need* + NP2 + *to*-infinitive clause in American and British English from EModE to PDE (raw data)

As regards the semantic/pragmatic contexts in which transitive constructions occur, the EModE example with *need*, in (472) above, is associated with a non-factual unrealised interpretation, which illustrates the most frequent context with this pattern, both diachronically and synchronically (see Table 95). The example of *need* with a factual realised meaning is from American LModE (478). In PDE, the construction is attested in factual unrealised contexts in one example in British English. In the case of *dare*, the three instances in LModE convey non-factual unrealised meanings, as in (477) above and (479) below. In American PDE, two of the three examples also have a non-factual unrealised interpretation and the third one, in (474) above, conveys a factual realised meaning.

	EModE	LModE		PDE	
	Non-factual unrealised	**Factual realised**	**Non-factual unrealised**	**Factual unrealised**	**Non-factual unrealised**
American	0	1	11	0	9
British	1	0	0	1	16

Table 95: Notional characterisation of *need* + NP2 + *to*-infinitive clause in American and British English from EModE to PDE (raw data)

(478) It hasn't happened, but we've had our lesson. And after this we're going slow and going straight. And *we don't need you to tell us how to do that.* We want you to go away -- on a month's vacation. (COHA, fic_1914_3214)

(479) And then, again you touch'd on duelling: What did you mean, by matters of that sort You spoke of? now *I dare you to report* (looking furiously at both) That speech entire in manner it was spoken. Knight. The Knight of the Rum Bottle (aside -- trembling) I fear that I shall get my calibash broken. (COHA, fic_1818_8886)

To conclude, the construction with subject of infinitive is marginal in the history of English, with a significant increase observed from EModE to PDE in the case of *need*, and from LModE to PDE in the case of *dare* in the American variety. In contrast, *dare* only occurs once in British LModE. American English leads the variation in both periods. The pattern with *need* in American PDE is favoured in contexts with affirmative polarity, non-animate objects, main-clause syntax and transitive lower verbs. British PDE shows a larger range of contextual possibilities and the data mirror the features of American English in LModE. British PDE thus lags behind with respect to polarity, object animacy, syntax and valency. The few examples with *dare* suggest the expansion of the construction to more complex contexts over time: greater distance between *dare* and the *to*-infinitive, explicit morphology and occurrence in adverbial clauses. *Dare* + NP2 + *to*-infinitive is also attested in factual realised contexts. More data may corroborate these trends.

4. *Help*

4.1 Introduction

This chapter consists of a corpus analysis of infinitival complementation with *help* from ME to PDE in the British and American varieties. The study focuses on the possible factors affecting the choice of infinitival complement in PDE and investigates the influence of semantic/pragmatic factors.

Section 4.2 contains a review of the relevant literature. The first part of Section 4.3 examines the general complementation options over time and in each variety of English and then focuses specifically on infinitival complementation. The second part of the section presents a multivariate synchronic-diachronic analysis of the factors affecting infinitival choice in each period and regional variant, including a description of the methodology, data and analysis, and discussion of the results. Section 4.4 analyses the diachronic and synchronic features affecting infinitival complement alternation specifically in relation to *help*. Finally, the most significant findings of the chapter are summarised in Section 4.5.

4.2 Literature review

This section presents a review of the literature on the alternation between BI and *to*-infinitive complementation governed by *help* in the history of English (Quirk et al. 1985; Mair 2002; McEnery and Xiao

2005; Lohmann 2011 and Levshina 2018), in preparation for the multivariate analysis of the variation in Section 3.3.

Quirk et al. (1985: 1205) classify *help* as a Type (iii) predicate, "a residual class of two verbs [*help*, *know*] which are optionally followed by a *to*-infinitive" and observe that *help* is more common with *to*-complements in British English, whereas BI complements are more frequent in American English (1985: 1206, note [b]).[51] The example in (480) illustrates the 'object + bare infinitive complementation' pattern.

(480) Sarah *helped* John (to) *give better speeches than that.* (Quirk et al. 1985: 1205)

Mair's (2002: 121–129) linguistic data from the 1960s corroborate Quirk et al.'s observations. However, the former's data from the 1990s reflect the increased frequency of BI complements in written and spoken British English, thus revealing a change from *to*-infinitive to BI complementation in both varieties. Mair (2002: 125) contends that British and American English are developing along the same lines and that the contrast in usage in each variety is a transitional phenomenon due to the differential rate of development of the phenomenon between them. While the distribution of BI and *to*-infinitive clauses after *help* remains mostly stable throughout the period 1600–1850 (Mair 2002: 123), a rapid increase in *help* with infinitive complements is observed from the mid-nineteenth century onwards, most notably in the case of BI clauses. Mair (2002: 123–124) attributes this to the semantic broadening of *help* "from 'somebody lends support to somebody else in performing some task' to a more general notion of 'contribute to/provide a favourable environment for' ". In his view, as the meaning conveyed by *help* becomes more general and abstract, its behaviour begins to resemble more that of a functional verb; *help* is "in the process of taking over quasi-auxiliary function in complex verb phrases". Mair considers that *help* plus BI is related to the 'auxiliation' process identified by Brinton (1988: 96 f), involving the reanalysis "of a loose concatenation of main verb plus verbal complement as a unified or frozen form". He also mentions that reanalysis "of a participle or infinitive as an 'auxiliate' " may

51 In the case of the intransitive construction, Quirk et al. (1985: 1206) mention no distinction in frequency of use between *help* + *to*-infinitive and *help* + BI clause.

explain cases in which the form *to help* is followed by the *to*-infinitive rather than by the expected BI clause.

McEnery and Xiao's (2005) dispute both Mair's semantic distinctions and his view that *help* is undergoing a process of grammaticalisation as a "modal idiom/catenative" or "quasi-auxiliary". They provide a diachronic description of *help* from 1961 to 1998 in American and British English as well as an analysis of register in both varieties using six corpora. McEnery and Xiao (2005) appear, however, to have misinterpreted some of Mair's (2002) arguments, which in turn brings their own results and conclusions into question. To begin with, McEnery and Xiao (2005: 173–174) challenge Mair's conclusions on grammatisalisation by asking: "In what way has grammaticalisation contributed to the increase in use of *HELP* with infinitives? Is it that only a grammatical word increases in use over time, while a lexically full verb does not?" Yet Mair (2002: 123–124), as noted previously, does not attribute the increase in use of *help* with infinitives to grammaticalisation but to the broadening of the verb's meaning. The new meaning with *help*, i.e. 'contribute to/provide a favourable environment for', eliminates the constraint of the previous meaning 'somebody lends support to somebody else in performing some task', in which non-animate subjects or objects had to be understood in a metaphorical way. Secondly, McEnery and Xiao (2005: 174) have also misunderstood Brinton's (1988: 96 f) term 'auxiliate' and Mair's (2002: 124–125) use of this concept to explain the sequence *to help to*-infinitive. Whereas Mair (2002: 125) argues that the main components of this sequence may be analysed as " 'auxiliates' in Brinton's sense, and not as two separate infinitival clauses arranged in sequences", McEnery and Xiao (2005: 174) state that "the infinitival verb following *HELP* must be definite" so that the sequence can be analysed as a modal idiom. McEnery and Xiao use the example of the quasi-modal *be going to* to state that *going* "cannot be replaced with *coming*" in that sequence. They look for examples in their database to show that there is no "clear pattern in the infinitival verbs following *to help*". McEnery and Xiao's understanding of 'auxiliates' therefore extends beyond the sequence *to help to*-infinitive, to include the subordinate verb which follows the *to*-infinitive, i.e. *to help to*-infinitive plus a 'definite' subordinate verb. Thirdly, McEnery and Xiao (2005: 174) use some of the morphosyntactic features of the verbs *need* and *dare* as evidence against Mair's argument in favour of the grammaticalisation process of *help* as a quasi-auxiliary. McEnery and Xiao contrast examples (481) and (482) with (483), and contend that whereas (481) and (482) may be used as either a main verb or a modal auxiliary, (483) is not acceptable in an auxiliary position.

(481) Do we need/dare to escape?

(482) Need we/Dare we escape?

(483) *Helped Mrs Arthur Goldberg sponsor the art gallery?

In PDE, auxiliary *do* marks the distinction between modal and non-modal verbs. Loureiro-Porto (2009), following Rissanen (1999: 239), points out that "this situation is the result of the emergence and development of the verb as an optional tense operator over the course of Middle and early Modern English". The use of *do* at the beginning of the seventeenth century is not still regulated in a strict way, and its presence or absence may be determined by a number of factors (Loureiro-Porto 2009: 190 quoting Barber 1997:196). The old negation pattern without *do* is increasingly rare by the seventeenth century, but is found with highly frequent verbs such as *say*, *know*, *mistake* and *matter*, as in (484) and (485) (see Denison 1993: 451 ff). Apart from these specific situations, "residual usage of *do*-less negation disappeared rapidly after 1800, though occasional instances of such semi-idiomatic expressions occur even in the last decades of the 19th c. and in the early 20th c." (Aart et al 2012: 9).

(484) What it means *I know not*. (1769 Woodforde, Diary I 95.8 (17 Dec))

(485) *I doubt not* of her happiness in a future Life (1785 Woodforde, Diary II. 171.18 (23 Jan))

Denison (1993: 451) argues that by the late seventeenth century and early eighteenth century, examples such as (486) should be interpreted as instances of operator + *not*, and that dummy auxiliary *do* and other operators were by then the standard way of negating a verb. Aarts et al. (2012: 8) observe that the last steps in the regulation of *do* were taken in the eighteenth and nineteenth centuries.

(486) ... her breakfast *would not stay* on her Stomach also (17 Woodforde, Diary II 301.30 (3 Feb))

In view of these arguments, McEnery and Xiao's comparison of the status of *help* in (483) and the two different stages of the grammaticalisation of *need* and *dare* seems problematic. My analysis in Chapter 3 demonstrated the reluctance of both *dare* and *need* to adopt the new strategy of negation/inversion with *do*-support and their preference for direct negation/inversion instead. In fact, my data also contain examples of *to*-infinitive and dummy *do* in PDE with *dare*, which prefers BI complementation in this context, as in (487). Example (487) is an instance of the blend construction, a possibility which McEnery and Xiao do not consider (see Bemposta-Rivas 2016).

(487) Mrs Baines said she could see the buildings burning 100 yards from the house. '*I didn't dare go out*, because I'm still getting over bronchitis,' she explained. (BNC Baby, CFC)

Fourthly, McEnery and Xiao's (2005: 175) interpretation of Mair's example (12), reproduced in (488) below, seems flawed, since Mair does not analyse the causative use of *help* in (488) as a modal auxiliary but simply comments on its causative status and its similarity to *make* to justify the unlikeliness of adding *to* before the infinitive in this context. Moreover, McEnery and Xiao's (2005: 175) counter-example, in (489), is not an example of causative *help*, owing to the non-agentivity of the subject *accountant's evidence*.

(488) 1976 Alyn & Deeside Observer 10 Dec. 5/2 Part of the fun of the game comes in 'sooping'. This is when the players sweep the ice with special brooms in front of a moving stone *to help it go* further. (Mair 2002: 125)

(489) Where the fund of damage is likely to be substantial, including future nursing costs and the like as well as loss of earnings, an accountant's evidence can *help the court to decide* the multiplier, as well as the multiplicand, for example in the case of a one-man business [. . .] (BNC) (McEnery and Xiao 2005: 175; emphasis in original).

Finally, in their explanation of *help* in the passive construction, McEnery and Xiao (2005: 182) analyse *help* with an overt subject of infinitive as a complex transitive verb in which the NP functions as the object and the infinitival complement as the object complement, rather than as a transitive verb in which the NP and the infinitival clause function as the object of *help*. In the passive construction, the NP object in the active pattern occupies the subject position and the infinitival complementation fulfils the function of subject complement. As a result, the *to*-infinitive "can no longer be omitted", which they illustrate by analogy with *make*, *let*, *see* and *hear*:

> Although verbs of the latter group almost always take a bare infinitive as the object complement, the infinitive marker is not normally omitted when these verbs occur in passive constructions (McEnery and Xiao 2005: 182)

Following Rohdenburg (2018), I contend that the use of *to*-infinitive with *help* in the passive construction is a result of the Complexity Principle (see Section 4.3.2). According to Rohdenburg (2018: 130), the passive voice is more complex than the active and favours the presence of the more explicit construction option in case of two rival options.

Lohmann's (2011) more recent study uses a multifactorial mixed-effects analysis to test the explanatory power of three principles in the BNC: the Complexity Principle, the distance principle and the avoidance of identity (see Chapter 2). Levshina (2018) investigates whether quantitative differences in the use of *to*-infinitive/BI clauses are in keeping with the different probabilistic constraints, and the extent to which infinitival alternation may be explained by the universal tendency to use less coding material when the information is predictable. Her study analyses *help* and the *to*-infinitive/BI clause in the English varieties of Australia, Ghana, Great Britain, India, Hong Kong, Jamaica and USA using a Bayesian regression analysis. None of these studies has examined infinitival complementation diachronically or diatopically through a comparison of American and British English using a multifactorial analysis. Additionally, the literature has only paid attention to the semantic predictor ANIMACY, whereas my study includes a more complete notional characterisation of the construction and an analysis of subject and object animacy in order to assess the grammaticalisation of *help*.

4.3 Synchronic and diachronic analyses

In this section I first provide a description of the different complementation options for *help* from ME to PDE in the American and British varieties, paying special attention to those involving clausal complements. It continues with an analysis of the statistical occurrence of *to*-infinitive/BI clauses diachronically and synchronically in both varieties, and ends with a detailed study of the two infinitival complementation options with respect to the potential linguistic and textual factors affecting the choice of infinitival.

4.3.1 Complementation options over time

This section deals with the distribution of *help* and the different types of complementation in the history of American and British English. The verb *help* exhibits thirteen complementation options from ME to PDE, which may be grouped into transitive, intransitive and elliptical uses. The transitive uses are divided into three subgroups depending on the type of complementation: nominal (490), oblique phrasal (491), and clausal. These clausal complements may be finite and non-finite. Finite complement clauses may be predicate-internal *that*-clauses, as in (492), extraposed *that*-clauses with subject dummy *it*, as in (493), or *wh* complement clauses, as in (494).

(490) and was wel bilouede of ryche and of pore, for *he* honourede þe riche and *halpe þe poer.* (PPCME2, CMBRUT3,29.872)
'and was well beloved by the rich and the poor, because he honoured the rich and helped the poor.'

(491) A 28-year-old man was later arrested and was last night *helping with inquiries* at Witham police station. (BNC Baby, E9S)

(492) Mooste humble beseching your Grace too *helpe thatt some noblemen and gentilmen of the Kingis hous and the south parties maye be sente hither though they bring no greate nombres with theym.* (PCEEC, ORIGIN1,226.036.630)

(493) *It* does not *help that Cherubini allows too little variety of pace, and that his lyrical gift is limited too.* (BNC Baby, A7S)

(494) and if you should send for me and oure cheldren, she will com to see me set forart, and *to helpe what she can*. (PCEEC, BASIRE,137.004.206)

Non-finite complementation patterns include: *to*-infinitive complement clauses (495); BI clauses (496); extraposition clauses, with dummy *it* as the syntactic subject and the infinitival clause as the semantic subject (497); *can/could* plus *help* and *-ing* complementation (498); *can/could* plus *help* followed by *but* plus a BI clause (499); and *-ed* complementation, as *paid* in (500).

(495) He says they *help companies to influence* government decisions and legislation. (BNC Baby, AB9)

(496) Hail and tornadoes inland, combined with hurricanes on the coast, *help make* Texas homeowners rates the highest in the country. (COHA, mag_1999_391789)

(497) When trying to figure out what could kill this victim quickest, *it* helps *to remember the ABC's of medical assessment*. (COHA, mag_1996_383805)

(498) You *cannot help noticing* that the incidence of fatalities among Boyd's artistes seems remarkably high, even by the alarming standards of the pop business. (BNC Baby, AL0)

(499) LOUIS I have a presentiment -- I ask you to listen -- ELOISE in her irritation almost screaming. How *can I help but listen*? And Anne, too! With a short laugh. (COHA, fic_1912_14258)

(500) It's in her name, she's, her father'*s helping her paid* the deposit or something and she clears the mortgage she has no right, he has no right to it all if she went to the police. (BNC Baby, KB7)

Help behaves intransitively when it does not select any complements, as in (501). Finally, examples such as (502), in which the elided verbs of the subordinate clauses can be retrieved from the pretext, are classified as ellipsis.

(501) Thus you see how I make my moane to you *as yf you could helpe*. (PCEEC, CHAMBER,I,254.016.671)

(502) Crav. Craveall To turn them into hard cash. -- Fine boy! fine boy! Yes, you have a head for contriving --you you shall be my help: but come along with me, and *help me home*, you young dog! you have hurt me confoundedly; come along. Exit Craveall led by Simeon. (COHA, fic_1819_8961)

Since the focus of my study is not the diachronic variation of *help* but its development when it selects infinitival complements, a detailed description of the frequencies per period and dialect of the thirteen types of complementation is not required here. Table 100 shows the distribution of *help* plus either a finite or a non-finite clausal complement in the periods under investigation in British and in American English. To give a clearer picture of the infinitival complementation options with *help*, Table 100 divides non-finite complementation into 'infinitival' and 'other non-finite' complement clauses. The 'infinitival' category comprises instances of *help* with *to*-infinitive and BI complementation, while 'other non-finite' includes infrequent non-finite complement clauses: extraposed clauses, *cannot help -ing*, *cannot help but* and *-ed* clauses. The classification of the infinitival extraposed clause in the 'other non-finite' category is justified by the fact that the *to*-infinite clause is the subject and not an internal complement of the verb. As Table 100 illustrates, only the 'infinitival' category is attested from ME to PDE.

	ME	**EModE**	**LModE**		**PDE**	
	British	**British**	**American**	**British**	**American**	**British**
Finite clause	7 (0.96)	8 (0.64)	2 (0.24)	0	0	3 (0.09)
Infinitival clause	89 (12.16)	117 (9.34)	82 (9.89)	22 (5.59)	326 (89.44)	574 (17.23)
Other non-finite complements	0	3 (0.24)	31 (3.74)	0	23 (6.31)	27 (0.81)
TOTAL	96 (13.11)	128 (10.22)	115 (13.88)	22 (5.59)	349 (95.76)	604 (18.14)

Table 100: *Help* patterns in British and American English from ME to PDE (raw and n.f./10,000 IP-MATs and <s> units)

As regards variation across type and variety, Figures 17 and 18 show the frequencies of finite and non-finite complementation types synchronically and diachronically in British and American English.

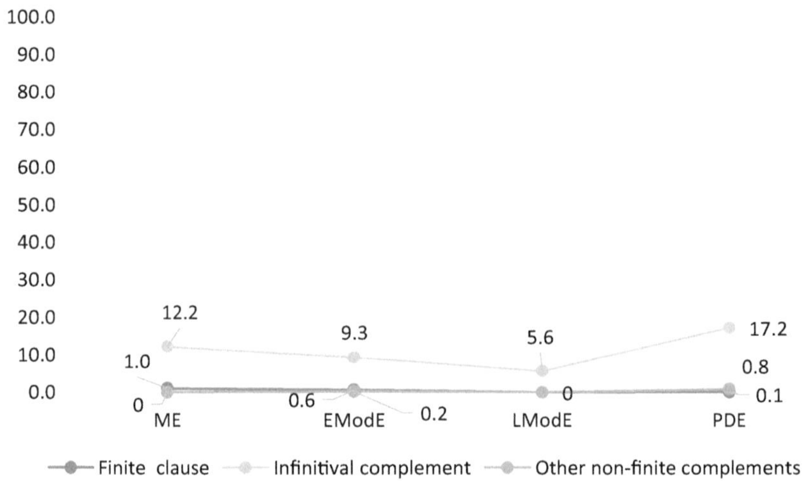

Figure 17: Types of clausal complementation of *help* in British English from ME to PDE (n.f./10,000 IP-MATs and <s> units)

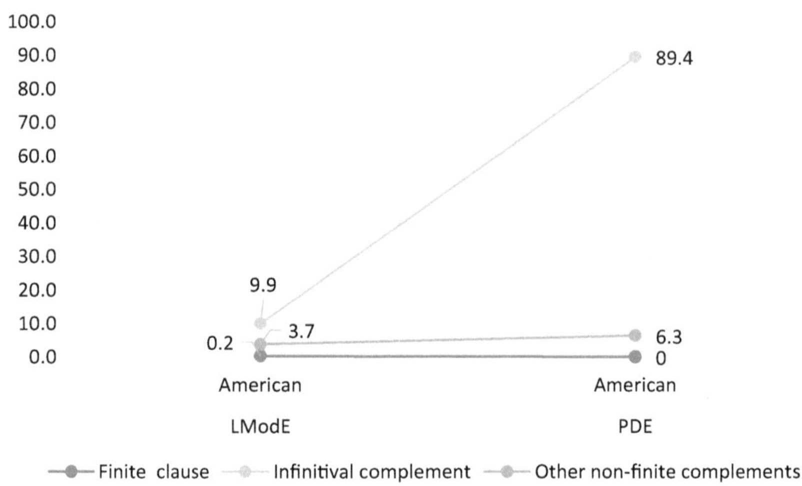

Figure 18: Types of clausal complementation of *help* in American English from LModE to PDE (n.f./10,000 IP-MATs)

Figures 17 and 18 reflect ongoing changes in the frequency of *help* plus infinitive clause in both varieties of English and, in particular, a steep increase in use already in LModE and in PDE. The normalised frequencies of the 'infinitival' type decrease slightly from ME (12.16 vs 13.11) to EModE (9.34 vs 10.22), but this change is not statistically significant ($\chi^2(1)$=0.01, P=0.7184; chi-square tests based on raw frequencies). In British English, the change is significant from EModE to LModE, when 'infinitival' is the only clausal complementation alternative in the data (5.59 vs 5.59 n.f.), and also from LModE to PDE (17.23 vs 18.14 n.f.). As regards the American variety, the occurrence of *help* and infinitival complementation shows a very significant increase from LModE to PDE ($\chi^2(1)$=37.77, P=<.0001). The increase in use of infinitival complementation is not at the expense of the finite or of the 'other non-finite' categories. Both 'finite' and 'other non-finite' constructions have low normalised frequencies diachronically, the former being more frequent in ME (0.96 vs 13.11) and the latter in American LModE (3.74 vs 13.88). The chi-square test can only be calculated for the 'finite' clause and 'infinitival' clause from ME to EModE and it shows that the difference is not statistically significant ($\chi^2(1)$=0, P=0.7913). In British LModE *help* is not attested with 'finite' clauses and only three examples of this type are found in PDE. In contrast, the 'infinitival' alternative can only be compared to the 'other non-finite' constructions in the American English data, the variation here proving statistically significant ($\chi^2(1)$=33.94, P=<.0001). Nonetheless, the increase in the 'infinitival' pattern is not at the expense of the 'other non-finite' constructions because the frequency of the latter also increases, though not as much as that of the infinitivals. These results demonstrate the need to examine the competition between the different non-finite complementation options governed by *help*.

Table 101 shows the variation with *help* between the two types of infinitive complements, i.e. *to*-infinitive and BI. Both types are found diachronically in the two regional varieties, but their frequencies are considerably different. The *to*-infinitive pattern is the preferred complementation type in ME and significantly increases in use in EModE with respect to the BI clause ($\chi^2(1)$=4.7, P=0.0163). By contrast, Fisher's Exact Probability Test indicates that the occurrence of *to*-infinitive/BI complementation remains stable from EModE to LModE (P=0.428).

	ME	EModE	LModE		PDE	
			British	American	British	American
BI	14 (1.91)	7 (0.56)	2 (0.51)	35 (4.22)	365 (10.96)	286 (78.47)
TO	72 (9.83)	111 (8.86)	20 (5.09)	47 (5.67)	191 (5.73)	40 (10.97)

Table 101: *Help* and the *to*-infinitive/BI complementation in British and American English from ME to PDE (raw and n.f./10,000 IP-MATs and <s> units)

The variation is statistically significant in British English from LModE to PDE, when the BI clause becomes the most frequent variant ($P=1.02e^{-7}$). In the American variety, the *to*-infinitive alternative is more frequent than BI in LModE, the difference between the two variants being less significant (P=0.0022) than that attested in British English. In American PDE, the change in favour of BI complementation is significant ($\chi^2(1)=76.59$, P=<.0001); in fact, the productivity of *to*-infinitive complements is significantly lower in American PDE than in British ($\chi^2(1)=50.7$, P=<.0001).

These findings demonstrate the need for a detailed analysis of the factors in order to assess their influence on both the increase in *help* plus infinitival complementation and diachronic and synchronic variation between the two varieties.

4.3.2 Multivariate analysis

The following section explains the distribution and statistical analysis of the data, and describes the potential factors affecting infinitival choice. Subsection 4.3.2.2.1 focuses on ME and EModE, subsection 4.3.2.2.2 on LModE, and subsection 4.3.2.2.3 on PDE.

4.3.2.1 Methodology

This chapter investigates the infinitival complementation governed by *help* diachronically, from ME to PDE, and diatopically, in American and British English. The data analysed are explored through three statistical models which include the four time periods and two varieties: *Model 1* is based on ME and EModE British data. The analysis of these two periods is carried out together because all of the ME and EModE examples in my database come from the British variety and, as illustrated in Table 100, the proportions of infinitival complementation do not vary significantly from ME to EModE. *Model 2* covers the LModE American data. The fact that there are only two examples of *help* plus BI in the LModE British data makes it impossible to apply a reliable statistical method to the data, so the multifactorial analysis for LModE is restricted to the American data and the comparison of the varieties is only feasible for PDE. *Model 3* explores the PDE data, with separate 'glm' analyses for British and American to ensure methodological consistency with the other two models.

The low number of examples, mainly in the earlier periods, makes it difficult to run a statistical model with a large number of predictors, and individual texts and lower verbs cannot be considered as random effects. The analysis of the predictors must, therefore, be carried out in two steps. *STEP 1* consists of a multifactorial analysis of the predictors proposed by Lohmann (2011) for British PDE, plus the predictor VALENCY of the infinitive verb (see Levshina 2018). Lohmann's findings corroborate the effect of the *horror aequi* principle on the verb *help*, as in (503), where the non-finite form *to help* is followed by the BI lower verb *pay for*. According to Lohmann, when the subject is animate, *help* favours BI. This is also the preferred complement choice when the infinitival complement has an explicit NP subject, as in (504). In example (504), *which* functions as the subject of *help* and *him* is the subject of the BI clause *gain election to his seat*. When there are no intervening NPs, the construction is labelled as 'intransitive' and the subject of the infinitival clause is understood to be co-referential with the subject of *help*, as in (505), where *The Sunday working at Sainsbury* is the grammatical subject of *helped* and the logical (covert) subject of *(to) maintain*.

(503) She also had to work in her spare time *to help pay for* her studies (BNC Baby, K3A)

(504) He should return every dime, every dollar given by Colorado Democrats in 1992 *which helped him gain* election to his seat. (COHA, news_1995_641091)

(505) *The Sunday working at Sainsbury helped* [(*to*)] *maintain* the household's income, she said. (BNC Baby, E9S)

Lohmann (2011: 55) also identifies a correlation between length of intervening material and pronominal/full-NP status of the intervening nominal constituents, concluding that "the length of the intervening NP influences the complexity of the construction and therefore leads to a preference for the full infinitive while pronoun status does not lead to a decrease in complexity". Lohmann's (2011: 17) study does not support Mair's conclusions, reasoning instead that "the assumption that the BI acquires new grammatical meaning is hard to reconcile with the result that instances with animate agents preferably employ the bare variant". In his conclusions, Lohmann (2011: 17–18) remarks that even though the *to*-drop results from "general functional constraints", entrenchment of the construction may account for the constraints on the verb *help* regardless of its lexical or grammatical function.

Levshina (2018) uses the following predictors in her regression analysis model: information content of the infinitive given the construction, information content of the construction given the infinitive, distance between *help* and the infinitive lower verb, consequences of the *horror aequi* principle, textual formality, morphology of *help* forms, presence/absence of the Helpee, and valency of the infinitive. To these fixed-effects predictors, Levshina adds the individual texts (websites) and verbs in the complement clauses as random variables. In addition, she models two interactions after the diagnostic tests: distance and *horror aequi*, and morphology and the presence/absence of the Helpee. Levshina (2018: 14–19) concludes that BI is the preferred complement type in the varieties in her study, with American English showing the highest proportion and Jamaican the lowest, just above British. As expected, complexity and *horror aequi* affect the type of infinitive complement in all of the varieties: the proportions of *to*-infinitive increase according to the length of the material intervening between *help* and the infinitive, the American variety reporting the lowest values for this effect. The presence of *to* before *help* decreases the productivity of *to*-infinitive, and the interaction between distance and *horror aequi* is positive when *help* is preceded by *to*, with American English once again showing the weakest effect. The second interaction analysed by Levshina indicates that *helping* without the Helpee increases the use of *to*-infinitive and that *help* without the Helpee is more frequently found with BI clauses, except in the Indian variety. The presence of the Helpee favours BI clauses, but it has a minor impact on the forms after the base form *help*. The probability of finding *to*-infinitive complements with transitive infinitives is high in Hong Kong, Indian and Jamaican English, followed by American English. Finally, with respect to the influence of the degree of formality of the texts on the model, Levshina reports that the average word length of the text has a positive effect on the preference for the *to*-infinitive alternative in all varieties except Indian English, which reveals the opposite trend.

STEP1, therefore, consists of the following predictors:

- presence/absence of an NP between *help* and the infinitival complement, i.e. SUBJECT OF INFINITIVE
- complexity of the object, i.e. OBJECT COMPLEXITY
- distance between *help* and the *to*/BI complement, i.e. DISTANCE
- *horror aequi* effect, i.e. HORROR AEQUI
- Principle of Rhythmic Alternation, i.e. RHYTHMIC ALTERNATION
- animacy of the subject
- animacy of the object
- argumental complexity of the lower verb, i.e. VALENCY
- present-tense morphology, i.e. PRESENT
- indicative mood of the *help* form, i.e. INDICATIVE

Three last points should be made about the selection of predictors for *STEP 1*. Firstly, despite the demonstrated effect of inflection on infinitival complement choice (see Lind 1983: 168, Rohdenburg 2009: 317, Lohmann 2011: 7, Levshina 2018), *STEP 1* uses the predictors PRESENT and INDICATIVE rather than the different morphological forms of *help* for three reasons: (i) BI is used categorically with the form (*to*) *help* in *Model 1*, with all 21 occurrences of *help* plus BI in ME and EModE containing infinitive forms of *help*: *to*-infinitive in 14 examples, as in (506), and BI after a modal verb in the remaining 7 examples, as in (507); (ii) PARADIGM cannot be added to the 'glm' regression in *Model 2* because of the small number of examples with the forms *helps* and *helping* plus BI; (iii) In *Model 3* the variables PRESENT, INDICATIVE and PARADIGM show collinearity, so I have opted to include only PRESENT and INDICATIVE to facilitate comparison with the diachronic data and between American and British English.

(506) and so þai senten to Gurmond, þere þat he was in Irland, þat he shulde come into Britaigne, and helpe ham aġeynes þe Britons, *to helpe ham deliuere* þat lande of ham; (PPCME2, CMBRUT3,93.2834)
'and so they sent to Gurmond, where he was in Ireland, that he should come into Britain and help them against the Britons so as to help them deliver their land'

(507) there willbe three great loades of it as he sayes. and aneighbour of his *will helpe* you carry one loade if you please; (PCEEC, OXINDE,I,72.044.592)
'there will be three great loads of it as he says, and a neighbour of his will help you carry one load if you please;'

Additionally, *to*-infinitive complements are attested in 40 examples in my American English database, which limits the ideal number of factors to 4 in *Model 3* for this variety. PRESENT and INDICATIVE are two predictors with only two levels each (present vs non-present, indicative vs non-indicative), and PARADIGM has four levels: *help*, *helps*, *helping* and *helped*. The literature on these variables is partial and limited. Callies (2013: 4) investigates PRESENT and INDICATIVE when he deals with complexity, while Lohmann (2011) and Levshina (2018) focus on the variant *help*, but none of them explains why BI clauses are more frequent with the form *help*. A qualitative study of all the variants is required to provide a more comprehensive account of all of the levels and predictors.

The third point in relation to the selection of predictors is that the proven collinearity between SUBJECT OF INFINITIVE, DISTANCE, OBJECT COMPLEXITY and OBJECT ANIMACY makes a *STEP 1* 'glm' analysis of these four predictors impossible. The unexpressed levels of OBJECT COMPLEXITY and OBJECT ANIMACY match both the covert level of SUBJECT OF INFINITIVE and 0-word DISTANCE between *help* and the infinitive clause. The levels pro and NP of OBJECT COMPLEXITY clash with the overt level, most of the examples containing animate objects and examples with 1-word DISTANCE. Finally, collinearity is also revealed among OBJECT ANIMACY, SUBJECT OF INFINITIVE and SUBJECT ANIMACY because the subjects of *help* and the infinitive clause are co-referential when the latter is not explicit. In consequence, when there are enough data, the predictors SUBJECT OF INFINITIVE, DISTANCE, OBJECT COMPLEXITY and OBJECT ANIMACY will be analysed separately, one analysis per predictor.

To improve the analysis of the variation in infinitival complement choices governed by *help*, *STEP 2* adds new complexity variables, semantic/pragmatic factors and interactions between variables to the multifactorial analysis in *STEP 1*. These are the added predictors in *STEP 1*:

- complexity of the subject, i.e. SUBJECT COMPLEXITY
- voice of the main and infinitive clauses, i.e. PASSIVISATION
- presence/absence of a relative clause, i.e. RELATIVE
- type of syntactic structure in which *help* plus complement is embedded, i.e. SYNTAX
- NOTIONAL CHARACTERISATION
- interaction between *horror aequi* and the number of words between the main verb and the infinitival clause, i.e. HORROR AEQUI: DISTANCE[52]

The ANOVA test is used to determine statistical optimality and whether the predictors which are collinear in *STEP 1* (SUBJECT OF INFINITIVE, DISTANCE, OBJECT COMPLEXITY and OBJECT ANIMACY) affect the variation in the same way or can be scaled in terms of explanatory power.

4.3.2.2 Data analysis and discussion

This section consists of three subsections that explore each of the time periods: ME and EModE in Section 4.3.2.2.1, LModE in Section 4.3.2.2.2 and PDE in Section 4.3.2.2.3. Each subsection presents a description of the variables in each model, the qualitative univariant analysis of the predictors that cannot enter the multifactorial model, and the 'glm' analyses and their results.

---

52 The interaction between register and subject complexity (REGISTER: SUBJECT COMPLEXITY) and between the *horror aequi* principle and the Principle of Rhythmic Alternation (HORROR AEQUI: RHYTHMIC_ALTERNATION) may have an influence on *to*-infinitive/BI choices. However, owing to the size of my database, these interactions cannot be added to the models as explanatory variables. Only HORROR AEQUI: DISTANCE is considered because of the significant findings reported for the PDE data.

4.3.2.2.1 Model 1: Middle English and Early Modern English

This section analyses the distribution of *help* plus *to*-infinitive/BI complement in ME and EModE, and assesses the influence and explanatory power of the factors that are claimed to account for the variation in PDE. The variable PERIOD with the levels ME and EModE is thus added to the predictors in *STEP1* (see Section 4.3.2.1). Table 136 in Appendix contains a summary of the data by predictor.

The data presented in Table 136 in Appendix reveal that *to*-infinitive is more frequent in both periods (89.71 per cent). *Help* plus infinitive complement is more frequent in EModE (57.84 per cent) and with covert subject of infinitive (65.2 per cent).

As regards SUBJECT and OBJECT COMPLEXITY, pro subjects are the most frequent ones. To measure the distance between *help* and the infinitival complementation type, the function 'log ()' was used. The most frequent scenario is 0 words with 60.78 per cent of the data, followed by 1-word subjects (29.41 per cent). However, the function estimates that the quantile of the data ranges from 1 word up to 7. This means that most of the data lie between 0 and 1 word. Two more complexity-related contexts which may favour *to*-infinitive complementation are the occurrence of passive main and/or subordinate verbs and the presence of relative clauses. Only 3.43 per cent of the data contain passive verbal groups, and relative clauses are attested in 8.82 per cent of cases. By contrast, the present tense and indicative mood levels within the predictors of the same name are considered less complex contexts and consequently favour the less explicit variant. The proportion of infinitival complements with present-tense and indicative-mood forms is also low, i.e. 8.33 and 13.73 per cent, respectively.

As regards the variable RHYTHMIC ALTERNATION, so-called unproblematic cases are the most productive in the data (69.61 per cent of instances). Critical contexts account for 30.39 per cent of the examples. The HORROR AEQUI predictor also analyses the avoidance of identical lexical and/or morphological forms in immediate adjacency (*to help to*-infinitive clause) and accounts for 27.94 per cent of the data. The statistical productivity of the SYNTAX predictor is quite even across all of its levels, with adverbial clauses slightly more frequent, i.e. 38.24 per cent. VALENCY shows that practically every lower verb requires an obligatory complement (88.24 per cent). Intransitive and coordinated lower clauses with (in-)transitive verbs are infrequent (7.35 and 4.41 per cent, respectively).

The data corresponding to the semantic/pragmatic factors SUBJECT ANIMACY, OBJECT ANIMACY and NOTIONAL CHARACTERISATION show that the success of *help* plus *to*-infinitive/BI clause is greater with animate subjects and objects (75 and 94.37 per cent, respectively), and with non-factual unrealised contexts (81.37 per cent). When only the construction with overt subject of infinitive is considered, animate objects represent 94.37 per cent of cases, in contrast to 5.63 per cent for non-animate objects.

The low number of examples of *help* plus BI in my ME and EModE database leads to a number of variables with fewer than 5 instances in each level. In consequence, these variables are described below from a qualitative and quantitative point of view, with an analysis of those admitted by *Model 1*. SUBJECT OF INFINITIVE, OBJECT COMPLEXITY and OBJECT ANIMACY are not included in the statistical analysis because *help* plus BI only occurs in 4 examples with a subject in the lower clause. SUBJECT OF INFINITIVE does not affect *to*-infinitive/BI variation significantly (P=0.0835), and the frequency of both infinitival complements is higher in the absence of an intervening subject of infinitive (see Table 102). The subject of the infinitive clause is animate in the four instances in which *help* selects BI clauses, as in (508) and (509). In one example the Helpee is a coordinated NP (*hare ken/ oþer hare uryendes* in (508)) and in the other three examples the subject is pronominal (for example, *us* in (509)). As in the case of BI complements, *to*-infinitive clauses are mostly restricted to animate subjects, and occur in only 4 (out of the 67) examples with non-animate Helpees, as in (510). When the Helpee is present, it frequently takes a pro form, as in (511).

	Transitive		**Intransitive**
	NPs	**Pro**	**Unexpressed**
BI	1 (0.05)	3 (0.15)	17 (0.86)
TO	8 (0.4)	59 (2.97)	116 (5.84)

Table 102: Transitivity and object complexity in ME and EModE (raw data and n.f./ 10,000 IP-MATs)

(508) Þe on is/ huanne hi wylleþ *helpe hare ken/ oþer hare uryendes/ an heġy* ine dingnetes/ of holi cherch. (PPCME2, CMAYENBI,42.714)
The one is when they will help their kin or their friends rise in dignities of holy church.
'One is when they will help their kin or their friends to rise in dignities of holy Church.'

(509) But now it has pleased God to reveale unto us the author of our frite, which was our maide in letting in young fellowes in to the house at unseasonable howers to riot with them both with our beare and bread, indide we did little suspect her becase she came up to *helpe us cry out* theves. (PCEEC, BARRING,174.119.2036)

(510) and Attempt it at least but doe it sincerely and doe not help *your passion* to master you. (PCEEC, OSBORNE,121.050.2774)

(511) In þe xv ġere of þis kyng, aftir tyme þe kyng of Frauns was slayn in batayle, whech he held ageyn Petir, kyng of Aragoyne, þan þe kyngis son sent aftir Edward þat he schuld come and helpe *him* to venge his fader deth. (PPCME2, CMCAPCHR,129.2996)
'In the xv year of this king, after the king of France was slain in battle, which he held in resistance to Peter, king of Aragone, the king's son sent after Edward so that he should come and help him to venge his father's death.'

SUBJECT COMPLEXITY is not included in my statistical analysis because NP subjects are only attested with *to*-infinitive complements in the two periods, as illustrated in (512) (see Table 103). Complex subjects occur just once with a BI clause in my database, as the genitive subject *aneighbour of his* in (507) above. In contrast, the *to*-infinitive type with complex subjects is attested in 15 (out of 183) examples, as in (513), with the *to*-infinitive complement *to direct the rest* and the 12-word subject *anyone of these Schollers, chiefly one of them who write the best*. Example (513) is also an instance of a construction with overt subject of infinitive, that is with the NP *the Master* occurring between *helpe* and the *to*-infinitive complement. The length of the subject of the main verb and the presence of a lower-clause subject leads to a complex clausal design in which the Complexity Principle may explain the preference for *to*-infinitive complements.

	Complex	NP	Pro	Unexpressed
BI	1 (0.05)	0	6 (0.29)	14 (0.67)
TO	15 (0.72)	19 (0.91)	109 (5.22)	40 (1.91)

Table 103: Subject complexity and *help* plus the *to*-infinitive/BI clause in ME and EModE (raw data and n.f./10,000 IP-MATs)

(512) The Toung is a carnous member, compounde and made of many Nerues, Lygamentes, Veines and Arteirs, ordeyned principally for three causes: The first is, that when a man eateth, the Toung *mighte helpe to turne* the meate tyll it were wel chewed: (PPCEME2, VICARY-E1-P2,43.18)

(513) Thus *anyone of these Schollers, chiefly one of them who write the best*, may helpe the Master *to direct the rest*. (PPCEME2, BRINSLEY-E2-P2,37.192)

Table 103 shows that BI complementation is significantly more frequent with (0-word) unexpressed subjects, as in (514), than with pro subjects ($\chi^2(1)$=13.18, P=0.0001). The subject of *healpe* in (514) is unexpressed but it corefers with *Sir Walter Rawleighe*. In 13 of the 14 examples with unexpressed main subjects and BI complements, *help* is preceded by a *to*-infinitive form, as in (514). The hypothesis here is that the preference for BI is accounted for the *horror aequi* principle. The number of examples is too small, however, to allow the addition of the interaction of SUBJECT COMPLEXITY and HORROR AEQUI to the model.

(514) Whereof one hundred I would have to be myners, and have written to *Sir Walter Rawleighe to healpe procure* them out of his jurisdiction in Cornwall and Devon. (PCEEC, LEYCEST,86.024.906)

PASSIVISATION is not included in the analysis because *to*-infinitive is the only variant attested in the 7 passive examples, as in (515). In (515) both *help* and the lower verb *berȝe(n)* are in the passive voice. Once again, this finding gives support to the correlation between complexity contexts and marked complementation choices.

(515) & ġiff þin macche iss wis & god, | | & tu wittlæs & wicke, | | Þa birrþ þin macche gætenn þe | | All þatt ġho maġġ fra sinne; | | Forr eġġþerr birrþ þurrh oþerr beon | | Hollpenn to wurrþenn borrġhenn,| (PPCME2, CMORM,I,214.1765)

'and if your wife is wise and good and you stupid and wicked, then your wife should preserve you all that she can from sin. Because each of you will be helped by the other to be saved.'

The presence of a relative clause also favours the marked *to*-infinitive variant, found in 17 (out of 18) relative clauses, as in (516). *A cloude* functions as the antecedent of *that* in (516), which is the subject of *help* and the infinitival clause. Example (517) is the only instance in which a BI clause and a relativiser (*which*) co-occur in my ME and EModE data.

(516) Can I discerne that it has made the trouble of your life, and cast *a cloude* upon mine *that* will help to cover mee in my grave; (PCEEC, OSBORNE,118.050.2699)

(517) I ensure yow by my soule I brake no mater to hym but of Ser Thomas vndoyng and hys aduersaries neuere the better, *whych* to my power *wold help make* it knowen to lordes and all othyrs of the cruell amerciementes, the cruell juge to be knowen as he ys, for I am of hys contrey (PCEEC, PASTON,II,178.345.9365)

The hypothesis that the less complex levels of the predictors PRESENT and INDICATIVE favour the less explicit complementation variant is not corroborated by my data in the two periods under scrutiny since the *to*-infinitive is the only variant favoured by the less complex value of those predictors. For this reason, these variables are not included in *Model 1*. The sentence in (518) contains two examples of *help* in the present tense and indicative mood co-occurring with the *to*-infinitive choice.

(518) The vtilitie of them are, that by them a man shal take the better holde: also *they helpe to clawe* the body when it needeth: Lastly, *they helpe to deuide* thinges, for lacke of other tooles, &c. (PPCEME, VICARY-E1-P1,24.200)

Figure 19 shows that the complexity of the lower clause does not influence *to*-infinitive/BI variation and variation between transitive/intransitive complement clauses is not statistically significant either (P=0.47). Regardless of the type of complement, *help* prefers infinitive transitive verbs in the lower clause, as in the case of *procure* in (519).

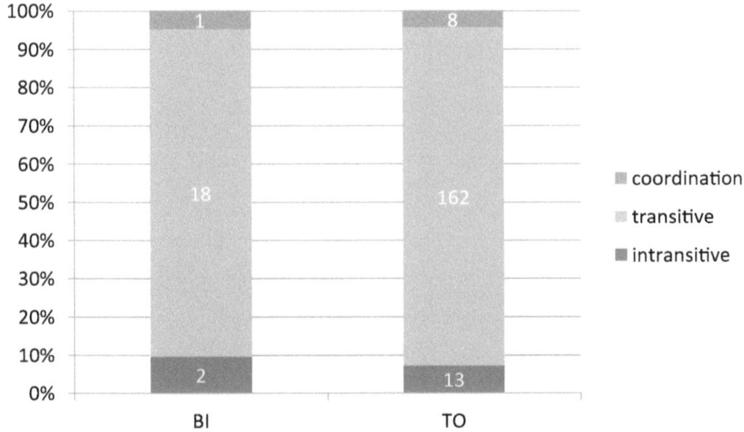

Figure 19: Valency of the *to*-infinitive/BI complement clause governed by *help* in ME and EModE

(519) Whereof one hundred I would have to be myners, and have written to Sir Walter Rawleighe to healpe *procure them out of his jurisdiction* in Cornwall and Devon. (PCEEC, LEYCEST,86.024.906)

The univariate analysis of the predictor SYNTAX shows that variation between complement alternatives in dependent clauses is not statistically significant in comparison to adverbial and main clauses ($\chi^2(1)=2.41$, P=0.0719 and P=0.246, respectively). The proportion of the BI clause alternative is higher in adverbial clauses, as in (519) above, whereas *to*-infinitive complements are preferred in main clauses, as in (518) (P=0.0057 when these two levels are compared; see Figure 20).

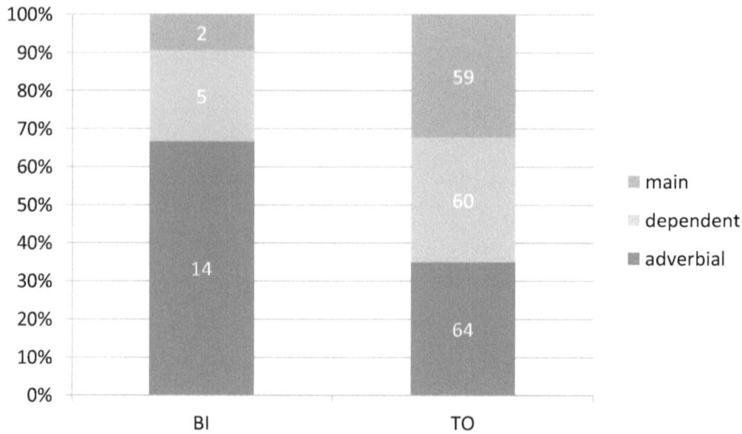

Figure 20: Syntactic dependency and *help* plus *to*-infinitive/BI clause in ME and EModE

The variable NOTIONAL CHARACTERISATION is not included in the analysis because no instances of *help* plus BI were found in factual unrealised contexts and the two examples with a factual realised interpretation take *to*-infinitive clauses, as in (520) (see Table 104). The proportions of *help* with either *to*-infinitive or BI complementation do not vary significantly with respect to NOTIONAL CHARACTERISATION (P=0.463), the non-factual unrealised level being the most frequent context.

(520) Þerfore seculer lordes schulde take awey the superfluyte of here possessiouns, and ġeve it to hem þat nedeþ, or elles whan þey knowen þat, þey beeþ cause and mayn-tenours of here evel dedes, seþþe *þey helpeþ nouġt to amende hit* while it is in hir power, what evere covetous preostes seyn. (PPCME2, CMPOLYCH,VI,465.3438)
'Therefore secular lords should take away the superfluities of their possessions and give it to those who need them, or else when they know that, they are cause and maintainers of their evil deeds, since they don't help to amend it while it is in their power, whatever covetous priests say'

	Factual realised	Factual unrealised	Non-factual unrealised
BI	3 (0.15)	0	18 (0.91)
TO	33 (1.66)	2 (0.1)	148 (7.46)

Table 104: Notional characterisation of *help* plus *to*-infinitive/BI clause in ME and EModE (raw data and n.f./10,000 IP-MATs)

The occurrence of *help* plus infinitival complementation in non-factual unrealised contexts is associated with the mood of the *help* verbal group: indicative mood is normally selected in factual contexts, while imperative and subjunctive moods tend to convey lack of factuality (see Chapter 2). In ME and EModE, the main verbal groups exhibit indicative mood in 29 instances, of which only 4 correspond to non-factual unrealised contexts, as in (521). In other words, of the 166 examples with non-factual unrealised meaning, *help* occurs 4 times in the indicative mood, and in the rest of the examples *help* is in the subjunctive, indeterminate (522), or imperative, or with a non-finite form (519) above.

(521) And if any thing considerable be done, it will be when your Majesty has almost certainty on your side, for they would help up the last steps, and care not for being at the expenses till they can say *this helped immediately to set him on his Throne.* (PPCEME2, DRUMMOND-E3-P1,2.4,206.74)

(522) He protested, that *although he* were of the Contrary faction to my lord of Essex, and *had helped to plucke him downe*, yet never had he a hande in his bloud, that is to saye, he was none of them that procured his death; (PCEEC, PORY,71.002.84)

RHYTHMIC ALTERNATION, HORROR AEQUI, PERIOD and DISTANCE are the variables with enough data in all of their levels to enter the statistical multivariate analysis. *Model 1* can accommodate two predictors because the BI level of the dependent variable comprises only 21 examples. The factor HORROR AEQUI is included in the model in order to assess its effect on the distribution of infinitival complements in ME and EModE, and to compare the effect observed in the PDE data. PERIOD is the other predictor selected in this diachronic study. The exclusion of RHYTHMIC ALTERNATION is justified by the fact that RHYTHMIC ALTERNATION is not statistically significant in the univariate analysis ($\chi^2(1)=0$,

P=0.8415) and also because, as contended by Lohmann (2011), it has not been shown to be significant in PDE, with greater productivity in unproblematic stress patterns observed with both infinitival complement alternatives (see Table 105).

	Critical	**Unproblematic**
BI	6 (0.3)	15 (0.76)
TO	56 (2.82)	127 (6.4)

Table 105: Rhythmic Alternation and *help* plus *to*-infinitive/BI clause in ME and EModE (raw data and n.f./10,000 IP-MATs)

DISTANCE is also discarded here because most of the examples in my data contain 0–1 words between *help* and the lower clause and, as explained in the description of SUBJECT OF INFINITIVE and OBJECT COMPLEXITY, in the only example with a BI complement, the *help* form and the complement are separated by three words (see Table 102). Table 106 presents the results of *Model 1*, which uses the variables PERIOD and HORROR AEQUI. The model reveals that these two predictors are sufficiently explanatory of infinitival alternation in the complement clauses in my data. The polarity of the estimate in each predictor in Table 106 shows the type of complement selected by *help*. Given that the '*to*' infinitive is the reference level of the response variable, negative estimates indicate that *help* favours *to*-infinitive complements, whereas positive estimates reflect a preference for BI complementation.

Predictor	**Estimate**	**P-value**	**OR**
Intercept	-3.5275	2.6e-12 ***	1/ 0.02937969 =34.0371
Period (Ref. Level: *EModE*) *ME*	1.2126	0.016634 *	3.36233
Horror Aequi (Ref. Level: *Other*) *Yes*	1.7005	0.000569 ***	5.4768

Table 106: *Model 1, STEP 1, help* plus *to*-infinitive/BI clause in ME and EModE

As illustrated by Table 106, periodisation and the *horror aequi* principle are significant predictors in the model. As the *to*-infinitive alternative is more frequent in the periods under study (see Table 107), while the productivity of the BI type is significantly higher in ME than in EModE (Pr(>|z|)=0.016634), where the probability of a BI clause is 3.362 percentage points higher with respect to EModE.

	ME	**EModE**
BI	14 (1.79)	7 (0.53)
TO	72 (9.21)	111 (8.48)

Table 107: Distribution of *help* plus *to*-infinitive/BI clause in ME and EModE (raw and n.f./10,000 IP-MATs)

The OR predicts a strong association between HORROR AEQUI and the response variable. *To help* is attested in 57 (out of 204) examples, of which 13 have BI complements, as in (523) (see Table 108). Even though the effect of the *horror aequi* principle is not pervasive in this context, this variable significantly favours BI complementation (Pr(>|z|)=0.000569). In other words, the probability of BI complementation increases by 5.477 percentage points with the *to*-infinitive form of *help* (see Table 106).

	to help	**Other**
BI	13 (0.62)	8 (0.38)
TO	44 (2.1)	139 (6.65)

Table 108: (*To*) *help* plus *to*-infinitive/BI clause in ME and EModE (raw and n.f./10,000 IP-MATs)

(523) Mr. Wylford wrote a letter to Partridg of Kent. *to help send* hym some victells. and therwith he sent a letter of your lordship to the commissioners of Kent. (PCEEC, LEYCEST.40.012.321)

As mentioned in my description of the variables, the BI alternative is not attested with present-tense or indicative-mood verbal forms. HORROR AEQUI has explained the preference for BI clauses governed by *to help* in 13 (out of 21) examples. In the other 8 examples, infinitive *help* is required by the presence of modal auxiliaries, as in (524). The data show that BI complementation is the default option with governing *to*-infinitive *help* forms in ME and EModE. While *to*-infinitive clauses complement main verbal groups headed by *help* in its different morphological forms, the non-finite form *help* is the most frequent, accounting for 80 per cent of the instances with *to*-infinitive complementation (see Table 109). The forms *helps* and *helping* are infrequent in my database (n.f. 0.1 and 0.19, respectively), as in (525) and (526); *helping* is only attested in two EModE examples in my data.

(524) Yef sho wyl noht o þis maner a-mende, bot wid pride defende hir dede, þan sal þabbes do als te sleze miri: wen sho hauis laid hir plaisters and hir vinemens wid faire wordis and te medicinis of haly writ, and cursid hyr, & berid, And *may noht helpe do* hir best, þabbes & al þe cuuent sal pray for hir to god, þat he make hyr hale. (PPCME2, CMBENRUL,23.774)
'If she will not in this manner amend, but with pride defend her deeds, then shall the abbots do as the cunning physician: when she has laid her plasters and her ointments with fair words and the medicines of holy writings and curse and beat her and she may not help do her best, the abbots and all the convent shall pray for her to god that he make her healthy.'

(525) Besydes, you know, 'tis saufest living, when we least inioye; and, sence *the sadnis of your condition helpes to secure* you are in the right way, for pitty, be content to goe att such a rate, as all your little flocke may see yr steps, and follow you; (PCEEC, TIXALL,20.006.148)
'Besides, you know, it is the safest living, when we enjoy the least; and, since the sadness of your condition helps to secure that you are in the right way, for pity, be content to go at such a rate, as all your little company may see your steps and follow you'

(526) Hee is now strangly delighted *in helping to macke* the Garlins and hopes to looke out att the winding to morow. (PCEEC, BROWNE,199.046.896)
'He is now strangely delighted in helping to make the gardens and hopes to look out at the winding the tomorrow'

	Non-finite *help*	**Finite *help***	***Helped***	***Helping***	***Helps***
BI	21 (1.01)	0	0	0	0
TO	146 (6.99)	12 (0.57)	19 (0.91)	2 (0.10)	4 (0.19)

Table 109: Paradigm forms of *help* plus *to*-infinitive/BI clause in ME and EModE (raw and n.f./10,000 IP-MATs)

To summarise, even though the *to*-infinitive alternative is more frequent in ME and EModE, the odds of the BI clause are significantly higher in ME. BI complements are favoured by the infinitive forms of *help*, especially the *to*-infinitive variant. *To*-infinitive complements are also attested with all of the morphological forms of *help*, and in a wider range of contexts, i.e. with non-animate subjects and in factual unrealised contexts. In line with the Complexity Principle, the more marked dependent variant, i.e. *to*-infinitive complementation, is attested in passive-voice contexts, with complex subjects and in relative clauses, while BI prefers unexpressed main-clause subjects, mainly because of the productivity of BI complementation when *help* is inflected as *to*-infinitive, particularly in adverbial clauses.

4.3.2.2.2 Model 2: Late Modern English

This section examines the LModE data and provides a qualitative description of British English and a more quantitative analysis of the American data. In my British English data, the complements are BI clauses in only 2 instances (out of 22), in (527) and (528), which illustrate the clause's occurrence with covert and overt subjects of infinitival clauses, respectively. The subjects of the main clauses in the two examples of *help* plus BI in British English are pronominal and animate, as is the subject of infinitive in (528). In the two examples in my British LModE data, BI *help* is preceded by modals, making them examples of BI complementation with non-present subjunctive-mood main verbs with non-factual unrealised interpretation. BI complementation in (527) triggers the violation of the Principle of Rhythmic Alternation as both *help* and *dress* show lexical stress. This is not the case in example (528), where the insertion of a stress-clash buffer is not necessary because of the presence of the unstressed subject of infinitive *me* between stressed *help* and *make*. As regards the syntactic properties of these instances, they are main clauses and the complement is transitive.

(527) – Lucy. Yes, Madam, and *I'll help dress you*, in order to be undrest again with more Pleasure than ever you was drest in your Life. (PPCMBE, STEVENS-1745.54.972)

(528) "So you must be very good to her, Violetta, and *you shall help me make* her clothes; but you need not be afraid I ever could love any one half or

one quarter as much as you, my own dear child, (PPCMBE, YONGE-1865.166.184)

The *to*-infinitive alternative is attested in the remaining 20 occurrences of my British LModE data, of which 11 show overt subject of infinitive and 9 the covert construction. The *to*-infinitive is more frequent with 0–1-word distance between the main verb and the infinitival clause (17 out of 20 examples). The length of the intervening words in the other instances is 2, 7 and 10 words, as in (534) below. Most of the main-clause subjects are pronouns (in 13 out of 20 instances), as in the case of *it* in (529), and the unexpressed pronoun (4 examples), illustrated in (533) and (534). One NP subject and two long complex subjects (9 and 24 words each) are attested, in (530).

(529) *It helps them to see* the point, to record it rapidly, and moreover it acts as a little anchor to the restless mind, (PPCMBE, BENSON-1908,51.154)

(530) *A moment's thought of what the highest religious truth must be –how large, how deep, how vastly greater than our power to embrace it* –will help us to see that it must be conveyed, or convey itself to us, not in a sentence, or in a moment, but by parts. (PPCMBE, TALBOT-1901.90.23)

Most of the examples of the *to*-infinitive complementation alternative have non-present and non-indicative *help* forms, in 16 and 14 (out of 20) instances, respectively, illustrated in (530) above. No examples are attested in passive-voice contexts and only two examples are found in relative clauses. As regards syntax, the *to*-infinitive fulfils a complement function in adverbial and main clauses, and only in two examples in constructions of syntactic dependency, as in (532) and (535) below, where it co-occurs with the relativisers *which* and *what* as the subjects of the relative clauses. In these *to*-infinitive clauses, the lower verbs are mainly transitive (15 out of 20 examples), *improve* in (531) and *service* and *maintain* in (532) illustrating intransitive and coordination uses, respectively.

(531) O Almighty God, inspire us with this divine Principle; kill in us all the Seeds of Envy and Ill-will; and *help us,* by cultivating within ourselves the Love of our Neighbour, *to improve* in the Love of Thee. (PPCMBE, BUTLER-1726,253.184)

(532) Indeed there are institutions, as I think so wisely, *which* take in only primiparae, and then *help the woman to service* and *to maintain her child herself* instead of sending it to the workhouse. (PPCMBE, NIGHTINGALE-189X,420.20)

With respect to RHYTHMIC ALTERNATION, the *to*-infinitive complements are distributed as follows: unproblematic contexts, 15 examples, as in (533) and (534); uncritical stress pattern, one example (535); and critical contexts, seven examples, as in (536). The unstressed pronoun *you* and the overshadowed particle of the phrasal verb *wash away* is the pattern in (533), while (534) contains material intervening between *us* and *to improve*. In (535), the *to*-complement is preceded and followed by unstressed syllables. Finally, in (536), the *to*-infinitive acts as a stress-clash buffer between *help* and *work*.

(533) if they go out of Town, they come *to help you to wash away* Sorrow; so that the good People are resolv'd to share both your Pleasure and your Pain. (PPCMBE, DAVYS-1716.29.178)

(534) Help *us, by the due Exercise of them, to improve* to Perfection; (PPCMBE, BUTLER-1726.254.187)

(535) What *helps us to evade* this may do us the worst moral mischief; and truth, if truth it be, cannot be more gravely misused. (PPCMBE, TALBOT-1901.111.290)

(536) The Captain of the Gloucester, detained *the Boat* and Men *to help to work* the Ship. (PPCMBE, OFFICER-1744.234.447)

The non-finite form *to help* is found in 4 (out of 20) examples with *to*-infinitive complementation. In two of these four instances, the *horror aequi* principle is violated, as in (536) above. In the other two, an NP intervening between *help* and the *to*-infinitive mitigates the effect of the co-occurrence of two items with identical morphology, as in (533) above with the pronoun *you*. As regards SUBJECT ANIMACY, 9 of the instances are animate (533), and 11 are non-animate (535). As explained in Chapter 2, the classification of the subject *the Boat and Men* as non-animate in example (536) above relies on the status of the first member of the coordination. All of the NP2 subjects of the complement clauses are animate. Finally, *help* plus *to*-infinitive is more frequently found with non-factual unrealised meanings (13 out of 20), as in (533) and

(534) above. Since no examples of *help* plus infinitive complement have a factual unrealised meaning in British LModE, the other 7 instances of *help* plus *to*-infinitive are factual realised, as in (535) and (536) above.

In American English, the number of the LModE examples allows the application of my 'glm' *Model 2*, using the methodology described in Section 4.3.2.1. *Model 2* includes the variables PRESENT and INDICATIVE, excluded from *Model 1* because of the categorical distribution of the ME and EModE data in those periods. Table 136 in Appendix shows the distribution of *help* plus infinitival complementation for the factors under analysis. The proportion of BI complementation in American LModE is significantly higher than in British English (42.68 vs 9.9 per cent). In American LModE, the distribution of the data according to the variable SUBJECT OF INFINITIVE shows that *help* is more frequently attested with covert subject of infinitive uses with infinitival clauses (59.76 per cent).

With respect to complexity, as revealed by the predictors SUBJECT COMPLEXITY and OBJECT COMPLEXITY, the productivity of pro subjects is higher in main (51.22 per cent) and lower clauses (75.75 per cent when only the construction with overt subject of infinitive is considered). Unexpressed subjects are also more frequent (26.83 per cent) than complex and NP subjects.

DISTANCE indicates that the construction disfavours the presence of intervening elements between *help* and the infinitival complement (57.32 per cent). In fact, when the length of intervening elements is 1–3 words, the productivity of the construction decreases to 42.68 per cent. The construction is infrequent in relative clauses (10.98 per cent) and absent in passive-voice contexts in either main or complement clauses. As regards PRESENT and INDICATIVE, the less complex present and indicative levels are attested in 21.95 and 40.24 per cent of the data.

The study of the RHYTHMIC ALTERNATION factor reveals that unproblematic contexts are the most common stress patterns, accounting for 68.29 per cent of the data, whereas the proportion of the so-called critical contexts is 31.7 per cent. HORROR AEQUI is operational in 24.39 per cent of instances. As for SYNTAX, the construction is favoured in main clauses (46.34 per cent), followed by dependent and adverbial clauses. The VALENCY factor reveals that most verbs are transitive in the complement clauses (87.8 per cent).

The semantic factor SUBJECT ANIMACY indicates that most main-clause subjects (64.63 per cent) and all of the NP2s between *help* and the infinitive clause have animate referents. In fact, the only complement clause with what is theoretically a non-animate subject, in (537), illustrates the metaphorical interpretation of the referent 'Italy' using the (animate) personal pronoun *her*. Finally, non-factual unrealised contexts are favoured by the construction in 56.1 per cent of the examples. Factual realised contexts account for 40.24 per cent of the data, whereas factual unrealised meanings are marginal (3.66 per cent) (see Table 136 in Appendix).

(537) Through the prohibition of emigration and through the return of hundreds of thousands of her sons from abroad to help *her* defend her rights and civilisation, *Italy* will have more population than when the war began, however great the losses caused by the war may prove. (COHA, news_1917_682980)

A number of variables cannot be included in *Model 2* because of the low frequencies in some of the factor levels. The variables excluded on this basis are SUBJECT COMPLEXITY, OBJECT COMPLEXITY, PASSIVISATION, RELATIVE, PRESENT, HORROR AEQUI, VALENCY and OBJECT ANIMACY. As mentioned above, my American LModE data contain no examples of passive voice contexts or non-animate objects. As regards SUBJECT COMPLEXITY, Table 110 shows an almost categorical preference by NP subjects for the *to*-infinitive alternative, and a significant frequency of pro and complex subjects also with *to*-infinitive complements, as in (538). BI, on the other hand, is more frequent with unexpressed subjects, as in (539) (P=0.0030 and P=0.000010 in comparison with pro and complex subjects, respectively; no significant difference is observed between complex and pro subjects, P=0.603). Example (538) contains a 24-word subject in which *the coacher* is postmodified by a relative clause introduced by *who*. Example (539) is coded as unexpressed because *help* is found in the non-finite form and preceded by a *to*-infinitive, the NP *a German locomotive engineer* being the logical subject of *help*. Unexpressed subjects with BI clauses occur in *horror aequi* contexts in 18 out of the 19 instances; in the other example (540), the selection of BI is affected by the presence of *to* in the catenative verb *intend*.

	Complex	NP	pro	Unexpressed
BI	3 (0.36)	1 (0.12)	12 (1.45)	19 (2.29)
TO	7 (0.84)	7 (0.84)	30 (3.62)	3 (0.36)

Table 110: Subject complexity and *help* plus *to*-infinitive/BI clause in the American LModE data (raw and n.f./10,000 IP-MATs)

(538) Beyond doubt *the coacher who can control and use the noise of a great crowd, and direct it upon some panicky player at the right instant,* can help his team to win. (COHA, mag_1911_430486)

(539) Returning from Berlin to Paris in February, I found myself alone, in a compartment on the train from Cologne to Spa, with *a German locomotive engineer* on his way *to help advise* the German armistice commission about the delivery of railway engines and cars to the Allies. (COHA, mag_1919_434026)

(540) He had *intended to* join the land forces of Mark Antony and *help crush* the rebellious Pompey, but Antony had done the trick alone; and only a few days before, word had come that Pompey was dead. (COHA, fic_1910_2859)

The *horror aequi* principle is almost categorical because *help* plus *to*-infinitive complementation is attested in only one out of 20 instances (541), where the distance between *to help* and the infinitival complement explains the selection of the *to*-infinitive alternative. When *help* selects a BI clause, more than half of the non-finite *help* forms are *to*-infinitives (19 out of 26). In contrast to the diachronic and synchronic British English data, in American LModE, not only the infinitive (*to*) *help* but also other non-finite and finite paradigmatic forms are attested with BI complementation (see Table 111). This reflects the spread of the BI alternative through contexts formerly restricted to the *to*-infinitive option.

(541) "He knew that he was not happy; but he might, like most people with whom life had not succeeded. often imagine himself so, and Marmaduke wanted *to help him*, if possible, *to imagine it*." (COHA, mag_1918_434258)

	Non-finite *help*	Finite *help*	Finite *helped*	Non-finite *helped*	*Helping*	*Helps*
BI	26 (3.14)	1 (0.12)	4 (0.48)	1 (0.12)	1 (0.12)	2 (0.24)
TO	17 (2.05)	4 (0.48)	6 (0.72)	5 (0.6)	5 (0.6)	10 (1.21)

Table 111: Paradigm forms of *help* plus *to*-infinitive/BI clause in American LModE (raw and n.f./10,000 IP-MATs)

The distribution of the data in relation to the predictor OBJECT COMPLEXITY shows that both complementation alternatives are more frequent with pro subjects in the complement clause (the *to*-infinitive/BI variation is not statistically significant with NP vs pro lower-clause subjects, P=0.240) (see Table 112). No instances of complex infinitive-clause subjects are attested.

	NP	pro	Unexpressed
BI	5 (0.6)	10 (1.21)	20 (2.41)
TO	3 (0.36)	15 (1.81)	29 (3.5)

Table 112: Object complexity and *help* plus *to-infinitive/BI clause* in American LModE (raw and n.f./10,000 IP-MATs)

The predictor RELATIVE is not included in *Model 2* because the *to*-infinitive alternative is categorical in the 9 examples of relative clauses (Table 136 in Appendix), in line with the Complexity Principle. For example, *a light* in (542) is the antecedent of the relativiser *that*, which functions as the subject of *helped*. However, the present-tense *help* forms, which are considered less complex in the verbal paradigm, favour *to*-infinitive and not BI complementation (P=0.010), as in (543) (see Table 113). The greater success of BI with non-finite forms of *help* explains this distribution (cf. Table 111).

	Present	Other
BI	3 (0.36)	32 (3.86)
TO	15 (1.81)	32 (3.86)

Table 113: Present and *help* plus *to*-infinitive/BI clause in American LModE (raw and n.f./10,000 IP-MATs)

(542) In her eyes was a light *that* helped to tell the great news. (COHA, fic_1914_3214)

(543) The plowing aerates the soil and *helps* to set plant food free. (COHA, nf_1913_773672)

With respect to VALENCY, BI clauses are restricted to transitive infinitive verbs, as is the case with *realize* in (544), which selects as its compulsory complement *the character of the individual and his work* (see Table 114). Conversely, the *to*-infinitive is only found with intransitive lower-clause verbs, as in the case of *die* in (545), resulting in the exclusion of VALENCY from *Model 2*. The coordination level, which only accounts for 4.88 per cent of the data, is found in one instance with a BI clause, in (546), with the coordinated verbs *pay* and *write*, and in three examples with *to*-infinitive complements, illustrated in (547) with *build* and *rebuild*.

	Intransitive	Transitive	Coordination
BI	0	34 (4.1)	1 (0.12)
TO	6 (0.72)	38 (4.58)	3 (0.36)

Table 114: Valency of the *to*-infinitive/BI complement clause governed by *help* in American LModE (raw and n.f./10,000 IP-MATs)

(544) These help us realize *the character of the individual and his work*. (COHA, nf_1919_771390)

(545) We need the patience -- that goes without saying; but it's the love that helps us to *die* gladly -- love for our cause, our pals, our family, our country. (COHA, nf_1918_755585)

(546) There's one thing only of you I beseech, To help me *pay* the printer -- *write* thy speech. (COHA, fic_1818_8886)

(547) They themselves helped *to build and rebuild* it. (COHA, nf_1916_751482)

Finally, the factor NOTIONAL CHARACTERISATION cannot be included in *Model 2* either because the *to*-infinitive clause is not found in examples with factual unrealised meanings. Example (548) is one of the three instances in which the proposition is factual but the infinitival clause in unrealised; the context following the construction in (548) indicates that *business* is delayed rather than stabilised. The relation between the variation and factual realised and non-factual unrealised meanings is not statistically significant ($\chi^2(1)=0.16$, P=0.527). *Help* is more frequent with non-factual unrealised meanings when it selects an infinitival complement, as in (549), with the *to*-infinitive clause. The conditional clause in example (549) conveys a non-factual meaning in which the proposition conveyed by the infinitival clause has not taken place.

	Factual realised	**Factual unrealised**	**Non-factual unrealised**
BI	12 (1.45)	3 (0.36)	20 (2.41)
TO	21 (2.53)	0	26 (3.14)

Table 115: Notional characterisation of *help* plus *to*-infinitive/BI clause in American LModE (raw and n.f./10,000 IP-MATs)

(548) About three months have elapsed since it was announced that it was the intention of the Redfield Committee to *help stabilize* business, but the only effect of this announcement and the deliberations since that time, has been to retard the development of business generally. (COHA, news_1919_684516)

(549) "If," I promised, "you *help us to escape and come* with us, we will give you not only money, but a job for life in Australia." (COHA, mag_1919_467032)

The *to*-infinitive/BI alternation is shown to be productive in all of the levels of the predictors SUBJECT OF INFINITIVE, DISTANCE, INDICATIVE, RHYTHMIC ALTERNATION, SUBJECT ANIMACY and SYNTAX. Following the methodology explained in Section 3.2.1, *STEP 1* tests whether the variables that were explanatory in PDE, i.e. SUBJECT OF INFINITIVE, DISTANCE, INDICATIVE, RHYTHMIC ALTERNATION and SUBJECT ANIMACY, are also significant in my American LModE data or not. Owing to the collinearity between SUBJECT OF INFINITIVE and DISTANCE, these predictors are tested separately against the non-collinear variables INDICATIVE, RHYTHMIC ALTERNATION and SUBJECT ANIMACY. ANOVA (P=0.233) shows that the addition of the *STEP 2* variable SYNTAX to *STEP 1* does not significantly improve *Model 2*. To avoid an overfitted regression model, only the predictors of *STEP 1* are analysed with my American LModE data. As in the case of *Model 1*, the *to*-infinitive alternative is taken as the reference level of the response variable, so negative 'Estimate' values indicate a preference for this level. Table 116 displays the results of these analyses after step "backward".

Predictor	**Estimate**	**P-value**	**OR**
Intercept	-1.1394	0.00503 **	1/0.320000= 3.125
Indicative	1.3442	0.00689 **	3.8352
(Ref. Level: *Indicative*)			
Other			

Table 116: *Model 2, STEP 1, help* plus *to*-infinitive/BI clause in American LModE (step "backward" results)

Model 2, STEP 1 shows that INDICATIVE is the only significant predictor (Pr(>|z|)=0.00689). This means that: (i) the probability of finding a *to*-infinitive/BI complement with covert subject of infinitive is similar to that with overt ones, as in (550) and (551), respectively; (ii) distance does not favour the marked alternative of complementation and, hence, the Complexity Principle is not corroborated; (iii) both types of complement are attested more frequently with animate subjects, as in, for example, *most of us* in (552) (cf. *The verdict of Italy* in example (550)); (iv) both complementation alternatives are found in unproblematic contexts, as in (551); and (v) *to*-infinitive/BI have similar chances of occurrence in all three syntactic contexts analysed.

(550) The verdict of Italy *helped to turn* the feeling of the civilized world against the pretensions of Germany. (COHA, news_1914_681503)

(551) So she does not wave it; she proceeds with an ostrichlike caution; all she wants to do is to *help the Finns restore* order. (COHA, news_1918_683757)

(552) "*Most of us have helped to brighten* your lives on other Christmas days. possibly by our gifts and our presence. Pew this year can give what they desire; none can be with you." (COHA, news_1917_683630)

As regards the significant variable INDICATIVE, *help* prefers BI complementation in non-indicative contexts, by 3.83 percentage points, as in (553) and (554). In fact, 19 (out of 27) examples with BI complements in non-indicative predicates are explained by *horror aequi*, as in (553) (see Table 117). Conversely, the odds of the *to*-infinitive are higher when the main verbal group has indicative mood, as in the case of *have helped* in (555) and *helps* in (556).

(553) I have told the President and the Secretary of War that I would be willing to raise and lower the limits whenever necessary *to help win* the war, but I wish it to be necessary, and I prefer to raise them before lowering them. (COHA, news_1918_684106)

(554) I *saw him help his mother climb* the wheel as she took her place on the seat. (COHA, fic_1910_2859)

(555) They *have helped to dispose* of the vile slanders against this city, that it is a place given over to vice and crime. (COHA, news_1911_679540)

(556) One of the big influences that *helps to keep* a soldier's soul sanitary is what is known in the British Army as "spit and polish. (COHA, nf_1918_755585)

	Indicative	Non-indicative
BI	8 (0.96)	27 (3.25)
TO	25 (3.01)	22 (2.65)

Table 117: Indicative and *help* plus *to*-infinitive/BI clause in American LModE (raw and n.f./10,000 IP-MATs)

In summary, the *horror aequi* principle is a very strong determinant in the American LModE data and exerts an indirect influence on the type of contexts in which BI clauses occur, i.e. with unexpressed main clause subjects, in non-present tense and non-indicative mood expressions. Unlike the synchronic and diachronic British English data, the American LModE data show early signs of forms like *helping*, *helps* and *helped* with BI complementation. When *help* is inflected for indicative mood, *to*-infinitive complement clauses are significantly higher, this being the preferred alternative with present-tense *help* as well. In addition, *help* plus *to*-infinitive occurs with simple and more complex subjects and lower verbal groups. Object complexity does not affect infinitival choice, whereas in relative clauses the *to*-infinitive level is categorical. Finally, the two complementation variants show a similar distribution with factual realised and non-factual unrealised meanings, with BI found to be categorical in the few examples conveying a factual unrealised interpretation.

4.3.2.2.3 Model 3: American and British PDE

For the purposes of consistency, *Model 3* repeats the predictors included in the previous models. However, two separate statistical analyses are run in this section, one for American PDE and another for British PDE. Table 136 in Appendix summarises the distribution of each predictor in *Model 3*.

PDE shows a trend reversal in favour of BI complementation with respect to the earlier periods and varieties analysed. As pointed out in Section 4.3.1, the proportion of BI is higher than that of the *to*-infinitive alternative in both varieties, and this is more pronounced in American English ($\chi^2(1)$=50.7, P=<.0001; the chi-square values are calculated by comparing the BI and *to*-infinitive data for each variety). The effect of the presence/absence of a subject of infinitive on the alternation is similar in both varieties, with over and covert subject of inifinitive uses representing approximately 50 per cent of the data.

The distribution of the four levels of SUBJECT COMPLEXITY is more even in American English. British English significantly favours pro subjects vs complex and NP subjects ($\chi^2(1)$=5.38, P=0.0155 and $\chi^2(1)$=7.36, P=0.0049, respectively). The difference between NP and unexpressed subjects is also significant, with British English having the lower proportion ($\chi^2(1)$=3.69, P=0.0434).

The four strategies of object complexity display a similar distribution in both varieties (see Table 136 in Appendix). The quantile established by the frequencies of the predictor DISTANCE between *help* and the infinitival clause is 1–7 words in British English and 2–7 words in American English. The proportion of examples occurring in relative clauses is similar in both varieties (12.23 per cent in British English and 13.5 per cent in American English). Passivisation is attested in British English on three occasions. Present-tense verbal groups are more frequent in American English ($\chi^2(1)=6.11$, P=0.0101) than in British English. Finally, mood exerts no influence on the variation in each variety, with non-indicative verbal groups showing a higher distribution in both.

In line with the tendency revealed by the diachronic data, *help* plus *to*-infinitive/ BI is more frequent in unproblematic stress patterns. Critical contexts represent 23.74 and 21.17 per cent of the data in British and American English, respectively. HORROR AEQUI is more significant in British English and accounts for 27.16 per cent of the examples, vs 20.86 per cent in American English ($\chi^2(1)=4.04$, P=0.0366).

The proportions of the construction according to syntactic context are quite similar in both varieties: most frequent in main clauses, followed by dependent and then adverbial contexts. With respect to the valency of the infinitive clause, more than 89 per cent of lower verbs are transitive and coordination is statistically marginal.

As regards ANIMACY, non-animate subjects and animate objects are preferred in both variants. Finally, as regards the predictor NOTIONAL CHARACTERISATION, so-called non-factual unrealised contexts are slightly preferred in British and in American English.

Model 3 analyses the variables SUBJECT OF INFINITIVE, DISTANCE, OBJECT COMPLEXITY and OBJECT ANIMACY separately plus the other *STEP1* factors. Owing to the low number of *to*-infinitive complement clauses (40 instances) in American English, only four factors may be included in the model of the American English data. In contrast, *to*-infinitive complementation is more productive in the British variety (191 examples) and so allows more predictors to be included in *Model 3* for British English. For comparability purposes, *Model 3* for British English is implemented first and step "backward" function applied to the results in order to identify the most significant factors in this variety and apply them in my analysis of the American English data. As shown in Table 136 in Appendix, BI is taken as the reference level because of its frequency.

4.3.2.2.3.1 Model 3: Help and to-infinitive/BI in British PDE

All of the predictors and levels in Table 136 in Appendix, with the exception of PASSIVISATION and NOTIONAL CHARACTERISATION, have enough examples to be included in *Model 3* for British PDE. The database contains three examples with passive verbal groups which have *to*-infinitive complements (n.f. 0.09); two contain passive main verbal group, such as *can be helped* in (557), while the other contains a passive infinitive clause (558).

(557) With AAS, new firms can be given cash incentives to set up in Tendring, or established ones *can be helped* to expand and create more jobs and opportunities. (BNC Baby, CFC)

(558) Fellow councillor Margaret Crooks said it was clear the bombing had been an "inside job" and she called for those who helped the bombers *to be ostracised* (BNC Baby, CBM)

As illustrated in Table 118, *help* plus *to*-infinitive occurs only twice with factual unrealised meanings, as in (559). However, the semantic/pragmatic context does not appear to affect the variation: *help* plus BI is slightly more frequent in non-factual unrealised contexts than in the factual realised ones, but the difference is not statistically significant ($\chi^2(1)=1.33$, P=0.2131). The difference between factual unrealised and the other two meanings is not significant either (P=0.28954 with respect to factual realised and P=0.40580 with respect to non-factual unrealised).

	Factual realised	**Factual unrealised**	**Non-factual unrealised**
BI	145 (4.35)	7 (0.21)	213 (6.4)
TO	87 (2.61)	2 (0.06)	102 (3.06)

Table 118: Notional characterisation of *help* plus *to*-infinitive/BI clause in British PDE (raw and n.f./10,000 <s> units)

(559) Any post-war government would have met Unionist critics in its reconsideration of Britain's imperial role, but the existence of a bipartisan policy *did not help to secure acceptance.* (BNC Baby, EW1)

The analysis of *Model 3, STEP 1* with the predictors SUBJECT OF INFINITIVE, DISTANCE, OBJECT COMPLEXITY and OBJECT ANIMACY reveals that

HORROR AEQUI, PRESENT and VALENCY are significant after step "backward". SUBJECT OF INFINITIVE and OBJECT COMPLEXITY are significant explainers of the distribution of *to*-infinitive/BI complements in their own 'glm'. DISTANCE is significant when it interacts with HORROR AEQUI. In the analysis with the interaction term, INDICATIVE is also shown to be a significant factor in the model. As explained below, OBJECT ANIMACY is the only non-significant variable in this group. ANOVA reveals that OBJECT COMPLEXITY creates a better model than the other three factors, the greatest difference being with the interaction (P=0.08926). However, given that the effect of OBJECT COMPLEXITY cannot be tested for American English owing to the low or null occurrence of instances in the NP and complex levels, respectively, SUBJECT OF INFINITIVE is selected for *STEP 2*, together with the other *STEP 1* factors in order to check whether SYNTAX, RELATIVE and SUBJECT COMPLEXITY have an effect on the variation or not. The results indicate that the *STEP 2* predictors are not significant either before or after the step "backward" function. My analysis therefore focuses on the significant variables from *STEP 1* and some relevant aspects of the non-significant factors.

Predictor	**Estimate**	**P-value**	**OR**
Intercept	1.1146	0.04258 *	3.0484
Subject of infinitive (Ref. Level: *Covert*) Overt	-0.4092	0.03935 *	1/0.6641953= 1.5055
Horror Aequi (Ref. Level: *Other*) Yes	-1.8185	6.22e-10 ***	1/0.1622684= 6.1626
Present (Ref. Level: *Other*) Present	0.5407	0.06105 .	1.7171
Valency (Ref. Level: *Coordination*) Intransitive	-0.9299	0.13617	1/0.3945851= 2.5343
Transitive	-1.5530	0.00276 **	1/0.2116212= 4.7254
Animacy (Ref. Level: *Animate*) Non-animate	0.2891	0.15467	1.3352057

Table 119: *Model 3, STEP 1*, significant factors with *help* plus *to*-infinitive/BI clause in British PDE (step "backward" results)

As shown in Table 119, HORROR AEQUI is the strongest predictor in *Model 3, STEP 1*. As with the diachronic data, the odds of the *to*-infinitive alternative decrease with *to*-infinitive *help* (by 6.16 percentage points). Even though it is not statistically significant, DISTANCE seems to have a mitigating effect on the *horror aequi* principle in British PDE (Pr(>|z|)= 0.13781; see Table 120); in fact, as Figure 21 illustrates, an increase in one word between *to help* and the infinitival clause favours the use of the *to*-infinitive clause, as in (560) with four intervening words (*members of the public*). When *help* is not preceded by a *to*-infinitive form, as in (561), distance favours the use of the BI clause in a statistically significant way (by 1.43 percentage points, Pr(>|z|)=0.01047) (see example (562)).

Predictor	**Estimate**	**P-value**	**OR**
Intercept	0.4076	0.42131	1.5031837
Distance:Horror	-0.3592	0.01047 *	1/0.6982598= 1.4321
Aequi =Other	0.2942	0.13781	1.3420817
Distance:Horror Aequi =Yes			
Indicative (Ref.	-0.4059	0.05417 .	1/0.6664079= 1.5005
Level: *Indicative*)			
Non-indicative			
Present (Ref. Level: *Other*)	0.6502	0.03928 *	1.9159
Present			
Valency (Ref.	-0.6756	0.23704	1/0.5088763= 1.9651
Level: *Coordination*)	-1.2584	0.00684 **	1/0.2841183= 3.5196
Intransitive			
Transitive			
Animacy (Ref.	0.2973	0.13286	1.3462
Level: *Animate*)			
Non-animate			

Table 120: *Model 3, STEP 1*, significant factors with *help* plus *to*-infinitive/BI clause in British PDE (step "backward" results)

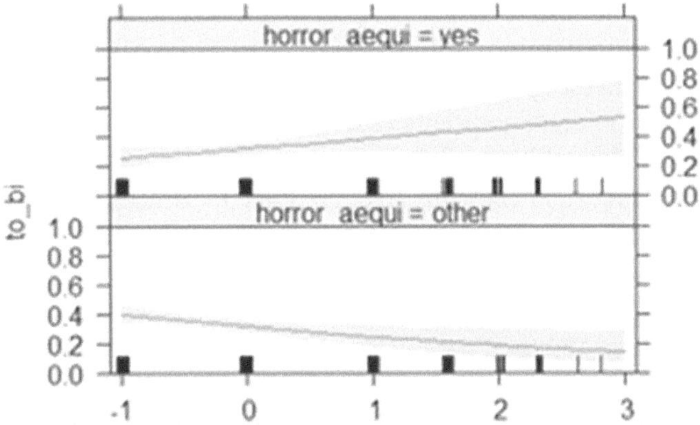

Figure 21: *Model 3, STEP 1*, interaction DISTANCE:HORROR AEQUI and *help* plus *to*-infinitive/BI clause in British PDE (step "backward" results)

(560) The objectives are to help *members of the public* to find their way through this information store and to transmit their orders for particular journeys or holidays to the providers of those services. (BNC Baby, CLP)

(561) The stock fell another 6 to 240p before Hoare Govett was reported to have issued a recommendation on the basis of a 9 p.c. yeild, *helping the price partially recover* to 242 ½p. (BNC Baby, AHB)

(562) In the letter, the President supports the envoy proposal, pledges to take a more active role in *helping to end* the violence and criticises the role of the British Government. (BNC Baby, K2N)

This result tallies with those produced by the SUBJECT OF INFINITIVE variable, according to which the presence of an NP between *help* and the infinitival complement significantly favours BI, as in (561) above (Pr(>|z|)=0.03935; see Table 119). The probability of *to*-infinitive in the construction with covert subject of infinitive increases by 1.5 percentage points, as in (562) above, in contrast to BI complementation (see also Table 121).

	Covert	**Overt**
BI	178 (5.34)	187 (5.61)
TO	108 (3.24)	83 (2.49)

Table 121: Presence/absence of an NP2 between *help* plus *to*-infinitive/BI clause in British PDE (raw and n.f./10,000 <s> units)

The analysis of the levels of the predictor OBJECT COMPLEXITY reveals that lower-clause complex subjects significantly favour the *to*-infinitive alternative, as in (560) above and (563) below, vs NP and pro subjects, by 5.56 and 4.47 percentage points (Pr(>|z|)=0.02620 and Pr(>|z|)=04937), respectively. The subjects of the complement clauses in (560) and (563) are complex because they involve PP post modification. Conversely, NP lower-clause subjects significantly prefer BI complements, as in (564), by 1.87 percentage points, and pro lower-clause subject favour BI clauses (565) (Pr(>|z|)=0.08250), vs unexpressed lower-clause subjects, as in (562) above and (566) below (see Figure 22). Finally, when complex and unexpressed lower-clause subjects are compared, the variation is not statistically significant; the results simply indicate that unexpressed subjects tend to select BI clauses (P=0.05360; see also Table 122).

(563) Mrs Thatcher has been convinced by her Environment Secretary, Mr Chris Patten, from his days at overseas development that there is an important role for Britain to play in helping *countries like Brazil* to manage its forests correctly. (BNC Baby, A7W)

(564) He looked a pale shadow of the commanding centre half who helped *Denmark* win the European championship, but said: 'I won't crack under the pressure. (BNC Baby, CH3)

(565) 'They don't have a lot left over for themselves and they see smoking as an affordable luxury which helps *them* cope.' (BNC Baby, K5C)

(566) Destined to run in Manchester, they will relieve traffic congestion and *help to reduce* the levels of carbon monoxide in the city centre, outlying suburbs and satellite towns of Bury, Altrincham, Salford, Oldham and Rochdale. (BNC Baby, A3M)

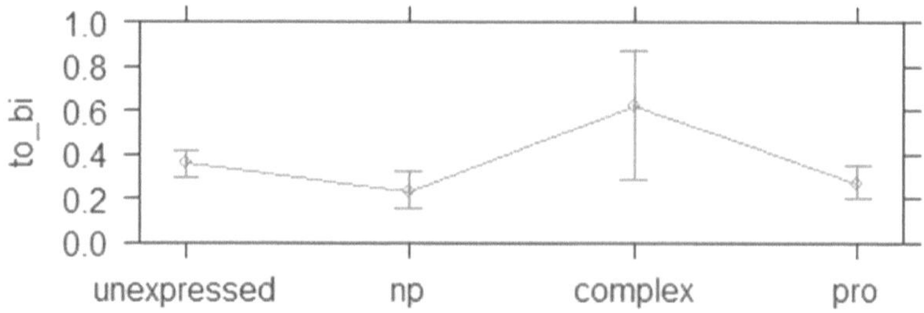

Figure 22: *Model 3, STEP 1,* OBJECT COMPLEXITY and *help* plus *to*-infinitive/BI clause in British PDE (step "backward" results)

	Complex	NP	Pro	Unexpressed
BI	5 (0.15)	82 (2.46)	100 (3)	178 (5.34)
TO	5 (0.15)	30 (0.9)	48 (1.44)	108 (3.24)

Table 122: Object complexity and *help* plus *to*-infinitive/BI clause in British PDE (raw and n.f./10,000 <s> units)

No significant differences are revealed by the models as regards animate complement-clause subjects in comparison with non-animate (Pr(>|z|)=0.12530) and unexpressed ones (Pr(>|z|)=0.13757; Figure 23). With unexpressed subjects, the differences in comparison with non-animate is statistically significant (Pr(>|z|)=0.01999). As with SUBJECT OF INFINITIVE, unexpressed subjects in lower complement clauses favour the *to*-infinitive alternative, as in (566) above, whereas non-animate ones opt for BI clauses, as in (561) above.

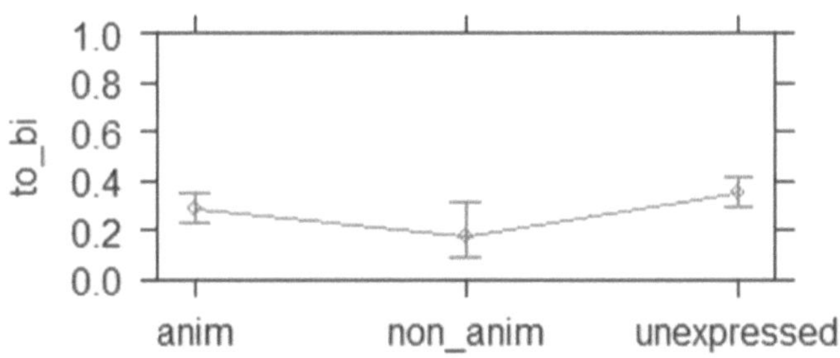

Figure 23: *Model 3, STEP 1,* OBJECT ANIMACY and *help* plus *to*-infinitive/BI clause in British PDE (step "backward" results)

The valency of the infinitival clause also explains the type of infinitive clause selected by *help* (see Table 123). The effect is significant when a comparison is made between coordination and transitive lower verbal groups (Pr(>|z|)=0.00276; see Table 119). The *to*-infinitive alternative is more frequently found with coordinated infinitives, such as *redress* and *bring back* in (567), whereas BI complementation prefers transitive verbs, in (568), by 4.72 percentage points. In comparison to complex lower verbal groups, the variation is not statistically significant when the lower verb is intransitive (Pr(>|z|)=0.13617), as in the case of *clear up* in (569). Variation is not significant when transitive and intransitive subordinate verbal groups are compared, but there is a trend in favour of the *to*-infinitive clause to occur with intransitive lower verbs (Pr(>|z|)=0.09943).

	Intransitive	Transitive	Coordinated
BI	21 (0.63)	336 (10.09)	8 (0.24)
TO	16 (0.48)	161 (4.83)	14 (0.42)

Table 123: Valency of the *to*-infinitive/BI complement clause governed by *help* in British PDE (raw and n.f./10,000 <s> units)

(567) "This will help *to redress* the balance and *bring* them *back* to a positive situation. Every little helps," he added. (BNC Baby, CBD)

(568) The historical background provided in this chapter helps us *understand some of these diagnoses as well as some of the prescriptions.* (BNC Baby, J57)

(569) Afterwards, when Billie had helped *clear up* and Adam had finished the list of instructions for Lily, they settled down in the living room with a large jug of coffee. (BNC Baby, G0L)

The predictor PRESENT is relevant to the variation in the analysis with the interaction DISTANCE:HORROR AEQUI (Pr(>|z|)=0.03928). Non-present *help* forms increase the use of BI complements by 1.91 percentage points, as illustrated by the past participle *helped* in (570). The *to*-infinitive alternative is significantly more frequent with present-tense *help* forms, as in (571) (see Table 124).

	Present	Non-present
BI	27 (0.81)	338 (10.15)
TO	36 (1.08)	155 (4.65)

Table 124: Present and *help* plus *to*-infinitive/BI clause in British PDE (raw and n.f./10,000 <s> units)

(570) Roycroft also claims – and many in the health authority agree with him – that relationships between the social services department and the health authority, both managerially and professionally, have long been good and *have helped* underpin a high level of community care. (BNC Baby, FT1)

(571) Pub *helps* to put its customers off alcohol. (BNC Baby, K3B)

Also, the interaction DISTANCE:HORROR AEQUI, INDICATIVE shows a tendency in the model (Pr(>|z|)=0.05417) (see Table 120). The odds of *to*-infinitive decrease by 1.5 percentage points when *help* is in the non-indicative mood, as in (572), in favour of the BI alternative, as in (573). A closer look at not only the morphological forms of *help* but also at finiteness in general helps to explain these results (see Figure 24). The univariate analysis indicates that the finiteness of *help* affects the variation: non-finite *help* strongly favours BI, whereas finite *help* significantly prefers *to*-infinitive ($\chi^2(1)=11.83$, P=0.0002). At the same time, third-person singular present *helps* and the form *helping* significantly favour *to*-infinitive complementation ($\chi^2(1)=7.69$, P=0.0033 and $\chi^2(1)=3.42$, P=0.0431, in comparison with the totals of the other (non-) finite forms in each case). Finite and non-finite *helped* do not exert a significant influence on non-finite complementation ($\chi^2(1)=0$, P=0.8625 for the finite form, and $\chi^2(1)=2.95$, P=0.0581 for the non-finite one). Only a univariate analysis is possible here, given the number of (non-) finite levels and the low number of instances per level.

(572) Thinking about the way a word is put together *can sometimes help you to remember* how to spell it. (BNC Baby, HXH)

(573) They hope that the fact they reported the matter *will help them avoid* a disqualification. (BNC Baby, CH3)

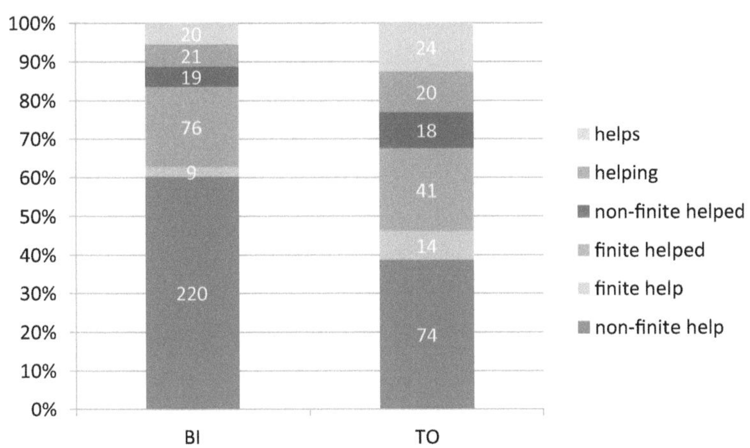

Figure 24: Paradigm forms of *help* plus *to*-infinitive/BI clause in British PDE

In summary, the results of the analysis of the British English data set reveal that *to*-infinitive/BI variation is explained by the *horror aequi* principle by demonstrating that identical morphological forms are avoided in the immediate contexts. DISTANCE mitigates the effect of the non-finite infinitive form *to help* and allows *to*-infinite complementation when the number of intervening words between forms with identical morphology is greater. The analysis of SUBJECT OF INFINITIVE shows that BI clauses are significantly preferred in constructions with overt lower subjects, where the complexity of the object also plays a role: when the NP intervening between *help* and the infinitival clause is complex, the chances of *to*-infinitive increase significantly in comparison with NP and pro lower-clause subjects; NP and pro subjects are also preferred with BI complementation in comparison to the unexpressed subjects, probably because the latter are, from a cognitive perspective, harder to process. Valency issues are also of importance here: the construction is, in general, more frequent with transitive lower verbs, BI is favoured when the verbs in the complement clauses are transitive, and the *to*-infinitive alternative is more successful when the lower verbs are coordinated. *To*-infinitive complementation is illustrated by the three examples involving passivisation, which is in keeping with the Complexity Principle. The univariate analysis indicates that BI is more frequent with infinitive *help* forms, either preceded by another *to*-infinitive element (in a *horror aequi* context) or preceded by a modal auxiliary. Finite *help*, *helps* and non-finite *helping* favour *to*-infinitive complements. The animacy of the infinitival-clause subject indicates that non-animate lower subjects prefer BI clauses, whereas unexpressed ones the *to*-infinitive clause. Finally, the semantic/pragmatic interpretation conveyed by the construction and the Principle of Rhythmic Alternation do not exert a significant influence on the variation. The model only suggests that *help* plus *to*-infinitive/BI is more frequent with non-factual unrealised meanings and in so-called unproblematic stress patterns.

4.3.2.2.3.2 Model 3: Help and to-infinitive/BI in American PDE

Model 3 for American English contains all of the significant variables in *Model 3*, *STEP 1* for British English except VALENCY; the database contains only three *to*-infinitive complements governed by intransitive verbs, as in (574), and two with coordinated complement clauses, as in

(575) (see Table 125). However, the variation is not statistically significant (P=0.693), not even when intransitive and transitive uses are contrasted (P=0.484) or when transitive and coordination valency levels are compared (P=0.524).

	Intransitive	Transitive	Coordination
BI	18 (4.94)	256 (70.24)	12 (3.29)
TO	3 (0.82)	35 (9.6)	2 (0.55)

Table 125: Valency of the *to*-infinitive/BI complement clause governed by *help* in American PDE (raw and n.f./10,000 IP-MATs)

(574) She ran to St. August and helped him *to sit down* to conserve energy (COHA, fic_1996_54389)

(575) By making river cleanup the focus of a multidisciplinary curriculum, the East Peoria project helps *to unite* the school, *give* traditional course work a special relevance, and *spark* student enthusiasm for conservation and community activism. (COHA, news_1996_658415)

A multivariate approach to OBJECT COMPLEXITY and OBJECT ANIMACY is not feasible either. As Table 126 shows, there are no instances of *to*-infinitive clauses with complex subjects, and NP subjects in lower clauses occur only three times, as in the case of the subjects *Amiel* and *the wine* in (576) and (577), respectively. Nonetheless, no significant differences are observed between NP and pro subjects (P=0.611). Non-animate objects, accounting for 8.44 per cent of the data, are attested in one example with the *to*-infinitive alternative, in (577) (see Table 127). Passivisation, found in three examples in British English, is not attested with the *to*-infinitive variant in the American variety.

	Complex	NP	Pro	Unexpressed
BI	6 (1.65)	51 (13.99)	89 (24.42)	140 (38.41)
TO	0	3 (0.82)	5 (1.37)	32 (8.78)

Table 126: Object complexity and *help* plus *to*-infinitive/BI clause in American PDE (raw and n.f./10,000 IP-MATs)

(576) Friends helped *Amiel* to cross into Turkey, where he set out for Istanbul, the main hub for immigrant smugglers in the region. (COHA, news_2000_660012)

(577) This also extracts tannins and other compounds which add flavor and help *the wine* to keep better. (COHA, mag_1995_426553)

Model 3 for American English can cope with DISTANCE as a fixed predictor but not with the interaction of this factor and HORROR AEQUI. Of the 68 potential scenarios of *horror aequi* in the data, the *to*-infinitive alternative is attested in one example, in (578). Distance between *help* and the *to*-infinitive complement may favour lack of compliance with *horror aequi* in example (578). As in the synchronic and diachronic analysis of the British English data, the factor HORROR AEQUI is significant in relation to the *to*-infinitive/BI alternation.

	Animate	**Non-animate**	**Unexpressed**
BI	134 (36.77)	12 (3.29)	140 (38.41)
TO	7 (1.92)	1 (0.27)	32 (8.78)

Table 127: Object animacy and *help* plus *to*-infinitive/BI clause in American PDE (raw and n.f./10,000 IP-MATs)

(578) Those that have it and those that don't. Butler: What advice would you give me *to help my community to do* that? (COHA, news_1999_639445)

(579) Growing up, Dole worked as a soda jerk, a janitor and sold milk *to help his struggling family make* ends meet. (COHA, news_1995_601143)

Two analyses were then implemented in *Model 3* in the American English variety, one with SUBJECT OF INFINITIVE and one with DISTANCE plus the three factors which were also significant in the British English *Model 3*: PRESENT and INDICATIVE. INDICATIVE does not explain the alternation in my American PDE data; in fact, this predictor is removed from the model after step "backward" in the two analyses. Table 128 shows the results of the analysis with SUBJECT OF INFINITIVE.

Predictor	Estimate	Std Error	z value	P-value	OR
Intercept	-1.7050	0.2238	-7.620	2.54e-14 ***	0.1817786 (1/ 0.1817786= 5.501198)
Subject of infinitive (Reference Level: *Covert*) Overt	-1.4805	0.4181	-3.541	0.000399 ***	0.2275142 (1/0.2275142= 4.39533)
Present (Reference Level: *Other*) Present	1.0637	0.3903	2.726	0.006419 **	2.8971593

Table 128: *Model 3, STEP 1*, significant factors with *help* plus *to*-infinitive/BI clause in American PDE (step "backward" results)

As in the British PDE data, SUBJECT OF INFINITIVE is shown to be a significant variable (Pr(>|z|)=0.000399) in this model. The estimate's negative value in Table 128 shows that the presence of an intervening NP2 increases the odds of the BI clause, as in *musicians Blaze, Riff and Surge* in (580) (4.39 percentage points). In contrast, the proportion of *to*-infinitive clauses is higher when the NP2 is absent (581) (see Table 129).

	Intransitive	Transitive
BI	140 (38.41)	146 (40.06)
TO	32 (8.78)	8 (2.19)

Table 129: Transitivity and *help* plus *to*-infinitive/BI clause in the American PDE data (raw and n.f./10,000 IP-MATs)

(580) So, claim your backstage pass' at the Zap venue and help *musicians Blaze, Riff and Surge* repair their equipment before the big concert. (COHA, mag_1998_390828)

(581) I think that "the puzzle" *helped to shape* my conception of the world and of life itself. (COHA, fic_1999_28238)

PRESENT also affects the distribution of *help* plus *to*-infinitive/BI (Pr(>|z|)=0.006419). The BI alternative is significantly favoured by the levels non-present tense (by 2.89 percentage points), simple past *helped* forms (582), and the presence of a modal auxiliary (583). By contrast, the *to*-infinitive level is more successful with present-tense, as the third-person present *helps* form in (584). The raw and the normalised frequencies are given in Table 130.

	Present	Non-present
BI	44 (12.07)	242 (66.40)
TO	13 (3.57)	27 (7.41)

Table 130: Present and *help* plus the *to*-infinitive/BI clause in the American PDE data (raw and n.f./10,000 IP-MATs)

(582) That status *helped push up* Chang's appearance fees and endorsement income, especially in tennis-crazy Asia, where the Chinese-American is arguably the continent 's most popular athlete. (COHA, mag_1997_428465)

(583) But it can not even deliver the first one because an agreement for loan guarantees from the Export-Import Bank in Washington that *would help pay* for the planes has lapsed. (COHA, news_1999_653855)

(584) The cool temperature of the refrigerator *helps to maintain* the freshness of perishable foods and keeps them safe by inhibiting or retarding the growth of most bacteria. (COHA, mag_1997_428180)

Following the methodology used in my analysis of the British PDE data, a univariate analysis of the paradigm forms of *help* is also necessary here (see Figure 25). The frequency of the BI option in American English is significantly higher with infinitive (*to*) *help* forms, as in (583) above, whereas finite *help* is more productive in sentences containing *to*-infinitive complements, as in (585) ($\chi^2(1)=9.29$, P=0.0005). Figure 25 also shows that non-finite *helped* clearly favours BI clauses, while the *to*-infinitive alternative is significantly preferred with non-finite *helping*, as in (586) ($\chi^2(1)=20.75$, P=<.0001). Unlike in British English, the variation shows similar proportions with *helps* ($\chi^2(1)=1.65$, P=0.1183) and finite *helped* forms ($\chi^2(1)=0$, P=0.8415). The chi-square values for the finite *helped, helping* and *helps* were calculated by comparing each of these forms with the totals for the other forms.

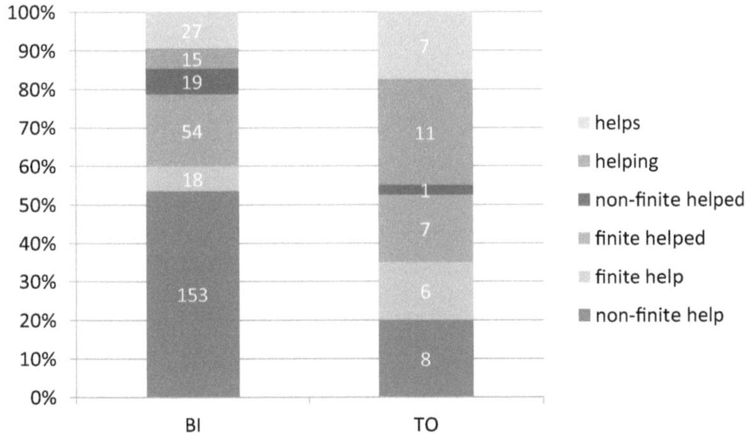

Figure 25: Paradigm forms of *help* plus *to*-infinitive/BI clause in American PDE

(585) The same factors *help to explain* the famous zadruga or family commune, which involves several generations of the same family living together (usually in a group of houses protected by an outer wall) and functioning as a single economic unit. (COHA, nf_1998_775159)

(586) With the radio collar attached to his neck, he began his new career, *helping to preserve* the jaguars and all the other creatures of la Selva Maya. (COHA, mag_2000_402540)

In the analysis with DISTANCE, in which this predictor replaces SUBJECT OF INFINITIVE, *Model 3* shows similar results for the variable PRESENT. As Table 131 illustrates, an increase of one word in distance significantly favours BI clause (by 2.51 percentage points).

Predictor	Estimate	Std Error	z value	P-value	OR
Intercept	-2.7124	0.3056	-8.875	< 2e-16 ***	0.06637709 (1/0.06637709= 15.06544)
Distance	-0.9191	0.3222	-2.852	0.00434 **	0.39886974 (1/0.39886974= 2.507084)
Present (Reference Level: *Other*) Present	1.0357	0.3850	2.690	0.00713 **	2.81716473

Table 131: *Model 3, STEP 1*, with DISTANCE and *help* plus *to*-infinitive/BI clause in American PDE (step "backward" results)

ANOVA confirms that the results of the analysis with DISTANCE are not statistically different from those for SUBJECT OF INFINITIVE. The distance between *help* and the complement clause is 0–1 words (see Table 132); the quantile is 1 log, which implies that the distance in 10 per cent of the examples is 2–7 words (see Figure 26 and Table 132). The *to*-infinitive complementation type is attested in constructions with up to three intervening words, as in (587), whereas distance when BI complements are present may be as much as seven words, as in (588).

(587) But simple physical geography also matters, helping *as it does* to explain both the seclusion of the area and, at the same time, its near-central importance. (COHA, nf_1998_775159)

(588) "The Big Salad" - Kramer helps *an athlete wanted for a brutal crime* flee police; guest Michelle Forbes. (COHA, news_1998_626723)

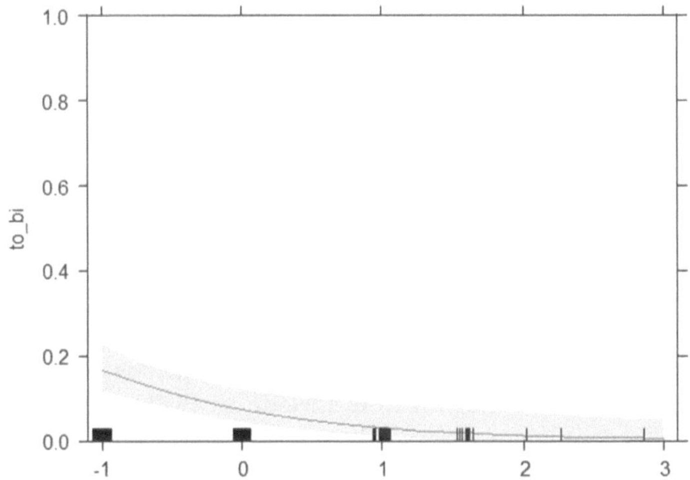

Figure 26: *Model 3, STEP 1,* DISTANCE and *help* plus *to*-infinitive/BI clause in American PDE (step "backward" results)

	0 words	1 words	2–7 words
BI	139 (38.14)	115 (31.55)	32 (8.78)
TO	32 (8.78)	5 (1.37)	3 (0.82)

Table 132: Distance and *help* plus *to*-infinitive/BI clause in American PDE (raw and n.f./10,000 IP-MATs)

In summary, the BI complementation alternative is more successful with overt subject of infinitive constructions and when there is intervening material between *help* and the infinitival clause. The *horror aequi* principle, which predicts 20.86 per cent of the data, is pervasive in my American PDE data, where BI is the only option. *Model 3* also reveals a preference for *to*-infinitive complement clauses with present-tense *help*, whereas BI is favoured with non-present-tense *help* forms. The univariate analysis shows that *helping* and finite *help* are more frequent with *to*-infinitive complements, while non-finite *help* and non-finite *helped* prefer BI complements. Finally, *helps* and finite *helped* are not explanatory for the PDE data.

4.4 Infinitival complementation governed by *help*: A diachronic and synchronic exploration

This section analyses the factors that affect *help* plus *to*-infinitive/BI in the three models discussed in Section 4.3.2.2 in relation to periodisation and regional variation. To begin with, the presence or absence of an NP between *help* and the infinitive clause is subject to variation from EModE to British LModE, with a significant decrease in the construction with covert subject of infinitive in the latter period ($\chi^2(1)=3.12$, P=0.0447; see Table 136 in Appendix). The frequency of covert NP2 in British English rises again from LModE to PDE, though the variation in this case is not statistically significant ($\chi^2(1)=0.11$, P=0.5839). Neither regional nor diachronic significant differences are observed in the data;[53] in fact, the proportion of constructions with overt NP2 remains stable in ME and PDE ($\chi^2(1)=2.71$, P=0.0783). In constructions with overt NP2, complex subjects are marginal in lower clauses (see Table 136 in Appendix), compared to the much higher frequency of pro subjects (more than 84 per cent from British ME to LModE). In PDE, the proportion of NP subjects increases significantly in British English, whereas the rise is not statistically significant in American English ($\chi^2(1)=1.29$, P=0.1797).

Horror aequi contexts account for less than 30 per cent of the data. The strength of this factor remains stable over time ($\chi^2(1)=0.2$, P=1 for ME vs EModE, P=0.249 for EModE and British LModE, P=0.252 for British LModE vs PDE, $\chi^2(1)=0.3$, P=0.488 for American English). The proportion of examples explained by *horror aequi* is higher in British than in American PDE ($\chi^2(1)=4.04$, P=0.0366; see Section 4.3.2.2.3). In fact, this is one of the strongest factors in the model, diachronically and synchronically, as demonstrated in Section 4.3.2.2.

The proportions of the levels of the predictors PRESENT and INDICATIVE are subject to diachronic variation: present-tense and indicative-mood *help* forms are only attested with *to*-infinitive complements in

---

53 The chi-square test reveals no significant differences between ME vs EModE ($\chi^2(1)=0.58$, P=0.3623) or American LModE vs PDE ($\chi^2(1)=1.03$, P=0.256).

ME and EModE; from LModE onwards, *help* selects BI clauses in non-indicative mood and non-present tense verbal groups in British and American English, possibly dragged by the general trend towards BI with non-finite *help* forms. The overall success of the construction when *help* exhibits present-tense forms has been constant in my study. The LModE data set has the highest proportions of present-tense forms, but the differences in the variation with respect to the response variable are not statistically significant between this period and either British EModE (P=0.1556) or British and American PDE (P=0.244 and $\chi^2(1)=0.6$, P=0.351, respectively) (see Table 136 in Appendix). Indicative-mood forms increase progressively from ME to PDE, especially in American English. This increase is not statistically significant in either British or American English, however ($\chi^2(1)=0.02$, P=0.7401 for ME vs EModE; $\chi^2(1)=1.4$, P=0.1345 for EModE vs British LModE; $\chi^2(1)=0.91$, P=0.2401 for British LModE vs PDE; $\chi^2(1)=0.1$, P=0.6547 for American LModE vs PDE). The analysis of the paradigm forms of *help* also reveals diachronic and synchronic variation (see Figure 27). Non-finite *help* is the most frequent form in my database: 82.5 per cent in ME and EModE. Over time, the construction starts to select other forms more frequently, resulting in a decrease in non-finite *help*. This variation is statistically significant from EModE to British LModE ($\chi^2(1)=2.99$, P=0.0437), but not from British LModE to PDE ($\chi^2(1)=0.6$, P=0.3222) or between British and American LModE ($\chi^2(1)=0.48$, P=0.3482) and PDE ($\chi^2(1)=0.87$, P=0.3173). In LModE, the frequency of the form *helps* increases (P=0.0265) with respect to the EModE data; the same trend is observed in the case of *helping* in the American variety, probably because of the growing success of the BI alternative in these contexts. In PDE, *helping* is also attested in British English, and the productivity of *helps* is not subject to significant variation in comparison with LModE (P=0.262). The increase in finite *helped* forms from LModE to PDE is not statistically significant in either variety (P=0.134 for British English, P=0.107 for American English). Conversely, finite *help* is statistically marginal in the data, with minor variations.

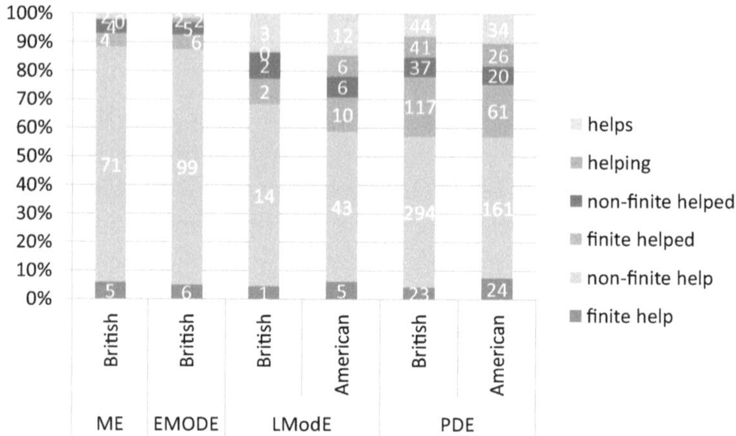

Figure 27: Paradigm forms of *help* plus *to*-infinitive/BI clause in British and American English from ME to PDE

The Principle of Rhythmic Alternation does not play a role in the distribution of the infinitival options in my data. The construction is attested with significantly higher proportions in critical contexts in EModE than in ME ($\chi^2(1)=7.09$, $P=0.0049$; see Table 136 in Appendix). The variation is not significantly significant from British EModE to LModE ($\chi^2(1)=0.1$, $P=0.5716$) or from LModE to PDE ($\chi^2(1)=0.38$, $P=0.3833$). The proportion in unproblematic contexts increases from LModE to PDE in my American data ($\chi^2(1)=3.51$, $P=0.0434$).

As regards SUBJECT ANIMACY, the univariate analysis detects a significant diachronic increase in non-animate subjects with *help*. The proportions are quite similar in ME and EModE ($\chi^2(1)=0.11$, $P=0.6242$), while the variation is significant from British EModE to LModE ($\chi^2(1)=3.91$, $P=0.0258$), and even from LModE to PDE ($\chi^2(1)=0.28$, $P=0.4503$). In LModE, the proportion of non-animate subjects is roughly the same in both regional varieties ($\chi^2(1)=1.01$, $P=0.2102$). In American English, where the proportion of animate subjects is higher in LModE, the number of non-animate subjects significantly increases in PDE, when distribution across both varieties is the same (see Table 136 in Appendix). The statistical behaviour of OBJECT ANIMACY also reveals a diachronic increase in non-animate objects (see Table 133).

	ME	EModE	LModE		PDE	
	British	**British**	**British**	**American**	**British**	**American**
Animate	33	34	12	32	230	141
Non-animate	0	4	0	1	40	13

Table 133: Object animacy and *help* plus *to*-infinitive/BI clause in British and American English from ME to PDE (raw data)

Finally, *help* plus *to*-infinitive/BI complementation is attested in 81.37 per cent of the data in non-factual unrealised contexts in ME and EModE, and this proportion decreases progressively over time to approximately 56.65 per cent of the data in PDE (see Table 136 in Appendix). In the British English data set, the increase in the construction with factual realised meanings is not statistically significant diachronically ($\chi^2(1)=0.85$, P=0.2674 for ME to EModE, $\chi^2(1)=0.83$, P=0.2334 for EModE to LModE, $\chi^2(1)=0.59$, P=0.3247 for LModE to PDE; see Table 136 in Appendix). The same trend is observed in the American data from LModE to PDE ($\chi^2(1)=0.06$, P=0.7083), in contrast to the period from EModE to American LModE, when the number of examples conveying a factual realised meaning increases significantly ($\chi^2(1)=9.56$, P=0.0011). Factual unrealised contexts, of which two examples are attested in ME, are not attested until LModE in the American variety and are marginal in PDE. Both types of infinitival complementation are found in factual realised and non-factual unrealised contexts in the periods covered by the study, and in factual unrealised contexts in PDE. The two ME examples have *to*-infinitive complements, while the three instances in American LModE select BI clauses.

4.5 Concluding remarks and discussion

The research reported in this chapter has shown that the occurrence of *help* constructions plus infinitival complementation in British and

American English over time is significantly affected by distance, complexity and the avoidance of identity. As observed in Section 4.3.1, infinitival clauses are the most productive type of non-finite complementation governed by *help* from ME to the present, with BI complementation increasing over time.

The frequency of the construction without an intervening NP between *help* and the complement clause decreases from EModE to LModE in British English. Although pronominal (pro) subjects are preferred in lower clauses in the periods studied, the frequency of NP subjects rises significantly from British LModE to PDE. *Horror aequi* contexts account for at least 30 per cent of the data, with higher frequencies in American PDE. With respect to tense and mood, while the frequencies of present-tense forms remain stable over time, indicative-mood forms show a gradual increase from ME to PDE, especially in American English. Non-finite *help* forms are the most frequent in the database, decreasing progressively over time in both varieties in favour of higher proportions of *helps* and *helping.*

The data also attest a significant increase from ME to EModE in examples classed as critical according to the Principle of Rhythmic Alternation. The effects of this principle remain stable in the British variety from EModE onwards, whereas in American English so-called unproblematic contexts increase from LModE to PDE.

The number of non-animate main-clause subjects and objects gradually increases in these periods. The productivity of the construction decreases with non-factual unrealised meanings from ME to PDE in favour of contexts conveying a factual realised meaning.

Regarding the complementation alternatives, *to*-infinitive clauses represent the most frequent variant in ME and EModE in all the levels considered in *Model 1.* The preference for this alternative is in keeping with the Complexity Principle because the *to*-infinitive complementation type is the variant attested in passive constructions and in examples involving relative clauses and complex subjects. The BI alternative, more frequent in ME than in EModE, is favoured in *horror aequi* contexts so as to avoid co-occurrence of a *to*-infinitive clause and a *to help* form in the nearby context. The success of *help* plus BI is consequently greater with unexpressed subjects. The BI option is also categorical with non-present tense and non-indicative mood verbal groups. Non-finite *help* is also the preferred solution when preceded by a modal auxiliary or a catenative verb. As regards syntactic contexts, *help* plus *to*-infinitive/BI is slightly more frequent in adverbial clauses, with *to*-infinitive clauses favoured in main clauses. In LModE, the *to*-infinitive alternative is more frequent in British English, with similar proportions in ME and in EModE. By contrast, BI clauses show a steep increase in American English due to its functionality in *horror aequi* contexts and main-clause verbal groups containing modal auxiliaries. The proportion of BI clauses lacking explicit subjects is significantly higher in adverbial clauses. Morphological forms such as *helping*, *helps* and (non-)finite *helped* increase in productivity over time, with significant co-occurrence of *to*-infinitive complements and present-tense and indicative-mood *helps* and *helped* forms. In American LModE, the data reveal the following tendencies with respect to complexity and semantics preferences: *to*-infinitive clauses are favoured when relative clauses are involved and when non-factual unrealised meanings are conveyed, while BI clauses, preferred in non-factual unrealised contexts, are the only alternative with factual unrealised meanings.

The PDE data reveal a trend reversal in favour of BI, particularly in American English. The presence/absence of an intervening NP between *help* and the infinitival complement is determining here: the BI alternative is preferred in constructions with overt subjects of infinitive and *to*-infinitive is favoured with the covert ones. In American English, distance does not play a role in the variation, as BI is successful even when lexical material intervenes between *help* and the complement. This is also the case in British English when *horror aequi* is not present. In British English, *help* does tend to be accompanied by *to*-infinitive clauses when *help* is preceded by a *to*-infinitive form and the complement clause is separated from the *help* verbal group. The complexity of the subject of the lower clause is a strong factor in British English: the *to*-infinitive is more successful with unexpressed and complex lower-clause subjects, which is consistent with the preference for *to*-infinitive clauses in constructions with covert subjects of infinitive and with the Complexity Principle (the marked *to*-infinitive alternative is favoured in complex contexts and BI more frequent with pro and NP subjects). The three examples with passive verbs and coordinated verbal groups in the British English data set also have *to*-infinitive complements. As regards verbal variation, the probability of BI complements is higher with non-present verbal forms in both varieties, BI is significantly more frequent with non-finite *help*, and finite *help* forms co-occur with *to*-infinitive complements. American English shows a higher occurrence of *to*-infinitive complements with *helping* and of BI complements with non-finite *helped*, while British English favours the *to*-infinitive alternative with *helping* and third-person singular present *helps*.

In summary, the empirical analysis carried out in this chapter reveals, firstly, that, from EModE onwards, the initially marginal variant of the complementation, BI, begins to occur in contexts previously dominated by the *to*-infinitive alternative. Additionally, the analysis shows evidence of BI with all of the paradigm forms of *help* and that *to*-infinitive/BI alternation is also subject to functional factors.

5. Summary, conclusion and avenues for further research

Non-finite complementation and, in particular, *to*-infinitive and BI complement clauses have been the subject of extensive investigation and debate. The aim of this study is to contribute to the existing literature by modelling the variation in relation to a selection of main-clause verbs that select *to*-infinitive and BI complements in the recent history of American and British English. Using the methodologies provided by corpus linguistics and multivariate analyses, this study attempts to account for the reasons why certain verbs show a preference for either *to*-infinitive or BI complementation from ME onwards, and to provide a comprehensive description of the factors that influence the choice of infinitival.

My study has shown that the transition from ME to EModE and from LModE to PDE witnessed changes in the complementation patterns of the verbs *dare*, *need* and *help*, including the choice of infinitival. The main findings of the empirical analysis of the infinitival complements governed by these verbs are summarised in Section 5.1. Section 5.2 offers a qualitative interpretation of the results and proposes some future avenues of research.

5.1 Findings

The research questions underpinning this thesis were presented in Chapter 1, which examined the variation between *to*-infinitive and BI complementation in relation to the morphosyntactic, semantic/pragmatic, processing-related, identity-avoidance, dialectal and diachronic factors explored in previous studies. The review of the literature on corpus linguistics in Chapter 2 demonstrated the appropriateness of the corpus-based/driven methodology adopted here. Section 2.1 described the corpora used for the empirical investigation: The Penn Corpora of Historical English, the Parsed Corpus of Early English Correspondence (PCEEC) and the British National Corpus Baby (BNC Baby) for British English, and the Corpus of Historical American English (COHA) for American English. In addition, examples from the Oxford English Dictionary (OED), the Middle English Dictionary (MED) and Visser ([1963] 1973) were used to provide a more comprehensive understanding of the linguistic phenomena under investigation. Software such as CorpusStudio and WordSmith Tools was used to extract all relevant examples, and the resulting data were enriched with language-internal and language-external information. In Section 2.2, the variables analysed were organised into the following categories: verb, metadata, main clause, complement clause and construction. Some of these variables and their levels had to be modified for the quantitative study based on logistic-regression modelling using the 'glm' function in R (R Core Team 2020), and preference was given to binary results whenever the merging of levels did not lead to linguistic oversimplification. Section 2.3 explained the normalisation units used for comparability purposes: IP-MATs for the Penn Corpora of Historical English and COHA, and <-s> units for the BNC Baby. The analysis of infinitival complementation in Chapters 3-4 offered a new perspective on the changes that took place from ME to PDE to shed light on the influence of grammatical, structural, semantic/pragmatic, identity-avoidance, and processing- and period-related factors on the infinitival alternation options with *dare*, *need* and *help*. Attention was also paid to the regularisation of variants and the consolidation of ongoing processes. Section 2.4 corroborated the effect of verb, diachrony and regional variation on the infinitival alternation in constructions headed by *dare*, *need* and *help*, and identified the factors that influenced the choice, in American and British ME to PDE. The variables VERB, PERIODISATION, REGIONAL VARIANT, DISTANCE and SUBJECT OF INFINITIVE, RHYTHMIC ALTERNATION, HORROR AEQUI, POLARITY, SYNTAX, VALENCY and NOTIONAL CHARACTERISATION are significant factors of complementation choice. The results show that *need* significantly prefer the *to*-infinitive clause in my data, whereas *help* and *dare* opt for BI clauses. As for PERIODISATION, the *to*-infinitive decreases in use from ME to EModE. Whereas the proportions remain stable in EModE and in LModE, the incidence of *to*-infinitive increases in PDE, showing a similar distribution of that of BI clauses. REGIONAL VARIANT also is also determinant of the alternation and shows that British English significantly prefer *to*-infinitive clauses. The productivity of the *to*-infinitive clause increases in the passive voice and factual unrealised or non-factual unrealised meanings. In contrast, BI clauses are found when there is an overt subject of infinitive or material between the main and lower clauses, in unproblematic stress patterns, *horror aequi* contexts, negative clauses, dependent and main syntax, and with intransitive and transitive lower verbs.

Chapters 3 and 4 were devoted to the study of specific verbs. Chapter 3 dealt with the verbs *dare* and *need* from ME to PDE in American and British English. The literature review on *dare* and pre-modals in Section 2 paved the way for the qualitative and quantitative analysis of the verbs *dare, need* and *tharf* in Section 3. Infinitival alternation was first attested at the end of ME: *dare* was attested with the old BI clauses and the new *to*-infinitive complementation alternative, whereas *need* was found with the old *to*-infinitive option and the new BI one. At the end of ME, pre-modal *dare* and lexical *need* began to show both lexical and modal features, such as alternation between *to*-infinitive and BI complementation, (c-)overt inflection and blend features. These changes, driven by frequency, were triggered by the phonological and orthographic similarity between *dare* and pre-modal *tharf*, competition between *tharf* and *need*, and the influence of *need* on *dare*. The frequency of *dare* increased continuously to the extent that it became the most frequent of the three verbs between M1 and E2. *Tharf* was the second most frequent verb in M1, but it decreased in use during the ME period and became obsolete in EModE. The hypothesis that the growing tendency towards *d*-spelling occurred at the expense of the *th-/þ* forms was supported by the confusion between *dare* and *tharf* between M1 and M4 and the stable occurrence of *need* at this time. With the obsolescence of *tharf* at the end of ME, the frequency of *need* increased significantly in E1 to levels comparable to those exhibited by *dare*. However, whereas *need* continued to increase from E2 to E3, *dare* decreased significantly over the same period. The six criteria analysed confirmed the relationship between *dare*, *tharf* and *need*:

(i) In line with the dictionary entries for *dare* and *tharf* and also with Molencki (2002: 378, 2005) and Loureiro-Porto (2009: 71–72), my data showed the *d*-spelling with necessity meanings in M4 and the *th-/þ*-spelling with a 'courage' meaning in M3.

(ii) *Dare* conveyed necessity meanings when it selected verbs such as *eisian* 'to frighten', *fear, shame, doubt, dread, grieve* and *seek* and expressions such as *be afraid, be ashamed* and *be frightened* as its complements in ME and EModE, even though its frequency was low in both periods (cf. MED s.v. *durren* 2a.(a)). *Tharf* showed the highest frequency in this context in ME and *need* gradually increased its frequency between the last two periods of ME and EModE when it was the most frequent of the three verbs.

(iii) Unlike *tharf, dare* and *need* were present in contexts expressing *fear* and *doubt*, typically associated with modal and subjunctive meanings; *dare* most frequently conveyed meanings of courage and boldness in these contexts.

(iv) Whereas no instances of *dare* were found in the Experiencer construction in my data, *tharf* and *need* were attested in this context with the highest frequencies in M3 and M4.

(v) Polarity and semantic/pragmatic factors influenced the evolution and behaviour of the three verbs. As regards polarity, the distribution of *dare* was stable from M1 to M4. *Dare* was significantly more frequent in affirmative clauses from M4 to E1 and in negative clauses from E1 to E2, when its productivity was similar in affirmative and negative clauses. *Dare* and *need* did not show variation with respect to polarity in M4. Nonetheless, *need*, which occurred in affirmative clauses in more than 60 per cent of the cases in ME, was more frequently attested in negative clauses in EModE. With respect to semantic/pragmatic factors, *dare* was found in the three contexts identified in my analysis, but it favoured non-factual unrealised meanings in ME. The gradual increase of *dare* in factual unrealised meanings over the ME period was significantly reverted in E1 in favour of factual realised and non-factual unrealised meanings; this situation remained stable during EModE. *Need* was frequently attested with non-factual unrealised meanings in ME and EModE. The distribution of *need* in factual realised and factual unrealised meanings significantly increased in E1, accounting for around 30 per cent of the data in E2 and E3. *Tharf* was restricted to negative clauses and non-factual unrealised meanings, and its obsolescence was directly related to the increase in negative clauses with *dare* and *need* in EModE.

(vi) As regards semantic contexts of necessity, possibility and volition (see MED s.v. *durren* 2, (a) and s.v. *thurven* 7. (a) and 8), *th-/þ*-spelling was found conveying volition. *D*-spelling was more frequent in necessity and obligation interpretations in both periods, but occurred most frequently in volition meanings in M2 and M3, and was also attested with possibility interpretations from M3 onwards. As a result, from late ME onwards, pre-modal *dare* showed lexical features such as *to*-infinitive and inflections, the lexical verb *need* occured with BI clauses and without overtly marked inflections, and both *dare* and *need* occurred in blend constructions, while *tharf* became obsolete.

Section 3.4 presented the qualitative and multivariate analysis of infinitival alternation over time: methodology used and the factors selected for the study of *dare* and *need*, the overall distribution of infinitival complementation options with each of the verbs, and the determinants of the variation in EModE, LModE and PDE in American and British English. In EModE, *dare* increased its use with *to*-infinitive complements and *need* with BI clauses. Morphology showed the strongest effect on infinitival alternation, with *dare* and *need* exhibiting similar frequencies in this regard. BI clauses were selected with covertly marked inflections, whereas the *to*-infinitive option was preferred with overt inflection. In the case of *dare*, the forms *dared* and *durst* were both found in simple past contexts, but *durst* was more frequent. Also, even though the *to*-infinitive was preferred with explicit forms, BI clauses were found with every type of non-finite form, and with the regularised third-person *s/–th* inflection and second-person singular present *–st* inflection. *Need* favourred BI complementation with other non-explicit forms, and the *to*-infinitive complement with the bare infinitive form and *needed*. When *need* contained inflection for the third-person singular, the verb selected either type of complement. *Do*-support was only attested with *dare* in two instances with the *to*-infinitive clause, a finding explained by analogy and the Principle of Rhythmic Alternation. DISTANCE favoured BI clauses with both *dare* and *need*, even though it was only a tendency in the case of *dare*; direct *not* negation and inversion with the subject were the factors found to explain this result. My data revealed that the *to*-infinitive option was not subject to complexity regulations in EModE, and that both *dare to* and *need to* were conceptualised as a unit and therefore not likely to accommodate intervening material. As regards passive and perfect constructions, *dare* and *need* continued to select the old variants, i.e. *dare* with BI clauses and *need* with *to*-infinitive. *Need* and *dare* also selected the old variants in non-factual unrealised contexts. With factual realised meanings, both verbs favoured BI clauses, and the *to*-infinitive was preferred with factual unrealised meanings. The new variants *to*-infinitive for *dare* and BI clauses for *need* were significantly favoured with non-animate main-clause subjects. These subjects were typically unexpressed in the case of *dare* because the construction occurred in adverbial clauses and the verbal form was *daring* in most instances. *Dare* and BI clauses were more frequent in main and dependent clauses. The Principle of Rhythmic Alternation was corroborated in the case of *need* because the *to*-infinitive was selected in critical stress patterns and acted as a stress clash buffer. *Need* plus *to*-infinitive was more frequent in critical and negative contexts, where a modal verb preceding *need* carried the negative particle. Finally, 'fear' verbs were barely attested with *dare* in this period, and the predictor was not shown to exert any influence on the alternation with *need* either.

In LModE, the frequencies for *dare* with *to*-infinitive complements and *need* with BI clauses increased significantly in American and British English and, in the case of *need*, more instances of the new variant were attested in British English. As in EModE, these verbs exhibited dichotomous morphologies: *to*-infinitives with explicit forms and BI clauses with non-explicit ones. In both varieties, *dare* plus BI was favoured with 'other' non-explicit forms. In American English, the *to*-infinitive/BI clause freely alternated with simple past forms and the third-person singular present, and *dare* significantly selected BI clauses with simple past forms; *durst* was preferred in British English, *-s* inflections being infrequent in this regional variety. *Dare* plus BI clause was preferred with covert inflection for third-person singular present in American English, while the form *daring* was restricted to *to*-infinitives. This complementation alternative was also more frequent with non-finite forms in American English, where the new regularised past-participial *–ed* forms were attested with both complementation variants. Like *dare*, *need* selected BI clauses with 'other' and covert third-person singular present forms in American English. *Do*-support was infrequent with *dare* and absent with *need* in British English, while in American English, dummy *do* occurred with the old variants, i.e. with *dare* plus BI, even though inversion and negation were the most frequent strategies with this complement. In this period, dummy *do* was attested with *need* for the first time in a context where the old *to*-infinitive complementation alternative was categorical. *Dare* opted for *to*-infinitive clauses when auxiliary and modal verbs were used in negative and interrogative clauses in American English, while in interrogative clauses in British English, *dare* occurred with BI clauses when it inverted with the subject. If *dare* was preceded by an auxiliary, it selected a *to*-infinitive complement. POLARITY did not affect the *dare*-construction in British English, which showed a slight preference for affirmative clauses. In contrast, the frequency of *need* in negative clauses was higher with BI clauses, the *to*-infinitive alternative being more frequent in affirmative clauses in British English. In American English, both *dare* and *need* favoured *to*-infinitives in affirmative clauses and BI complements in negative ones. DISTANCE was shown to be relevant to the alternation with *dare* in American English, which selected BI clauses when there was a distance increase of one word. The most frequent linguistic items that occurred between *dare* and the complement clauses were *not* and inverted subjects, which explains why the most explicit *to*-infinitive variant is not used in this complex context. Similarly, the predictor RHYTHMIC ALTERNATION revealed that *to*-infinitives occur in critical contexts as stress clash buffers, usually in affirmative and negative and interrogative clauses with auxiliary support where the *to*-infinitive clause was placed between the stressed forms of the main verb and the infinitive, whereas BI clauses were found in unproblematic stress patterns in American English. While NOTIONAL CHARACTERISATION did not exert any influence on *dare* in LModE, it did affect *need*, which frequently selected the old variant with non-factual unrealised meanings and BI clauses with factual realised interpretations in both varieties. Only a few instances were attested of *need* with factual unrealised meanings in British English, and *need* selected BI clauses in every case. In American English, POLARITY explained the variation with non-factual unrealised meanings and confirmed the results of the semantic/pragmatic analysis for EModE: the *to*-infinitive was more frequent in affirmative clauses and BI clauses were favoured in negative ones. As regards the perfect construction and the occurrence of 'fear' verbs, *need* selected BI clauses in both varieties. With passive-voice predicates, *need* only showed significant results with the *to*-infinitive clause in British English. The old BI alternative was selected in the two passive examples with *dare* in my data. SUBJECT COMPLEXITY showed that *dare* preferred *to*-infinitives with non-basic (mainly unexpressed) subjects, typically opting for the verbal form *daring* in this context in American English. Also in the American variety, SYNTAX revealed that *need* preferred BI clauses in main clauses and the more marked variant in dependent clauses, and the *to*-infinitive was also the preferred complement with *need* in contexts of relativisation.

The frequencies for *dare*- and *need*-constructions developed in opposite directions in PDE: the former decreased and reached its lowest productivity since EModE, while the latter became more frequent. Both verbs selected their old variants in PDE. As in the diachronic analysis, BI clauses were still more frequent with *dare*. In contrast, *need*'s preference for *to*-infinitives contradicts the trend observed until the end of the LModE period. In keeping with the diachronic results, *dare* and *need* continued to select BI clauses with non-explicit inflected forms and *to*-infinitive complements with explicit forms. The proportion of *dare* predicates with explicit forms increased in both complementation alternatives in PDE. The equal distribution of *need* plus *to*-infinitive with explicit inflection indicated that regularisation and paradigmatic expansion were underway in both verbs. The forms *dares* and *needs* typically co-occurred with BI clauses with covert forms. *Dare* plus BI complementation was more frequent with the non-finite base form *dare*, and *daring* tended to be associated with the *to*-infinitive alternative in British English. In the American variety, the non-finite base form *dare* had similar distribution with *to*-infinitive and BI complements. With *dared*, the frequencies of the two complementation alternatives were practically identical in American and British English. In PDE, the frequency of *need* plus *to*-infinitive and BI clauses was very high with 'other' non-explicit forms. The form *needed* was mostly restricted to the *to*-infinitive option in British English and categorical with the simple past form in American English. The past participle form *needed* was attested in PDE not only in the perfect construction but also, for the first time, in passive-voice predicates and with non-finite modifiers. Non-finite *need* forms were infrequent and mostly co-occurred with *to*-infinitive clauses. *Do*-support was more productive with *need* in PDE and also in contexts of emphatic polarity. *Need* plus *to*-infinitive was restricted to instances of auxiliary support in negative and interrogative contexts, whereas inversion and direct negation were still the most frequent strategies with BI clauses. American English showed similar proportions of the infinitival complementation variants in context with *dare* plus either *do*- or auxiliary support. In contrast, *do*-support was almost categorical with *dare* in British English, the use of auxiliaries, direct negation or inversion not being statistically significant with BI clauses. The Principle of Rhythmic Alternation was not corroborated by the *dare* data, therefore, because BI clauses occurred more frequently in negative and critical contexts with auxiliary support, leading to stress clash patterns. *Dare* plus *to*-infinitive was significantly more frequent in affirmative and unproblematic contexts in British English. However, POLARITY did not explain the alternation with *dare* in either of the regional variants and *do*-support was also attested with *dare* in negative imperative clauses. In contrast to *dare*, direct *not* negation and subject-inversion acted as stress clash buffers in negative unproblematic stress patterns with *need*. This was also the effect of the *to*-infinitive clause when *need* occurred in affirmative/negative critical and affirmative unproblematic contexts, since auxiliaries were used in negative clauses with *to*-infinitive complements. POLARITY proved the strongest effect predictor for *need*, with *to*-infinitives in affirmative clauses and with BI complements in negative ones. POLARITY also affected the results for NOTIONAL CHARACTERISATION and, as observed in the diachronic analysis, explained the findings for contexts conveying non-factual unrealised meanings. In affirmative factual realised contexts in both varieties and in negative factual unrealised contexts in British English, *need* was attested with both variants. *Need* plus BI significantly favoured negative factual realised interpretations in the British variety, but the same pattern was not attested in American English. NOTIONAL CHARACTERISATION did not account for the variation with *dare* in American English, where infinitival complementation was more frequent with factual realised meanings. In British English, *dare* plus *to*-infinitive was used in factual realised and factual unrealised contexts, whereas its use with BI clauses led to non-factual unrealised meanings. SYNTAX was not found to exert a strong influence on complementation governed by *need* in British and American English. The only apparent trend was that dependent clauses preferred *to*-infinitives and adverbial clauses favoured BI complements. In the case of *dare*, BI complements were preferred in main clauses in both varieties, and *to*-infinitives were favoured in adverbial clauses in British English and in dependent clauses in American English. In the perfect construction, *need* selected BI clauses in British English, and passive-voice lower clauses took *to*-infinitives. Lower clauses marked for progressive aspect were attested with *need* plus *to*-infinitive in American and British PDE for the first time. In keeping with the diachronic results, *dare* plus *to*-infinitive preferred non-basic unexpressed subjects, mostly with the form *daring* in adverbial clauses. The subjects with *dare* plus BI were typically basic, and were attested in main-clauses. As regards *need*, the only significant finding in American English was the correlation between non-basic subjects and BI complementation, and between basic subjects and *to*-infinitives. SUBJECT ANIMACY did not play a role in the alternation with *dare* in either of the variants, and with *need* in American English, both verbs opt for animate subjects. In British English, *need* selected *to*-infinitives with animate subjects, and BI clauses with non-animate ones.

Section 3.4.4 dealt with the most significant factors affecting *dare* and *need* plus infinitival complementation in the two varieties from EModE to PDE and summarised the main findings. Morphologically, the *to*-infinitive alternative was associated with explicitly inflected verbal forms, whereas BI complementation was more probable with non-explicit forms. However, the significant rise of explicit forms, independently of the variant, revealed that regularisation and paradigm expansion were well underway in PDE. The same situation was observed in the case of *do*-support, which significantly increased in use in PDE and was more frequent with both complement types in *dare* predicates. In the case of *need*, *to*-infinitive was the preferred complementation alternative in contexts of emphatic polarity and auxiliary-verb support. BI complementation was frequent with direct *not* negation and subject-verb inversion with both verbs. *Dare* plus infinitival complementation was mainly found with affirmative polarity in the periods under investigation, with a higher occurrence of negative clauses in British PDE. *Need* plus infinitival complement clause was usually attested in negative clauses in LModE, and increased in frequency in affirmative clauses in PDE. In the case of *need*, the old *to*-infinitive form was associated with affirmative clauses diachronically and diatopically, whereas BI clauses were found in negative clauses, a trend favoured by the obsolescence of *tharf* in EModE. The results of the factor RHYTHMIC ALTERNATION with the verb *need* were as follows: BI clauses were frequent in so-called unproblematic examples in LModE, whereas *to*-infinitives were preferred in critical contexts in PDE. The *dare* data revealed greater productivity of critical contexts in British English, and of unproblematic stress patterns in American English. As regards semantic/pragmatic categorisation, non-factual unrealised meanings were frequent in the LModE data, and increased in both varieties with *need* in PDE and in the British variety with *dare*. The old forms were more frequent in non-factual unrealised contexts, with the exception of *dare* in American PDE, which favoured factual realised meanings with both variants.

Finally, Section 3.5 described the main features and contexts of the less frequent construction *dare*/*need* + NP2 + *to*-infinitive complementation. This pattern showed a significant increase in frequency over time, particularly in American English. The subject of infinitive construction governed by *need* in American PDE was preferred in contexts of affirmative polarity, and with non-animate objects, main-clause syntax and transitive lower verbs, whereas the range of contextual possibilities was larger in British PDE. The British data mirrored the patterns revealed by the American English LModE data set. *Dare* + NP2 + *to*-infinitive was associated with factual realised contexts, with an increase in more complex contexts over time, i.e. in adverbial clauses, with explicit morphology, and when the distance between *dare* and the *to*-infinitive was larger.

The organisation of Chapter 4, focusing on the verb *help*, was similar to that adopted in Chapter 3. Following a summary of the main findings of the literature in Section 4.2, Section 4.3 provided an analysis of the complementation variants of *help* over time in both varieties, and justified the methodology used and the variables selected for the analysis. Section 4.4 examined the factors affecting the variation with *help* from diachronic and diatopic perspectives.

Help differs from *dare* and *need* in that the frequency of *to*-infinitive complements significantly increased from ME to EModE, with more instances attested in subject of infinitive constructions. With the rise of *to*-infinitive complementation, the construction was found in more critical contexts owing to the *to*-infinitive's function as a stress clash buffer. This change in favour of the more marked infinitive option was not accompanied by differences of subject animacy in the main clause or semantic/pragmatic meaning since the construction continued to favour animate subjects and non-factual unrealised meanings.

The empirical investigation carried out in Chapter 4 revealed two waves of diachronic variation affecting *help* plus *to*-infinitive/BI complementation: from ME-EModE to LModE and from LModE to PDE. For the first wave, the data confirmed the increase in frequency of transitive constructions and non-animate main-clause subjects in British English, of *helping* forms in American English, and of *helps* in both varieties. During the same period, the data showed a decrease in non-finite *help* forms. The formerly marginal BI alternative was attested in contexts which previously favoured the *to*-infinitive alternative, i.e. with the forms *helping*, *helps* and *helped* and the non-finite form *help* in newspapers. Later on, in PDE, the number of NP lower-clause subjects and their occurrence with *helping* forms increased in the British variety.

In PDE, the number of *horror aequi* contexts increased in British English, as did that of unproblematic stressed contexts explained by the Principle of Rhythmic Alternation in American English. However, whereas *help* selected BI clauses in *horror aequi* contexts, Rhythmic Alternation was not found to affect the variation. In general, *help* plus the infinitival complement tended to occur with non-animate subjects and objects and with factual realised meanings. The gradual diachronic decrease evinced by the construction in predicates with non-indicative mood was explained by its increasing frequency in factual realised contexts. *To*-infinitive clauses were significantly preferred with non-finite *help* and *helping* forms in both varieties, and with the form *helps* and passive voice predicates in British English. BI was especially frequent with non-finite *help* forms in my data, but begins to be attested with all paradigmatic forms in PDE.

My diachronic study provided empirical support for Lohmann's (2011) claims regarding complementation preferences in *help* predicates in British PDE. Lohmann contended that *to*-omission was triggered by entrenchment and, consequently, by ease of processing. Semantic/pragmatic features were not found to affect the variation, contrary to Mair's (2002: 123–124) claim of the grammaticalisation of *help* as a quasi-auxiliary in PDE. The analysis showed that *to*-infinitive/BI complementation alternation governed by *help* was affected by paradigmatic features and general constraints such as *horror aequi*.

5.2 Qualitative analysis

The verbs investigated in this dissertation were attested with either complementation alternative from ME. In EModE *dare* increased its use with *to*-infinitive complements and *need* with BI clauses. *Help* differs from *dare* and *need* in that the frequency of *to*-infinitive complements significantly increased from ME to EModE, with more instances attested in transitive constructions. *Dare* and *need* significantly selected BI clauses in LModE in British and American English, whereas *help* favoured the *to*-infinitive alternative. In PDE, *need* shows more instances of the *to*-infinitive option in both American and British English. In contrast, *help* and *dare* in British English typically govern BI clauses.

These differences in the productivity and distribution of the variants were corroborated by the statistical models and analyses used in this investigation. The variation is probabilistic with most of the factors analysed, and the significance of the predictors varied depending on the verb, period and variety.

The diachronic analysis revealed an increase in the frequency of *to*-infinitive complementation in PDE and a change dialectically with respect to BI complementation, which became more productive in PDE in American English than in British, in contrast to the relative parity of distribution of both alternatives in each variety in EModE and LModE.

As regards the weight of internal linguistic features in the alternation from ME to PDE, *horror aequi* was found to be the strongest predictors diachronically and synchronically. BI clauses typically occurred in *horror aequi* contexts, particularly when there was no distance between the main clause and the lower clause (to avoid co-occurrence of identical morphological forms). *Help* favours BI complementation in *horror aequi* contexts from ME onwards, and the *horror aequi* effect explains why *help* plus BI in LModE is associated with unexpressed main-clause subjects and non-present tense and non-indicative mood forms. *Dare* and *need* were barely attested in my data in contexts with preceding *to*-infinitive markers. The passive voice was also a significant predictor and was mainly associated with *to*-infinitive clauses. Examples of all of the verbs in the passive voice were attested in my data and typically governed *to*-infinitive clauses, with the exception of *dare*, which was infrequent in passive contexts and selected the less marked BI complementation alternative. *Dare* and *need* were attested in only a few examples with intervening NP2, mainly from LModE onwards and always with *to*-infinitive complements. In contrast, *help* was more frequent with BI clauses when an NP2 was present in PDE. From a cognitive perspective, subject of infinitive constructions were easier to process than those with unexpressed NP2, which may explain the preference for the BI alternative. The contribution of the complexity of the NP2 subject to the variation was relevant to the *help* examples in British PDE (see Lohmann 2011 in this respect). As regards the animacy of these NP2 subjects, the verbs in my data were associated with animate NP2 subjects. The factor SUBJECT ANIMACY also affected the alternation: *dare* tended to favour the *to*-infinitive clause with non-animate subjects in EModE and *need* seemed to favour BI complements with non-animate main-clause subjects in EModE and British PDE. As regards other contexts exhibiting linguistic complexity, *need* and *help* in American English selected the more marked *to*-infinitive clause in contexts of relativisation in LModE, in keeping with the Complexity Principle. Coordinated lower-clause verbs were mainly found with *to*-infinitive complements to mark the beginning of these complex clauses with the verb *help* in PDE. The results for DISTANCE suggested that the construction with the *to*-infinitive complement was conceptualised as a unit when this was governed by the verbs *dare* and *need* in EModE and LModE. In PDE, *help* replicated this trend in American English. However, distance mitigated the effect of *horror aequi*, which explained the preference for the *to*-infinitive alternative in this context. The Principle of Rhythmic Alternation proved to be a determining factor of the variation with the verb *need* in EModE and in LModE in the constructions governed by *dare* and *need* in American English. These verbs selected *to*-infinitive clauses in so-called critical contexts. In PDE, the *to*-infinitive alternative was more frequent only with *need*, which was most likely linked to the increase in *to*-infinitive clauses and the necessity to avoid stress clash contexts. Polarity and the way in which negation was operationalised in the data also explained the variation with *need* and *dare* in relation to the factor RHYTHMIC ALTERNATION: *to*-infinitives were favoured in affirmative clauses and in negative clauses with auxiliary or *do*-support because the *to*-infinitive marker acted as a stress clash buffer, whereas BI clauses were favoured in unproblematic contexts and in negative clauses with direct negation or subject-verb inversion. Polarity was a significant factor in the alternation with *dare* and *need* in the whole database: *Need* preferred *to*-infinitives with affirmative polarity in both regional varieties in LModE and PDE, and *dare* typically governed *to*-infinitival complements in affirmative sentences in American LModE. The factor NOTIONAL CHARACTERISATION influenced the alternation with the verb *dare* and *need* in EModE, which favoured the *to*-infinitive complement in factual unrealised and non-factual unrealised meanings, respectively, and the verbs *need* and *help* in LModE, which opted for BI clauses with factual unrealised meanings. *Need* also selected BI clauses with factual realised meanings and *to*-infinitives with non-factual unrealised ones in both regional varieties diachronically. The semantic/pragmatic interpretation of the examples was only a determining factor of the variation with *dare* in British

PDE, where BI complementation was associated with non-factual unrealised meanings, and *to*-infinitive clauses with factual realised ones. In PDE, the distribution of the variants with *dare* and *need* mirrored the preferences observed in the LModE data, and the predictor NOTIONAL CHARACTERISATION did not influence the alternation with *help*.

The variation between *to*-infinitive and BI clausal complementation has been mainly explained in terms of diachronic, diatopic, grammatical and cognitive factors. My data indicate that passivisation and the *horror aequi* effect were the strongest factors in the alternation across both periods and varieties, except in *dare* and *need* predicates. The classification of the meaning conveyed by the examples according to the factuality of the proposition (factual vs non-factual) and the realisation of the event in the subordinate clauses (realised vs unrealised) led to a better understanding of the contexts in which clausal complementation is accepted with *dare*, *need* and *help*. However, since semantic/pragmatic factors were not found to be decisive in the models, no correlation may be drawn between meanings and complementation alternation based on my data. This study has revealed a number of tendencies and correlations regarding the *to*-infinitive/BI clausal complementation alternation governed by the verbs *dare*, *need* and *help* from ME to PDE in American and British English. Further research on the complementation patterns governed by these verbs in earlier periods of the English language may offer additional insights into the variation between *to*- and bare-infinitival complements and into the reasons for the alternation in contemporary English. This research could also benefit from a study of the alternation in World Englishes and of how these patterns are acquired in L2 English(es).

Appendix

Predictor	DARE					
	EModE	LModE		PDE		
		American	British	American	British	Coding
COMPLEMENTATION	N=488 BI (94.21 %); N=30 TO (5.79 %)	N=187 BI (69 %); N=84 TO (31 %)	N=44 BI (70.97 %); N=18 TO (29.03 %)	N=12 BI (54.55 %); N=10 TO (45.45 %)	N=63 BI (67.74 %); N=30 TO (32.26 %)	Categorical: BI=ref. level
MORPHOLOGY	N=210 explicit (40.54 %); N=308 non-explicit (59.46 %);	N=135 explicit (49.82 %); N=136 non-explicit (50.18 %)	N=29 explicit (46.77 %); N=33 non-explicit (53.23 %)	N=18 explicit (81.82 %); N=4 non-explicit (18.18 %)	N=73 explicit (78.49 %); N=20 non-explicit (21.51 %)	Categorical: Explicit=ref. level
POLARITY	N=289 positive (55.79 %); N=229 negative (44.21 %)	N=188 positive (69.37 %); N=83 negative (30.62 %)	N=40 positive (64.52 %); N=22 negative (35.48 %)	N=15 positive (68.18 %); N=7 negative (31.82 %)	N=45 positive (48.39 %); N=48 negative (51.61 %)	Categorical: Positive=ref. level

Table 134: *Continued*

Predictor	DARE					
	EModE	LModE		PDE		
		American	British	American	British	Coding
SYNTAX	N=128 adverbial (24.71 %); N=157 dependent (30–31 %); N=233 main (44.98 %)	N=38 adverbial (14.02 %); N=53 dependent (19.55 %); N=180 main (66.42 %)	N=12 adverbial (19.35 %); N=16 dependent (25.81 %); N=34 main (54.84 %)	N=2 adverbial (9.09 %); N=8 dependent (36.36 %); N=12 main (54.55 %)	N=18 adverbial (19.35 %); N=18 dependent (19.35 %); N=57 main (61.29 %)	Categorical: Adverbial=ref. level
VALENCY	N=54 intransitive (10.42 %); N=456 transitive (88.03 %); N=8 coordination (1.54 %)	N=31 intransitive (11.44 %); N=234 transitive (86.34 %); N=6 coordination (2.21 %)	N=1 intransitive (1.61 %); N=55 transitive (88.71 %); N=6 coordination (9.68 %)	N=7 intransitive (31.82 %); N=12 transitive (54.55 %); N=3 coordination (13.64 %)	N=17 intransitive (18.28 %); N=76 transitive (81.72 %); N=0 coordination	Categorical: Coordination=ref. level
RHYTHMIC ALTERNATION	N=376 unproblematic (72.59 %); N=142 critical (27.41 %)	N=184 unproblematic (67.9 %); N=87 critical (32.1 %)	N=29 unproblematic (46.77 %); N=33 critical (53.23 %)	N=15 unproblematic (68.18 %); N=7 critical (31.82 %)	N=44 unproblematic (47.31 %); N=49 critical (52.69 %)	Categorical: Critical=ref. level

PASSIVISATION	N=513 active (99.03 %); N=5 passive (0.97 %)	N=270 active (99.63 %); N=1 passive (0.37 %)	N=61 active (98.39 %); N=1 passive (1.61 %)	No instances	No instances	Categorical: Active=ref. level
PERFECT INFINITIVE	N=505 other (97.49 %); N=13 perfect (2.51 %)	No instances	No instances	No instances	No instances	Categorical: Other=ref. level
RELATIVE	N=432 other (83.4 %); N=86 relative (16.6 %)	N=206 other (76.01 %); N=65 relative (23.99 %)	N=48 other (77.42 %); N=14 relative (22.58 %)	N=15 other (68.18 %); N=7 relative (31.82 %)	N=84 other (90.32 %); N=9 relative (9.68 %)	Categorical: Other=ref. level
DISTANCE	*Min*=-1 log (0 words; N=241; 46.53 %); *Mean*=-0.3099805 logs (0.8066527 words); *Quantile*=1 logs (2 to 16 words; N=53; 10.23 %)	*Min*=-1 log (0 words; N=159; 58.67 %); *Mean*=-0.434965 logs (0.7397117 words); *Quantile*=0 logs (1 to 16 words; N=112; 41.33 %)	*Min*=-1 log (0 words; N=41; 66.13 %); *Mean*=-0.6451613 logs (0.6394213 words); *Quantile*=0 logs (1 to 2 words; N=21; 33.87 %)	*Min*=-1 log (0 words; N=15; 68.18 %); *Mean*=-0.6363636 logs (0.6433325 words); *Quantile*=0 logs (1 to 2 words; N=7; 31.82 %)	*Min*=-1 log (0 words; N=79; 84.95 %); *Mean*=-0.8324198 logs (0.5615865 words); *Quantile*=0 logs (1 to 3 words; N=14; 15.05 %)	Quantitative, logarithmically transformed with natural base; values of zero were assigned a score of -1 (log_words_mv_inf)

Continued

Table 134: *Continued*

Predictor	DARE					
	EModE	LModE		PDE		
		American	British	American	British	Coding
SUBJECT COMPLEXITY	N=39 non-basic (7.53 %); N=479 basic (92.47 %)	N=19 non-basic (7.01 %); N=252 basic (92.99 %)	N=6 non-basic (6.45 %); N=56 basic (90.32 %)	N=2 non-basic (9.09 %); N=20 basic (90.91 %)	N=14 non-basic (15.05 %); N=79 basic (84.95 %)	Categorical: Basic=ref. level
SUBJECT ANIMACY	N=496 animate (95.75 %); N=22 non-animate (4.25 %)	N=255 animate (94.1 %); N=16 non-animate (5.9 %)	N=61 animate (98.39 %); N=1 non-animate (1.61 %)	N=22 animate (100 %)	N=88 animate (94.62 %); N=5 non-animate (5.38 %)	Categorical: Animate=ref. level
FEAR	N=515 other (99.42 %); N=3 fear verbs (0.58 %)	N=269 other (99.26 %); N=2 fear verbs (0.74 %)	No instances	No instances	No instances	Categorical: Fear=ref. level

NOTIONAL CHARACTERISATION	N=184 factual realised (35.52 %); N=139 factual unrealised (26.83 %); N=195 non-factual unrealised (37.64 %)	N=81 factual realised (29.89 %); N=43 factual unrealised (15.87 %); N=147 non-factual unrealised (54.24 %)	N=23 factual realised (37.1 %); N=11 factual unrealised (17.74 %); N=28 non-factual unrealised (45.16 %)	N=11 factual realised (50 %); N=5 factual unrealised (22.73 %); N=6 non-factual unrealised (27.27 %)	N=19 factual realised (20.43 %); N=19 factual unrealised (20.43 %); N=55 non-factual unrealised (59.14 %)	Categorical: Factual realised=ref. level

Table 134: Summary of predictors affecting *dare* plus infinitival complementation from EModE to PDE

Predictor	NEED					
	EModE	LModE		PDE		
		American	British	American	British	Coding
COMPLEMENTATION	N=195 BI (55.71 %); N=155 TO (44.29 %)	N=149 BI (78.01 %); N=42 TO (21.99 %)	N=91 BI (93.81 %); N=6 TO (6.19 %)	N=20 BI (8.58 %); N=213 TO (91.42 %)	N=116 BI (11.6 %); N=884 TO (88.4 %)	Categorical: BI=ref. level
MORPHOLOGY	N=139 explicit (39.71 %); N=211 non-explicit (60.29 %);	N=31 explicit (16.23 %); N=160 non-explicit (83.77 %)	N=8 explicit (8.25 %); N=89 non-explicit (91.75 %)	N=117 explicit (50.21 %); N=116 non-explicit (49.79 %)	N=458 explicit (45.8 %); N=542 non-explicit (54.2 %)	Categorical: Explicit=ref. level
POLARITY	N=90 positive (25.71 %); N=260 negative (74.29 %)	N=79 positive (41.36 %); N=112 negative (58.64 %)	N=39 positive (40.21 %); N=58 negative (59.79 %)	N=209 positive (89.7 %); N=24 negative (10.3 %)	N=820 positive (82 %); N=180 negative (18 %)	Categorical: Positive=ref. level
SYNTAX	N=43 adverbial (12.29 %); N=104 dependent (29.71 %); N=203 main (58 %)	N=8 adverbial (4.19 %); N=30 dependent (15.71 %); N=153 main (80.1 %)	N=1 adverbial (1.03 %); N=23 dependent (23.71 %); N=73 main (75.26 %)	N=17 adverbial (7.3 %); N=55 dependent (23.61 %); N=161 main (69.1 %)	N=66 adverbial (6.6 %); N=238 dependent (23.8 %); N=696 main (69.6 %)	Categorical: Adverbial=ref. level

VALENCY	N=33 intransitive (9.43 %); N=309 transitive (88.29 %); N=8 coordination (2.29 %)	N=40 intransitive (20.94 %); N=149 transitive (78.01 %); N=2 coordination (1.05 %)	N=24 intransitive (24.74 %); N=72 transitive (74.23 %); N=1 coordination (1.03 %)	N=43 intransitive (18.45 %); N=174 transitive (74.68 %); N=16 coordination (6.87 %)	N=203 intransitive (20.3 %); N=756 transitive (75.6 %) N=41 coordination (4.1 %)	Categorical: Coordination=ref. level
RHYTHMIC ALTERNATION	N=266 unproblematic (76 %); N=84 critical (24 %)	N=163 unproblematic (85.34 %); N=28 critical (14.66 %)	N=89 unproblematic (91.75 %); N=8 critical (8.25 %)	N=147 unproblematic (63.09 %); N=86 critical (36.91 %)	N=620 unproblematic (62 %); N=380 critical (38 %)	Categorical: Critical=ref. level
PASSIVISATION	N=333 active (95.14 %); N=17 passive (4.86 %)	N=155 active (81.15 %); N=36 passive (18.85 %)	N=80 active (82.47 %); N=17 passive (17.53 %)	N=198 active (84.98 %); N=35 passive (15.02 %)	N=835 active (83.5 %); N=165 passive (16.5 %)	Categorical: Active=ref. level
PERFECT INFINITIVE	N=335 other (95.71 %); N=15 perfect (4.29 %)	N=189 other (98.95 %); N=2 perfect (1.05 %)	N=95 other (97.94 %); N=2 perfect (2.06 %)	No instances	N=989 other (98.9 %); N=11 perfect (1.1 %)	Categorical: Other=ref. level

Continued

Table 135: *Continued*

Predictor	NEED					
	EModE	LModE		PDE		
		American	British	American	British	Coding
RELATIVE	N=310 other (88.57 %); N=40 relative (11.43 %)	N=177 other (92.67 %); N=14 relative (7.33 %)	N=87 other (89.69 %); N=10 relative (10.31 %)	N=209 other (89.7 %); N=24 relative (10.3 %)	N=891 other (89.1 %); N=109 relative (10.9 %)	Categorical: Other=ref. level
DISTANCE	*Min*=-1 log (0 words; N=133; 38 %); *Mean*=-0.2301113 logs (0.8525691 words); *Quantile*=1 logs (2 to 16 words; N=36; 10.28 %)	*Min*=-1 log (0 words; N=95; 49.74 %); *Mean*=-0.4389009 logs (0.7376964 words); *Quantile*=0 logs (1 to 6 words; N=96; 50.26 %)	*Min*=-1 log (0 words; N=5; 22.68 %); *Mean*=-0.1631966 logs (0.8930441 words); *Quantile*=0 logs (1 to 3 words; N=75; 77.32 %)	*Min*=-1 log (0 words); *Mean*=-0.9073607 logs (0.5331596 words); *Quantile*=-1 logs (0.5 words)	*Min*=-1 log (0 words); *Mean*=-0.8840163 logs (0.5418569 words); *Quantile*=-1 logs (0.5 words)	Quantitative, logarithmically transformed with natural base; values of zero were assigned a score of -1 (log_words_mv_inf)
SUBJECT COMPLEXITY	N=9 non-basic (2.57 %); N=341 basic (97.43 %)	N=21 non-basic (10.99 %); N=170 basic (89.01 %)	N=7 non-basic (7.22 %); N=90 basic (92.78 %)	N=24 non-basic (10.3 %); N=209 basic (89.7 %)	N=99 non-basic (9.9 %); N=901 basic (90.1 %)	Categorical: Basic=ref. level

SUBJECT ANIMACY	N=319 animate (91.14 %); N=31 non-animate (8.86 %)	N=142 animate (74.35 %); N=49 non-animate (25.65 %)	N=76 animate (78.35 %); N=21 non-animate (21.65 %)	N=170 animate (72.96 %); N=63 non-animate (27.04 %)	N=751 animate (75.1 %); N=249 non-animate (24.9 %)	Categorical: Animate=ref. level
FEAR	N=283 other (80.86 %); N=67 fear verbs (19.14 %)	N=182 other (95.29 %); N=9 fear verbs (4.71 %)	N=90 other (92.78 %); N=7 fear verbs (7.22 %)	No instances	N=998 other (99.8 %); N=2 fear verbs (0.2 %)	Categorical: Fear=ref. level
NOTIONAL CHARACTERISATION	N=53 factual realised (15.14 %); N=39 factual unrealised (11.14 %); N=258 non-factual unrealised (73.71 %)	N=40 factual realised (21.05 %); N=5 factual unrealised (2.63 %); N=145 non-factual unrealised (76.32 %)	N=16 factual realised (16.49 %); N=9 factual unrealised (9.28 %); N=72 non-factual unrealised (74.23 %)	N=17 factual realised (7.3 %); N=11 factual unrealised (4.72 %); N=205 non-factual unrealised (87.98 %)	N=59 factual realised (5.91 %); N=27 factual unrealised (2.7 %); N=913 non-factual unrealised (91.39 %)	Categorical: Factual realised=ref. level

Table 135: Summary of predictors affecting *need* plus infinitival complementation from EModE to PDE

Predictor	HELP					
	ME/EModE	LModE	PDE			
		American	American	British	Chi-square/ Fisher Exact Probability Test	Coding
COMPLEMENTATION	N=21 BI (10.29 %); N=183 TO (89.71 %)	N=35 BI (42.68 %); N=47 TO (57.32 %)	N=286 BI (87.73 %); N=40 TO (12.27 %)	N=365 BI (65.65 %); N=191 TO (34.35 %)	$\chi^2(1)=50.7$, P=<.0001	
PERIOD	N=86 ME (42.16 %); N=118 EModE (57.84 %)					Categorical: EModE=ref. level
SUBJECT OF INFINITIVE	N=133 overt (65.2 %); N=71 covert (34.8 %)	N=33 overt (40.24 %); N=49 covert (59.76 %)	N=172 overt (52.76 %); N=154 covert (47.24 %)	N=286 overt (51.44 %); N=270 covert (48.56 %)	$\chi^2(1)=0.1$, P=0.71	Categorical: Explicit=ref. level
SYNTAX	N=78 adverbial (38.24 %); N=65 dependent (31.86 %); N=61 main (29.9 %)	N=18 adverbial (21.95 %); N=26 dependent (31.71 %); N=38 main (46.34 %)	N=70 adverbial (21.47 %); N=104 dependent (31.9 %); N= 152 main (46.63 %)	N=127 adverbial (22.84 %); N=192 dependent (34.53 %); N=237 main (42.63 %)	Adv vs Dep: $\chi^2(1)=0$, P=0.9203; Dep vs main: $\chi^2(1)=0.95$, P=0.2921; main vs Adv: $\chi^2(1)=0.55$, P=0.4028	Categorical: Adverbial=ref. level

VALENCY	N=15 intransitive (7.35 %); N=180 transitive (88.24 %); N=9 coordination (4.41)	N=6 intransitive (7.32 %); N=72 transitive (87.8 %); N=4 coordination (4.88 %)	N=21 intransitive (6.44 %); N=291 transitive (89.26 %); N=14 coordination (4.29 %)	N=37 intransitive (6.65 %); N=497 transitive (89.39 %); N=22 coordination (3.96 %)	Intrans vs Trans: $\chi^2(1)=0$, P=0.9203; Trans vs Coord: $\chi^2(1)=0$, P=0.8065; Coord vs Intrans: $\chi^2(1)=0$, P=0.7913	Categorical: Coordination=ref. level
RHYTHMIC ALTERNATION	N=142 unproblematic (69.61 %); N=62 critical (30.39 %)	N=56 unproblematic (68.29 %); N=26 critical (31.7 %)	N=257 unproblematic (78.83 %); N=69 critical (21.17 %)	N=424 unproblematic (76.25 %); N=132 critical (23.74 %)	$\chi^2(1)=0.64$, P=0.3802	Categorical: Critical=ref. level
HORROR AEQUI	N=147 other (71.08 %); N=57 yes (27.94 %)	N=62 other (75.61 %); N=20 yes (24.39 %)	N=258 other (79.14 %); N=68 yes (20.86 %)	N=405 other (72.84 %); N=151 yes (27.16 %)	$\chi^2(1)=4.04$, P=0.0366	Categorical: Other=ref. level
PASSIVISATION	N=197 active (96.57 %); N=7 passive (3.43 %)	N=82 active (100 %); N=0 passive	N=326 active (100 %); N= 0 passive	N=553 active (99.46 %); N= 3 passive (0.54 %)		Categorical: Active=ref. level
RELATIVE	N=186 other (91.18 %); N=18 relative (8.82 %)	N=73 other (89.02 %); N=9 relative (10.98 %)	N=282 other (86.5 %); N=44 relative (13.5 %)	N=488 other (87.77 %); N= 68 relative (12.23 %)	$\chi^2(1)=0.19$, P=0.5839	Categorical: Other=ref. level

Continued

Table 136: *Continued*

Predictor	HELP					
	ME/EModE	LModE	PDE			
		American	American	British	Chi-square/ Fisher Exact Probability Test	Coding
PRESENT	N=187 other (91.67 %); N=17 present (8.33 %)	N=64 other (78.05 %); N=18 present (21.95 %)	N=269 other (82.52 %); N=57 present (17.48 %)	N=493 other (88.67 %); N=63 present (11.33 %)	$\chi^2(1)=6.11$, P=0.0101	Categorical: Other=ref. level
INDICATIVE	N=176 other (86.27 %); N=28 indicative (13.73 %)	N=49 other (59.76 %); N=33 indicative (40.24 %)	N=186 other (57.06 %); N=140 indicative (42.94 %)	N=335 other (60.25 %); N=221 indicative (39.75 %)	$\chi^2(1)=0.74$, P=0.351	Categorical: Indicative=ref. level
DISTANCE	*MiN*=-1 log (0 words; N=124; 60.78 %); *MeaN*=-0.4630979 logs (0.7254269 words); *Quantile* =0 logs (1 to 7 words; N=80; 39.22 %)	*MiN*=-1 log (0 words; N=47; 57.32 %); *MeaN*=-0.4979277 logs (0.7081232 words); *Quantile* =0 logs (1 to 3 words; N=35; 42.68 %)	*MiN*=-1 log (0 words; N=171; 52.45 %); *MeaN*=-0.3865678 logs (0.7649473 words); *Quantile* =1 logs (2 to 7 words; N=35; 10.74 %)	*MiN*=-1 log (0 words; N=284; 51.08 %); *MeaN*=-0.4979277 logs (0.7081232 words); *Quantile* =0 logs (1 to 7 words; N=272; 48.92 %)		Quantitative, logarithmically transformed with natural base; values of zero were assigned a score of -1 (log_words_ mv_inf)

SUBJECT COMPLEXITY	N=16 complex (7.84 %); N=19 NP (9.31 %); N=115 pro (56.37 %); N=54 unexpressed (26.47 %)	N=10 complex (12.2 %); N=8 NP (9.76 %); N=42 pro (51.22 %); N=22 unexpressed (26.83 %)	N=71 complex (21.78 %); N=83 NP (25.46 %); N=87 pro (26.69 %); N=85 unexpressed (26.07 %)	N=96 complex (17.27 %); N=106 NP (19.06 %); N=192 pro (34.53 %); N=162 unexpressed (29.14 %)	complex vs pro: $\chi^2(1)=5.38$, P=0.0155; NP vs pro: $\chi2(1)=7.36$, P=0.0049; NP vs complex: $\chi^2(1)=0.03$, P=0.7913 NP vs unexpressed: $\chi^2(1)=3.69$, P=0.0434; complex vs unexpressed $\chi^2(1)=2.45$, P=0.0949 pro vs unexpressed: $\chi^2(1)=0.48$, P=0.431	Categorical: Complex=ref. level
OBJECT COMPLEXITY	N=9 NPs (4.41 %); N=62 pro (30.39 %); N=133 unexpressed (65.19 %)	N=8 NP (9.75 %); N=25 pro (30.48 %); N=49 unexpressed (59.75 %)	N=6 complex (1.84 %); N=54 NP (16.56 %); N=94 pro (28.83 %); N=172 unexpressed (52.76 %)	N=10 complex (1.79 %); N=112 NP (20.14 %); N=148 pro (26.61 %); N=286 unexpressed (51.44 %)	complex vs pro: $\chi^2(1)=0.03$, P=0.9203; NP vs pro: $\chi^2(1)=1.44$, P=0.1923; NP vs complex=$\chi^2(1)=0.02$, P=0.6892; NP vs unexpressed: $\chi^2(1)=1.12$, P=0.2488; complex vs unexpressed $\chi^2(1)=0.07$, P=1; pro vs unexpressed: $\chi^2(1)=0.06$, P=0.7401	Categorical: NPs =ref. level

Continued

Table 136: *Continued*

Predictor	HELP					
	ME/EModE	LModE	PDE			
		American	American	British	Chi-square/ Fisher Exact Probability Test	Coding
SUBJECT ANIMACY	N=153 animate (75 %); N=51 non-animate (25 %)	N=53 animate (64.63 %); N=29 non-animate (35.37 %)	N=116 animate (35.58 %); N=210 non-animate (64.42 %)	N=233 animate (41.91 %); N=323 non-animate (58.09 %)	$\chi^2(1)=3.18$, P=0.0636	Categorical: Animate=ref. level
OBJECT ANIMACY	N=67 animate (32.84 %); N=4 non-animate (1.96 %); N=133 unexpressed (65.2 %)	N=32 animate (39.02 %); N=1 non-animate (1.22 %); N=49 unexpressed (59.76 %)	N=141 animate (43.25 %); N=13 non-animate (3.99 %); N=172 unexpressed (52.76 %)	N=230 animate (41.37 %); N=40 non-animate (7.19 %); N=286 unexpressed (51.44 %)	animate vs non-animate: $\chi^2(1)=3.08$, P=0.0564	Categorical: Animate=ref. level
NOTIONAL CHARACTERISATION	N=36 factual realised (17.65 %); N=2 factual unrealised (0.98 %); N=166 non-factual unrealised (81.37 %)	N=33 factual realised (40.24 %); N=3 factual unrealised (3.66 %); N=46 non-factual unrealised (56.1 %)	N=142 factual realised (43.56 %); N=4 factual unrealised (1.23 %); N=180 non-factual unrealised (55.21 %)	N=232 factual realised (41.73 %); N=9 factual unrealised (1.62 %); N=315 non-factual unrealised (56.65 %)	Fact real vs fact unr: P=0.416 Fact unreal vs non-fact unr: P=0.462 Non-fact unr vs fact real: $\chi^2(1)=0.17$, P=0.6242	Categorical: Factual realised=ref. level

Table 136: Summary of predictors affecting *help* plus infinitival complementation from EModE to PDE

References and sources

Aarts, Bas, María José López-Couso and Belén Méndez-Naya. 2012. 'Late Modern English Syntax'. In *Historical Linguistics of English, Vol. II*, edited by Alex Bergs and Laurel Briton, 869–887. Berlin and New York: De Gruyter Mouton.

Allen, Cynthia. 1995. *Case Marking and Reanalysis. Grammatical Relations from Old to Early Modern English.* Oxford: Clarendon Press.

Anderson, John. 1986. A Note on Old English Impersonals. *Journal of Linguistics* 22: 167–177. https://doi.org/10.1017/S0022226700010604

Bemposta-Rivas, Sofía. 2016. '*Dared*-headed Blend Constructions in Middle and Early Modern English'. *SKASE Journal of Theoretical Linguistic*, Vol. 13(1): 24–39.

Beths, Frank. 1999. 'The History of *Dare* and the Status of Unidirectionality'. *Linguistics* 37: 1069–1110. https://doi.org/10.1515/ling.37.6.1069

Biber, Douglas, Stig Johansson, Geoffrey Leech, Susan Conrad and Edward Finegan. 1999. *Longman Grammar of Spoken and Written English.* London: Longman.

Bloomfield, Leonard. 1933. *Language.* New York: Henry Holt.

Bouzada-Jabois, Carla and Javier Pérez-Guerra. 2016. 'Towards a Unified Constructional Characterisation of the Nonfinite Periphery. On Verbal Free Adjuncts and Absolutes in English'. In *Outside the clause. Form and Function of Extra-clausal Constituents*, edited by Gunther Kältenbock, Evelien Keizer and Arne Lohmann, 175–202. Amsterdam: John Benjamins.

Brinton, Laurel J. 1988. *The Development of English Aspectual Systems. Aspectualizers and Post-verbal Particles.* Cambridge: Cambridge University Press.

Burnard, Lou. 2008. R*eference Guide to BNC Baby (second edition).* http://www.natcorp.ox.ac.uk/corpus/baby/manual.pdf.

Callies, Marcus. 2013. 'The Verb Phrase in English: Bare Infinitival Complements in Present-Day English'. *Philosophy*. DOI:10.1017/CBO9781139060998.011

Campbell, Alistair. 1959. *Old English Grammar*. Oxford: Oxford University Press.

Cuyckens, Hubert and Hendrik De Smet. 2007. '*For*. . .*to*-infinitives from Early to Late Modern English'. In *Of Varying Language and Opposing Creed: New Insights into Late Modern English*, edited by Javier Pérez-Guerra, Dolores González-Álvarez, Jorge L. Bueno-Alonso and Esperanza Rama-Martínez, 77–102. Suíza: Peter Lang.

Cuyckens, Hubert, Frauke D'hoedt and Benedikt Szmrecsanyi. 2014. 'Variability in Verb Complementation in Late Modern English: Finite vs. Non-finite Patterns'. In *Late Modern English Syntax*, edited by Marianne Hundt, 182–203. Cambridge: Cambridge University Press.

Denison, David. 1990. 'The Old English Impersonals Revived'. In *Papers of the 5th International Conference on English Historical Linguistics*, edited by Anna G. Ramat, Onofrio Carruba and Guiliano Bernini, 123–136. Amsterdam: John Benjamins.

Denison, David. 1993. *English Historical Syntax: Verbal Constructions*. London: Longman.

Denison, David. 1998. 'Syntax'. In *The Cambridge History of the English Language, Volume IV: 1776*–1997, edited by Suzanne Romaine, 92–329. Cambridge: Cambridge University Press

Denison, David. 2004. 'Do Grammars Change When they Leak? In *New Perspectives on English Historical Linguistics. Volume I: Syntax and Morphology*, edited by Christian J. Kay, Simon Horobin and Jeremy J. Smith, 15–30. Amsterdam and Philadelphia: John Benjamins Publishing Company.

Dirven, René. 1989. 'A Cognitive Perspective on Complementation'. In *Sentential Complementation and the Lexicon*, edited by Dany Jaspers, Wim Klooster, Yvan Putseys and Pieter Seuren, 113–139. Dordrecht: Foris.

Dixon, Robert Malcolm Ward. 1991. *A New Approach to English Grammar, on Semantic Principles*. Oxford: Clarendon Press.

Dixon, Robert Malcolm Ward and Alexandra Yurievna Aikhenvald. 2006. *Complementation: A Cross-linguistic Typology*. Oxford: Oxford University Press.

Duffley, Patrick J. 1992. *The English Infinitive*. London: Longman.

Duffley, Patrick J. 1994. 'Need and Dare: The Black Sheep of the Modal Family'. *Lingua* 94: 213–243. https://doi.org/10.1016/0024-3841(94)90010-8

Egan, Thomas. 2008. *Non-finite Complementation. A Usage-based Study of Infinitive and -Ing Clauses in English*. Amsterdam: Rodopi.

Fanego, Teresa. 1996. 'The Gerund in Early Modern English: Evidence from the Helsinki Corpus'. *Folia Linguistica Historica* 17: 97–152.

Fanego, Teresa. 1998. 'Developments in Argument Linking in Early Modern English Gerund Phrases'. *English Language and Linguistics* 2: 5–55.

Fanego, Teresa. 2004. 'Is Cognitive Grammar a Usage-based Model? Towards a Realistic Account of English Sentential Complements'. *Miscelánea: A Journal of English and American Studies* 29: 23–58.

Fanego, Teresa. 2017. 'The Trolley Rumbled Through the Tunnel: On the History of the English Intransitive Motion Construction'. *Folia Linguistica Historica* 38: 29–73.

Fischer, Olga and Max Nänny. 1999. 'Iconicity as a Creative Form in Language Use'. In *Form Miming Meaning: Iconicity in Language and Literature*, edited by Max Nänny and Olga Fischer, 26–36. Amsterdam: John Benjamins.

Fromkin, Victoria. 2000. *Linguistics: An Introduction to Linguistic Theory*. Oxford: Blackwell.

Gelman, Andrew and Jennifer Hill. 2007. *Data Analysis Using Regression and Multilevel/Hierarchical Models*. Cambridge: Cambridge University Press

Givón, Talmy. 1995. *Functionalism and Grammar*. Amsterdam: John Benjamins.

Haegeman, Liliane. 2006. *Thinking Syntactically. A Guide to Argumentation and Analysis*. Oxford: Blackwell Publishing.

Hamawand, Zeki. 2002. *Atemporal Complement Clauses in English: A Cognitive Grammar Analysis*. Muenchen: Lincom Europa.

Hamawand, Zeki. 2003. 'The Construal of Atemporalisation in Complement Clauses in English'. *Annual Review of Cognitive Linguistics* 1: 59–85.

Harris, Alice C. and Lyle Campbell. 1995. *Historical Syntax in Cross-linguistic Perspective*. Cambridge: Cambridge University Press.

Heine, Bernd. 1993. *Auxiliaries: Cognitive Forces and Grammaticalization*. New York: Oxford University Press.

Hilpert, Martin. 2014. *Construction Grammar and its Application to English*. Edinburgh: Edinburgh University.

Hockett, Charles F. 1958. *A Course in Modern Linguistics*. New York: Macmillan.

Hopper, Paul J. 1991. 'On Some Principles of Grammaticalization'. In *Approaches to Grammaticalization, Vol. I*, edited by Elizabeth Closs Traugott and Heine Bernd, 17–35. Amsterdam and Philadelphia: John Benjamins.

Hopper, Paul J. and Elizabeth Closs Traugott. 2003. *Grammaticalization*. Cambridge: Cambridge University Press.

Huddleston, Rodney, Geoffrey K. Pullum, Laurie Bauer, Betty Birner, Ted Briscoe, Peter Collins, David Denison, David Lee, Anita Mittwoch, Geoffrey Nunberg, Frank Palmer, John Payne, Peter Peterson, Lesley Stirling, and Gregory Ward. 2002. *The Cambridge Grammar of the English Language*. Cambridge and New York: Cambridge University Press.

Hundt, Marianne and Anne Gardner. 2017. 'Corpus-based Approaches: Watching English Change'. In *English Historical Linguistics: Approaches and Perspectives*, edited by Laurel Brinton Cambridge: University Press.

Jacobsson, Bengt. 1974. 'The Auxiliary *Need*'. *English Studies* 55: 56–63. https://doi.org/10.1080/00138387408597603

Komen, Erwin R. 2014. *Corpus Studio Manual v3.3*. Nijmegen: Radboud University (Centre for Language Studies, English Language Department).

Kroch, Anthony, Beatrice Santorini and Ariel Diertani. 2010. *The Penn Parsed Corpus of Modern British English (PPCMBE)*. Department of Linguistics, University of Pennsylvania. https://www.ling.upenn.edu/hist-corpora/PPCMBE2-RELEASE-1/index.html (November 28, 2016.)

Krug, Manfred. 2000. *Emerging English Modals: A Corpus-based Study of Grammaticalization*. Berlin: De Gruyter Mouton. https://doi.org/10.1515/9783110820980

Langacker, Ronald W. 1977. 'Syntactic Reanalysis'. In *Mechanisms of Syntactic Change*, edited by Charles Li, 57–139. Austin: University of Texas Press.

Langacker, Ronald W. 1990. *Concept, Image, and Symbol: The Cognitive Basis of Grammar*. Berlin: Mouton Gruyter.

Langacker, Ronald W. 1991. *Foundations of Cognitive Grammar: Descriptive Application Vol. II*. Stanford. California: Stanford University Press.

Levshina, Natalia. 2015. *How to Do Linguistics with R. Data Exploration and Statistical Analysis*. Amsterdam and Philadelphia: John Benjamins.

Levshina, Natalia. 2018. 'Probabilistic Grammar and Constructional Predictability: Bayesian Generalized Additive Models of *Help* + (*to*) Infinitive in Varieties of Web-based English'. *Glossa: a Journal of General Linguistics* 3(1), 55: 1–22, DOI: https://doi.org/10.5334/gjgl.294

Lightfoot, David W. 1979. *Principles of Diachronic Syntax*. Cambridge: Cambridge University Press.

Lind, Age. 1983. 'The Variant Forms of *help to/help Ø*'. *English Studies* 64. 263–275. DOI:https://doi.org/10.1080/00138388308598255

Lohmann, Arne. 2011. 'Help vs. Help to - a Multifactorial, Mixed-effects Account of Infinitive Marker Omission'. *English Language and Linguistics* 15(3): 499–521.

Los, Bettelou. 2005. *The Rise of the To-infinitive*. Oxford: Oxford University Press.

Loureiro-Porto, Lucía. 2009. *The Semantic Predecessors of* Need *in the History of English (c750–1710)*. Oxford: Wiley Blackwell.

Loureiro-Porto, Lucía. 2010. 'A Review of Early English Impersonals: Evidence from Necessity Verbs'. *English Studies* 91(6): 674–699.

Mair, Christian. 2002. 'Three Changing Patterns of Verb Complementation in Late Modern English: A Real-time Study Based on Matching Text Corpora'. *English Language and Linguistics* 6: 105–132.

Mair, Christian. 2003. 'Gerundial Complements after *Begin* and *Start* Grammatical and Sociolinguistic Factors, and How they Work against Each Other'. In *Determinants of Grammatical Variation in English*, edited by Günter Rohdenburg and Britta Mondorf, 329–346. Berlin: De Gruyter Mouton.

Matthews, Peter. 1981. *Syntax*. Cambridge: Cambridge University Press.

Matthews, Peter. 2007. *Syntactic Relations. A Critical Survey*. Cambridge: Cambridge University Press.

McEnery, Anthony and Zhonghua Xiao. 2005. 'HELP or HELP to: What do Corpora have to Say? *English Studies* 86(2): 161–187.

Méndez-Naya, Belén and María José López-Couso. 1997. 'What is Really Meant by Impersonal? On Impersonal and Related Terms'. *Atlantis* XIX/2: 185–191.

Mitchell, Bruce. 1985. *Old English Syntax* (2 vols.). Oxford: Claredon Press. https://doi.org/10.1093/acprof:oso/9780198119357.001.0001

Molencki, Rafał. 2002. 'The Status of Dearr and Tearf in Old English'. *Studia Anglica Posnaniensia* 38: 363–379.

Molencki, Rafał. 2005. 'The Confusion between Tharf and Dare in Middle English'. In *Rethinking Middle English: Linguistic and Literary Approaches*, edited by Nikolas Ritt and Herbert Schendl, 147–160. Frankfurt am Main: Peter Lang.

Mustanoja, Tauno F. 1960. *A Middle English Syntax*. Helsinki: Société Néophilologique.

Nagle, Stephen J. 2003. 'Double Modals in the Southern United States: Syntactic Structure or Syntactic Structures?' In *Modality in Contemporary English*, edited by Roberta Facchinetti, Frank Palmer and Manfred Krug, 349–372. Berlin and New York: De Gruyter Mouton

Norde, Muriel. 2011. 'Degrammaticalization'. In *The Oxford Handbook of Grammaticalization*, edited by Heiko Narrog and Bernd Heine, 475–546. Oxford: Oxford University Press.

Palmer, Frank Robert. 1990. *Modality and the English Modals*. London: Longman.

Quirk, Randolph, Sidney Greenbaum, Geoffrey Leech, and Jan Svartvik. 1985. *A Comprehensive Grammar of the English Language*. London: Longman.

R Core Team. 2020. *R: A Language and Environment for Statistical Computing*. Vienna: R Foundation for Statistical Computing. https://www.R-project.org.

Rissanen, Matti. 1999. 'Syntax'. In *The Cambridge History of the English Language Vol. III: 1746–1776*. Edited by Roger Lass, 187–331. Cambridge: Cambridge University Press.

Rohdenburg, Günter. 1996. 'Cognitive Complexity and Increased Grammatical Explicitness in English'. *Cognitive Linguistics* 7: 149–182.

Rohdenburg, Günter. 2003. 'Cognitive Complexity and *Horror Aequi* as Factors Determining the Use of Interrogative Clause Linkers in English'. In *Determinants of Grammatical Variation in English*, edited by Günter Rohdenburg and Britta Mondorf, 205–249. Berlin: De Gruyter Mouton.

Rohdenburg, Günter. 2009. 'Grammatical Divergence between British and American English in the Nineteenth and Early Twentieth Centuries'. In *Current Issues in Late Modern English*, edited by Ingrid Tieken-Boon van Ostade and Wim van der Wurff, 301–329. Bern: Peter Lang.

Rohdenburg, Günter. 2014. 'Relative Clauses of Reason in British and American English. *American Speech* 89: 288–311. DOI: 10.1215/00031283-2848978

Rohdenburg, Günter. 2018. 'The Use of Option Complement Markers in Present-day English. The Role of Passivization and other Complexity Factors'. In *Changing Structures: Studies in Constructions and Complementation*, edited by Mark Kaunisto, Mikko Höglund and Paul Rickman, 129–149. Amsterdam: John Benjamins.

Rohdenburg, Günter and Schlüter, Julia. 2000. 'Determinanten grammatischer Variation im Frühund Spätneuenglischen'. *Sprachwissenschaft* 25: 443–496.

Rohdenburg, Günter and Julia Schlüter. 2009. 'Introduction'. In *One Language, Two Grammars? Differences between British and American English*, edited by Günter Rohdenburg and Julia Schlüter, 1–12. Studies in English Language: Cambridge.

Rudanko, Juhani. 2000. *Corpora and Complementation*. Lanham, MD: University Press of America.

Rudanko, Juhani. 2011. *Changes in Complementation in British and American English. Corpus-based Studies on Non-finite Complements in Recent English*. London: Palgrave MacMillan.

Ruppenhofer, Josef. 2005. 'Regularities in Null Instantiation'. Retrieved August, 2020, from https://citeseerx.ist.psu.edu/viewdoc/download?doi=10.1.1.515.8486&rep=rep1&type=pdf

Schlüter, Julia. 2005. *Rhythmic Grammar. The Influence of Rhythm on Grammatical Variation and Change in English*. Berlin: De Gruyter Mouton.

Schlüter, Julia. 2010. 'To Dare To or Not To: Is Auxiliarization Reversible?' In *Formal Evidence in Grammaticalization Research*, edited by An van Liden, Jean-Christophe Verstraete, and Kristin

Davidse, 289–325. Amsterdam: John Benjamins. https://doi.org/10.1075/tsl.94.11sch

Smith, Michael B. and Joyce Escobedo. 2001. 'The Semantics of *To*-infinitival vs. *–ing* Verb Complement Constructions in English'. In *The Proceedings from the Main Session of the Chicago Linguistic Society's Thirty-seventh Meeting*, edited by Mary Andronis, Christopher Ball, Heidi Helston and Sylvain Neuvel, 549–563. Chicago: Chicago Linguistic Society.

Taeymans, Martine. 2004a. 'DARE and NEED in British and American Present-Day English: 1960s-1990s'. In *New Perspectives on English Historical Linguistics: Selected Papers from 12 ICEHL, Glasgow, 21–26 August 2002, Vol.1: Syntax and Morphology*, edited by Christian J. Kay, Simon Horobin and Jeremy J. Smith, 215–227. Amsterdam: John Benjamins.

Taeymans, Martine. 2004b. 'An Investigation into the Marginal Modals DARE and NEED in British Present-day English: A Corpus-based Approach'. In *Up and down the Cline – The Nature of Grammaticalization*, edited by Olga Fischer, Muriel Norde and Harry Perridon, 97–114. Amsterdam: Benjamins.

Taeymans, Martine. 2006. *An Investigation into the Emergence and Development of the Verb* Need *from Old to Present-Day English: A Corpus-based Approach*. Unpublished Doctoral dissertation. Belgium: Universiteit Antwerpen.

Tesnière, Lucien. [1959] 1969. *Éléments de Syntaxe Structurale*. Paris: Klincksieck.

Traugott, Elizabeth Closs. 1992. 'Syntax'. In *The Cambridge History of the English Language, Vol. I: The Beginnings to 1066*, edited by. R. M. Hogg, 168–289. Cambridge: Cambridge University Press.

Traugott, Elizabeth Closs and Graeme Trousdale. 2013. *Constructionalization and Constructional Changes*. Oxford: Oxford University Press

van der Auwera, Johan and Gabriele Diewald. 2012. 'Methods for Modalities'. In *Methods in Contemporary Linguistics*, edited by Andrea Ender, Adrian Leemann and Bernhard Wälchli, 121–142. Berlin and Boston: De Gruyter Mouton

Van der Auwera, Johan and Vladimir A. Plungian. 1998. 'Modality's Semantic Map'. *Linguistic Typology* 2: 79–124.

Verspoor, Marjoijn. 1996. 'The Story of *–Ing*: A Subjective Perspective'. In *The Construal of Space in Language and Thought*, edited by Martín Pütz and René Dirven, 417–454. Berlin: De Gruyter Mouton.

Verspoor, Marjolijn. H. 1999. '*To* infinitives'. In *Issues in Cognitive Linguistics*, edited by Leon de Stadler and Christoph Eyrich, 505–526. Berlijn and New York: De Gruyter Mouton.

Visser, Frederikus Thomas. [1963] 1973. *An Historical Syntax of the English Language. Vol. I-III.* (2nd ed). Leiden: E.J. Brill.

Vosberg, Uwe. 2006. *Die große Komplementverschiebung. Außersemantische Einflüsse auf die Entwicklung satzwertiger Ergänzungen im Neuenglischen*. Tübingen: Narr.

Wahlén, Niels. 1925. *The Old English Impersonalia, Part I.* Götteborg: Flanders.

Warner, Anthony. 1993. *English Auxiliaries. Structure and History.* Cambridge: Cambridge University Press. https://doi.org/10.1017/CBO9780511752995

Wischer, Ilse. 2019. 'Old English *Wolde* and *Sceolde*: A Semantic and Syntactic Analysis'. In *Developments in English Historical Morpho-Syntax*, edited by Claridge Claudia and Birte Bös, 111–128. Amsterdam and Philadelphia: John Benjamins.

Zaenen, Annie, Jean Carletta, Gregory Garretson, Joan Bresnan, Andrew Koontz-Garboden, Tatiana Nikitina, M. Catherine O'Connor and Tom Wasow. 2004. 'Animacy Encoding in English: Why and How'. In *ACL 2004. Workshop on Discourse Annotation*, edited by Bonnie Webber and Donna K. Byron, 118–125. Barcelona: Association for Computational Linguistics.

Linguistic Insights

Studies in Language and Communication

This series aims to promote specialist language studies in the fields of linguistic theory and applied linguistics, by publishing volumes that focus on specific aspects of language use in one or several languages and provide valuable insights into language and communication research. A cross-disciplinary approach is favoured and most European languages are accepted.

The series includes two types of books:

- Monographs – featuring in-depth studies on special aspects of language theory, language analysis or language teaching.
- Collected papers – assembling papers from workshops, conferences or symposia.

Each volume of the series is subjected to a double peer-reviewing process.

Vol. 1 Maurizio Gotti & Marina Dossena (eds)
Modality in Specialized Texts. Selected Papers of the 1st CERLIS Conference.
421 pages. 2001. ISBN 3-906767-10-8 · US-ISBN 0-8204-5340-4

Vol. 2 Giuseppina Cortese & Philip Riley (eds)
Domain-specific English. Textual Practices across Communities and Classrooms.
420 pages. 2002. ISBN 3-906768-98-8 · US-ISBN 0-8204-5884-8

Vol. 3 Maurizio Gotti, Dorothee Heller & Marina Dossena (eds)
Conflict and Negotiation in Specialized Texts. Selected Papers of the 2nd CERLIS Conference.
470 pages. 2002. ISBN 3-906769-12-7 · US-ISBN 0-8204-5887-2

Vol. 4 Maurizio Gotti, Marina Dossena, Richard Dury, Roberta Facchinetti & Maria Lima
Variation in Central Modals. A Repertoire of Forms and Types of Usage in Middle English and Early Modern English.
364 pages. 2002. ISBN 3-906769-84-4 · US-ISBN 0-8204-5898-8

Editorial address:

Prof. Maurizio Gotti Università di Bergamo, Dipartimento di Lingue, Letterature e Culture Straniere Piazza Rosate 2, 24129 Bergamo, Italy
Fax: +39 035 2052789, E-Mail: m.gotti@unibg.it

Vol. 5 Stefania Nuccorini (ed.)
Phrases and Phraseology. Data and Descriptions.
187 pages. 2002. ISBN 3-906770-08-7 · US-ISBN 0-8204-5933-X

Vol. 6 Vijay Bhatia, Christopher N. Candlin & Maurizio Gotti (eds)
Legal Discourse in Multilingual and Multicultural Contexts.
Arbitration Texts in Europe.
385 pages. 2003. ISBN 3-906770-85-0 · US-ISBN 0-8204-6254-3

Vol. 7 Marina Dossena & Charles Jones (eds)
Insights into Late Modern English. 2nd edition.
378 pages. 2003, 2007.
ISBN 978-3-03911-257-9 · US-ISBN 978-0-8204-8927-8

Vol. 8 Maurizio Gotti
Specialized Discourse. Linguistic Features and Changing Conventions.
351 pages. 2003, 2005.
ISBN 3-03910-606-6 · US-ISBN 0-8204-7000-7

Vol. 9 Alan Partington, John Morley & Louann Haarman (eds)
Corpora and Discourse.
420 pages. 2004. ISBN 3-03910-026-2 · US-ISBN 0-8204-6262-4

Vol. 10 Martina Möllering
The Acquisition of German Modal Particles. A Corpus-Based Approach.
290 pages. 2004. ISBN 3-03910-043-2 · US-ISBN 0-8204-6273-X

Vol. 11 David Hart (ed.)
English Modality in Context. Diachronic Perspectives.
261 pages. 2003. ISBN 3-03910-046-7 · US-ISBN 0-8204-6852-5

Vol. 12 Wendy Swanson
Modes of Co-reference as an Indicator of Genre.
430 pages. 2003. ISBN 3-03910-052-1 · US-ISBN 0-8204-6855-X

Vol. 13 Gina Poncini
Discursive Strategies in Multicultural Business Meetings.
2nd edition. 338 pages. 2004, 2007.
ISBN 978-3-03911-296-8 · US-ISBN 978-0-8204-8937-7

Vol. 14 Christopher N. Candlin & Maurizio Gotti (eds)
Intercultural Aspects of Specialized Communication.
2nd edition. 369 pages. 2004, 2007.
ISBN 978-3-03911-258-6 · US-ISBN 978-0-8204-8926-1

Vol. 15 Gabriella Del Lungo Camiciotti & Elena Tognini Bonelli (eds)
Academic Discourse. New Insights into Evaluation.
234 pages. 2004. ISBN 3-03910-353-9 · US-ISBN 0-8204-7016-3

Vol. 16 Marina Dossena & Roger Lass (eds)
Methods and Data in English Historical Dialectology.
405 pages. 2004. ISBN 3-03910-362-8 · US-ISBN 0-8204-7018-X

Vol. 17 Judy Noguchi
The Science Review Article. An Opportune Genre in
the Construction of Science.
274 pages. 2006. ISBN 3-03910-426-8 · US-ISBN 0-8204-7034-1

Vol. 18 Giuseppina Cortese & Anna Duszak (eds)
Identity, Community, Discourse. English in Intercultural Settings.
495 pages. 2005. ISBN 3-03910-632-5 · US-ISBN 0-8204-7163-1

Vol. 19 Anna Trosborg & Poul Erik Flyvholm Jørgensen (eds)
Business Discourse. Texts and Contexts.
250 pages. 2005. ISBN 3-03910-606-6 · US-ISBN 0-8204-7000-7

Vol. 20 Christopher Williams
Tradition and Change in Legal English. Verbal Constructions in Prescriptive Texts.
2nd revised edition. 216 pages. 2005, 2007. ISBN 978-3-03911-444-3.

Vol. 21 Katarzyna Dziubalska-Kolaczyk & Joanna Przedlacka (eds)
English Pronunciation Models: A Changing Scene.
2nd edition. 476 pages. 2005, 2008. ISBN 978-3-03911-682-9.

Vol. 22 Christián Abello-Contesse, Rubén Chacón-Beltrán, M. Dolores López-Jiménez & M. Mar Torreblanca-López (eds)
Age in L2 Acquisition and Teaching.
214 pages. 2006. ISBN 3-03910-668-6 · US-ISBN 0-8204-7174-7

Vol. 23 Vijay K. Bhatia, Maurizio Gotti, Jan Engberg & Dorothee Heller (eds)
Vagueness in Normative Texts.
474 pages. 2005. ISBN 3-03910-653-8 · US-ISBN 0-8204-7169-0

Vol. 24 Paul Gillaerts & Maurizio Gotti (eds)
Genre Variation in Business Letters. 2nd printing.
407 pages. 2008. ISBN 978-3-03911-681-2.

Vol. 25 Ana María Hornero, María José Luzón & Silvia Murillo (eds)
Corpus Linguistics. Applications for the Study of English.
2nd printing. 526 pages. 2006, 2008. ISBN 978-3-03911-726-0

Vol. 26 J. Lachlan Mackenzie & María de los Ángeles Gómez-González (eds)
Studies in Functional Discourse Grammar.
259 pages. 2005. ISBN 3-03910-696-1 · US-ISBN 0-8204-7558-0

Vol. 27 Debbie G. E. Ho
Classroom Talk. Exploring the Sociocultural Structure of Formal ESL Learning.
2nd edition. 254 pages. 2006, 2007. ISBN 978-3-03911-434-4

Vol. 28 Javier Pérez-Guerra, Dolores González-Álvarez, Jorge L. Bueno-Alonso & Esperanza Rama-Martínez (eds)
'Of Varying Language and Opposing Creed'. New Insights into Late Modern English.
455 pages. 2007. ISBN 978-3-03910-788-9

Vol. 29 Francesca Bargiela-Chiappini & Maurizio Gotti (eds)
Asian Business Discourse(s).
350 pages. 2005. ISBN 3-03910-804-2 · US-ISBN 0-8204-7574-2

Vol. 30 Nicholas Brownlees (ed.)
News Discourse in Early Modern Britain. Selected Papers of CHINED 2004.
300 pages. 2006. ISBN 3-03910-805-0 · US-ISBN 0-8204-8025-8

Vol. 31 Roberta Facchinetti & Matti Rissanen (eds)
Corpus-based Studies of Diachronic English.
300 pages. 2006. ISBN 3-03910-851-4 · US-ISBN 0-8204-8040-1

Vol. 32 Marina Dossena & Susan M. Fitzmaurice (eds)
Business and Official Correspondence. Historical Investigations.
209 pages. 2006. ISBN 3-03910-880-8 · US-ISBN 0-8204-8352-4

Vol. 33 Giuliana Garzone & Srikant Sarangi (eds)
Discourse, Ideology and Specialized Communication.
494 pages. 2007. ISBN 978-3-03910-888-6

Vol. 34 Giuliana Garzone & Cornelia Ilie (eds)
The Use of English in Institutional and Business Settings.
An Intercultural Perspective.
372 pages. 2007. ISBN 978-3-03910-889-3

Vol. 35 Vijay K. Bhatia & Maurizio Gotti (eds)
Explorations in Specialized Genres.
316 pages. 2006. ISBN 3-03910-995-2 · US-ISBN 0-8204-8372-9

Vol. 36 Heribert Picht (ed.)
Modern Approaches to Terminological Theories and Applications.
432 pages. 2006. ISBN 3-03911-156-6 · US-ISBN 0-8204-8380-X

Vol. 37 Anne Wagner & Sophie Cacciaguidi-Fahy (eds)
Legal Language and the Search for Clarity / Le langage juridique et la quête de clarté. Practice and Tools / Pratiques et instruments.
487 pages. 2006. ISBN 3-03911-169-8 · US-ISBN 0-8204-8388-5

Vol. 38 Juan Carlos Palmer-Silveira, Miguel F. Ruiz-Garrido & Inmaculada Fortanet-Gómez (eds)
Intercultural and International Business Communication.
Theory, Research and Teaching.
2nd edition. 343 pages. 2006, 2008. ISBN 978-3-03911-680-5

Vol. 39 Christiane Dalton-Puffer, Dieter Kastovsky, Nikolaus Ritt & Herbert Schendl (eds)
Syntax, Style and Grammatical Norms. English from 1500–2000.
250 pages. 2006. ISBN 3-03911-181-7 · US-ISBN 0-8204-8394-X

Vol. 40 Marina Dossena & Irma Taavitsainen (eds)
Diachronic Perspectives on Domain-Specific English.
280 pages. 2006. ISBN 3-03910-176-0 · US-ISBN 0-8204-8391-5

Vol. 41 John Flowerdew & Maurizio Gotti (eds)
Studies in Specialized Discourse.
293 pages. 2006. ISBN 3-03911-178-7

Vol. 42 Ken Hyland & Marina Bondi (eds)
Academic Discourse Across Disciplines.
320 pages. 2006. ISBN 3-03911-183-3 · US-ISBN 0-8204-8396-6

Vol. 43 Paul Gillaerts & Philip Shaw (eds)
The Map and the Landscape. Norms and Practices in Genre.
256 pages. 2006. ISBN 3-03911-182-5 · US-ISBN 0-8204-8395-4

Vol. 44 Maurizio Gotti & Davide Giannoni (eds)
New Trends in Specialized Discourse Analysis.
301 pages. 2006. ISBN 3-03911-184-1 · US-ISBN 0-8204-8381-8

Vol. 45 Maurizio Gotti & Françoise Salager-Meyer (eds)
Advances in Medical Discourse Analysis. Oral and Written Contexts.
492 pages. 2006. ISBN 3-03911-185-X · US-ISBN 0-8204-8382-6

Vol. 46 Maurizio Gotti & Susan Šarcević (eds)
Insights into Specialized Translation.
396 pages. 2006. ISBN 3-03911-186-8 · US-ISBN 0-8204-8383-4

Vol. 47 Khurshid Ahmad & Margaret Rogers (eds)
Evidence-based LSP. Translation, Text and Terminology.
584 pages. 2007. ISBN 978-3-03911-187-9

Vol. 48 Hao Sun & Dániel Z. Kádár (eds)
It's the Dragon's Turn. Chinese Institutional Discourses.
262 pages. 2008. ISBN 978-3-03911-175-6

Vol. 49 Cristina Suárez-Gómez
Relativization in Early English (950-1250). the Position of Relative Clauses.
149 pages. 2006. ISBN 3-03911-203-1 · US-ISBN 0-8204-8904-2

Vol. 50 Maria Vittoria Calvi & Luisa Chierichetti (eds)
Nuevas tendencias en el discurso de especialidad.
319 pages. 2006. ISBN 978-3-03911-261-6

Vol. 51 Mari Carmen Campoy & María José Luzón (eds)
Spoken Corpora in Applied Linguistics.
274 pages. 2008. ISBN 978-3-03911-275-3

Vol. 52 Konrad Ehlich & Dorothee Heller (Hrsg.)
Die Wissenschaft und ihre Sprachen.
323 pages. 2006. ISBN 978-3-03911-272-2

Vol. 53 Jingyu Zhang
The Semantic Salience Hierarchy Model. The L2 Acquisition of Psych Predicates
273 pages. 2007. ISBN 978-3-03911-300-2

Vol. 54 Norman Fairclough, Giuseppina Cortese & Patrizia Ardizzone (eds)
Discourse and Contemporary Social Change.
555 pages. 2007. ISBN 978-3-03911-276-0

Vol. 55 Jan Engberg, Marianne Grove Ditlevsen, Peter Kastberg & Martin Stegu (eds)
New Directions in LSP Teaching.
331 pages. 2007. ISBN 978-3-03911-433-7

Vol. 56 Dorothee Heller & Konrad Ehlich (Hrsg.)
Studien zur Rechtskommunikation.
322 pages. 2007. ISBN 978-3-03911-436-8

Vol. 57 Teruhiro Ishiguro & Kang-kwong Luke (eds)
Grammar in Cross-Linguistic Perspective.
The Syntax, Semantics, and Pragmatics of Japanese and Chinese.
304 pages. 2012. ISBN 978-3-03911-445-0

Vol. 58 Carmen Frehner
Email – SMS – MMS
294 pages. 2008. ISBN 978-3-03911-451-1

Vol. 59 Isabel Balteiro
The Directionality of Conversion in English. A Dia-Synchronic Study.
276 pages. 2007. ISBN 978-3-03911-241-8

Vol. 60 Maria Milagros Del Saz Rubio
English Discourse Markers of Reformulation.
237 pages. 2007. ISBN 978-3-03911-196-1

Vol. 61 Sally Burgess & Pedro Martín-Martín (eds)
English as an Additional Language in Research Publication and Communication.
259 pages. 2008. ISBN 978-3-03911-462-7

Vol. 62 Sandrine Onillon
Pratiques et représentations de l'écrit.
458 pages. 2008. ISBN 978-3-03911-464-1

Vol. 63 Hugo Bowles & Paul Seedhouse (eds)
Conversation Analysis and Language for Specific Purposes.
2nd edition. 337 pages. 2007, 2009. ISBN 978-3-0343-0045-2

Vol. 64 Vijay K. Bhatia, Christopher N. Candlin & Paola Evangelisti Allori (eds)
Language, Culture and the Law.
The Formulation of Legal Concepts across Systems and Cultures.
342 pages. 2008. ISBN 978-3-03911-470-2

Vol. 65 Jonathan Culpeper & Dániel Z. Kádár (eds)
Historical (Im)politeness.
300 pages. 2010. ISBN 978-3-03911-496-2

Vol. 66 Linda Lombardo (ed.)
Using Corpora to Learn about Language and Discourse.
237 pages. 2009. ISBN 978-3-03911-522-8

Vol. 67 Natsumi Wakamoto
Extroversion/Introversion in Foreign Language Learning.
Interactions with Learner Strategy Use.
159 pages. 2009. ISBN 978-3-03911-596-9

Vol. 68 Eva Alcón-Soler (ed.)
Learning How to Request in an Instructed Language Learning Context.
260 pages. 2008. ISBN 978-3-03911-601-0

Vol. 69 Domenico Pezzini
The Translation of Religious Texts in the Middle Ages.
428 pages. 2008. ISBN 978-3-03911-600-3

Vol. 70 Tomoko Tode
Effects of Frequency in Classroom Second Language Learning.
Quasi-experiment and stimulated-recall analysis.
195 pages. 2008. ISBN 978-3-03911-602-7

Vol. 71 Egor Tsedryk
Fusion symétrique et alternances ditransitives.
211 pages. 2009. ISBN 978-3-03911-609-6

Vol. 72 Cynthia J. Kellett Bidoli & Elana Ochse (eds)
English in International Deaf Communication.
444 pages. 2008. ISBN 978-3-03911-610-2

Vol. 73 Joan C. Beal, Carmela Nocera & Massimo Sturiale (eds)
Perspectives on Prescriptivism.
269 pages. 2008. ISBN 978-3-03911-632-4

Vol. 74 Carol Taylor Torsello, Katherine Ackerley & Erik Castello (eds)
Corpora for University Language Teachers.
308 pages. 2008. ISBN 978-3-03911-639-3

Vol. 75 María Luisa Pérez Cañado (ed.)
English Language Teaching in the European Credit Transfer System. Facing the Challenge.
251 pages. 2009. ISBN 978-3-03911-654-6

Vol. 76 Marina Dossena & Ingrid Tieken-Boon van Ostade (eds)
Studies in Late Modern English Correspondence. Methodology and Data.
291 pages. 2008. ISBN 978-3-03911-658-4

Vol. 77 Ingrid Tieken-Boon van Ostade & Wim van der Wurff (eds)
Current Issues in Late Modern English.
436 pages. 2009. ISBN 978-3-03911-660-7

Vol. 78 Marta Navarro Coy (ed.)
Practical Approaches to Foreign Language Teaching and Learning.
297 pages. 2009. ISBN 978-3-03911-661-4

Vol. 79 Qing Ma
Second Language Vocabulary Acquisition.
333 pages. 2009. ISBN 978-3-03911-666-9

Vol. 80 Martin Solly, Michelangelo Conoscenti & Sandra Campagna (eds)
Verbal/Visual Narrative Texts in Higher Education.
384 pages. 2008. ISBN 978-3-03911-672-0

Vol. 81 Meiko Matsumoto
From Simple Verbs to Periphrastic Expressions: The Historical Development of Composite Predicates, Phrasal Verbs, and Related Constructions in English.
235 pages. 2008. ISBN 978-3-03911-675-1

Vol. 82 Melinda Dooly
Doing Diversity. Teachers' Construction of Their Classroom Reality.
180 pages. 2009. ISBN 978-3-03911-687-4

Vol. 83 Victoria Guillén-Nieto, Carmen Marimón-Llorca & Chelo Vargas-Sierra (eds)
Intercultural Business Communication and Simulation and Gaming Methodology.
392 pages. 2009. ISBN 978-3-03911-688-1

Vol. 84 Maria Grazia Guido
English as a Lingua Franca in Cross-cultural Immigration Domains.
285 pages. 2008. ISBN 978-3-03911-689-8

Vol. 85 Erik Castello
Text Complexity and Reading Comprehension Tests.
352 pages. 2008. ISBN 978-3-03911-717-8

Vol. 86 Maria-Lluisa Gea-Valor, Isabel García-Izquierdo & Maria-José Esteve (eds)
Linguistic and Translation Studies in Scientific Communication.
317 pages. 2010. ISBN 978-3-0343-0069-8

Vol. 87 Carmen Navarro, Rosa Mª Rodríguez Abella, Francesca Dalle Pezze & Renzo Miotti (eds)
La comunicación especializada.
355 pages. 2008. ISBN 978-3-03911-733-8

Vol. 88 Kiriko Sato
The Development from Case-Forms to Prepositional Constructions in Old English Prose.
231 pages. 2009. ISBN 978-3-03911-763-5

Vol. 89 Dorothee Heller (Hrsg.)
Formulierungsmuster in deutscher und italienischer Fachkommunikation. Intra- und interlinguale Perspektiven.
315 pages. 2008. ISBN 978-3-03911-778-9

Vol. 90 Henning Bergenholtz, Sandro Nielsen & Sven Tarp (eds)
Lexicography at a Crossroads. Dictionaries and Encyclopedias Today, Lexicographical Tools Tomorrow.
372 pages. 2009. ISBN 978-3-03911-799-4

Vol. 91 Manouchehr Moshtagh Khorasani
The Development of Controversies. From the Early Modern Period to Online Discussion Forums.
317 pages. 2009. ISBN 978-3-3911-711-6

Vol. 92 María Luisa Carrió-Pastor (ed.)
Content and Language Integrated Learning. Cultural Diversity.
178 pages. 2009. ISBN 978-3-3911-818-2

Vol. 93 Roger Berry
Terminology in English Language Teaching. Nature and Use.
262 pages. 2010. ISBN 978-3-0343-0013-1

Vol. 94 Roberto Cagliero & Jennifer Jenkins (eds)
Discourses, Communities, and Global Englishes
240 pages. 2010. ISBN 978-3-0343-0012-4

Vol. 95 Facchinetti Roberta, Crystal David, Seidlhofer Barbara (eds)
From International to Local English – And Back Again.
268 pages. 2010. ISBN 978-3-0343-0011-7

Vol. 96 Cesare Gagliardi & Alan Maley (eds)
EIL, ELF, Global English. Teaching and Learning Issues
376 pages. 2010. ISBN 978-3-0343-0010-0

Vol. 97 Sylvie Hancil (ed.)
The Role of Prosody in Affective Speech.
403 pages. 2009. ISBN 978-3-03911-696-6

Vol. 98 Marina Dossena & Roger Lass (eds)
Studies in English and European Historical Dialectology.
257 pages. 2009. ISBN 978-3-0343-0024-7

Vol. 99 Christine Béal
Les interactions quotidiennes en français et en anglais. De l'approche comparative à l'analyse des situations interculturelles.
424 pages. 2010. ISBN 978-3-0343-0027-8

Vol. 100 Maurizio Gotti (ed.)
Commonality and Individuality in Academic Discourse.
398 pages. 2009. ISBN 978-3-0343-0023-0

Vol. 101 Javier E. Díaz Vera & Rosario Caballero (eds)
Textual Healing. Studies in Medieval English Medical, Scientific and Technical Texts.
213 pages. 2009. ISBN 978-3-03911-822-9

Vol. 102 Nuria Edo Marzá
The Specialised Lexicographical Approach. A Step further in Dictionary-making.
316 pages. 2009. ISBN 978-3-0343-0043-8

Vol. 103 Carlos Prado-Alonso, Lidia Gómez-García, Iria Pastor-Gómez & David Tizón-Couto (eds)
New Trends and Methodologies in Applied English Language Research. Diachronic, Diatopic and Contrastive Studies.
348 pages. 2009. ISBN 978-3-0343-0046-9

Vol. 104 Françoise Salager-Meyer & Beverly A. Lewin
Crossed Words. Criticism in Scholarly Writing?
371 pages. 2011. ISBN 978-3-0343-0049-0.

Vol. 105 Javier Ruano-García
Early Modern Northern English Lexis. A Literary Corpus-Based Study.
611 pages. 2010. ISBN 978-3-0343-0058-2

Vol. 106 Rafael Monroy-Casas
Systems for the Phonetic Transcription of English. Theory and Texts.
280 pages. 2011. ISBN 978-3-0343-0059-9

Vol. 107 Nicola T. Owtram
The Pragmatics of Academic Writing. A Relevance Approach to the Analysis of Research Article Introductions.
311 pages. 2009. ISBN 978-3-0343-0060-5

Vol. 108 Yolanda Ruiz de Zarobe, Juan Manuel Sierra & Francisco Gallardo del Puerto (eds)
Content and Foreign Language Integrated Learning. Contributions to Multilingualism in European Contexts
343 pages. 2011. ISBN 978-3-0343-0074-2

Vol. 109 Ángeles Linde López & Rosalía Crespo Jiménez (eds)
Professional English in the European context. The EHEA challenge.
374 pages. 2010. ISBN 978-3-0343-0088-9

Vol. 110 Rosalía Rodríguez-Vázquez
The Rhythm of Speech, Verse and Vocal Music. A New Theory.
394 pages. 2010. ISBN 978-3-0343-0309-5

Vol. 111 Anastasios Tsangalidis & Roberta Facchinetti (eds)
Studies on English Modality. In Honour of Frank Palmer.
392 pages. 2009. ISBN 978-3-0343-0310-1

Vol. 112 Jing Huang
Autonomy, Agency and Identity in Foreign Language Learning and Teaching.
400 pages. 2013. ISBN 978-3-0343-0370-5

Vol. 113 Mihhail Lotman & Maria-Kristiina Lotman (eds)
Frontiers in Comparative Prosody. In memoriam: Mikhail Gasparov.
426 pages. 2011. ISBN 978-3-0343-0373-6

Vol. 114 Merja Kytö, John Scahill & Harumi Tanabe (eds)
Language Change and Variation from Old English to Late Modern English. A Festschrift for Minoji Akimoto
422 pages. 2010. ISBN 978-3-0343-0372-9

Vol. 115 Giuliana Garzone & Paola Catenaccio (eds)
Identities across Media and Modes. Discursive Perspectives.
379 pages. 2009. ISBN 978-3-0343-0386-6

Vol. 116 Elena Landone
Los marcadores del discurso y cortesía verbal en español.
390 pages. 2010. ISBN 978-3-0343-0413-9

Vol. 117 Maurizio Gotti & Christopher Williams (eds)
Legal Discourse across Languages and Cultures.
339 pages. 2010. ISBN 978-3-0343-0425-2

Vol. 118 David Hirsh
Academic Vocabulary in Context.
217 pages. 2010. ISBN 978-3-0343-0426-9

Vol. 119 Yvonne Dröschel
Lingua Franca English. The Role of Simplification and Transfer.
358 pages. 2011. ISBN 978-3-0343-0432-0

Vol. 120 Tengku Sepora Tengku Mahadi, Helia Vaezian & Mahmoud Akbari
Corpora in Translation. A Practical Guide.
135 pages. 2010. ISBN 978-3-0343-0434-4

Vol. 121 Davide Simone Giannoni & Celina Frade (eds)
Researching Language and the Law. Textual Features and Translation Issues.
278 pages. 2010. ISBN 978-3-0343-0443-6

Vol. 122 Daniel Madrid & Stephen Hughes (eds)
Studies in Bilingual Education.
472 pages. 2011. ISBN 978-3-0343-0474-0

Vol. 123 Vijay K. Bhatia, Christopher N. Candlin & Maurizio Gotti (eds)
The Discourses of Dispute Resolution.
290 pages. 2010. ISBN 978-3-0343-0476-4

Vol. 124 Davide Simone Giannoni
Mapping Academic Values in the Disciplines. A Corpus-Based Approach.
288 pages. 2010. ISBN 978-3-0343-0488-7

Vol. 125 Giuliana Garzone & James Archibald (eds)
Discourse, Identities and Roles in Specialized Communication.
419 pages. 2010. ISBN 978-3-0343-0494-8

Vol. 126 Iria Pastor-Gómez
The Status and Development of N+N Sequences in
Contemporary English Noun Phrases.
216 pages. 2011. ISBN 978-3-0343-0534-1

Vol. 127 Carlos Prado-Alonso
Full-verb Inversion in Written and Spoken English.
261 pages. 2011. ISBN 978-3-0343-0535-8

Vol. 128 Tony Harris & María Moreno Jaén (eds)
Corpus Linguistics in Language Teaching.
214 pages. 2010. ISBN 978-3-0343-0524-2

Vol. 129 Tetsuji Oda & Hiroyuki Eto (eds)
Multiple Perspectives on English Philology and History of Linguistics.
A Festschrift for Shoichi Watanabe on his 80th Birthday.
378 pages. 2010. ISBN 978-3-0343-0480-1

Vol. 130 Luisa Chierichetti & Giovanni Garofalo (eds)
Lengua y Derecho. líneas de investigación interdisciplinaria.
283 pages. 2010. 978-3-0343-0463-4

Vol. 131 Paola Evangelisti Allori & Giuliana Garzone (eds)
Discourse, Identities and Genres in Corporate Communication.
Sponsorship, Advertising and Organizational Communication.
324 pages. 2011. 978-3-0343-0591-4

Vol. 132 Leyre Ruiz de Zarobe & Yolanda Ruiz de Zarobe (eds)
Speech Acts and Politeness across Languages and Cultures.
402 pages. 2012. 978-3-0343-0611-9

Vol. 133 Thomas Christiansen
Cohesion. A Discourse Perspective.
387 pages. 2011. 978-3-0343-0619-5

Vol. 134 Giuliana Garzone & Maurizio Gotti
Discourse, Communication and the Enterprise. Genres and Trends.
451 pages. 2011. ISBN 978-3-0343-0620-1

Vol. 135 Zsuzsa Hoffmann
Ways of the World's Words.
Language Contact in the Age of Globalization.
334 pages 2011. ISBN 978-3-0343-0673-7

Vol. 136 Cecilia Varcasia (ed.)
Becoming Multilingual.
Language Learning and Language Policy between Attitudes and Identities.
213 pages. 2011. ISBN 978-3-0343-0687-5

Vol. 137 Susy Macqueen
The Emergence of Patterns in Second Language Writing.
A Sociocognitive Exploration of Lexical Trails.
325 pages. 2012. ISBN 978-3-0343-1010-9

Vol. 138 Maria Vittoria Calvi & Giovanna Mapelli (eds)
La lengua del turismo. Géneros discursivos y terminología.
365 pages. 2011. ISBN 978-3-0343-1011-6

Vol. 139 Ken Lau
Learning to Become a Professional in a Textually-Mediated World.
A Text-Oriented Study of Placement Practices.
261 pages. 2012. ISBN 978-3-0343-1016-1

Vol. 140 Sandra Campagna, Giuliana Garzone, Cornelia Ilie & Elizabeth Rowley-Jolivet (eds)
Evolving Genres in Web-mediated Communication.
337 pages. 2012. ISBN 978-3-0343-1013-0

Vol. 141 Edith Esch & Martin Solly (eds)
The Sociolinguistics of Language Education in International Contexts.
263 pages. 2012. ISBN 978-3-0343-1009-3

Vol. 142 Forthcoming.

Vol. 143 David Tizón-Couto
Left Dislocation in English. A Functional-Discoursal Approach.
416 pages. 2012. ISBN 978-3-0343-1037-6

Vol. 144 Margrethe Petersen & Jan Engberg (eds)
Current Trends in LSP Research. Aims and Methods.
323 pages. 2011. ISBN 978-3-0343-1054-3

Vol. 145 David Tizón-Couto, Beatriz Tizón-Couto, Iria Pastor-Gómez & Paula Rodríguez-Puente (eds)
New Trends and Methodologies in Applied English Language Research II. Studies in Language Variation, Meaning and Learning.
283 pages. 2012. ISBN 978-3-0343-1061-1

Vol. 146 Rita Salvi & Hiromasa Tanaka (eds)
Intercultural Interactions in Business and Management.
306 pages. 2011. ISBN 978-3-0343-1039-0

Vol. 147 Francesco Straniero Sergio & Caterina Falbo (eds)
Breaking Ground in Corpus-based Interpreting Studies.
254 pages. 2012. ISBN 978-3-0343-1071-0

Vol. 148 Forthcoming.

Vol. 149 Vijay K. Bhatia & Paola Evangelisti Allori (eds)
Discourse and Identity in the Professions. Legal, Corporate and Institutional Citizenship.
352 pages. 2011. ISBN 978-3-0343-1079-6

Vol. 150 Maurizio Gotti (ed.)
Academic Identity Traits. A Corpus-Based Investigation.
363 pages. 2012. ISBN 978-3-0343-1141-0

Vol. 151 Priscilla Heynderickx, Sylvain Dieltjens, Geert Jacobs, Paul Gillaerts & Elizabeth de Groot (eds)
The Language Factor in International Business. New Perspectives on Research, Teaching and Practice.
320 pages. 2012. ISBN 978-3-0343-1090-1

Vol. 152 Paul Gillaerts, Elizabeth de Groot, Sylvain Dieltjens, Priscilla Heynderickx & Geert Jacobs (eds)
Researching Discourse in Business Genres. Cases and Corpora.
215 pages. 2012. ISBN 978-3-0343-1092-5

Vol. 153 Yongyan Zheng
Dynamic Vocabulary Development in a Foreign Language.
262 pages. 2012. ISBN 978-3-0343-1106-9

Vol. 154 Carmen Argondizzo (ed.)
Creativity and Innovation in Language Education.
357 pages. 2012. ISBN 978-3-0343-1080-2

Vol. 155 David Hirsh (ed.)
Current Perspectives in Second Language Vocabulary Research.
180 pages. 2012. ISBN 978-3-0343-1108-3

Vol. 156 Seiji Shinkawa
Unhistorical Gender Assignment in Lahamon's *Brut.* A Case Study of a Late Stage in the Development of Grammatical Gender toward its Ultimate Loss.
186 pages. 2012. ISBN 978-3-0343-1124-3

Vol. 157 Yeonkwon Jung
Basics of Organizational Writing: A Critical Reading Approach.
151 pages. 2014. ISBN 978-3-0343-1137-3.

Vol. 158 Bárbara Eizaga Rebollar (ed.)
Studies in Linguistics and Cognition.
301 pages. 2012. ISBN 978-3-0343-1138-0

Vol. 159 Giuliana Garzone, Paola Catenaccio, Chiara Degano (eds)
Genre Change in the Contemporary World. Short-term Diachronic Perspectives.
329 pages. 2012. ISBN 978-3-0343-1214-1

Vol. 160 Carol Berkenkotter, Vijay K. Bhatia & Maurizio Gotti (eds)
Insights into Academic Genres.
468 pages. 2012. ISBN 978-3-0343-1211-0

Vol. 161 Beatriz Tizón-Couto
Clausal Complements in Native and Learner Spoken English. A corpus-based study with Lindsei and Vicolse. 357 pages. 2013. ISBN 978-3-0343-1184-7

Vol. 162 Patrizia Anesa
Jury Trials and the Popularization of Legal Language. A Discourse Analytical Approach.
247 pages. 2012. ISBN 978-3-0343-1231-8

Vol. 163 David Hirsh
Endangered Languages, Knowledge Systems and Belief Systems.
153 pages. 2013. ISBN 978-3-0343-1232-5

Vol. 164 Eugenia Sainz (ed.)
De la estructura de la frase al tejido del discurso. Estudios contrastivos español/italiano.
305 pages. 2014. ISBN 978-3-0343-1253-0

Vol. 165 Julia Bamford, Franca Poppi & Davide Mazzi (eds)
Space, Place and the Discursive Construction of Identity.
367 pages. 2014. ISBN 978-3-0343-1249-3

Vol. 166 Rita Salvi & Janet Bowker (eds)
Space, Time and the Construction of Identity.
Discursive Indexicality in Cultural, Institutional and Professional Fields.
324 pages. 2013. ISBN 978-3-0343-1254-7

Vol. 167 Shunji Yamazaki & Robert Sigley (eds)
Approaching Language Variation through Corpora. A Festschrift in Honour of Toshio Saito.
421 pages. 2013. ISBN 978-3-0343-1264-6

Vol. 168 Franca Poppi
Global Interactions in English as a Lingua Franca. How written communication is changing under the influence of electronic media and new contexts of use.
249 pages. 2012. ISBN 978-3-0343-1276-9

Vol. 169 Miguel A. Aijón Oliva & María José Serrano
Style in syntax. Investigating variation in Spanish pronoun subjects.
239 pages. 2013. ISBN 978-3-0343-1244-8

Vol. 170 Inés Olza, Óscar Loureda & Manuel Casado-Velarde (eds)
Language Use in the Public Sphere. Methodological Perspectives and Empirical Applications
564 pages. 2014. ISBN 978-3-0343-1286-8

Vol. 171 Aleksandra Matulewska
Legilinguistic Translatology. A Parametric Approach to Legal Translation.
279 pages. 2013. ISBN 978-3-0343-1287-5

Vol. 172 Maurizio Gotti & Carmen Sancho Guinda (eds)
Narratives in Academic and Professional Genres.
513 pages. 2013. ISBN 978-3-0343-1371-1

Vol. 173 Madalina Chitez
Learner corpus profiles. The case of Romanian Learner English.
244 pages. 2014. ISBN 978-3-0343-1410-7

Vol. 174 Chihiro Inoue
Task Equivalence in Speaking Tests.
251 pages. 2013. ISBN 978-3-0343-1417-6

Vol. 175 Gabriel Quiroz & Pedro Patiño (eds.)
LSP in Colombia: advances and challenges.
339 pages. 2014. ISBN 978-3-0343-1434-3

Vol. 176 Catherine Resche
Economic Terms and Beyond: Capitalising on the Wealth of Notions.
How Researchers in Specialised Varieties of English Can Benefit from Focusing on Terms.
332 pages. 2013. ISBN 978-3-0343-1435-0

Vol. 177 Wei Wang
Media representation of migrant workers in China. Identities and stances
198 pages. 2018. 978-3-0343-1436-7

Vol. 178 Cécile Desoutter & Caroline Mellet (dir.)
Le discours rapporté: approches linguistiques et perspectives didactiques.
270 pages. 2013. ISBN 978-3-0343-1292-9

Vol. 179 Ana Díaz-Negrillo & Francisco Javier Díaz-Pérez (eds)
Specialisation and Variation in Language Corpora.
341 pages. 2014. ISBN 978-3-0343-1316-2

Vol. 180 Pilar Alonso
A Multi-dimensional Approach to Discourse Coherence. From Standardness to Creativity.
247 pages. 2014. ISBN 978-3-0343-1325-4

Vol. 181 Alejandro Alcaraz-Sintes & Salvador Valera-Hernández (eds)
Diachrony and Synchrony in English Corpus Linguistics.
393 pages. 2014. ISBN 978-3-0343-1326-1

Vol. 182 Runhan Zhang
Investigating Linguistic Knowledge of a Second Language.
207 pages. 2015. ISBN 978-3-0343-1330-8

Vol. 183 Hajar Abdul Rahim & Shakila Abdul Manan (eds.)
English in Malaysia. Postcolonial and Beyond.
267 pages. 2014. ISBN 978-3-0343-1341-4

Vol. 184 Virginie Fasel Lauzon
Comprendre et apprendre dans l'interaction. Les séquences d'explication en classe de français langue seconde.
292 pages. 2014. ISBN 978-3-0343-1451-0

Vol. 185 Forthcoming.

Vol. 186 Wei Ren
L2 Pragmatic Development in Study Abroad Contexts
256 pages. 2015. ISBN 978-3-0343-1358-2

Vol. 187 Marina Bondi & Rosa Lorés Sanz (eds)
Abstracts in Academic Discourse. Variation and Change.
361 pages. 2014. ISBN 978-3-0343-1483-1

Vol. 188 Giuditta Caliendo
Rethinking Community. Discourse, Identity and Citizenship in the European Union.
240 pages. 2017. ISBN 978-3-0343-1561-6

Vol. 189 Paola Evangelisti Allori (ed.)
Identities in and across Cultures.
315 pages. 2014. ISBN 978-3-0343-1458-9

Vol. 190 Erik Castello, Katherine Ackerley & Francesca Coccetta (eds).
Studies in Learner Corpus Linguistics. Research and Applications for Foreign Language Teaching and Assessment.
358 pages. 2015. ISBN 978-3-0343-1506-7

Vol. 191 Ruth Breeze, Maurizio Gotti & Carmen Sancho Guinda (eds)
Interpersonality in Legal Genres.
389 pages. 2014. ISBN 978-3-0343-1524-1

Vol. 192 Paola Evangelisti Allori, John Bateman & Vijay K. Bhatia (eds)
Evolution in Genre. Emergence, Variation, Multimodality.
364 pages. 2014. ISBN 978-3-0343-1533-3

Vol. 193 Jiyeon Kook
Agency in Arzt-Patient-Gesprächen. Zur interaktionistischen Konzeptualisierung von Agency
271 pages. 2015. ISBN 978-3-0343-1666-8

Vol. 194 Susana Nicolás Román & Juan José Torres Núñez (eds)
Drama and CLIL. A new challenge for the teaching approaches in bilingual education.
170 pages. 2015. ISBN 978-3-0343-1629-3

Vol. 195 Alessandra Molino & Serenella Zanotti (eds)
Observing Norm, Observing Usage. Lexis in Dictionaries and in the Media.
430 pages. 2015. ISBN 978-3-0343-1584-5

Vol. 196 Begoña Soneira
A Lexical Description of English for Architecture. A Corpus-based Approach.
267 pages. 2015. ISBN 978-3-0343-1602-6

Vol. 197 M Luisa Roca-Varela
False Friends in Learner Corpora. A corpus-based study of English false friends in the written and spoken production of Spanish learners.
348 pages. 2015. ISBN 978-3-0343-1620-0

Vol. 198 Rahma Al-Mahrooqi & Christopher Denman
Bridging the Gap between Education and Employment. English Language Instruction in EFL Contexts.
416 pages. 2015. ISBN 978-3-0343-1681-1

Vol. 199 Rita Salvi & Janet Bowker (eds)
The Dissemination of Contemporary Knowledge in English. Genres, discourse strategies and professional practices.
171 pages. 2015. ISBN 978-3-0343-1679-8

Vol. 200 Maurizio Gotti & Davide S. Giannoni (eds)
Corpus Analysis for Descriptive and Pedagogical Purposes. ESP Perspectives.
432 pages. 2014. ISBN 978-3-0343-1516-6

Vol. 201 Ida Ruffolo
The Perception of Nature in Travel Promotion Texts. A Corpus-based Discourse Analysis.
148 pages. 2015. ISBN 978-3-0343-1521-0

Vol. 202 Ives Trevian
English suffixes. Stress-assignment properties, productivity, selection and combinatorial processes.
471 pages. 2015. ISBN 978-3-0343-1576-0

Vol. 203 Maurizio Gotti, Stefania Maci & Michele Sala (eds)
Insights into Medical Communication.
422 pages. 2015. ISBN 978-3-0343-1694-1

Vol. 204 Carmen Argondizzo (ed.)
European Projects in University Language Centres. Creativity, Dynamics, Best Practice.
371 pages. 2015. ISBN 978-3-0343-1696-5

Vol. 205 Aura Luz Duffé Montalván (ed.)
Estudios sobre el léxico. Puntos y contrapuntos.
502 pages. 2016. ISBN 978-3-0343-2011-5

Vol. 206 Maria Pavesi, Maicol Formentelli & Elisa Ghia (eds)
The Languages of Dubbing. Mainstream Audiovisual Translation in Italy.
275 pages. 2014. ISBN 978-3-0343-1646-0

Vol. 207 Ruth Breeze & Inés Olza (eds)
Evaluation in media discourse. European perspectives.
268 pages. 2017. ISBN 978-3-0343-2014-6

Vol. 208 Vijay K. Bhatia & Maurizio Gotti (eds)
Arbitration Discourse in Asia.
331 pages. 2015. ISBN 978-3-0343-2032-0

Vol. 209 Sofía Bemposta-Rivas, Carla Bouzada-Jabois, Yolanda Fernández-Pena, Tamara Bouso, Yolanda J. Calvo-Benzies, Iván Tamaredo (eds)
New trends and methodologies in applied English language research III. Synchronic and diachronic studies on discourse, lexis and grammar processing.
280 pages. 2017. ISBN 978-3-0343-2039-9

Vol. 210 Francisco Alonso Almeida, Laura Cruz García & Víctor González Ruiz (eds)
Corpus-based studies on language varieties.
285 pages. 2016. ISBN 978-3-0343-2044-3

Vol. 211 Juan Pedro Rica Peromingo
Aspectos lingüísticos y técnicos de la traducción audiovisual (TAV).
177 pages. 2016. ISBN 978-3-0343-2055-9

Vol. 212 Maria Vender
Disentangling Dyslexia. VenderPhonological and Processing Deficit in Developmental Dyslexia.
338 pages. 2017. ISBN 978-3-0343-2064-1

Vol. 213 Zhilong Xie
Bilingual Advantages. Contributions of Different Bilingual Experiences to Cognitive Control Differences Among Young-adult Bilinguals.
221 pages. 2016. ISBN 978-3-0343-2081-8

Vol. 214 Larissa D'Angelo
Academic posters. A textual and visual metadiscourse analysis.
367 pages. 2016. ISBN 978-3-0343-2083-2

Vol. 215 Evelyne Berger
Prendre la parole en L2. Regard sur la compétence d'interaction en classe de langue.
246 pages. 2016. ISBN 978-3-0343-2084-9

Vol. 216 David Lasagabaster and Aintzane Doiz (eds)
CLIL experiences in secondary and tertiary education: In search of good practices.
262 pages. 2016. ISBN 978-3-0343-2104-4

Vol. 217 Elena Kkese
Identifying Plosives in L2 English: The Case of L1 Cypriot Greek Speakers.
317 pages. 2016. ISBN 978-3-0343-2060-3

Vol. 218 Sandra Campagna, Elana Ochse, Virginia Pulcini & Martin Solly (eds)
Languaging in and across Communities: New Voices, New Identities. Studies in Honour of Giuseppina Cortese.
507 pages. 2016. ISBN 978-3-0343-2073-3

Vol. 219 Adriana Orlandi & Laura Giacomini (ed.)
Defining collocation for lexicographic purposes. From linguistic theory to lexicographic practice.
328 pages. 2016. ISBN 978-3-0343-2054-2

Vol. 220 Pietro Luigi Iaia
Analysing English as a Lingua Franca in Video Games. Linguistic Features, Experiential and Functional Dimensions of Online and Scripted Interactions.
139 pages. 2016. ISBN 978-3-0343-2138-9

Vol. 221 Dimitrinka G. Níkleva (ed.)
La formación de los docentes de español para inmigrantes en distintos contextos educativos.
390 pages. 2017. ISBN 978-3-0343-2135-8

Vol. 222 Katherine Ackerley, Marta Guarda & Francesca Helm (eds)
Sharing Perspectives on English-Medium Instruction.
308 pages. 2017. ISBN 978-3-0343-2537-0

Vol. 223 Juana I. Marín-Arrese, Julia Lavid-López, Marta Carretero, Elena Domínguez Romero, Mª Victoria Martín de la Rosa & María Pérez Blanco (eds)
Evidentiality and Modality in European Languages. Discourse-pragmatic perspectives.
427 pages. 2017. ISBN 978-3-0343-2437-3

Vol. 224 Gilles Col
Construction du sens : un modèle instructionnel pour la sémantique.
292 pages. 2017. ISBN 978-3-0343-2572-1

Vol. 225 Ana Chiquito & Gabriel Quiroz (eds)
Pobreza, Lenguaje y Medios en América Latina.
362 pages. 2017. ISBN 978-3-0343-2142-6

Vol. 226 Xu Zhang
English Quasi-Numeral Classifiers. A Corpus-Based Cognitive-Typological Study.
360 pages. 2017. ISBN 978-3-0343-2818-0

Vol. 227 María Ángeles Orts, Ruth Breeze & Maurizio Gotti (eds)
Power, Persuasion and Manipulation in Specialised Genres. Providing Keys to the Rhetoric of Professional Communities.
368 pages. 2017. ISBN 978-3-0343-3010-7

Vol. 228 Maurizio Gotti, Stefania Maci & Michele Sala (eds)
Ways of Seeing, Ways of Being: Representing the Voices of Tourism.
453 pages. 2017. ISBN 978-3-0343-3031-2

Vol. 229 Dino Selvaggi
Plurilingual Code-Switching between Standard and Local Varieties.
A Socio-Psycholinguistic Approach
371 pages. 2018. ISBN 978-3-0343-2663-6

Vol. 230 Anca-Cristina Sterie
Interprofessional interactions at the hospital. Nurses' requests and reports of problems in calls with physicians.
371 pages. 2017. ISBN 978-3-0343-2734-3

Vol. 231 Xiaodong Zhang
Understanding Chinese EFL Teachers' Beliefs and Practices in the Textbook-Based Classroom.
189 pages. 2017. ISBN 978-3-0343-3053-4

Vol. 232 Manuela Caterina Moroni & Federica Ricci Garotti (Hrsg.)
Brücken schlagen zwischen Sprachwissenschaft und DaF-Didaktik.
345 pages. 2017. ISBN 978-3-0343-2667-4

Vol. 233 Dimitrinka Georgieva Níkleva
Necesidades y tendencias en la formación del profesorado de español como lengua extranjera
401 pages. 2017. ISBN 978-3-0343-2946-0

Vol. 234 Juan Santana-Lario & Salvador Valera (Hrsg.)
Competing patterns in English affixation.
272 pages. 2017. ISBN 978-3-0343-2701-5

Vol. 235 Francisco Salgado-Robles
Desarrollo de la competencia sociolingüística por aprendices de español en un contexto de inmersión en el extranjero
241 pages. 2018. ISBN 978-3-0343-2323-9

Vol. 236 Maria Chiara Janner
Sguardi linguistici sulla marca. Analisi morfosintattica dei nomi commerciali in italiano
345 pages. 2017. ISBN 978-3-0343-2667-4

Vol. 237 Bárbara Herrero Muñoz-Cobo & Otman El Azami Zalachi
La primavera del árabe marroquí.
192 pages. 2017. ISBN 978-3-0343-3104-3

Vol. 238 Consuelo Pascual Escagedo
El papel del oyente en la construcción de la conversación espontánea de estudiantes italianos en su interlengua y en su lengua materna
295 pages. 2017. ISBN 978-3-0343-3186-9

Vol. 239 Stefania M. Maci
The MS Digby 133 *Mary Magdalene*. Beyond scribal practices: language, discourse, values and attitudes.
336 pages. 2017. ISBN 978-3-0343-3256-9

Vol. 240 Eliecer Crespo-Fernández
Taboo in Discourse. Studies on Attenuation and Offence in Communication.
326 pages. 2018. ISBN 978-3-0343-3018-3

Vol. 241 Jana Altmanova, Maria Centrella, Katherine E. Russo (eds)
Terminology & Discourse / Terminologie et discours.
424 pages. 2018. ISBN 978-3-0343-2417-5

Vol. 242 Xavier Blanco et Inès Sfar (dir.)
Lexicologie(s) : approches croisées en sémantique lexicale.
442 pages. 2018. ISBN 978-3-0343-3056-5

Vol. 243 Yunfeng Ge
Resolution of Conflict of Interest in Chinese Civil Court Hearings.
A Perspective of Discourse Information Theory.
302 pages. 2018. ISBN 978-3-0343-3313-9

Vol. 244 Carla Vergaro
Illocutionary Shell Nouns in English
322 pages. 2018. ISBN 978-3-0343-3069-5

Vol. 245 Paolo Frassi
L'adjectif en français et sa définition lexicographique.
270 pages. 2018. ISBN 978-3-0343-3394-8

Vol. 246 Suwilai Premsrirat and David Hirsh (eds)
Language Revitalization. Insights from Thailand
328 pages. 2018. ISBN 978-3-0343-3497-6

Vol. 247 Wei Wang
Researching Learning and Learners in Genre-based Academic Writing Instruction
282 pages. 2018. ISBN 978-3-0343-3297-2

Vol. 248 Isusi Alabarte, Alberto & Lahuerta Martínez, Ana Cristina (eds)
La comprensión lectora de lengua extranjera
Estudio de los factores de familiaridad, interés, género y métodos de evaluación
336 pages. 2018. ISBN 978-3-0343-3493-8

Vol. 249 Mercedes Eurrutia Cavero
Approche didactique du langage techno-scientifique
Terminologie et discours
374 pages. 2018. ISBN 978-3-0343-3512-6

Vol. 250 Aurora Ruiz Mezcua (ed.)
Approaches to Telephone Interpretation
Research, Innovation, Teaching and Transference
268 pages. 2018. ISBN 978-3-0343-3330-6

Vol. 251 Morini Massimiliano
A Day in the News
A Stylistic Analysis of Newsspeak
188 pages. 2018. ISBN 978-3-0343-3507-2

Vol. 252 Ignacio Guillén-Galve & Ignacio Vázquez-Orta (eds.)
English as a Lingua Franca and Intercultural Communication
Implications and Applications in the Field of English Language Teaching
414 pages. 2018. ISBN 978-3-0343-2763-3

Vol. 253 Bianca Del Villano
Using the Devil with Courtesy
Shakespeare and the Language of (Im)Politeness
216 pages. 2018. ISBN 978-3-0343-2315-4

Vol. 254 David Hirsh (ed.)
Explorations in Second Language Vocabulary Research
252 pages. 2018. ISBN 978-3-0343-2940-8

Vol. 255 Tania Baumann (ed.)
Reiseführer - Sprach- und Kulturmittlung im Tourismus / Le guide turistiche - mediazione linguistica e culturale in ambito turistico
270 pages. 2018. ISBN 978-3-0343-3402-0

Vol. 256 Ariadna Sánchez-Hernández & Ana Herraiz-Martínez (eds)
Learning second language pragmatics beyond traditional contexts
376 pages. 2018. ISBN 978-3-0343-3437-2

Vol. 257 Albert Bastardas-Boada, Emili Boix-Fuster, Rosa Maria Torrens (eds)
Family Multilingualism in Medium-Sized Linguistic Communities
336 pages. 2019. ISBN 978-3-0343-2536-3

Vol. 258 Yuyang Cai
Examining the Interaction among Components of English for Specific Purposes Ability in Reading. The Triple-Decker Model
296 pages. 2020. 978-3-0343-2913-2

Vol. 259 Catia Nannoni
Participe présent et gérondif dans la presse française contemporaine
176 pages. 2019. ISBN 978-3-0343-3631-4

Vol. 260 Nieves Rodríguez Pérez & Bárbara Heinsch (eds.)
Contextos multilingües. Mediadores interculturales, formación del profesorado de lenguas extranjeras
289 pages. 2019. ISBN 978-3-0343-3768-7

Vol. 261 Giuliana Elena Garzone, Mara Logaldo, Francesca Santulli (eds.)
Investigating Conflict Discourses in the Periodical Press
244 pages. 2020. ISBN 978-3-0343-3668-0

Vol. 262 Laura Nadal
Lingüística experimental y contraargumentación
233 pages. 2019. ISBN 978-3-0343-3791-5

Vol. 263 Claudia Claridge & Merja Kytö (eds.)
Punctuation in Context – Past and Present Perspectives
288 pages. 2019. ISBN 978-3-0343-3790-8

Vol. 264 Maurizio Gotti, Stefania Maci, Michele Sala (eds.)
Scholarly Pathways
530 pages. 2020. ISBN 978-3-0343-3860-8

Vol. 265 Ruth Breeze, Ana M. Fernández Vallejo (eds.)
Politics and populism across modes and media
350 pages. 2020. ISBN 978-3-0343-3707-6

Vol. 266 Jean Marguerite Jimenez
Understanding the Effects of Immediate Electronic Corrective Feedback on Second Language Development
252 pages. 2020. ISBN 978-3-0343-3815-8

Vol. 267 Sergio Rodríguez-Tapia, Adela González-Fernández (eds)
Lenguas y turismo: estudios en torno al discurso, la didáctica y la divulgación
380 pages. 2020. ISBN 978-3-0343-3881-3

Vol. 268 Ana Bocanegra-Valle (ed.)
Applied Linguistics and Knowledge Transfer. Employability, Internationalisation and Social Challenges
344 pages. 2020. ISBN 978-3-0343-3714-4

Vol. 269 Beatrice Garzelli
La traducción audiovisual español-italiano.Películas y cortos entre humor y habla soez
202 pages. 2020. ISBN 978-3-0343-4013-7

Vol. 270 Iván Tamaredo
Complexity, Efficiency, and Language Contact. Pronoun Omission in World Englishes
292 pages. 2020. ISBN 978-3-0343-3902-5

Vol. 271 Silvia Domenica Zollo,
Origine et histoire du vocabulaire des arts de la table. Analyse lexicale et exploitation de corpus textuels
239 pages. 2020. ISBN 978-3-0343-3890-5

Vol. 272 Paola Paissa, Michelangelo Conoscenti, Ruggero Druetta, Martin Solly (eds.)
Metaphor and Conflict / Métaphore et conflit
385 pages. 2021. 978-3-0343-4068-7

Vol. 273 María Martínez-Atienza de Dios,
Entre el léxico y la sintaxis: las fases de los eventos
178 pages. 2021. 978-3-0343-4173-8

Vol. 274 Noelia Castro-Chao,
Argument Structure in Flux. The Development of Impersonal Constructions in Middle and Early Modern English, with Special Reference to Verbs of Desire.
300 pages. 2021. 978-3-0343-4189-9

Vol. 275 Gabriella Carobbio, Cécile Desoutter, Aurora Fragonara (eds.)
Macht, Ratio und Emotion: Diskurse im digitalen Zeitalter / Pouvoir, raison et émotion: les discours à l'ère du numérique
246 pages. 2020. 978-3-0343-4184-4

Vol. 276 Miguel Fuster-Márquez, José Santaemilia, Carmen Gregori-Signes, Paula Rodríguez-Abruñeiras (eds.)
Exploring discourse and ideology through corpora
293 pages. 2021. 978-3-0343-3969-8

Vol. 277 Tamara Bouso
Changes in Argument Structure
The Transitivizing Reaction Object Construction
392. 2021. 978-3-0343-4095-3

Vol. 278 Maria Luisa Maggioni, Amanda Murphy (eds.)
Back to the Future. English from Past to Present
250 pages. 2021. 978-3-0343-4273-5

Vol. 279 Luisa Chierichetti
Diálogos de serie. Una aproximación a la construcción discursiva de personajes basada en corpus
246 pages. 2021. 978-3-0343-4274-2

Vol. 280 Cristina Lastres-López
From subordination to insubordination. A functional-pragmatic approach to if/si-constructions in English, French and Spanish spoken discourse
258 pages. 2021. 978-3-0343-4220-9

Vol. 281 Eleonora Federici, Stefania Maci (eds.)
Gender issues. Translating and mediating languages, cultures and societies
500 pages. 2021. 978-3-0343-4022-9

Vol. 282 José Mateo, Francisco Yus (eds.)
Metaphor in Economics and specialised Discourse
354 pages. 2021. 978-3-0343-4048-9

Vol. 283 Nicholas Brownlees (ed.)
The Role of Context in the Production and Reception of Historical News Discourse
376 pages. 2021. 978-3-0343-4181-3

Vol. 284 Catalina Fuentes Rodriguez, María Ester Brenes Peña, Víctor Pérez Béjar (eds.)
Sintaxis discursiva: construcciones y operadores en español
396 pages. 2021. 978-3-0343-4306-0

Vol. 285 Dominic Stewart
Frequency in the dictionary. A corpus-assisted contrastive analysis of English and Italian
176 pages. 2021. 978-3-0343-4368-8

Vol. 286 Carla Bouzada-Jabois
Nonfinite supplements in the recent history of English
320 pages. 2021. 978-3-0343-4226-1

Vol. 287 Sofía Bemposta-Rivas
Verb-governed infinitival complementation in the recent history of English
320 pages. 2022. 978-3-0343-4227-8

www.ingramcontent.com/pod-product-compliance
Ingram Content Group UK Ltd.
Pitfield, Milton Keynes, MK11 3LW, UK
UKHW041449071026
15587UKWH00010B/713

9 783034 342278